TROPHY KILL
THE "SHALL WE DANCE" MURDER

TROPHY KILL
THE "SHALL WE DANCE" MURDER

THE TRIAL AND REVELATIONS OF
A PSYCHOPATHIC KILLER

* * * * *

DAN ZUPANSKY

PROHYPTIKON
PUBLISHING INC.

TORONTO

Trophy Kill: The "Shall We Dance" Murder, The Trial and Revelations of a Psychopathic Killer, by Dan Zupansky.

PROHYPTIKON TRUE MURDER Series
Editor: Carmina M. Dragomir

For design credits and environmental commitment information, see backmatter, page 388.

I./2. 2010.

ISBN 978-1-926801-00-1 (Trade Paperback)

PROHYPTIKON TRUE MURDER
www.PROHYPTIKON.com

"We have decided from now on to stress the rehabilitation of individuals rather than protection of society... and create a more relaxed atmosphere... This new policy will probably involve some risk."

Canada's Solicitor General, Jean-Pierre Goyer
October 7, 1971.

TABLE OF CONTENTS

LIST OF FIGURES

TROPHY KILL
THE "SHALL WE DANCE" MURDER

THE TRIAL AND REVELATIONS OF
A PSYCHOPATHIC KILLER

*   *   *   *   *

Acknowledgements

SPECIAL THANKS TO ROBYN MAHARAJ, AGNEW JOHNSTON, SHERRY WATSON, George Jacub, Steve McIntosh, Dan Caldwell, Allen Smitty, Susie Moloney, Ross Read, Dave, Allen and Don Abbott.

I would also like to thank my publishers Colin and Carmina for having faith in me and this book and providing all of their expertise.

Figure 1: July 2003, Jennifer Lopez on the set of *Shall We Dance* waves at appreciative fans. Courtesy of Sun Media.

1

The Day in Question

WINNIPEG IN THE PROVINCE OF MANITOBA IS A COSMOPOLITAN CITY with a rich history, the capital of the province and the eighth largest city in Canada. Situated in the Red River Valley in the geographical center of North America, it covers over 145 square miles. The population in 2003 was almost 700,000 people, comparable in size and population to the city of Seattle, Washington, without Seattle's vastly more populated surrounding suburban area.

The prairie city has a very diverse cultural mix with the major representation by Ukrainian, French-Canadian, Filipino, Asian and Aboriginal people. Winnipeg has the single largest Aboriginal population in Canada making up almost ten percent of Winnipeg's total population.

For decades the license plate for the province read 'Friendly Manitoba' and for many years running, Winnipeg has held the distinction of having the highest per capita murder rate in Canada.

After quite a few years of a slow but steady migration of people out of Winnipeg to booming oil-rich Alberta—namely Calgary and Edmonton—Winnipeg recently had been experiencing modest but steady growth. During the time that twice-elected Winnipeg mayor Glen Murray was in office, the city had been turned around. People were moving to Winnipeg, homes began to sell—new businesses and industries were encouraged to locate in Winnipeg.

One industry, which was offered major incentives to do business in Winnipeg, was the film industry. The province of Manitoba had initiated a program where movie production companies would receive in effect substantial subsidies for filming in the province; coupled with the very significant dollar exchange difference between the U.S. and Canada, Winnipeg was especially attractive to foreign, primarily American filmmakers.

The *Miramax* movie *Chicago* starring Richard Gere, Renee Zellweger and Catherine Zeta-Jones won six Oscars in 2002. It had been primarily shot in Toronto. Clearly hoping to benefit from the success of *Chicago*, Miramax began production on another dance-themed movie called *Shall We Dance* starring Jennifer Lopez, Susan Sarandon and again Richard Gere—it was to have been filmed in Toronto also.

In March 2003, reports of health care workers with unexplained pneumonia in Vietnam and Toronto initiated an international investigation of the infection that came to be known as SARS or Severe Acute Respiratory Syndrome.

During the outbreak, transmissions in hospitals and infection persisted in Toronto and Taiwan. Consequently by April 2003 the World Health Organization imposed an international travel ban on Toronto. With panic spreading almost as quickly as the virus, incoming travel and tourism were shut down, with restaurants, theatres and nightclubs virtually empty.

Near the end of May a new cluster of SARS cases were detected in Toronto.

With the definite possible health risks associated with filming in Toronto, which was to start in June, Miramax decided to move the filming of *Shall We Dance* to Winnipeg instead.

Jennifer Lopez, one of the stars of the movie, was a dancer, a successful recording artist and a beautiful, sought after Hollywood actress—a worldwide mega-celebrity. She was engaged to actor Ben Affleck.

The ravenous paparazzi descended on Winnipeg anxious for any photo or any story involving Jennifer Lopez and fellow cast members, Susan Sarandon and Richard

Figure 2: Winnipeg, July 2003, Susan Sarandon attends baseball game as fans snap photos. Courtesy of Sun Media.

Gere. The paparazzo's focus was on Jennifer Lopez, however, even though Sarandon and Gere were huge stars in their own right. Lopez's performing career and especially her personal life had captured the imagination of millions of fans everywhere. There was a definite buzz in the air in Winnipeg since the movie began shooting the second week of June. Hundreds of actor and dancer hopefuls had tried out for coveted parts as extras in the movie. Most every day, the local papers featured on their front pages photographs of the stars waving to fans, shaking hands and enthusiastically signing autographs. A legion of young movie fans had just been let out for summer holidays.

*　　*　　*　　*　　*

IT WAS CANADA DAY, JULY 1ST, 2003; A MAN NAMED ROBIN ROBERT GREENE WAS in Winnipeg. He was visiting from the Shoal Lake Reserve in Ontario, a couple of hours drive east of Winnipeg, just the other side of the Manitoba border.

Greene was a 38-year old aboriginal man who had the free time and wanted to visit Winnipeg for the July 1st Canada Day festivities. He was anxious to hear the bands that were to play at The Forks and later to see the fireworks display.

The Forks is a cultural landmark in Manitoba, a long established meeting place for the earliest people who resided in or traveled through the area; today it's a mix of restaurants, garden markets and specialty shops, with an outdoor main stage for music and cultural events.

Robin Greene was outside early that morning of July 1st. It was a gorgeous sunny day. The *Shall We Dance* film crew was set up a few blocks away from The Forks at an outdoor location near the Provincial Legislative Building. Filming had begun at 8:00 and by around 10:00 fans had gathered near the outdoor site trying to get a glimpse of one of the stars of the movie.

Susan Sarandon and her personal assistant were in her trailer, changing clothes after having filmed some scenes. Sarandon the veteran Oscar winning actress had been in Winnipeg for almost two weeks and she was finding the city very enjoyable. She had frequented various restaurants, shopped in some boutiques and had even gone to a baseball game.

Susan removed her two gold earrings; her engraved silver bracelet and the antique gold necklace with pendant and put them on the counter. Her assistant Maria gathered the jewelry and put it in a Ziploc bag and then placed it into one of the cupboards. The two then left the trailer.

Robin Greene was out walking near the area and came upon a group of anxious fans assembled behind a barricade manned by a half-dozen security personnel, about a block from the outdoor movie location. Robin had to ask someone what all the excitement was about. He was told that people were there to see Richard Gere and Susan Sarandon. He hung with the excited crowd for a while but no one had a chance to see Susan Sarandon, Richard Gere or any of the other stars of the movie.

Robin eventually wandered away from the assembled crowd, walked a block and a half or so north and then came upon a group of trailers parked side by side. He

7

Figure 3: The Woodbine Hotel where the killer met the victim, next door to the dance studio where Gere and Lopez rehearsed their dance steps.

walked around the trailers for a few minutes and didn't notice any security staff and decided to enter the biggest and nicest trailer of the many that were there.

Inside were changes of clothes, a small wall mounted television, a small bar fridge and some magazines. Greene searched the room quickly and found the Ziploc bag with jewelry in it in one of the cupboards. Greene grabbed the Ziploc bag, stuffed it into his pant pocket and exited the trailer. He walked quickly, heading downtown to Main Street.

A little while later Sarandon's assistant Maria went to the trailer to drop off some clothing and was surprised to discover one of Susan's gold earrings on the floor. Thinking it unusual that Sarandon would have returned to the trailer to retrieve her jewelry—she went to the set and told Sarandon that she had found one of her earrings on the floor of the trailer. Sarandon, confused, stated that she hadn't been back there since taking off the jewelry. They both rushed to the trailer and realized that someone must have stolen the jewelry, dropping the one gold earring on the floor as they left. Sarandon contacted security on set and they in turn notified Winnipeg Police.

It was about 11 in the morning by the time Robin Greene made his way to The Woodbine, an older drinking establishment on Main Street, right next door to Ted Motyka Dance Studio, where Richard Gere was spending most of his off camera time getting what he felt was necessary extra dance rehearsals. Once inside the bar Greene moved from table to table asking patrons if they would like to buy a gold necklace for fifteen dollars.

Sidney Teerhuis, a 33-year-old aboriginal man, had been in the bar since just after 9 that morning. He was close to 5'8 and weighed about 220 lbs. He was overweight with a chubby face and a third chin. He wore silver colored thin, wire rimmed glasses and had short, slightly wavy, dark brown hair. He was clean-shaven and had a boyish, dimpled face. He may have been a handsome man once but the years and the extra weight had changed that.

Sidney had been employed as a chef for almost ten years in Vancouver and Edmonton and most recently had worked in Kenora, Ontario. He had just lost his job there and after a long absence was back in Winnipeg where he was originally raised. He was planning to return to Edmonton as soon as he could. He had been up all night drinking alcohol and smoking crack cocaine.

Sidney was sitting with a man and a woman at a table when Greene approached them to buy a gold necklace for fifteen dollars. Sidney told Greene to have a seat next to him while he examined the gold necklace closely. It was a thick gold chain with amber colored pendant attached to a thin gold bar. It looked quite old. Sidney declined to buy it but convinced Greene to put the necklace away and poured half a beer in a glass for him to drink.

Greene put his hand on Sidney's knee and smiled. Sidney found Greene attractive and after drinking and talking for a while they decided to leave the Woodbine and go to his room at the Royal Albert Arms. Sidney told Greene that he had beer in his room to drink. When the two got outside Greene introduced himself as 'Robin' and Sidney introduced himself as 'Seth'. By the time they had arrived at the hotel, not a block away, Sidney had already forgotten Robin's name.

Once upstairs in the room, Sidney asked Robin to sit down on the chair and take off his clothes. Robin was around 5'8, average weight and not especially muscular. He had long straight jet-black hair, halfway down his back. Sidney watched him undress completely and then offered him a beer as Robin sat naked and they talked. Sidney then got on his knees and performed oral sex on him while he ran his hands all over Robin's body.

Sidney had three disposable cameras in the room and took provocative photos of Robin in different poses—some were of him modelling underwear and others of him naked lying in the bathtub. Sidney asked Robin if he wanted to move in with him, that way they could have sex every night. Robin replied enthusiastically, "Yes."

Figure 4: The Royal Albert Arms Hotel and the scene of the murder-horror spectacle.

They kissed and held each other. Robin pulled Susan Sarandon's gold necklace from his pant pocket and placed it around Sidney's neck. Sidney moved in front of the dresser mirror to see how the necklace looked. It was obviously a woman's necklace. He thought that Robin's gesture though was "kind of sweet."

Eventually Sidney took off the necklace and put in on the dresser. A little while afterwards Robin said that he was tired and wanted to sleep. It was about half-past 2 p.m. by that time. Sidney was okay with Robin wanting to get some shut-eye and decided to go downstairs to the bar for a few drinks, and to kill some time.

Dianne Last, the head bartender was working, as usual. She had worked for some thirty years as a waitress and bartender and her face seemed to reveal that fact she looked like she had near seen it all. Dianne was maybe 5'4, a bigger, yet sturdy woman with long, dry blond hair, mid-fifties.

Since Sidney had moved in some four weeks earlier, she seemed to be there all the time. Always pleasant to Sidney, engaging him in friendly small talk whenever he happened to be in the bar.

Sidney asked for a beer, she stated the price—two eighty-five. He gave her the exact change, thanked her and grabbed his beer and walked over to a table where the evening bartender Damien and his girlfriend Sherry and another man were sitting. Sidney said something to them and then sat down and joined them at the table.

He sat there talking with them for about half an hour and then the three of them went out the back entrance to the parking lot for a cigarette. They were outside for about 5 minutes and then returned to the table. Another ten minutes later Sidney finished his beer, left the bar and headed back to his room.

Back at the room Sidney found Robin awake. They both had a by now warm beer that was in the room and Robin commented that it was a beautiful day, and that they should get outside. It was getting hot. Sidney locked the door and he and Robin left the hotel.

Figure 5: Front entrance of Royal Albert Arms Hotel and restaurant.

They walked a few blocks north, stopped and bought some beer at the Windsor Hotel and headed to the Millennium Library, a couple of blocks away. The newly built library was a fine example of modern architecture featuring a grand courtyard with many flower gardens, numerous high-back benches and a huge water fountain. They sat in the shade of a large elm tree and took a few swigs of their beers. Robin took off his white t-shirt and they kissed as a steady breeze provided some relief from the increasing heat.

After a short stay outside the library they continued walking to the Assiniboine River and finally made it to Bonnycastle Park situated behind the Hotel Fort Garry's Royal Crown Restaurant. The Park on Assiniboine Avenue just off Main Street is a popular meeting place for homosexuals. The barricades and the security for *Shall We Dance* were just a few blocks down the street.

Robin and Sidney sat at a picnic table talking and drinking beer. The park was well maintained, with plenty of colorful flowerbeds and neatly trimmed hedges. The grass was freshly cut and clipped around the cement sidewalk. An older couple lounged on one of the park benches while Sidney and Robin sat there quietly, soaking up the sun.

Robin got up, stretched and slowly sauntered down toward the river. Sidney watched his new friend stop to chat with a young, blond guy. They talked for a few minutes and then Robin walked back to the picnic table and told Sidney the young guy was a hustler, and that he wanted to take him back to the room. Sidney refused saying that the guy was too young and suggested that just the two of them should head back to the hotel. Robin agreed.

By then it was late afternoon, around 5:00, numerous cars adorned with Canadian flags, packed with families, headed to the Forks for the July 1st festivities. The revellers drove past the two men as they walked northbound on Main Street to the Royal Albert Hotel. It was stifling hot by now, as they slowly made their way back to Sidney's room.

They entered the hotel lobby and walked towards the elevator just a few feet away from the bar entrance.

Sidney spotted Dianne and motioned Robin to follow him and they walked over to the stand-up bar where she was working. He introduced Robin as his cousin so that she wouldn't suspect that he was gay. Sidney was a self-avowed homosexual but when in bars in downtown Winnipeg, he liked to keep that to himself.

Sidney then asked Dianne, "Can you keep an eye on him? I'm going to get some ice." She nodded yes. He was worried that his new acquaintance might get into trouble or just wander off. He walked through the bar to take the stairs to the basement. While he was gone Dianne noticed Sidney's 'cousin' was swaying back and forth, quite unsteady on his feet.

Sidney was gone a few minutes and returned with a bucket of ice.

They said their goodbyes to Dianne and walked to the elevator heading to room 309. Sidney planned to have a few more drinks and have some more sex—after all, the night was still young.

2

The Very Next Day

THE NEXT MORNING, JULY 2ND, AROUND 9:30, SIDNEY TEERHUIS WALKED through the visitor's entrance into the Winnipeg Remand Center. The Remand Center sits directly across from the Law Courts Building and is the facility where those persons currently in custody attending trials, or awaiting bail hearings are held. Two male guards were at the front desk and when Sidney got to the desk one of the guards asked,

"Can I help you?"

"I would like to speak to someone," Sidney replied.

The guard picked up the phone and said, "There is a gentleman here that wishes to speak to somebody. What about? I don't know," he said. Soon another guard named Donald Steenson came out from the back offices and upon approaching Sidney asked, "Can I help you Sir?"

Sidney replied matter-of-factly, "I found a body chopped up in my bathtub. I've turned myself in because I've killed somebody."

The guard stunned, replied, "Don't say another word. I'm not the person you should be telling this to!" He then handed the phone to Sidney, gave him the number for the Public Safety Building and instructed him to call.

The operator on the line Robyn Sabanski answered, "Winnipeg police, how can I help you?"

Sidney calmly replied, "My name is Sidney Teerhuis and I killed someone yesterday."

"How did you do it?"

"I chopped up the guy. I blacked out and when I woke up I found the body in the bathtub."

"What type of weapon did you use to kill the victim?"

"I used a knife."

"Where is the knife now?"

"I left it on the floor of the bathroom."

"Where did this occur?"

"The Royal Albert Arms Hotel, room 309."

"And where are you now?"

"The Remand Center."

"Sir, police officers are on their way."

About twenty minutes or so had elapsed by the time the two police officers, August Marin and his partner Sylvia Shroeder arrived at the Remand Center. He had been a cop in Winnipeg for almost 8 years; she had been for 4 years. As soon as they walked into the facility the guard at the front desk pointed to Sidney sitting on a small couch not too far from the entrance. They approached Sidney and asked him to explain his story.

Besides what the two officers had already been informed of by the 911 operator Sabanski, Sidney told them that he had met the victim, they had gone to his room for drinks and consensual sex—and eventually he had passed out intoxicated. When he awoke he went to the washroom and in the bathtub was the dismembered body. No more details were given to the officers and the two of them proceeded to the Royal Albert Arms Hotel and Sidney's room.

The hotel was not very far from the Remand Center by car and they arrived there in a few minutes. The hotel was built in 1913 making it one of the oldest hotels in Winnipeg. The hotel had seen better days however; the rooms were typically rented to welfare recipients and low-income residents. Besides catering to the hotel residents the beer-soaked barroom was also a fixture of the punk and hardcore metal music scene for years in Winnipeg.

Constable Beach, a beat patrol officer joined Shroeder and Marin at the hotel and the three officers and Sidney went through the front entrance, past the now dark, closed barroom to the elevator and up to the third floor. The halls were quite narrow and the floors uneven, the walls covered with graffiti, the room doors haphazardly painted off-white. Officer Marin asked Sidney for the key to the room and Sidney handed it to him. The cleaning lady was down the hall, cleaning another tenant's suite.

Marin opened the room door and walked in first and officer Shroeder followed. Constable Beach remained in the hallway with Sidney. It was a small room, littered with beer bottles and numerous pairs of bloodstained underwear. Shroeder found a bed sheet on the floor covered in blood and the mattress had several deep knife cuts and was soaked with blood.

There was blood splatter all over the wall by the bed and the wall leading to the washroom. Marin quickly completed looking about the room and proceeded to the washroom. The light shone in from the washroom window and when he pushed open the door—he froze.

In the antique claw-foot bathtub Robin Greene was displayed, lying on his back facing the doorway. He had been dismembered and posed crudely reassembled. The decapitated head with long, straight coarse black hair sat atop the neck and torso. One of the eyeballs was gone and the other punctured. The mouth was frozen wide open.

The body was sawn in half at the waist. The severed forearms were positioned close to the elbows as well as the severed legs, which had been chopped just below the knees. The penis and testicles were removed together and placed in their usual position. The chest had dozens of deep stab wounds carved in a figure-eight pattern. The right nipple was cut off and the right forearm and hand partially dissected.

There was one huge cut from the neck clear to the waist and the chest and abdominal cavity were completely empty. Flesh hung from the two rib cages. The skin's color was an ashen gray. All of the internal organs, the intestines, everything that normally would have been in a body, was gone. There was no blood inside the cavity or on any of the body parts.

Officer Marin stood there for two or three minutes transfixed—unable to move or say anything. His mind could simply not process what he was witnessing. Despite the fact that he had grown up in rough-and-tumble Winnipeg, despite his extensive police training and almost 8 years working the streets of Winnipeg, despite having being told by Sidney that there would be a chopped up body in the bathtub, the scene was overwhelming. The big, strong, tough and trained veteran officer found himself short of breath, his chest tight, sweating, shaking and needing to vomit. The sight and smell of the rotting corpse, surrounded by a horde of flies began to finally snap him back to reality. Initial shock turned to cold-hard recognition and then finally, revulsion.

He finally stumbled out of the washroom, to the main room and then out into the hallway. He tried his best to compose himself, steadying himself in the doorway, trying to catch his breath and finally told officer Beach, "Cuff him", and he did. Referring to the washroom he told his partner, "Don't go inside there. You really don't need to see that." Officer Marin locked the door and gave the key to officer Beach so he could remain, keeping the room secure. The two officers and Sidney walked to the elevator and traveled downstairs to the lobby and then outside to the police car.

Officer Shroeder placed Sidney in the backseat and then concerned, asked her partner, "Are you okay?" Shaking, the officer wiped the tears from his face and replied, "No I'm not—not after seeing something like that!"

After officer Shroeder had called headquarters to report the murder and arrest she and her shell-shocked partner and Sidney sat together in the police car. Officer Marin asked Sidney if he wanted to contact a lawyer and Sidney said that he did.

Soon the Coroner's van pulled up. Three Ford Crown Victoria police cars showed up shortly after the Coroner arrived and four crime scene technicians, the Coroner, Shroeder and Marin entered the hotel and went to room 309. A crowd had started to gather outside the hotel, soon after CTV News showed up. Not long after the other television news organizations began to arrive and with them came the many curious onlookers. Someone was heard asking if the scene was being filmed, as part of a movie.

Sidney Teerhuis sat handcuffed in the backseat of the police car taking in the whole scene—no one seemed to really take notice of him sitting quietly there in the cop car. After about 10 minutes or so, the two officers appeared from the hotel and returned to the cruiser. The three of them then proceeded in silence to the Public Safety Building.

Crime scene investigators searching the room had discovered Susan Sarandon's stolen gold necklace in the midst of the murder-horror spectacle.

3

I Dare Enter the Arena

I ARRIVED BACK IN WINNIPEG ON THE FOURTH OF JULY AFTER SPENDING Canada Day in Thunder Bay and saw the Winnipeg Sun newspaper with the headline **VICTIM CUT IN PIECES, Stolen Film Jewelry In Bizarre Tale Of Murder.** The following days saw the murder/dismemberment story make the front pages and then on July 12th, Sidney Teerhuis made again the front page, with his smiling face and the headline **I AM NOT A MONSTER** and inside another caption, **I'm Not Jeffrey Dahmer** and then on page 3, with the headline, **ROYAL ALBERT HELL, Accused Killer Has No Recall Of Grisly Events.**

I read the story about the gruesome murder and the statements made by Teerhuis saying he had passed out and had no memory of the killing. I cut the articles from the newspapers and put them with the other related clippings that I had been saving. This case was of particular interest to me—I was producing and hosting a talk radio program called Off the Cuff on the University of Manitoba Radio Station CJUM for almost three and a half years, and had worked as Chairman of Media and Policy Affairs for a Winnipeg-based law-reform group called People for Justice.

I was a vocal critic of the Canadian judicial system and I felt this case would demonstrate clearly one of the most important issues raised by People for Justice. Based on the fact that Sidney claimed to not recall anything whatsoever of the killing due to intoxication—I believed that the Prosecution would not be able to successfully convict Teerhuis of murder. They would have to settle for a manslaughter conviction.

With double credit given for pre-trial custody and sentences typically around ten years with one-third time off for good behavior—even without parole, which he would be eligible for after serving one third of his sentence—Sidney would be out in 4 years or less.

I saw murder charges routinely reduced to manslaughter via plea agreements, supposedly because of the difficulty successfully prosecuting murder. Right from the first time I read about Sidney and this case, it seemed absolutely absurd that anyone would accept that a person could do such an incredible act and not be cognizant of their actions. Given the fact that there were no eyewitnesses to the killing, I felt the story Sidney had put forth about the killing would be the only story ever told.

*   *   *   *   *

DON ABBOTT WAS AN OLD HIGH SCHOOL ACQUAINTANCE FROM THUNDER BAY who had moved to Winnipeg a couple of years earlier than I had which was 1994. Over the past few years we had bumped into each other occasionally, and a couple of different times in August and September of 2003, he had visited me at my home.

In November I received a phone call from Don who was calling from the Winnipeg Remand Center. He explained that he had been charged with two criminal offences and went on to claim innocence regarding the more serious charge. I tended to believe him based on his explanation and I agreed to let him call me from jail. We talked every few days.

Don was to be in jail for Christmas. Despite his predicament—on the phone he seemed to be faring well. I was returning to Thunder Bay to spend the holidays with family and friends.

One day, a couple of weeks after Christmas I received a phone call from Don and he asked me to guess who was in his jail range with him. I asked him whom he was referring to and he said "Sidney Teerhuis." The name didn't ring a bell immediately until Don explained, "Sidney Teerhuis—he's the person who had chopped up that guy at the Royal Albert!"

I was surprised and immediately expressed my interest in interviewing Sidney and asked Don to see if he could somehow arrange an interview.

A few days later Don called to say that Sidney would be interested in being interviewed at some point in the future. I told Don to tell Sidney that I was interested in his story and the murder trial.

I pondered Sidney's case and this unexpected prospect of a unique journalistic opportunity. I began to think much more ambitiously and decided to write a book. I discussed the idea with Don and asked him what he thought. I told him that, based solely on the details of the murder and the celebrity angle, there would be many people that would be interested in the story. I believed that offering a share of the potential profits from the sale of the proposed book would motivate both Don and Sidney more effectively than anything else would.

Legislation was just being drafted by government in the province to prevent criminals from profiting from the notoriety of their crimes.

Don approached Sidney with my proposal and Sidney told Don he was interested in participating in the book project.

I asked Don to request to share a cell with Sidney so he would be able to begin the research needed for the project.

The next day the request to share a cell with Sidney Teerhuis was granted.

Don and Sidney used their time together to document Sidney's life from the time he was a child living in Winnipeg, up to and including his time spent in Vancouver and Edmonton. Don was assigned the task of befriending Sidney and encouraging him to write about his past. Anything else he could glean by living with him everyday could turn out to be important.

Within a few weeks Sidney asked if I wanted to visit him in person. I told him that I was interested. He gave me the phone number to call so I could book a visit.

I called the next day and provided my particulars.

The following day I called and booked a visit for March 9th, 2004.

I had no idea what to expect. I knew what he looked like and what crime he had committed. I knew that he wanted to talk. I had planned to visit Sidney often so as to establish a rapport, so this first visit was simply to meet, and to demonstrate that I was serious about undertaking the book project with him.

On the afternoon of March 9th I arrived at the Winnipeg Remand Centre. It is a modern looking building built in 1992. Unless you had been told otherwise, there wasn't any real indication that this building was in fact a jail. I walked through the front doors of the Remand Centre, the same doors that Sidney had walked through, mistakenly thinking he was entering the Public Safety Building. I approached the guard at the front desk who asked for my name, which he located on the list. He then asked me to show him some identification. After that was done I was told to have a seat and he'd let me know when they were ready for the visit.

Perhaps fifteen minutes or so had passed when he called me to the desk, and another guard came out from a back office and motioned for me to follow him down a fairly long corridor which led to a series of small visiting rooms within a larger barred cell. The rooms were simply equipped with a narrow bench, flush to the bulletproof Plexiglas window, which separated the two parts of the room. A telephone was situated on both sides of the glass.

The guard ushered me into the room, and then left. I sat down and watched as Sidney entered the adjoining room. I was immediately struck by how non-threatening he appeared. My first impression was that he somewhat resembled comedic actor Drew Cary. He was about 5'9 and maybe 220 lbs. overweight and out of shape. He had short dark brown hair with sort of a baby face, not so much youthful, but unhardened. Sidney was soft-spoken and had a very effeminate voice.

"Hi, nice to meet you. Thanks for coming to visit me," he said as he smiled and sat down.

Sidney started off with telling me that he was aboriginal and had been adopted when he was three years old by a Dutch family in Winnipeg. However he didn't look aboriginal in appearance given his fair complexion.

He was originally from a reserve in northern Manitoba called Little Grand Rapids. He said he had just met his biological father a few years before. He felt that it was a big disappointment; despite having looked forward to the meeting, he described his father as 'a bum on welfare.'

He talked about the cocaine problem he had when he lived in Vancouver, overdosing some seven or eight times. He said he still did cocaine on and off, but told me that he had quit drinking in 2002 because of health problems involving his heart. The other reason he gave for quitting was that alcohol got in the way of him holding down a steady job.

Sidney also claimed that he had beaten bone cancer a few years earlier. I asked him if he had ever blacked out from alcohol and done anything regrettable and he answered, "no". He said he had never been in trouble with the law.

Sidney told me he had been a chef since 1996, and upon graduating he had worked and resided in Vancouver, Edmonton, Winnipeg, and the Yukon, and most recently Kenora.

Sidney claimed that while still in chef's school in Vancouver, because his instructor had been a personal friend of advertising mogul Jim Pattison of Pattison Signs, Sidney had worked a dinner party on Pattison's yacht, the Nova Vista, which George Bush Sr. and his wife Barbara had attended.

He went on to tell me that his older brother had sexually abused him starting at four years of age, and while growing up, his mother had invited him to touch her. He also said that when he was 18 or 19, a significant sexual incident involving his mother had occurred. Furthermore Sidney stated that two friends of the family had also sexually abused him until he was 17, so had a music teacher at elementary school.

Sidney claimed that he was homosexual, only having sex with six women in his life. "My mother screwed that up," he said. He stated he had endured both physical and mental abuse from his father—Sidney said that his father called it the 'Teerhuis Religion'.

There were reports in the newspaper article I'd read that claimed police had found disposable cameras in the rented room—and that there had been photos taken of the victim before and after the killing. I was very interested in discovering exactly what photos Sidney had taken after the murder. Based on that information I asked Sidney if he was interested in photography. He simply said, "no" and quickly changed the subject.

Sidney told me that he had a new lawyer named Greg Brodsky to defend him. He had fired his initial lawyer Amanda Sansregret because he had heard stories from other inmates about her dealings and because she didn't want to travel the distance to the Brandon jail, about 100 miles from Winnipeg, where he had been sent for assessment.

He commented how he felt safer at the Remand Center in an open cell block than he did in Brandon even though there he was in protective custody (a segregated individual jail cell). He told me he could hear the guards talking down the echoing hallway, "The guards talk about me like I was Charles Manson!" I simply listened to him and tried to appear as though much of our conversation was not surprising to me. He seemed oblivious to the fact that his singular murder spectacle could be considered nearly as bizarre, senseless and shocking as the murder spectacles that Charles Manson had orchestrated.

Sidney told me that he enjoyed living in Vancouver and that out there people were open minded about sex and many other things. He was interested in sadomasochism and once paid a guy three hundred dollars to spank him. He went on to say that he was not always submissive and could play either role and that his sexual fetishes went as far as water sports but that was all. He mentioned that he would have to know someone quite well before discussing the S & M subject.

Sidney again changed subjects and said that his hobbies included cooking and gardening. I found it particularly strange, in that he was speaking to me like I was interviewing him for his biography where people would be interested in those personal details.

He mentioned that his next court appearance was May 18th, but the case was nowhere near the preliminary trial stage. I told him that typically court cases could take three years or more to wind through the courts and he seemed surprised to learn that it would take that long.

Sidney told me that he had been asked for interviews from American media companies, which included 20/20 (Barbara Walters) and Celebrity Justice. His new lawyer had instructed Sidney not to read the newspaper articles concerning his case and he claimed he hadn't. He was also advised by his lawyer not to speak to any news agencies any further, after having already been interviewed by the Winnipeg Sun shortly after he was arrested and charged. Sidney said that he told the requesting parties that he would not speak to them at that time.

He told me that the phone used at the actual visit could very well have been listened in on by authorities; and since letters that were both sent and received were not read, written correspondence would be preferable when divulging confidential information.

Not long after that was said, the guard came by and told us that the visit was over. I told Sidney that it was nice to meet him, and he smiled and said, "it was finally nice to put a face together with the voice." All in all I thought the visit went very well.

*　　*　　*　　*　　*

In April Don Abbott's charges against him were withdrawn and he was released from Headingley Correctional Center. Don needed a place to stay and I had a room to rent so I invited him to move in.

I tried to ask Don questions whenever I had the chance, about his impression of Sidney and just what it was really like for him. Don just stated that it was disturbing sleeping every night in the same cell as someone capable of such a thing.

Don understandably wanted to get back to his life again—he was working full-time, and didn't seem to have very much time for my questions. I decided that I could always discuss things with him later. I felt indebted to Don for going to the lengths he did to convince Sidney that I could be trusted to convey his story accurately. One day when we were talking, Don commented, "You owe me big time!"

I began to interview Sidney by telephone regularly but more importantly he started to send me letters and with each letter Sidney revealed a little bit more about himself and his life up to the present time. He was very candid about all aspects of his personal life.

In October 2004 I received a letter that shed much more light on the facts surrounding the case. As a result I became much more aggressive and probing with my questions.

Each subsequent letter I received gradually revealed that Sidney could definitely remember the actual killing, dismemberment and whereabouts of the missing internal organs. I kept pushing for more information, for more answers.

In December, I received two letters from Sidney, which included detailed drawings and very graphic descriptions of what really transpired in that hotel room that fateful night.

Sidney had instructed me many months before that he wanted the information he had sent me to be revealed after his murder trial had been decided. I had also been led to believe that the information he had provided to me was of an exclusive nature. It seemed amazing that I would have all this information that neither the prosecuting Crown Attorney, the police, Sidney's lawyer nor the defense psychiatrist would know anything about. Armed with this crucial evidence I felt certain it would greatly alter the outcome of his trial if this information were to be known. I had definitely gained Sidney's trust but I was still shocked that Sidney had revealed as much as he did, which was tantamount to a written confession, an absolute admission of guilt—and much more.

On Tuesday, January 18th, I received a letter from Sidney telling me he had just recently spoken to a Dr. Kent Somers. Somers was a psychologist who had interviewed him when he was first charged and it was now apparently Sidney's intention to divulge certain information regarding the murder and post-murder, which up until that point I thought he would only impart to me. I was very surprised—I didn't really know how to assess this most recent revelation. I believed this admission would change a great many things.

That very night I spoke to Sidney on the telephone. I told him I was quite surprised to learn about his planned admission to Dr. Somers and I asked if his lawyer had been given the same information as I had been given. He acknowledged that his lawyer had been informed sometime in the summer of 2004.

As a result of this development, I consulted two veteran legal professionals to ask them about Sidney's lawyers' responsibility. Did he need to disclose to the Crown the information regarding the missing organs?

Agnew Johnston is a former defense lawyer and Crown Attorney from Thunder Bay, Ontario. He felt definitely that the admission by Sidney to his lawyer should have been shared with the Crown Attorney as it pertained directly to physical evidence, and almost in the same breath he implored me to contact the Crown Attorney involved with this case immediately. He said that I could potentially be charged for withholding evidence or I could possibly jeopardize the case.

A couple of days later I contacted Alan Young by telephone. Young is a Harvard educated law professor teaching law at Osgoode Hall and criminology at the University of Toronto. He is the author of *Justice Defiled — Perverts, Potheads, Serial Killers & Lawyers*. In regards to the admission by Sidney to his lawyer of the whereabouts of the victim's internal organs, Young felt that since the lawyer did not actually see or possess the actual physical evidence, he did not necessarily have a legal obligation to disclose that information to the Crown Attorney. Young stated that was his legal opinion but that the issue was not without controversy.

He agreed with Johnston that I had a responsibility to come forward with the evidence that I did possess as soon as possible.

However, there was still more information I needed to know, and I decided that I would continue questioning Sidney—I wouldn't contact the Crown Attorney quite yet.

The defense attorney representing Sidney was Greg Brodsky. Brodsky is a Winnipeg native, a 49-year veteran of criminal law. He has by his own count, defended accused in more murder trials than any other attorney in the English-speaking world. He is known especially for his unapologetic defense of killers and the most heinous of offenders—he worked for the defense in the Paul Bernardo trial. His impressive success rate and effective courtroom tactics have earned him a formidable reputation in the Canadian judicial system.

Working closely alongside Greg Brodsky on many court trials including murder, was veteran Winnipeg psychiatrist Dr. Fred Shane. Dr. Shane, working with Greg Brodsky, was most well known for the first successful use in Canada of the precedent-setting defense of Battered Women's Syndrome in murder cases. Of special interest to me was the successful use of the defense of Automatism by Mr. Brodsky and Dr. Shane in murder trials. I felt that given Sidney's contention that he could not remember the gruesome killing and dismemberment, that his legal team could use this defense. Automatism focuses not on the accepted medical definition, but rather the quite different 'legal' definition of unconsciousness. This court-defined unconsciousness transformed Sidney into an automaton (a robot), during the entire event: the murder, mutilation, dismemberment and the removal of all the internal organs and—as the media had reported—the photographing of the body after the killing.

What I thought would happen at the trial is despite the absurdity of Sidney's claim that he had passed out and could not remember anything of the commission of this murder/horror spectacle—Mr. Brodsky, with the expert testimony of Dr. Shane, would try to prove that very claim.

I found myself directly involved in a modern day murder mystery, not the classic "who done it?" But rather "Why had he done it?" Sidney gave me crucial information in bits and pieces, turning this into what seemed an elaborate puzzle. He was more than happy to cooperate, never really refusing to answer any question put to him, only deferring some questions to a later date—with the assurance that he would answer them in the foreseeable future.

In many ways this crime didn't seem to make sense despite all the information Sidney had given me in regard to the motive—I thought that there might be more to the story.

As I had requested, Sidney had referred to in his most recent letter the interrogation at the police station, which occurred after he was formally charged with murder. The police had questioned Sidney about other murder investigations in Vancouver and Edmonton, which involved several murdered young males that shared striking similarities regarding the killing and dismemberment. According to Sidney one of the detectives involved with the questioning had became so frustrated with Sidney's denials that he finally insisted that Sidney had killed all the young men.

Sidney had also told me about a serial killer from England named Dennis Nilsen who had murdered and dismembered 15 men and about best selling author Ann Rule who had written twenty-two books about serial killers and their cases, starting with Ted Bundy. I researched Nilsen's crimes to learn whatever I could. Maybe there was something specific that Sidney wanted me to discover, some shared characteristic, something that Nilsen had done that had influenced Sidney. I thought there was good reason why Sidney had seemingly directed me to two 'experts' on serial murder. I thought about what the police had said as I began drafting much different questions to ask Sidney, bearing in mind the distinct probability that he had killed before.

4
Serial Killing

IN JANUARY 2002, I HAD THE GREAT PLEASURE TO INTERVIEW ROBERT K. Ressler for my radio program. Considered the world's leading authority on violence in contemporary society, Robert Ressler is the founder and former director of the FBI's acclaimed *Violent Criminal Apprehension Program*. He is an expert on serial-killers (a phrase he coined) and sexual homicides, and is the acknowledged true-life hero of the movie *Silence of the Lambs*. The television series *The X Files* was inspired by Ressler's work at the FBI's Behavioral Science Unit. He is the coauthor of international best sellers *Sexual Homicide: Patterns and Motives, Crime Classification Manual, Whoever Fights Monsters, I Have Lived in the Monster* and *Justice is Served*.

Robert was in Winnipeg as a guest speaker at the University of Manitoba, giving a talk titled *Inside the Criminal Mind*.

We covered a lot of things in our one hour interview, including the origins of criminal profiling which date back to the Second World War, where the forerunner of the C.I.A. began compiling dossiers on enemy leaders to be able to make some predictions regarding their behavior and their actions. Understanding the enemy being the key to preventing further carnage.

The F.B.I. utilized this technique and applied it to the study of those who had committed multiple murders. Robert working as a special agent for the F.B.I. had interviewed extensively the most notorious and infamous serial killers in the world including Ted Bundy, John Wayne Gacy, Jeffrey Dahmer, Charles Manson, David Berkowitz (Son of Sam) along with 30 others.[1] Studying all the information resulted in two books that are required reading and have been essential tools in criminology and forensic psychology for years. One of those books is *Sexual Homicide: Patterns and Motives* (1988).

The following is from our radio interview:

> **Dan:** I am very interested in the John Wayne Gacy case. Dahmer seems to be more of a psych case, rather than Gacy, where you say he was more organized, and say that

---

1 In Ann Rule's *Stranger Beside Me*, there is a letter that Ted Bundy had written to Ann Rule criticizing her for naivety regarding serial killers and their motivations. Bundy stated that the only person that he believed that truly understood serial killers was Robert K. Ressler.

Dahmer was a combination of organized and disorganized. Maybe you can tell us a bit more about the John Wayne Gacy case, and how some of the information garnered from the interview would be used in particular, to be specific in profiling this person. Say you were looking for a person that had similar types of crimes, we'll say methodology; what had you garnered from the Gacy interview that would lead to a concrete criminal personality profile?

Ressler: The main difference between Gacy and Dahmer is that where Gacy was totally resistant to admitting his crimes, and based on his ego, and how long you would spend with him, he would start making admissions and painting himself into corners; but essentially right up to his execution, he was lying and deceiving and rationalizing that a lot of the young men that died-deserved to die. As he said, they were "just trash"; he was rationalizing the lives and the worth of these people, by down-playing their just general worth in society. In other words, he claimed that killing these people really didn't do any harm to society.

Dahmer, now on the other side of the coin, fully admitted his crimes. Where Gacy was a 'sexual psychopath', Dahmer was more mentally disordered, and actually offered insight into some of the things he had done and why he had done them.

By interviewing them you begin gleaning information from these individuals about their personalities that you can then apply to other like-crimes. Just the dynamics and circumstances of the disappearances of the young guys, with Gacy and Dahmer it would have been tough because both of them, their victims were disappearing from the face of the earth. Gacy had 29 of them buried under his house, 4 more in rivers that he had dumped; so until they really had a disappearance of a young boy in this drugstore where Gacy was working that particular day; there was no indication that Gacy had committed other offences. With Dahmer, his victims were all decapitated, eviscerated and dismembered, and body parts were disposed of; so again there was no finding of bodies where there would be evidence to review by law enforcement, so both those cases were extremely difficult. The dynamics of personalities of those two individuals gives you great clues to the types of people who would commit those types of crimes.

Dan: How prominent was the fact that they used marginalized people, or like you said, people that wouldn't be missed in their crimes; how prevalent was that in the interviews you did with these people?

Ressler: Quite prevalent because the most successful serial killers would select victims that would not lead back to them; and like you say, women engaged in prostitution, picking up and leaving on short notice and going to another area; gay transients who are riding buses around the country, and again within the gay community a person who disappears is often thought to have run off with somebody; people with lifestyles that are high risk often times become victims of serial killers because they're not going to be missed quite as readily as say somebody from the traditional part of the community. A lot of people like this are selected for victims because the killer intellectually decides that these people are going to be missed least by conventional law enforcement, or by society at large, and so they protect themselves.

There are three types of serial killer: Organized, disorganized and mixed, with the killer exhibiting characteristics of both organized and disorganized such as Jeffrey Dahmer.

Organized serial killers typically are above average in intelligence and they are known to plan out their murders very methodically.

They typically lure and then abduct their victims, killing them and then disposing of their bodies, targeting strangers, prostitutes, run-a-ways and transients.

They usually have a good grasp of forensic science and police investigation, which helps them avoid detection and capture.

These killers will follow media coverage closely, with great interest and they will take pride in their 'accomplishments'.

Organized serial killers are typically socially adequate, often marrying and having children and their murderous behavior seemingly out of character to those around them, as was in the case of Ted Bundy and John Wayne Gacy.

Disorganized serial killers on the other hand are often below average in intelligence and tend to commit their murders impulsively when they feel an opportunity has presented itself.

They rarely dispose of the victim's body and there is typically a blitz type of attack used, an obvious overkill.

Afterwards they perform whatever rituals they feel compelled to carry out such as necrophilia, mutilation and cannibalism.

They are often introverted being socially inadequate with few friends and may have a history of mental illness.

Mixed serial killers are those that exhibit both characteristics of organized and disorganized serial killers. These killers may move from organized to disorganized behavior as their murders continue, carrying out murders methodically in the beginning, but becoming careless and impulsive as their murderous compulsion takes over their lives.

In interviews conducted by Ressler, Douglas and others, serial killers have stated that the act of murder was never as good as their fantasies and that there was always something that didn't happen as planned or that could have been more gratifying. The killer would then murder again, escalating the violence, increasing the spectacle, taking more chances or approaching the media or authorities.

An environment of harsh discipline where the child grows up internalizing hurt, anger and fear beset with poor self-image characterizes the serial killer's childhood. They see themselves as underachievers, having never lived up to their potential.

They reject the society they felt rejected them.

The 'posing' of a victim by a disorganized serial killer is part of their 'signature'. The signature is a personal detail that is unique to the individual—the thing that fulfills them emotionally.

"We don't get that many cases of posing, treating the victim like a prop to leave a specific message. These are crimes of anger, of power... It's the thrill of the hunt, the thrill of the kill and it's the thrill afterwards of how the subject leaves that victim, and how he's basically beating the system."

(John Douglas 1997, p. 26, Mind Hunter-Pocket Books)

The U.S.A. represents just 6% of the world's population yet has three quarters of all serial killers. Canada, with a population about one tenth that of the U.S. has also experienced a marked increase in serial murder; especially evident with such notorious murderers as Clifford Olsen, Paul Bernardo and Karla Homolka, and now Robert Pickton.

There are other convicted serial killers in Canada who are not well known, other serial killers who have not been identified as such, and serial killers who remain free.

The motivations to kill include those that can be considered *Visionaries*, who act in response to voices, which instruct the subject to kill. These killers are usually schizophrenic and psychotic.

Another group are *Missionaries* who believe that it is their destiny to rid society of unwanted elements. Still another group are *Hedonists* who kill because it gives them pleasure. There are also *Gain Killers* who simply kill for personal gain and *Power Seekers* who kill to exert control over the life and death of others. There are the *Thrill Killers* who kill merely for the thrill or experience and *Lust Killers* who kill for sexual gratification with acts that are usually sadistic.

Definitions:

Psychopath: *a mentally ill or unstable person, especially a person having a psychopathic personality.*

Psychopathic Personality 1: *an emotionally and behaviorally disordered state characterized by clear perception of reality except for the individual's social and moral obligations and often by the pursuit of immediate personal gratification in criminal acts, drug addiction, or sexual perversion.* 2: *an individual having a psychopathic personality.*

Insane 1: *mentally disordered: exhibiting insanity.* 2: *used by, typical of, or intended for insane persons.* 3: *absurd.*

Insanity 1a: *a deranged state of the mind usually occurring as a specific disorder (as schizophrenia) and usually excluding such states as mental deficiency, psychoneurosis, and various character disorders.* b: *a mental disorder.* 2: *such unsoundness of mind or lack of understanding as prevents one from having the mental capacity required by law to enter into a particular relationship, status, or transaction or as removes one from criminal or civil responsibility.* 3a: *extreme folly or unreasonableness.* b: *something utterly foolish or unreasonable.*

*   *   *   *   *

SIDNEY WAS ARRESTED AND BROUGHT TO THE PUBLIC SAFETY BUILDING INITIALLY for questioning and processing. Sidney did not have a lawyer at the time and an attorney named Amanda Sansregret was assigned to him.

A woman in her thirties (reminded me of Princess Leia, with bad hair) introduced herself as Amanda Sansregret. One of the first things she said to me was "you tell them nothing! Nothing! They are the enemy." She pulled out a yellow note pad from a large black leather briefcase. It looked very expensive. She started writing notes down. She was very stern when asking questions. "Did you tell them anything?" she asked "No", I replied. "Don't!" she said. "We are talking about the rest of your life, tell them nothing." (We discussed many things as she wrote it down). Amanda already knew they did not follow proper procedure. "Did they take samples from you?" she asked. "Yes" I said. "Fuck" she said as she slammed her fist on the table. "Don't worry Sidney" she said "I won't leave you during the interrogation." "This is going to be a very long day for you." Amanda left the room momentarily, came back disappointed. "They won't let me stay", she said giving me her card. "Call me if you need help, remember tell them nothing. They will twist everything you say around", and she left.

The two detectives entered the room and locked the door. I sat across from them, wearing paper clothes. They started asking questions, I'd reply, "My lawyer said not to say anything." One of them replied, "I understand that but we're trying to do our job here." They persisted for a while. I ended up saying that I had met Greene at the Woodbine, he was trying to sell a necklace, we had a beer together, and we were sitting with a man and a woman. We then left for the Albert to have consensual sex. I remember one of the detectives had on navy blue dress pants; I could tell he had a huge cock from the enormous bulge in his crotch. They asked questions like "why did you do it?" If I couldn't remember anything they'd say, "try to remember." They said things like "you caused this guy a lot of pain" or "he had his whole life ahead of him and you took it away." I remember at one point the detective wearing the navy blue pants held a gun to my head and threatened to use it. They left the room, came back with a photocopy of something. They asked, "Do you recognize this?" I looked, couldn't tell what it was, replied "no". The taller detective claimed it was a very famous piece of jewelry. At first I thought what does this have to do with me? Then I remembered Greene trying to pawn off the necklace at the Woodbine. "It belongs to Susan Sarandon," said the detective. "It was reported stolen." I can't remember what else he said, but it had been found at the Albert in room 309. They were really interested as to why Greene had been chopped up and where the missing organs were. I was taken to another room down the hall, (there's something grim about nineteen seventies architecture) where I was weighed, took five blood samples, scanned my eyes, and fingerprinted my hands, palms, fingers, even my feet. There was a woman behind a large desk computer; all this info was fed into the computer. The woman asked, "What's the charge"? The detective replied as if he got all A's on his school report card, "First degree." He asked if I had any charges on record. She replied, "Nothing, no record."

I was brought back to the interrogation room; they brought me a sub sandwich and some water. They started all over again with the questioning, only this time they added a few things. They had a series of cold case files they wanted to dump on me. According to the detectives, in B.C. and Alberta there were similar murders, where young men had been chopped up or mutilated. One case in particular was of a young nineteen-year-old male who was found some years ago almost in the same condition as they found Greene. I could see where this was leading. They said something like they wanted to put the cases to rest for the victim's families. They got up and walked toward the door and said, "think about it, we hope you'll do the right thing, we'll be waiting for you to knock on the door." They left. I sat there for a long time, my mind a complete blank.

When they said they were done I was escorted to the basement where I was handcuffed. The detective in the navy blue dress pants kept on asking questions. I replied, "I thought the interview was over?" He became tumult and insisted that I killed all those young men. I told him I didn't have to answer any more questions; yet he persisted. He asked where I had worked in Vancouver, I told him "A Kettle Of Fish," a restaurant (Ivana Trump while in Vancouver as a guest star in TV series Beggars and Choosers dined there).

We left the Public Safety Building; it was one in the morning. For some odd reason they drove right by the Royal Albert Arms Hotel. It was hot; the streets were deserted, drove by the Convention Center and entered the parkade of the Winnipeg Remand Center. I met a young Aboriginal male in the holding cell, named Baptiste. Turns out he knew my cousin Delilah and my half-sister Cookie and my biological father George Moar from Little Grand Rapids. Small world.

Sidney

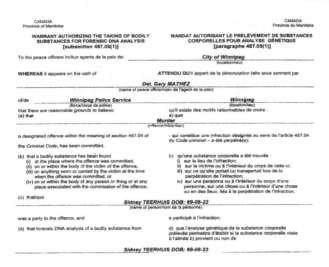

Figure 6: DNA Warrant for Sidney Teerhuis.

5

The Defence Team: Psychopathic Advocates

"Psychopaths are often found in positions of imposture. They are attracted to certain vocations having great opportunity for exerting power such as politics, the law, or medicine."

(Gordon Banks-1990)

NOVEMBER 6, 1999

Lawyer believes appeal has merit, by KATHLEEN MARTENS – Courts Reporter – Winnipeg Sun. "Everyone's entitled to a defence", says Greg Brodsky.

THE STORY STARTED WITH ANNOUNCING THAT WINNIPEG LAWYER Greg Brodsky had agreed to help convicted killer rapist Paul Bernardo get a new trial believing that there was merit to his appeal. Brodsky was quoted as saying, *"The law is blind. Justice isn't meted out to those we like. The people we like today may not be the people we like tomorrow. I don't think anyone should be excluded from justice. That's for the courts to decide."*

The article mentioned the 550 murder cases that Brodsky had been involved with in his 40-year career and stated he had been compared to Jake Lamotta, the 'Raging Bull' for his brawling courtroom style. *"He puts his head down and just belts away,"* said former Brodsky partner Saul Simmonds. *"There might be people with fancier footwork or sweeter to watch, but Greg has proved his prowess in the courtroom."*

The reporter wrote that Brodsky had taken on many controversial cases in Manitoba, including that of a Winnipeg man found not criminally responsible for killing and cannibalizing his wife. Brodsky claimed that he was not concerned about his client list damaging his reputation.

"I've talked to Bernardo. He's anxious for his appeal to go forward and has admitted that to which he is guilty of and wants to have a new trial on the balance. He understands that it is difficult for the public to look at his case with an unjaundiced eye."

RECOGNIZED AS TOP DEFENSE LAWYERS IN CANADA FOR 2006

BRODSKY & COMPANY IS CURRENTLY RECOGNIZED AS MANITOBA AND North Western Ontario's premier boutique criminal law firm. Founded in 1999, our firm traces its roots back to the legendary Walsh Micay and

Company, who represented leaders in the 1919 Winnipeg General Strike. Building on this strong tradition, we advocate for people from all walks of Canadian life in a progressive and liberal manner. Brodsky & Company also has extensive experience in appellate work, appearing regularly in the Manitoba and Ontario Courts of Appeal, as well as in the Supreme Court of Canada. The firm is headed by Greg Brodsky, Q.C., who has revolutionized Canadian Law over the past 45 years with cases such as R. v. Lavallee, creating a battered wife defence, R. v. Starr, redefining reasonable doubt and clarifying Canada's principled approach to

Figure 7: Greg Brodsky

the admission of hearsay in court proceedings, and R. v. Chaulk, modernizing the not criminally responsible defence. Brodsky also has litigated over 600 homicide cases in his career, a record in the English-speaking world.

Brodsky & Company combines the knowledge and expertise of five creative, talented and progressive lawyers. Backed by a staff of students and administrative support, our lawyers work as a litigation team, undertaking a detailed and thorough investigation of your case to identify and pursue all legal and factual issues and opportunities. Although you are assigned an individual lawyer, you will be able to interact with the entire litigation team throughout the various stages of your case, during meetings, bail applications, court appearances and trials.

We take pride in our responsiveness and try to communicate with our clients at least once a week. Most importantly, we focus on each individual case and client. We understand the implications of criminal action and we work with you to understand your situation and your goals.

Overall, our philosophy is to focus on providing responsive service and sophisticated strategies to achieve the desired results for our clients. Our commitment to hard work and excellence has lead to success in every level of the Canadian judicial system, including precedent setting cases in the Supreme Court of Canada.

Hope Buset Originally from Thunder Bay, Ontario, Hope Buset first attended the University of Western Ontario where she graduated with honors with a Bachelor of Arts degree (Philosophy). In 2005, Hope Buset received her Bachelor of Laws degree from the University of Manitoba, with recognition in Aboriginal Law.

After graduating from the University of Manitoba, Hope articled in Thunder Bay, Ontario at Buset & Partners LL.P, where she worked primarily in the area of civil litigation. She received her Ontario Call to the Bar in July 2006.

After returning to Winnipeg in August of 2006, Hope received her Manitoba Call to the Bar and joined the Brodsky legal team in November 2006.

Hope has appeared at every level of Court in Manitoba, including the Provincial Court, the Court of Queen's Bench and the Manitoba Court of Appeal.

Figure 8: Brodsky & Company, Defence Team.

*   *   *   *   *

Dan,

THE WHITE MAN'S DEFINITION OF LAW IS PREMISED ON THE BELIEF THERE *will be conflict. Crown Attorney Liz Thomson speaks "w' geewi-animah", they don't want facts. Our legal system tells lies and half-truths, they do not look at the big picture, people like Finlayson want expedient justice but forget most judicial delays are the fault of the Crown and Winnipeg Police. They cry foul over Greg Brodsky's workload claiming such cases are taking too long.*

Winnipeg police feel they do not have to justify their tumultuous behavior. I was brutally beaten by Detective Gary Mathez on August nineteen, 2004 when a warrant was presented for my DNA. After one year they claim to have found a bodily substance in the hotel room at the Royal Albert Arms, on the deceased.

The media is quick to point out that the taxpayer is flipping the bill for my legal fees, medical and time in custody. They are forgetting to mention that Crown Attorney Liz Thomson and my lawyer Greg Brodsky are lining their pockets and getting rich off taxpayer money as well! The longer I am kept remanded the more money Thomson and the courts make. If the average Canadian, Aboriginal, Jew etc. knew how corrupt our justice system works, they would be appalled.

Ann McLellan said it's time to review how Canada's Corrections system operates. Bruce Miller, a racist pig from the Ottawa Police Association claims there are too many "club-fed" prisons in Canada. Miller wants Ottawa to pay more attention to the victims of crime. Well, I am a victim of crime, there is a lot more at stake here. Ottawa needs to look at why there are so many individuals who commit crimes (rape, murder, incest)—nobody is born a killer or rapist, something happened to that individual, and for whatever reason they find themselves in the company of misadventure.

Sidney

FROM SEGREGATION (THE HOLE) IN REMANDED CUSTODY.

Dan,

MR. BRODSKY CAME TO SEE ME, SAID HE WAS WORRIED ABOUT MY WELL-being. We discussed topics on my charges (I needed to be more concise on the events that took place after Greene died). We talked about my state of mind during the transgression, having sex with the corpse. I spoke how Liz Thomson (Crown Attorney) needed to look at a broader picture as to why this took place. For the first time I did most of the talking, then Mr. Brodsky told me his stratagem. We needed or I need to go for more psychological evaluation. Brodsky said he was going to send over Dr. Shane again, we needed to start all over again. I don't care for Shane he is too crafty. Mr. Brodsky was having problems with legal aid on getting Shane to see me at Headingley.

A doctor from Stony Mountain is coming in a couple of weeks. This following Monday a very sexy young man from Brodsky's office came to see me on a few matters of the goings-on at Headingley. I mentioned being injected with PETHIDINE, that I would say this in court. I had also mentioned I did not want Dr. Shane, I wanted my former psychiatrist Dr. Fast (I was his patient when I attempted suicide at age thirteen). He said Mr. Brodsky would get in touch with me.

After reading the report on my duration at the Public Safety Building, I have proof now that they did not get a bench warrant for my D.N.A. Nor does it mention anywhere that one of the detectives held a loaded gun to my head, or that my interrogation lasted fifteen hours—there's proof the videotape had been tampered with and edited.

Regardless of anything I will keep a strong mind, and fight Mr. Brodsky. I will do whatever it takes to be the first to allow the media to have cameras in the courtroom. If I'm going to do fifteen to life or five for NCR, I'm going to make Canadian History for change in our court system. It's time Canada grew up. Just look at our Government in Ottawa, what a joke! If our American neighbors allow cameras in the courtroom so can we.

I still expect someone, a friend of yours to sell T-shirts outside the courthouse. You have to make sure you can get a hold of Marilyn Manson to write a song about me, it's release date has to coincide with the trial date. I want you to mention on your radio show about my upcoming trial and get a public poll: Should the courts allow cameras in the courtroom? I say yes, the public has a right to know what goes on during a court proceeding.

Sidney Teerhuis

My lawyer, Greg Brodsky comes to see me every now and then or he sends his assistant Bonnie. It's been almost a year now, the Crown can't decide on a preliminary hearing, yet alone a trial date. Over time a witness will move or o.d. on crack, vital evidence gets lost or goes missing. I really hate to say it but people die all the time or go missing. The Crown makes it sound like I'm some terrible person (yet they embellish and twist the facts around.) In any case, Brodsky better get a haircut soon, he's starting to look like Crypt Keeper. If he can afford to run around town in a fancy little ragtop sports car, he certainly can afford himself a haircut or transplant.

When I first met Greg he struck me as the stereotypical Jew. I actually hated him for the longest time. Recently we've had an almost non-legal conversation, I made him laugh, seeing the man behind the legal facade. I'm sure not too many individuals have that opportunity.

Court appearances are awkward. I enter the courtroom all shackled up—usually the ankle jewelry is on too tight. The pit of my stomach tightens up and I usually feel my neck muscles constricting. The room is always packed, I see Greg and Bonnie, then look over to the Crown.

Where the public sits I've seen a guy who looks like Robin, perhaps his brother. There was a tall native woman standing by the entrance, she wore a black leather, three-quarter-length jacket and held a black leather purse. She had a perm, just the way she stood there told me a lot.

In the front row, was an elderly couple, maybe Greene's parents? I felt my heart hit the floor. The man wore a fisherman-like plaid jacket—he had a glossy forlorn look. The woman had curly hair, she hid behind dark glasses, had very strong native features to her face (a stoic look) hands clasped upon her lap. I kept looking at her red nail polish for some odd reason. The image of those two is forever imbedded in my mind.

It's funny how tongues wag. The guards at the law courts are totally convinced I'm some deranged Susan Sarandon fan. They have come to the conclusion I had stolen the necklace. Others argued it belonged to Jennifer Lopez. Then there's the sock on MuchMusic who claims Greene was my boy friend. To top it all, some skinner inmate started a rumor that I ate some of Robin's body parts. Cardinal goes around telling people I ate the guy's cock and balls. Obviously he hasn't seen the forensic photos of the postmortem examination. I have. Greene's penis, pubic hair and testicles are intact, just not connected to the body. The gruesome reality, Greene is in many pieces from his hollow chest cavity to him cut in half above the pelvis.

In the photos, Greene's remains didn't look human any more. It was like a pile of raw meat and bone on the examining table. I could see the inside of the rib cage and the spinal column. The genitals were neatly laid out on the table, in proximity between the thighs that were cut off at the knee. Another photo showed the gaping hole where the neck was, the jugular veins, windpipe and chunk of spine jutted out. His right nipple was cut off. A mid-view of the pelvic area at the

waistline depicted the kidneys and bladder, still intact, there was a lot of red meat
that was the buttock tissue, a thin layer of human fat then the epidermis (flesh).
Brodsky's assistant showed me photos of clothing, Greene's and mine.
There were pictures of Greene hours before his death, he was posing nude.
Other photos he was masturbating, modeling various pairs of underwear.
Greene's lungs, heart, liver and intestines were nowhere to be found. I've had
so many court appearances to date, most of which determine the next court
appearance.

Sidney

APRIL 2/04

SIDNEY SAID THAT HIS LAWYER AND THE PSYCHIATRIST HAD REFERRED TO A REALLY traumatic experience occurring in regards to his case. The psychiatrist, Dr. Shane was convinced that the 68 stab wounds were done in a pattern, with a figure eight being carved into the chest of the victim.

Sidney stated that Dr. Shane felt that the murder was premeditated and a sick fantasy for him and mentioned that the doctor's report would go to his lawyer.

He spoke of undergoing psychiatric testing involving building blocks and flash cards.

Sidney gave permission for Dr. Shane to speak to only one family member and that was one of his sisters. He told me that the Crown thinks the murder was premeditated and planned and the psychiatrist thinks he has a mental disorder.

He noted that the dismembered body parts displayed on the autopsy table were very shrunken when he was shown a photo of the parts by Brodsky's assistant Bonnie and said that she had also brought a book of human anatomy for him to look at.

APRIL 6/04

SIDNEY TALKED ABOUT BEING IN BRANDON CORRECTIONAL CENTER WHERE HE claimed he was placed in a straight-jacket strapped to a chair for 12-20 hours. He was restrained because of an allegation of assaulting a female corrections officer and he was subsequently criminally charged.

JUNE /04

SIDNEY SPOKE OF THE INTERVIEW WITH DR. KENT SOMERS THAT OCCURRED IN January of 2004. He said it was basic psychological tests, which included building blocks. The interview lasted about an hour. He said there were also tests with multiple-choice (a b c) questionnaires. The same questions were asked different ways and every fourth or fifth question concerned suicide. Dr. Somers only asked questions relating to the killing at the end of the interview.

He told Sidney that he worked at Stony Mountain penitentiary and had seen Sidney in Brandon Correctional Centre and informed him that he would have to see him again.

Dr. Kent Somers is a psychologist, employed by the federal government but who also has an independent practice. Both the Crown and the Defense often hire him and is often asked to do a risk assessment, which is part of an overall mental health assessment.

Sidney then spoke of his second interview with Dr. Fred Shane. He said that while he was spilling his guts to him, Shane would not make eye contact with him. He seemed distracted, not taking any notes. Sidney was talking about what happened in the room that day, "the official story". He went on to talk about waking up and opening the bathroom door to find the horrific scene, which he told Shane, "hit him like a ton of bricks."

"Go on", Shane said. Sidney gave a lot of details but still Shane didn't take any notes and then supposedly in a quite obvious skeptical tone said, "Come on now, I'm a pro, I've been doing this for twenty years!" Sidney said that he got very angry with Shane because he felt he wasn't listening to him. "He seemed to only listen to what he wanted to."

Shane insisted that there was a definite U and an 8 pattern evident in the stabbing. Sidney said that he emphatically stated "No" in response to that allegation and asked Shane sarcastically, "Aren't you listening?" Shane's contention was that Sidney had set out to meet someone and kill them. Sidney said that he became very mad about that accusation, yelling and swearing at him, pounding his fists on the table. Shane just simply sat there staring at him.

The interview was the second one with Shane and it occurred about three months after Sidney had been charged, the first interview being conducted after about six weeks.

I asked again about what happened to Greene's missing organs and Sidney said, "It's too early to go into that."

He asked again about whether I thought the courts would ever allow cameras in the courtroom.

July 11/04

SIDNEY HAD JUST RECENTLY MET WITH GREG BRODSKY AND WHEN HE CALLED HE told me what they had spoken about. Brodsky said that there would be two stages of the trial—that being 'self defense' and 'not criminally responsible.'

Sidney had sent a detailed letter to The Assembly of First Nations regarding his involvement in the alleged assault of a female corrections officer and the mistreatment and discrimination he claimed to have experienced.

He went on to mention that a significant anniversary had just recently passed and that being July 2nd, the day through adoption, some thirty-one years earlier, Sidney Owens had become Sydney Teerhuis.

He failed to mention another significant anniversary on July 2, the date in 2003 that Sidney had been arrested for the shocking murder of Robin Greene.

November 16/04

SIDNEY RECALLED HIS FIRST CONVERSATIONS WITH DR. SHANE. HE SAID THAT Shane bragged about his 20 years as a professional. While speaking to Sidney he took no notes. Shane had interviewed him four times he said. Their first introductory meeting lasted about 15 minutes. The next interview was approximately thirty minutes. The third interview lasted about the same amount of time and the fourth meeting lasted only five minutes.

Sidney mentioned again that during their first interview Shane insisted that the stabbing was not random but rather there was a definite pattern to the 68 stab wounds that Sidney had inflicted on his victim. Sidney said that he denied it.

Sidney claimed that Shane was "fishing for info" and looking for consistency in Sidney's answers to the psychiatrist's questions. He also said that Shane was very transparent in his methodology with regards to questioning and that he had read the psychiatrist's report and the police report.

In February or March Brodsky and his assistant visited and showed Sidney the autopsy photos but there was no conversation regarding any of the information that was shown to him.

Brodsky told Sidney that he "wasn't happy about the psychiatric report" and that it was inconclusive and would have to be re-done. He said that Shane owed him a favor and that he wouldn't have to be paid to re-do the report.

In the report Sidney said that there was a psychiatric label attached to his behavior, and he had read it in June in the 6 or 7 page report that Sidney said, "covered everything."

JANUARY 14/05

SIDNEY SPOKE OF HIS INTERVIEW WITH DR. KENT SOMERS, WHICH HAPPENED the day before. He was given a multiple-choice questionnaire, true, mostly true, very true, etc. Somers re-introduced himself from the previous year; he spoke of seeing Sidney in January of 2004 in Brandon.

There was no talk of any conclusions from the first visit or anything about the meeting other than re-capping. The questionnaire took a couple of hours—Sidney got to work on it on his own. Sidney stated that Somers was more thorough than Shane who he said, "just went through the motions" and "just had to be there." Somers on the other hand, spent about forty-five minutes asking him about his job, school and about the kinds of people he had cooked for.

They discussed what Sidney's family was like; they talked about the abuse and touched on his relationship with 'Mother'.

Somers said he was going to meet with him again on Monday January 17th and told Sidney that he wanted to discuss what happened in the hotel room that fateful day.

JANUARY 13/05

Dan,

DR. KENT SOMERS CAME TO SEE ME FROM STONY MOUNTAIN. WE'LL HAVE *a couple more visits. I see him next Monday Jan. 17/05. Today we talked about what we'll do in the other meetings; we'll talk about the voices, and* the gory details of dissecting and having sex with Greene's dead body. I'm going to leave a message with Dr. Somers to bring the photos of Greene, before and after death. I'll try to sneak a photo of Greene's dismembered carcass on the examining table. Even Dr. Somers commented I did a pretty good job on Greene's body, saying it was very thorough.

I was given a bunch of tests to do: One was a PDS (Bidr version 7) by Delray L Paulus Ph.D.; it's 40 questions, multiple-choice. I managed to peel off the front page to see what was underneath, it's a score sheet grid, one side says Profile: General population, the other says Profile: Prison Entrants and has a bunch of numbers to add up. Looks kind of confusing. Then there is the MCMI–III Multiaxial Inventory, by Theodore Millian Ph.D. It's like the tests you do at the end of the year in high school (aptitude tests shade the most logical answer). Then a Personality Assessment Inventory, response booklet by Leslie C. Morey, Ph.D. It has 344 questions, multiple-choice from F false, ST somewhat true. MT mostly true and VT very true (e.g. question 118: "sometimes I have trouble keeping different thoughts separate" F ST MT VT). I'm beginning to hypothesize that these tests may not have anything to do with Pen placement. I am going to ask Dr. Somers his view if he sees me going to the Pen or a Mental Health Facility.

I would at some point like to go on the radio show Crime and Punishment on CJOB, talk about what the papers have said and speculated, that a camera should be allowed in the courtroom, perhaps my views on rehabilitation in the provincial penal system (what a joke!). Why I think this case should be heard by an Aboriginal Tribunal, or be heavily influenced by Aboriginal doctrine.

Write Soon,
Sidney

JANUARY 21/05

THE MEETING THAT WAS TO TAKE PLACE ON MONDAY THE 17TH DID NOT HAPPEN. There was no reason given for the cancellation, nor any notice of a re-scheduled interview. He said, "Somers is more interested in the facts, in the voices". I expressed surprise about this mention of 'voices', which he said he planned discussing with Somers at their next meeting. When I asked about it Sidney said that he had written about the 'voices' in past letters sent to me. I requested that he talk more about these 'voices' in his next letter.

Sidney stated that he didn't tell Dr. Shane any details about the actual murder when he spoke to him at the Remand Center in January of 2004. He mentioned again that he didn't like Shane—he didn't trust him and he would not be divulging anything concerning the murder to him whatsoever.

I asked him when he began to recall certain events and he replied that things came back to him in bits and pieces. Sidney stated, "At first I didn't remember, you know, when you're drinking?" Sidney however did say that Brodsky was aware of as much information as I was, having been informed about the details of the killing in the summer of 2004.

Sidney said he came across a book that explained some things about Greg Brodsky called Conspiracy of Silence. It spoke a lot about him. He said, "A lot of lawyers think he has a love for the microphone." Sidney said that Brodsky also had been made aware of the 'voices'.

$$* \quad * \quad * \quad * \quad *$$

UNBEKNOWNST TO THE KILLER'S ATTORNEY GREG BRODSKY WAS THE 'RELATIONSHIP' that I had been cultivating with his client via regular correspondence of letters, visits and telephone calls since March 2004. In my role as Host/Producer of my weekly talk radio program *Off the Cuff*, I asked Greg Brodsky for an interview and he agreed. The interview took place on March 7, 2005. I posed questions about novel defense strategies that he had employed in defending clients, such as Automatism but I focused quite a bit in the one-hour interview on the responsibility of the Defense Attorney to determine the truthfulness of their client's story.

Of particular interest to myself, and possibly the Prosecution is the claim in a letter from Sidney Teerhuis, in which the killer told his attorney about the location of actual physical evidence (the victim's internal organs). In the controversial trial of Paul Bernardo and Karla Holmolka, Bernardo's defense attorney was told about the location of physical evidence (the videotapes of the rape and murder victims). He retrieved the videotapes and then suppressed that evidence. He was charged for that offence, but was eventually acquitted, however his legal career was over as a result of the Bernardo trial.

THE GREG BRODSKY INTERVIEW – MARCH 7/05

> Good evening, this is your host Dan Zupansky for the program Off the Cuff, here on the University of Manitoba Radio, 101.5 UMFM. Our program today is with esteemed Winnipeg criminal defense lawyer Greg Brodsky. He has practiced law since 1963 and is one of the most successful and well-known lawyers in Canada. He is well known for defending those considered the worst of the worst, the most heinous offenders, often those accused of the most bizarre crimes. We will be talking to Greg Brodsky about how he defends some of those offenders, what the defense of insanity really means, and what is automatism. Thank you Mr. Greg Brodsky for agreeing to this interview.
> **Greg:** You are very welcome. It's a pleasure to be with you.
> **Dan:** Thank you. Now as far as I understand it, part of the defense team that you assemble includes one or more psychiatrists, what rules apply regarding your choice of psychiatrists?
> **Brodsky:** Well number one I don't always use psychiatrists and two when I do I use them to see whether I can accept

instructions from my client, some of them aren't able to understand what court proceedings are or aren't able to assist in their own defense, and that's one reason I'll have a psychiatrist involved and the second is to see if he's criminally responsible. He may at the time have been off his medication or in some kind of psychotic interlude and that's another reason for a psychiatrist. He may be better now or back on his medication and the third reason is obviously to mitigate the sentence that would otherwise be imposed.

Dan: Are there any rules applying to how many psychiatrists you can use or are there any other guidelines to how you would be able to use a psychiatrist in the defense of say a serious offence like murder?

Brodsky: Well number one legal aid only authorizes whatever, one or two. Second is that it would depend on what the defense is that I want to use, whether I'm going to get a local psychiatrist or not and three, sometimes the psychiatrist I use is the provincial psychiatrist, from time to time, even though when my client talks to that psychiatrist and that psychiatrist writes a report, the report goes to the Crown and the courts. If my client goes to see a private psychiatrist, then the report comes to me, it doesn't go to the courts and I 'sever post' to use it, which means that if it doesn't work out with the first psychiatrist, I can go to another one only if it's on a private basis, and my client can afford it.

Dan: You have said for the record that you are critical of the judicial system with regards to the length of sentences given to those sentenced to a mental facility as compared to those sentenced to a federal penitentiary. Could you please repeat your position regarding this issue?

Brodsky: Sure. What I mean by that is if someone is found not criminally responsible and goes to the Selkirk Mental Hospital, the forensic unit there--he's held there and the issue for his release is his risk to the community. So that is if he might commit an offence or if he might be dangerous, they hold him. If my client were to be convicted of a criminal offence and didn't use insanity as a defense, and went to the penitentiary--the situation is altogether different because in the penitentiary he can eat in the cafeteria, he can play cribbage with the people on his range. He has to do something wrong before that privilege is taken away from him. The parole board will release him when his parole eligibility comes unless there is a substantial risk that he's not going to comply with parole conditions. If the hospital doesn't agree with the findings of the court, which happens in a not infrequent basis, he is just locked up. He doesn't get to play cribbage because he's locked up. He doesn't get to go out to the cafeteria--his food is brought to him. He doesn't get to watch whatever program he wants on T.V. He doesn't get the same kind of freedom he does in a penitentiary. I think that is inappropriate and I think that is wrong.

Dan: Okay given your answer there, your profession dictates that you work in your client's best interest, is that correct? If your client were potentially to be sentenced to a penitentiary term rather than sentenced to a term in a mental facility--would the prospect of a lesser sentence given for the penitentiary term influence your decision as to how to proceed with the defense of your client?

Brodsky: Well sure, in one case we presented a not criminally responsible defense, it did not succeed and the man was convicted of murder. We then had to sit down and decide whether he was going to appeal and we decided he wasn't going to appeal. He was better off in the penitentiary. The reason for that is a psychiatrist won't treat him for something he thinks he doesn't have because it was a contested matter in the court. He was going to be sent to Selkirk, they wouldn't treat him for something he doesn't have. He would be in that position that we discussed earlier--that is where he would just be warehoused subject to no freedoms that are available in the penitentiary. In the penitentiary he gets minimum wage, he can buy a T.V. In the hospital he doesn't get that, he can't buy a T.V. he can't have anything that the hospital won't give him. He decided not to appeal.

Dan: (This is the actual prepared question that I had meant to ask). Would you choose to pursue a penitentiary sentence rather than a mental facility sentence because the time your client would receive in actual terms would be less and hence more beneficial to your client? (Instead I essentially asked the same question mistakenly adding a reference to a psychiatrist stating his determination of insanity during the trial).

Brodsky: Let me talk to you about a case I did a long time ago. He had two defenses. One was an accident two was insanity. You cannot use them both because once you use the insanity defense and he's found to be insane, the consequences are automatic referral to the Selkirk Mental Hospital. In that case despite the fact the insanity defense was available, we opted to fight the case based on the defense of accident. In fact the jury found it was an accident and he was released. Sometimes your clients come to you and they have two or three or four defenses. You can't put them all forward because then you will succeed with none. Sometimes you have to decide what your defense will be in this case. Sometimes it will be the insanity and sometimes as I've already indicated, it'll be for instance accident or self-defense or whatever.

Dan: Now you spoke of and you know I don't think a lot of people know this, and I certainly didn't know, when you talk about your client actually giving you two or three possible defenses, all of them possibly contradicting each other, "As a lawyer you are ethically bound to not support or tell a lie, you must not say a client is innocent if you know the client is not innocent, nor may you as a lawyer put the client on the witness stand to tell what you as the lawyer knows to be a lie." As a lawyer what is your responsibility in determining the truthfulness of your client's story, how far do you go in discerning whether your client is being untruthful concerning their guilt in the crime they have been accused of committing?

Brodsky: Let me breakdown that for you a little bit. First of all a lawyer cannot put a defense forward that he knows to be false. Second he can't put someone on the stand to tell a lie, he can't put a perjured defense before the court. What you said before though about I can't say he's (the client) innocent if he's not--that's not right. I don't decide on the innocence of my client, the court does. I'm only his lawyer and whether I believe in his defense or not is totally irrelevant. What I do is put forth the best defense that I can for him, subject to the ethics of my profession, and I let the courts decide whether it's going to accept it or not.

Dan: Now let's talk about... (interrupted)

Brodsky: Let me talk about something else, because you are making an assumption, at least I hear in the back of what you are saying, an assumption that when a client says he did it, he's telling you the truth. That's what I hear you saying or thinking and I have to tell you-- that's not accurate.

Dan: (Interrupting) In all cases.

Brodsky: I have clients that have told me that they are guilty or they want to plead guilty, some of them tell me that because they want to get their case over with and some of them, for instance--one fellow told police on five separate occasions that he was guilty of this murder and explained how he did it. The reason there were five statements, he couldn't get the place right or get the instrument right because he didn't do it. He was such an insignificant person in his life that he wanted the charge because for the first time in his life he was relevant. He was somebody and that was hard. We had to go in that case and find the real killer.

Dan: You say it's not the rule, but the thing is that it's just about as likely that many people that come to you that say they are not guilty of a crime--most of those are guilty and most of the people that say they have committed a crime have indeed committed that crime.

Brodsky: That's true, and maybe it was lucky for me that when I started out I went to the Health Sciences Center, it was called General Hospital then. The facts were as related to me by the police and by my client that my client's wife ran away and he chased her all over the United States. He came back to Canada. He caught up with her in the Maryland Hotel--she was there with her boyfriend. He knocked on the door, the door opened and the boyfriend was in the corner. He said to the boyfriend, "Now I got you". The boyfriend according to the story, told me, jumped up and he shot him twice. That was the story. I said, "How did you get injured?" "Well he ran over and we were fighting and in the fight I hurt my hand." Well you would think with that story he told me, and the bullet in the fellow, my client was a goner. The fact of the matter is that the ballistics expert from the R.C.M.P established that the injury to my client was a bullet. It went into the back of the hand he told me he was holding the gun in. The fellow who had been shot had gun shot residue that meant he hadn't been shot from the other side of the room, and that my guy's story was all wrong. He was acquitted.

I acted for a lady named Easter in Ontario and she told Winnipeg Police that she had stabbed her husband to death. She made again four statements: Winnipeg Police, two to the Ontario Provincial Police and one to a Justice of the Peace in Kenora. She said she stabbed her husband to death, and low and behold her husband was stabbed, she was full of the blood, and he was full of blood, and whatever. The jury acquitted that lady, who believes to this day she's guilty. We argued to the jury that the reason that she believes it is that she was confabulating--that is filling in the blank in her memory with what must have happened, and when she woke up and saw her husband dead and nobody else around, she assumed she was the guilty person. We said what about this and what about that and where the heck is the knife and the jury acquitted her. So the fact my client told me that he was guilty, or in this case, she's not guilty. Just take it in consideration, you don't stop looking, you see what the physical facts are and then you go to court. It's like you have eyewitnesses as to a car accident--the answer to me is no. What you rely on is the skid marks on the road because they are not subject to the foibles of eyewitness identification, and you can't fool the skid marks, they are physical evidence of the track of the car and what happened. They're what counts, not what your client tells you happened.

Dan: Now I was interested in the defense that you have used, and maybe you can tell us how many times that you have successfully used this, or attempted to use this-- was automatism? Automatism basically for our audience, is a state of involuntariness, a state of unconsciousness, not in a medical sense but a legal sense.

Brodsky: Automatism means that you didn't intend the act. The act is not yours. That happens sometimes when someone gets a bang on the head with a hammer, or a psychological shock such as people in wartime get, and the result is they are acting in an automatic way, not volitional, it's not thinking, it's an automatic way. It's not because of disease of the mind because that would make it insanity, or what we used to call insanity, which we now call not criminally responsible. That person is what we call an automaton, and if he didn't intend his act and it was involuntary--then the verdict the jury will deliver is not guilty. The difference between that and an involuntary act done by someone who is psychotic, (psychosis n a severe mental disorder affecting a person's whole personality psychotic adj.) is that person, the psychotic person will be found insane, what we call not criminally responsible, and go to a mental hospital. If you're found not guilty because you're an automaton, you just go home. Obviously if you're dangerous and if the crime could be repeated, there could be issues of civil commitment where you could be locked up if you are a danger to yourself or others, under the Mental Health Act.

Dan: How do they make the determination between non-insane automatism and insane automatism?

Brodsky: It's whether it's a disease of the mind or not.

Dan: How do they make the determination that it's a disease of the mind?

Brodsky: Well a disease of the mind--you're right, that's a legal term not a medical term.

Dan: Right.

Brodsky: Nobody goes to the hospital and has on their chart, disease of the mind.

Dan: No.

Brodsky: Disease of the mind is an ancient term and it usually refers to a long-term disability caused by improper functioning in your brain either because you have a legitimate organic disease or because your thinking is skewed (skew adj. slanting askew. v make skew; turn or twist around). If you get drunk and act in an involuntary way you don't walk away from the crime, your charge is reduced from murder to manslaughter, and then you can get up to a life sentence. If you have drugs and you get stoned out of your mind, that's not an automaton, that's caused by an impairment that will reduce your charge again, not murder but manslaughter if it's a murder case, and gives the judge the discretion in sentencing. On the other hand we had a case in Ontario, in Toronto where a fellow drove across the city and killed somebody. His defense was an automatism defense and it was called sleepwalking. That fellow was just acquitted. In order to succeed with that kind of defense, you would obviously need some medical evidence to show that the fellow had a history of sleepwalking--why he was subject to sleepwalking--what he had done in the past that was not criminal in that sleepwalking state, and why in this case the jury should believe that what he did was in an unconscious way. That is, how could an unconscious person drive across the city, how could an unconscious person stop at red lights, how could an unconscious person do this and that? The jury accepted that, that's a case called Park.

Dan: Right, and that involved somnambulism, and that seems understandable I think because it's an extremely rare example.

Brodsky: Right, the automatism defense has been referred to by judges as the last refuge of a helpless defendant because it is so rarely accepted, that we just don't use it anymore.[2]

Dan: When you talk about rarely accepted--how many times have you successfully used the defense of automatism?

Brodsky: I have only been successful with it two or three times, and I would say that I haven't even raised it in the last twenty years.

Dan: Oh really, hmm okay (I was very surprised at this admission, as I had been told by veteran journalist George Jacub that he had covered murder trials in which Brodsky had successfully used the automatism defense many times. I simply assumed that the trials he was referring to were more recent).

When you talked about the long-term disability of the person with a mental disorder, would that long-term disability have to be determined, for example by a doctor previous to the incident of automatism, where the person was unconscious?

Brodsky: No, sometimes because of their peculiar behavior they withdraw, and they don't go outside, and they don't want to see a doctor, and it's because of their peculiar behavior. So they are not diagnosed until something bad happens. Until the police come. What happens then is that you have to go back and talk to the people whom the person was dealing with to see what strange behavior they then can recollect. You don't need a diagnosis in advance of the criminal act, or what would be a criminal charge--sometimes you can work it backwards, and we do that from time to time.

Dan: Now when, this as far as I could see was unsuccessful, as this person was convicted of manslaughter, in the case where a person claimed that they could not remember the crime, the forty-seven stab wounds occurred as a result of what a court had to consider as a severe psychological blow. Also in the definitions you read, "weakness in the accused psychological or emotional makeup". So the thing is, isn't this a little bit open to interpretation?

Brodsky: Yes that's why we have juries.

Dan: Okay and that's where we get to a point I wanted to make--is that do you really think that the jury is capable--if a person like myself, a regular layman, and other people that only have the benefit of the daily newspaper and the nightly news to understand how things really work in court--do you think then, the jury being just an example of those same people, somewhat ignorant about how things really work, and then employing that same jury to be able to deal with and understand the concepts, of legal concepts rather than medical concepts, determining whether it's a severe psychological blow or a weakness in the accused's psychological or emotional

2 There were two cases in early 2006 where an automatism defense was successful.

makeup? Isn't some of this stuff open to interpretation, and hence maybe a problem for the jury?

Brodsky: Well number one, it is open to interpretation, but that's what court cases are and two, I have more respect for the jury system than I suppose the average person. I don't consider them a collection of my morons or idiots. I consider them reasonable people, and that's why I have my experts not talk like they're doing the 'grand rounds' but talk to the people in a way that's understandable. Hopefully the jury will be in a position to weigh the evidence and make the determination. On the other hand, the last couple of insanity cases we did, I did without a jury. The problem with juries is not what you are raising so much if they see a dangerous person in the prisoner's box they are very reluctant, no matter how many times you tell them about reasonable doubt, no matter how many times you tell them about the presumption of innocence. If they see what they perceive as a dangerous person in the prisoner's box, they don't want to let him go, they don't want him living next door to them, or next to their children's houses. They don't want him babysitting their grandkids. They're not going to let him go so easily. It's harder for them to get a fair trial than the average person.

Dan: If the accused you are representing--there is no eye-witness to the crime itself, and this accused has made no statements concerning their guilt one way or another, and the Prosecution come Preliminary, it is revealed that they have little physical evidence and no evident motive at this Preliminary. Now both you and your client look at the evidence, discuss the evidence. What are you obliged to share with the Prosecution, if anything, of what you've been told by your client?

Brodsky: Nothing. Why should I? Number one, I recognize we're in a courtroom; we're not in a church. I recognize that the issue to be tried in a courtroom is whether the Crown has sufficient evidence to satisfy a court, beyond a reasonable doubt of the guilt of my client. That's the test, does the Crown have enough evidence to establish beyond a reasonable doubt that my client is guilty. Notice I didn't say that my client did the dirty deed-- that's not the test. The test is not what I would do in the (same) circumstances, the test is: Does the Crown have sufficient evidence to prove beyond a reasonable doubt that my client is guilty, and I am entitled to argue: No they don't. The word innocent does not equate to: He didn't do it. The word innocent means there is insufficient proof.

Dan: Now would you have a problem, hypothetically, if a client were to lie fairly well, and stick to his story, like I had said, and have no eyewitness?

Brodsky: (Interrupting) What difference in your case, what difference would it make what my client told me? If the Crown's case is so deficient that they can't prove it, why do I have to tell the judge, "Wait a minute, my client confessed to me. I mean, what do you do then with solicitor/client privilege?

Dan: Your client definitely... it could be under the premise that he's telling you the truth and gave you a lie, that's why I say he could be a fairly good liar...

Brodsky: He could...

Dan: Now, what is your responsibility?

Brodsky: I am not the judge! I'm not the judge! My client tells me this, my client tells me that, so what? That's not the issue. I don't say to the judge, "Wait a minute, the Crown doesn't have enough proof to convict my client, I have to tell you my client really did it, never mind what the police think or don't think, or the evidence they have or they don't. I tell you that my client should be convicted. What do you need a lawyer for?

Dan: I'm just trying to get to your responsibility, if any at all, say he came up with an implausible, fanciful tale...

Brodsky: (Interrupting) They do that. My clients often lie to me...

Dan: (Interrupting) And you're still obliged to go with that?

Brodsky: Absolutely not, absolutely not.

Dan: Well like I said, how far do...

Brodsky: I tell them, "Number one, you tell me that, I'm not going to fly with that", and I tell them, "I can't put forward a defense I know to be false or perjured, and I don't know. So he says to me, "How can you defend me then?" And I say, "I can challenge the quality of the Crown's proof", and that's what I do. Because it has nothing to do with what my client tells me. I can say to the witnesses, "Are you sure you saw the person? Are you sure it was my client?" The witness says, "Well I'm not so sure it was your client." If that's the issue, of identity, I say to the judge, "So how can you convict my client if she says she's not sure, and the Crown has to prove its case beyond a reasonable doubt?" I don't have my client say, "Hey, it was me, it was me!" I don't have him yell out that from the back of the courtroom.

Dan: No. In the case of a client having one story, and then say a year later or two years later, whatever it is before the trial, but at some point comes up with, like you said, came up with another alternative...

Brodsky: Yeah. They looked at the facts that the Crown has and they want to figure out what they now should be saying. People try to squirm and figure, and try to out-lawyer the lawyer. That's normal. I still don't put forward a defense I know to be perjured.

Dan: And so, you said—you will have that conversation with him and say, "Listen, this is where I stand: I believe part of what you say, I don't believe the rest of it, and as a matter of fact, I'm not going to court with this."

Brodsky: Right. Okay, "And the option for you client is you can still have me as a lawyer or you can go to another lawyer."

45

Dan: The book that Truman Capote wrote called In Cold Blood, which documents the senseless murders of an entire family back in the 50's would barely raise an eyebrow or sell many books today. Do you believe that there has been an escalation in serious crime, in the severity of crimes and the increase in senseless murders?

Brodsky: That's very hard to talk about now, in view of the recent killings of four Mounties in Alberta. The public sees more and hears more about crime than they ever did. That's not a function of more crime taking place or more violence on the street. That's a function of more exploration of it by the media. We're inundated with it now, so it seems like there's more.

Dan: What kinds of crimes would qualify for an actual life sentence, where this person would never see the light of day, and what kind of criminal would qualify as being unable to be rehabilitated in your mind, from your experience?

Brodsky: Well in murder cases, it doesn't matter whether he can rehabilitate himself or not because the sentence is automatic, and that is life in prison. There are two kinds of murder, second-degree murder, where the minimum time he has to wait to make his first parole application is ten years. And there's first-degree murder and the minimum time he has to wait to make his first parole application is twenty-five years. Those have nothing to do with rehabilitation--they have to do with legislative enactments. And again, the dangerous offender that we spoke of, that has nothing to do with rehabilitation, that's a sentence that's imposed by law, and parole that's regulated by law.

Dan: Now if a person is convicted of two say heinous murders, is that person able to be deemed a dangerous offender or long-term offender?

Brodsky: If he's convicted of two murders, separate murders, he can't under the legislation that exists now, even apply for Faint Hope. We used to have something called the Faint Hope Clause, which said if you get a life sentence with no parole eligibility for twenty-five years yet you could still apply after fifteen years to have that twenty-five years reduced, and you take that before a jury. If you are convicted of two murders, homicides actually, they don't have to be murders, you're not eligible for the Faint Hope Clause. (Homicide n. killing of one person by another. Murder n. intentional unlawful killing.)

Dan: Now with some of these defenses that your sometime psychiatric partner, Dr. Shane has done--I want to ask you if you were involved with the defense of 'Catastrophic Rage' that Dr. Shane had put forth, involving a gentleman who stabbed his father forty-seven times--I believe after years of this gentleman abusing his mother?

Brodsky: Dr. Shane has been a witness that I've put forward in connection with a variety of cases and the reason for that is because we don't have that many psychiatrists who do forensic work. It's hard to tell your family that, "I'm going to court today so that people will be throwing stones at me, people will be vilifying me, people with paid warriors will be cross-examining me to make me look foolish, unreliable and ignorant." It's hard to get psychiatrists who want to put themselves in that forum, but you need them. Dr. Shane as you will recall, or your listeners may know, was one of the doctors I used when we first had a 'Battered Wife's Syndrome' presented to a court and successfully was upheld by the Supreme Court of Canada. And the reason that it went to the Supreme Court was because the Crown took the position that the 'Battered Wife Syndrome' was common sense and anyone could understand it. And the courts then argued that the psychiatric evidence shouldn't be accepted. I argued those things that bound a woman to her torturer, bound a woman to her abuser, were beyond the jurors kin, and without expert explanation they wouldn't understand her actions and the Supreme Court accepted that, and from that Angelique-Lynn Lavalee became the cornerstone in our judicial system of the 'Battered Wife' defense; it's the case, the seminal case, and Dr. Shane was the psychiatrist that we used in that case to explain what was not otherwise understandable. Without Dr. Shane and the psychiatrist who testified, there would be no 'Battered Woman' defense.

Dan: I think a lot of people are quite critical of some of the novel and controversial psychiatric-based defenses, but I think in the case that you point out, and some of the cases that have used a similar 'Battered Woman' defense, Syndrome defense--I think, I have to give you both credit, Dr. Shane and yourself for putting that kind of defense forward because I think it's an appropriate defense, despite the feeling maybe from most people that some of the defenses are a little bit too liberal, we'll say at the very least. But at least this one is very, very understandable for the public I find, so you've done a good job, I think, in taking a kind of case that people could understand and empathize with. But then again you can see the inherent dangers with this defense, when you see Karla Homolka, even in your words, I think it's ironic that you are commenting on a case, you've spearheaded a case in the first place, and then you're taking the definition of 'Battered Woman's Syndrome' to absurd heights if you can include Karla Homolka as a 'Battered Woman.'

Brodsky: And I think that's probably the reason, in fact I know that's the reason that I was hired in the first place. Not to argue that she's a 'Battered Woman' but to argue that I've had enough of these cases in my experience to know when some one is trying to put it over on you. So the argument there was that she wasn't, not that she was.

Dan: That's right (pause). This has been a very, very informative interview, and I want to thank you very much Mr. Greg Brodsky for this opportunity to interview you about all these things that we've talked about in this last hour.

Brodsky: Well you're very welcome. I'm glad to have been a guest on your show.

Dan: Thank you, have a good night.

6

The Cell-Mate

APRIL 7/04

Dear Dan,

I HAVE SPENT ABOUT 60 DAYS NEAR AND AROUND SIDNEY EITHER AT BRANDON CC OR Headingley CC. We have had a lot of conversations about numerous subjects. In my experiences with Sidney I have found him to be of more than average intelligence generally. He is meticulous sometimes to the point of seeming compulsive with his living space and his personal self. He possesses a quick temper and when aroused it has a feeling of great depth and passion behind it. Scary eyes. Very emotional, he told me about being startled by someone one time and having beaten them to the ground in tears and pain before he was aware he'd done it.

He is very open about his sexuality and is very much the effeminate being. 'Baby Cakes' is very definitely a Queen. He offers sexual favors regularly around the jail range, and claims a surprising degree of success. Living in such a confined space (jail cell) I observe him closely. Personal hygiene is a very big thing with Sidney, when he urinates he uses toilet paper to hold himself while he relieves his bladder.

He claims to not be racist but does not care for Afro-Americans and has large hope and visions of First Nations' people becoming very powerful in the future. He espouses an agenda for First Nations much as Hitler did for Aryans.

Don Abbott

*　　*　　*　　*　　*

Dear Dan,

WELL THE WEEKEND IS UPON US AND THIS IS WHEN I DO THE BULK OF MY LETTER WRITING. Its difficult to write much given what I have to draw upon for material, so having received a letter to respond to is well, overwhelming, my joy knows no bounds, in fact, honestly the pleasure of returning a reply is well, it feels so good. I'm going to drag it out till Sunday afternoon.

First things first, you will have found a few pages here for Sidney, please forward them to him. I saw the article in Friday March 13th paper about convicted criminals no longer being able to profit from their crimes. Read the few lines I wrote him if you wish.

You are absolutely *right about this situation and I will do all I can to help out.* I'm absolutely *sure you can compile enough material out of this to take it somewhere profitable. If its okay with you I will assist any way I can. So we'll see what comes out of a little correspondence with him.*

It is now Friday evening and that being all of this letter that I am dedicating to Mr. Teerhuis. I will set it aside to play an exciting game of cards. Write you later.

My being here at Headingley isn't all that bad a thing; you know sometimes a change is as good as a day off!

Don Abbott

*   *   *   *   *

Dear Dan,

SHORTLY BEFORE I JOINED SIDNEY AGAIN HIS LAWYER'S ASSISTANT BONNIE AND THE defense psychiatrist reviewed morgue photos with him, he stated that this upset him, and for 4 or 5 days it bothered him. The corpse was reconstructed (laid out) on a stainless steel morgue table. 8 pieces, head, arms at elbows, legs at the knees, torso at waist, front section of genital areas (if I understand him right).

He told me the following about this meeting: Forensic Investigation performed on Sidney. Besides the standard mug shot and prints, they (Winnipeg Police Services) photographed his entire body (naked) from head to toe.

As well they took a swab wipe from his head and had him stand on white paper barefoot (to footprint him). He was not surprised by this, as he walked around crime scene barefoot. He says the missing parts were probably just overlooked.

The psychiatrist says that the 47 stab wounds are not as random as Sid would say. He (Sidney) doesn't see any pattern himself even when shown to him. He says they claim the letter U and the number 8. He does not see this nor can he think of a reason for it to be there.

The only thing that bothers him or thing that he couldn't get over is the amount of shrinkage that had occurred in the body where the joints had been separated from each other. From the time he has seen them last, to when the photos were taken, he says the shrinkage was unbelievable, he could not get over it. He said he was only mildly surprised by the yellow color tint, but it was haunting. I wonder what his skin tone looks like in the four photos Sidney took of him posing naked alive in the hotel room.

I don't want to ask him too much but he asked me what I thought would affect the outcome most of all for him and I told him I believed the manner of separating the joints would be the biggest sway to the jury if it got right down to competency. Chopped in pieces or separated with demonstrable skill, he asked me why; we talked. He remembers a lot more that he claims—sick fuck.

Don Abbott

*   *   *   *   *

Don's Letter to Sidney

Hello there Sidney,

JUST A FEW LINES TO LET YOU KNOW THAT YOU DO CROSS MY MIND. HE TOLD ME THAT you are residing at Winnipeg Remand Centre. I'm happy that you are no longer in that ditch Brandon. How did you make out over Miss Jackson? I've seen a paper you had with a Brandon court appearance but there was no outcome given.

How is the novel coming along? You are still writing it are you not? I read on Friday (March 13th) an article about people convicted of a crime in Manitoba no longer being able to profit by it.

I am at Headingley now. I'm sure if you sent a letter for me to Dan; he would forward it to me here. Being in jail yourself I know you realize how much a little correspondence can cheer a person up.

Anyhow Sidney other than these few lines not much has really changed.

I still look towards a future of semi-retirement aboard my own charter vessel in the Caribbean and rest assured there will be a spot for a high quality chef aboard.

Until then stay in touch I promised you that I would and you must admit that I am keeping up my end. I would also urge you to cultivate your relationship with Dan. I have known him since 1976 and in all that time I can only say that he has always treated me in an honorable way and I am proud to list him among my few true friends. He treats people right and I'm glad you two now know each other.

Do drop me a few lines, it is your turn.

In friendship,
Don

*　　*　　*　　*　　*

Don's Letter to Dan

SITTING IN A JAIL CELL AWAITING AN OUTCOME/FUTURE AND THINKING ABOUT UPCOMING trial, any sort of resolution that will allow Sidney to be in attendance at the Vancouver Olympics in 2010 is the ultimate at this point.

On jury selection he hopes that the make-up of his jury will be close to:

1 Afro-American

60% Native American

3 Females

Balance-Asian and 1 East Indian

At the end of each period/employment/location of Sidney's life he has found himself stranded/broke/unemployed/strung out/starting over/ in a strange place halfway back to where he wanted to be and having to find a job and a place to stay in order to finish the proverbial trip home. He has through out his life left behind supports and friends whom he knew that he could quite likely depend on. Why?

"I have always hurt the people I loved the most."

As far as background goes what is here is what I got from Sidney. I think I've (we've) done all right as far as background goes. As you read this through the first few times you will come across references that as events unfold will indicate how honest Sidney has been with me (us).

Last night we talked about success of the project, and I put forth the thought that to a degree it depended partly on unsolved issues remaining that way. He then said for the second time that Winnipeg Police Services search methods were inadequate and he insists he never consumed his victim. This single thing he feels should fuel rumors and cause doubts that should ensure financial success.

I will talk to you soon by phone. I have had pretty much all I can take of this Dan and look forward to being away from Sidney. I have begun to have his nightmares (twice now).

Yours,

Don

7

The Victim

THE SALTEAUX OJIBWAY PEOPLE ARE THE ANCESTORS OF SHOAL LAKE #40 First Nation people and inhabitants of the Ontario portion of the area subsequently covered by the Northwest Angle Treaty of 1873. Their economy was based on fishing, hunting, gathering, trapping, the harvesting of wild rice and some horticulture, until the late 18th century when they became involved in the fur trade with the Hudson's Bay company. The Ontario government confirmed Shoal Lake #40 in 1915.

Major industries today include trapping, fishing and work at the water pumping station (Shoal Lake is the source of Winnipeg's drinking water). The community also has a tourist camp and a general store. In September 2006 there were 164 registered males and 142 females residing on the reserve. Located off of the Trans-Canada Highway about 45 km west of Kenora, down a winding dirt road, which leads to a sign announcing the community of Iskatewizaagegan (Shoal Lake) #40 First Nation.

Robin Robert Greene Sr. was born on Big Island, Lake of the Woods, on May 16th, 1932, before moving as a baby to Shoal Lake with his parents Ko-kum and Shomis who taught him the traditional values and culture. He gained an appreciation for the outdoors as his family made its livelihood by fishing, trapping and picking wild rice. In the 1980s, he stepped back in time by building a secluded cabin on Shoal Lake without hydro or running water, which allowed him to spend time away from the community. His wife Kathleen, 54, is a member of the Opaskwayak Cree First Nation in Manitoba, but has lived in Shoal Lake for 13 years. The couple worked together as counselors, healers and teachers.

Robin Robert Greene Sr. passed away in a Kenora hospital on April 25th, 2009. He was regarded as a humble spiritual leader, teacher, healer and advisor devoting his whole life to helping others, including Aboriginal activism. He was instrumental with the inclusion of Treaty Rights in the Canadian Constitution, embarking on his political journey at the age of 16 when he became a Councilor for Shoal Lake, He was also Chief of Shoal Lake for years, and then became Grand Chief of Treaty #3 for many years, and received the title of Honorary Grand Chief of Grand Council Treaty #3.

Robin Robert Greene Jr. was born in 1965. His mother was Mable Redsky. He was born and raised on the Shoal lake reserve. He died on July 1st, 2003. Canada Day.

TUESDAY OCTOBER 4/05

I SPOKE TO MY FRIEND ALLAN SMITTY, A WINNIPEG FILMMAKER WHO HAPPENS to work with a man named Jesse Greene. Smitty had discovered that Jesse Greene was a cousin of Robin Greene and that Jesse was originally from Shoal Lake, the reserve that Robin was from. Jesse told Smitty that he did not really know Robin at all but that his father would be a much better person to talk to about him. Smitty had recently interviewed Billy Joe Green, Jesse's father during the Juno Awards (the Canadian equivalent of the Grammy Awards), which were held in Winnipeg the spring of 2005. Smitty called Billy Joe and explained whom I was and that I was interested in interviewing someone from Robin's family for my proposed book.

Smitty called me to tell me that Billy Joe had said that he was appreciative of the fact that Smitty and myself had followed the appropriate manner in which to approach the family concerning my request for an interview. Billy Joe told Smitty that he would contact Robin's father who is also named Robin and ask him about the request and get back to us in a few days. He also told Smitty that the father Robin Greene Sr. was a highly respected elder in Shoal Lake and was considered a 'healer'.

I asked if Billy Joe had fully understood my intentions and Smitty said that Billy Joe did seem to understand. Despite Smitty's assurances, I called Billy Joe myself to see if I could at least reinforce what Smitty may have said and possibly add something that may not have been conveyed or may not have been so effectively conveyed by Smitty when speaking to Billy Joe.

I told Billy Joe that I had worked for a law reform group called People for Justice and that through my investigative work on this story that I had become the most important witness for the Prosecution in this murder case as I was responsible for providing evidence which will effectively help prosecute this accused for second-degree murder rather than a lesser charge of manslaughter. I told him that I wanted to portray Robin in a favorable light because in the course of this trial he would be portrayed in a negative light, while the killer would be portrayed in a somewhat favorable light.

I told Billy Joe that as the author of this book I would be able to control how Robin would be portrayed as well as how Sidney would be. Billy Joe asked if Sidney was aboriginal as he had heard and I acknowledged that was true. I told him that he was adopted by a non-aboriginal family and lived in Winnipeg. I also mentioned that Sidney had spoke of being tried by an Aboriginal Tribunal and Billy Joe stated that the Tribunal was normally a good idea but that this murder was not appropriate to be dealt with by the Tribunal. I thought that our conversation was very positive and hopefully I was able to express enough of the essence of what I wanted to express to the family so as to get an interview about the victim Robin Greene. Billy Joe said that he would contact Robin Greene Sr. and that he would call me back in a few days with an answer.

FRIDAY OCTOBER 14/05

I CALLED BILLY JOE AND HE SAID THAT HE HAD NOT BEEN ABLE TO CONTACT Robin Greene Sr. as of yet. I told Billy Joe that I felt it might be better if I were able to send him directly an E-mail outlining my involvement in this case and exactly what I wanted and why; and he could forward that E-mail to Robin Greene Sr. I felt that Billy Joe would not be as effective potentially as I would to be able to properly explain and state my case. Billy Joe agreed to forward the E-mail once he received it. He simply asked that the E-mail not be too long. I thanked him for his help and proceeded to E-mail to him my message:

```
Hello Billy Joe,

I will outline briefly what I am interested in and why.
You can hopefully E-mail this message to Mr. Greene.

    My name is Dan Zupansky.
    ...
    I want to present the story of your son in my
book, as you and your family would want. I want you to
have control over what I write about your son and your
son's life. You would have final approval about what
gets written about your son. I just want to provide an
opportunity for readers to understand who this victim
was and at the same time only talk about Teerhuis' crime
and very little else. I want the reader to not sympathize
with the killer at all and instead feel for the victim,
your son. Hopefully I will get to write this book to be
able to tell this story about the courts and maybe this
book can be a catalyst for a necessary serious debate
about how the courts fail to protect the rights of the
public while coddling the violent offender.
    I am sorry that your son was killed and that your
family will have to hear all the details during the
trial. You and your family will certainly not feel that
justice will have been served at the end of all of
this, I offer the opportunity to at least set the record
straight concerning your son and if you would like to
make some comments concerning the entire process I would
welcome that as well. I can only begin to imagine what
you and your family are going through and this E-mail
must also be hard to read. The potential for the book to
be published is not for certain at all but I am writing
the book regardless; my intentions in writing this book
are honest and sincere.
    Please consider my request and if you would like
to talk to me about this either E-mail me or my phone
number is ***-**** (work) or ***-**** (home). Thank you
for considering my request and I apologize for bothering
you and your family at this sensitive time.
```

I did not receive a reply from Billy Joe Green or the Greene family.

8

Blueprint for Disaster

MARIJETTE KLASSKE PELS WAS BORN JANUARY 12,1925 IN JAKARTA, Indonesia (Dutch East Indies). Her father Martinus Pels was an engineer in charge of a large sugar plantation. Her mother Dina studied piano at one of the finest schools in the Netherlands, hoping to become a concert pianist; she was also a close relative to the Dowe Egberts Coffee Empire. Case was her only brother, they live a privileged life of long vacations, the annual furlough back to the Netherlands by ship. Sailed into the ports of India, Sudan and the Suez Canal.

During the outbreak of WWII, Marijette and Case were sent to Alkmaar, in North Holland to be with her Uncle Peter Pels. Back in Indonesia her parents were making preparations to evacuate. They constructed a large crate, placed their valuables, furnishings on the plantation property and buried it, hoping to return after the war. Dina had the boat tickets ready; the Japanese army came to the plantation house and captured the two, placing them in concentration camps. Her mother was laid to rest in a mass grave, her father Martinus died the day the war ended.

Marijette Klasske Pels married Gerrit Teerhuis on July 10th, 1947; they had a champagne wedding. Shortly after her brother Case committed suicide on her doorstep. He shot himself in the head. There were enough bullets in the revolver to shoot Marijette, Gerrit and baby Martin (her first born of three children and one miscarriage, Isabel and Sidney would be adopted in the early seventies).

TEERHUIS, Sidney

Figure 9: Sidney Teerhuis, 1984 Yearbook entry.

She made a home in 1952. Originally Edmonton was to be the destination but the Immigration Hall was full. They lived in the East Kildonan area. Soon Foxdale Avenue became the Teerhuis homestead. At first 369 Foxdale, and then the infamous 373 Foxdale. The new house was a gift to Mother from Mr. Teerhuis. Within a couple of years Mrs. Teerhuis became involved with the Children's Aid Society of Winnipeg. She had an obsession with a foster child named Susan Watson, (mother spoke of Susan up until her death in 1990). Isabel Teresse Buffs was adopted first, then "Sidney Owens" came into foster care on September 12,1969. Sidney was nineteen days old.

Diane Basstiansen worked at New Faces on Henderson Highway; I believe there is a different Family Services at the same location.

1972 – The Boy Under the Glass Table

Mother told me I was always special, in more ways than one. A woman used to come visit from time to time. Her name was Mrs. Roberts. I still remember her big beehive hairdo.

I would contend with a Tonka tow-truck on the blue carpet near mother's feet. I was having my picture taken, I had red and white striped short-sleeved shirt. Mother explained (in a way only a child could understand) there was a family in St. James that wanted to adopt me. She said the lady with the red hair (Mrs. Roberts) was going to ask me a few questions. I recall going to the Children's Aid to see Dr. Barsky before the adoption took place.

One day in July 1972, mother said she was going to keep me. I remember lying on the blue shag carpet, under the glass table watching the two women sign the final adoption papers. "I became Sidney Teerhuis on July 2,1972. Judge Malloy signed it. When Mrs. Roberts left, after the papers had been signed, I remember mother holding me in her arms for what seemed like an eternity. I was puzzled as to why she was crying. Years later, for my 18th birthday she gave me the original copy of the adoption papers.

*   *   *   *   *

Saturday mornings we'd play in the basement. Izzy used to chase me around holding mother's panties, singing "Watch out for the pinties" over and over. It was a losing battle. I usually gave up having mothers soiled panties smothered all over my face. I'd go upstairs crying. Mother would yell at me and Izzy stood in the back hall laughing at me. Another time, Izzy made me drink her piss after bedtime. I went to go tell mother but I barfed all over the kitchen floor and got a severe beating from Mr. Teerhuis. I couldn't sit for a week.

I felt ashamed of being adopted. Izzy would always tell new neighborhood kids we were adopted. We'd get into some pretty intense fights. Isabel and Cathy Storimans spelled FUCK *across my belly in black ink. I stepped on Izzy's finger and broke her fingernail. Mother locked me naked in the broom closet for three days and fed me dinner and water in an old dog dish. R. Teerhuis put me in a burlap sack and locked me in the trunk of the car overnight for pushing Izzy down the stairs.*

Around 1977 — Early Years

In Grade 2, I joined Cub Scouts. I stayed in Cubs for two years. On our initiation night we had a dinner at the community centre. It was the only time Mr. Teerhuis and I participated in an event outside the family setting. During spring break the Cubs had a sleepover at the church (We had a baseball game the next day). During the night I was woken up an older boy who had unbuttoned my pajama pants and touched my prick. I just stared at him while he did that, and never made much of it the next morning.

During that same summer, there was a high-rise apartment beside the Norvilla hotel on Henderson Highway; a woman had been stabbed to death 47 times. Her body was found in the bathtub. My sister Izzy, neighbor Cathy Storimans and me got on our bikes and rode to the field behind the high rise. We tried to see what floor it happened on. We were scared shitless while we sat there. After sometime of hypothesizing, we rode over to Fredrick's, an old convenience store on Henderson Highway, got ourselves a couple of Danishes (a white chocolate bar) and Pixy Stix.

Grade 2

Around this time I first heard of Ted Bundy. I heard mother reading the paper out loud about the sorority murders.

Around 1973 — on Peter Mansbridge

Bun's Creek was at the back of our property. There had been a big shootout involving some bootleggers and police. The liquor from their distillery got in the ground water and contaminated our well water. He covered the story and interviewed mother in the kitchen. I think at the time he was with CKY news. Mother was holding me on her right arm. Mansbridge was a rookie at the time and had a full head of hair. That was my first television appearance. Now look where Mansbridge is today.

Jodi (Dan, as the preliminary unfolds and trial, you will hear more about Jodi).

From the time I could start remembering as a young child, I felt like I wasn't quite alone. My first recollection so far of Jodi was during a thunderstorm in the middle of the night. He hit my left shoulder and told me there were animals under my bed. He'd tell me things while I played in my sandbox. I used to make up words with him (years later I found out they were actual Cree words). I'd go out in the bush and spend hours collecting rocks. Jodi would tell me where to find things and I would actually find them. (An old leather boot and a bunch of shell casings from a rifle). As I got older, I learned not to pay much attention to him. He's always there.

Early Years — 373 Foxdale — early 70s (73-74)

Mother and I would cuddle from time to time. I'd nuzzle my face on her breasts. I always thought mothers and sons stuck their tongues in each other's mouths.

I could sense resentment from Mr. Teerhuis. Throughout the years, he'd comment on how much time we would spend together. I could sense a lot of jealousy from him. I have very few if any happy memories of Gerrat Teerhuis.

Early 80s (I was about 14)

Maurice owned an antique shop in the exchange district. We met at the Hill. I was with a bunch of other street hustlers, the weather was turning for the worse and my feet were getting numb. I got in his station wagon, he offered me a smoke and we headed for the antique shop. (Why did pervs always ask if I had my own place?) We waited at a stoplight in front of Eaton's. It was like we were the only two on the road. As I listened to Cindy Lauper's "All Through the Night" Maurice began to get friendly.

Once inside the shop it was warm and dark. The antique furnishings cast haunting shadows on the ceiling. He poured me brandy and we shared some pot. We talked about ourselves for a bit, had some more brandy; it felt warm in my stomach. I lay down on a huge antique four-poster bed. There was an enormous dusty mirror beside it. By now I was pretty buzzed. I watched the perv perform his pleasures in the mirror. The something weird happened. I smiled at myself in the mirror. "You little slut," I thought, and began to indulge my guilty pleasure. Maurice seemed happy. He gave me 90 bucks. I rolled on my stomach and had a cigarette. I was in no hurry to get up. He had his jeans on already. I happened to peer over the side of the bed, to my surprise; there was a little mountain of boy's underwear and a bunch of used condoms. Guess I wasn't the only one who frequented the shop. I didn't really care any more. They all said pretty much the same thing: "You're cute, you're young, nice body."

My favorite was, "I want to make you move." Yeah, right, like that other perv at the Westin who made me fuck his Asian wife. He sat in a chair and told her what to do. I could tell she wasn't enjoying herself. At least the sicko gave me $150. I headed for the liquor store on Ellis, had some woman get me a bottle of rye, then I headed back to the hill.

Other times we would party at some drag queen's place off Sherbrook, or walk over to Winners in St. Boniface. I knew this native chick named Cha Cha. She'd tell me street-smart stories. We'd get high sometimes. I think she was really looking for a friend.

Mr. Teerhuis

"A man cannot be comfortable without his own approval."

Growing up, my classmates went fishing or to ball games with their dads, they played sports. (I had a childhood fantasy; my dad bought me a big red balloon, we'd be riding down the highway in a blue convertible listening to Micky Finn on cassette. It never happened.)

I was jealous of my schoolmates; they had loving fathers. Mine was cold, abusive; he ran the house like a concentration camp. On the surface, we looked like your typical happy family. Behind closed doors, it was a different story. I couldn't stand being in the same room with him. I even poisoned him. I wanted him dead. I told mother one time that I wished he were dead. At age 14, I fixed the breaks on his car, hoping he'd die in a car accident, but nothing happened. Then I poisoned him again, mother caught me, and she threatened to send me to a group home.

1981-82

It started off around the beginning of November 1981 (Dan, this has reference to the music teacher for Grade 6 at Donwood Elementary. I was 11.) The school was to put on a Christmas play, "Christmas on Angel Street." Mr. Dyck (music teacher) had asked me to stay behind after class. He asked if I wanted to be in the school play. He also suggested that I needed extra singing lessons. *The first couple of lessons seemed okay, and then he would undo my trousers and rub his hands all over my abdomen. He would do the same, undo his pants. I could see his erect penis making an enormous bulge in his bikini underwear. He told me to pull them down and I did. His penis sprang up. It was huge. I ran my fingers through his pubic hair and began to massage his male organ.*

That night I lay in bed, I felt strange, numb. I couldn't comprehend what had happened and didn't sleep. I remember the next day at lunch, Mr. Dyck said, "Hi Sid," as I entered the lunchroom. I ignored him.

So now, through those, so-called, singing lessons, we would go into a storage room. He'd have me stripped down to my under shorts. He'd French kiss me rubbing his hands all over my smooth young body, getting me sexually aroused. That's when he would suck me off. I tensed up and felt my cock explode in his mouth. He would lick my balls and comment on how my body was changing, that he loved seeing me naked. We would say things like, "I love your body" or "You like that don't you."

He stole my red satin gym shorts. I found them in his desk drawer along with other boys' gym shorts.

It got to the point that he'd follow me home from school. A few times we'd go for a drive and have sex in the car (a blue 4-door Parisienne). I think the other students knew what was going on, at recess a boy named Corey asked, "So, Sidney, did you have fun with Mr. Dyck?"

Near the end of the school year, during one of our encounters, (what makes this even more twisted), while I stood there naked as he sucked me in the dark storage room, I remember thinking to myself, "I can't believe I'm having my cock sucked."

There were times I really enjoyed him doing things to me. He told me he loved me. He said I had a nice cock and that he liked my body. He said I was special. The sick part of it all was that I believed him.

When I told about these incidents at age 17, it was discovered about 14 other boys suffered as well. I had a chance to meet with one of them at New Faces Agency with the help of a social worker named Diane Bastianssen.

Siblings

Ann Teerhuis: The man in the moon refers to the piano teacher, "Mr. Taylor."
When Jodi would talk to me after the lights went out, I would tell Jodi "The man in the moon fucked my sister."

I distinctly remember Ann sitting on the back hall steps crying, saying she didn't want to go downstairs for her piano lesson with Mr. Taylor. He'd get extremely upset if mother wanted to watch Ann play piano, saying she was interfering. Both mother and Gerrit (Mr. Teerhuis) knew what was going on and turned a blind eye. They would sit at the dining room table drinking their coffee, exchanging glances; they did nothing to stop the molestation of Ann.

Izzy (Isabel) Teerhuis: Born Sept. 6, 1966.[3]

At Concordia Hospital, there is a psychiatrist named Dr. Fast. He may have some interesting background information on me.

Sidney Teerhuis

---

3   Note: *Dan, I will elaborate more on Jodi before the preliminary. I will send you an envelope.*

* * * * *

Dan,

I FEEL CONSTANTLY ABIDING IS MOST APPROPRIATE AS A BOOK TITLE. I WOULD LIKE TO
know some of your ideas for a book cover. On a page all by itself before the July 1ˢᵗ Chapter
(that will contain how I met Robin Greene, the sex we had, the nude photos, Greene's
gruesome demise, me having sex with the corpse, and what happened in room 309 at the
Royal Albert.) I would like this printed centre page in Gothic lettering.

"Now the deeds of the flesh are evident,
Which are: immorality, impurity, and sensuality?"

Galatians' 5:19

CONSTANTLY ABIDING

MY (ADOPTED) FAMILY HAD BEEN MORE DEMANDING ON ME, MORE THAN ANYONE ELSE.
Did they not know, I'm sure mother meant well, yet she did more damage than good.

Constantly: I had been compared to my non-related siblings. I was treated like a
heretic for my beliefs, my sexuality, the longing to be my own person.

Abiding: I listened to mother's voice, her strict lessons in love. Fear I would be sent
away if I did something to displease dear mother.

Constantly: My adopted siblings stole my self-esteem, as if it were a game to them. In
everything I did, they told me I had to prove myself to them. They were the answer and they were
the light (the Teerhuis Religion).

Abiding: Mr. Teerhuis laid down the family law. His callous hand was a weapon he
used often, and both Izzy and I feared him.

Constantly: I have always been misunderstood. They could not see outside their
protected bubble. (They had selective hearing and saw only what they wanted to, nothing
bad ever happened, it was always someone else's problem, not theirs.) What a wake-up
call when mother died, and Martin and Judy's infidelities became known, as well as Peter's
extra marital affair in Windsor. That name Teerhuis fell off its own pulpit.

Abiding: I carried the personal baggage they have bestowed upon me. For years I've
lived under the iron thumb of a father I have grown to hate. I will never forgive him for his
wicked ways throughout my childhood. I was Constantly Abiding.

EARLY TO MID-80s — JUNIOR HIGH (I WAS 13)

ONCE LUNCH HOUR WE WENT OVER TO MICHELLE'S AND SMOKED HER MOM'S WEED. I
had shops that afternoon, so I decided to skip class. I went to the Bay downtown to the fifth
floor men's room. I sucked off a Winnipeg Transit employee. Then I met some old perv. He
drove me over to his place in Garden City. He offered me a few drinks. I allowed him to
take Polaroid snapshots of me while I undressed.

I remember lying on his bed stark naked staring at the ceiling wondering why I was doing
this. I looked down and watched him suck my dick. It felt really good and I exploded into his
mouth. When it was all over the perv drove me to McIvor Mall in East Kildonan. He slipped

SID TEERHUIS: Amb.: To become a fashion designer. Fate: A garbage man; Likes: Rich people, parties, freedom; Dislikes: Heavy Metal, leather jackets, and commoners.

NHL; Fate: T .... n the .... ong .. 3.

Figure 10: 'Sid' Teerhuis, 1985 Yearbook entry; (bottom-right) close-up.

me a $50-bill. That got me thinking. There must be more pervs out there willing to pay to have a young boy fool around with them, so I began to frequent the Hill and the men's room at the Bay. I became an avid "Le Chateau" shopper. I'd lie to my adoptive parents and say I got the clothes on sale or at a clearance. I soon became one of the best-dressed students in school.

I'd go to the liquor store on Ellice and convince some drunk to get me a bottle of rye. I'd give him the money and pray he'd come back with the goods. This native man at the time got me the rye, and asked if I wanted to party with him. Being only 13 at the time, I said why not.

He took me to a room at the Royal Albert Arms and we drank and had sex. He put on his jeans and said he'd be right back. The door swung open and he came in with two other native men in their late 40s, maybe 30s. They were all drunk. One guy's teeth were all rotten. They sat at the table and told me to get up. I was still naked. They spoke in their language and made some jokes. One guy grabbed me and roughly ran his hands all over my body. The guy from the liquor store assured me they weren't going to hurt me, they just wanted to fool around. I was passed back and fourth while they played with my cock. When I said I was going to come, the guy with the rotten teeth fell to his knees and sucked hard. It hurt but I came anyway. He put his arms around me, kissed me (I could taste my own juice on his tongue and whisky) and said I tasted good. I put my underwear back on and sat on his lap for the rest of the afternoon. We drank, they made me dance for them and they took turns having me on the bed. As I sat on the bus going over the Disraeli Freeway, the thought occurred to me that I was just raped. I felt sick to my stomach. When I got off the bus on Rothesay and McIvor, I cried almost all the way home. The smell of those three native men was still on me. I had to listen to mother's long lecture for skipping class. I went to bed early and cried myself to sleep.

Mr. Teerhuis and I were not or very rarely on speaking terms. They didn't know and understand what I was going through, even though I continued to go to the Hill. I was accosted a few more times, and then I smartened up. I started to carry a knife with me. Some old perv started choking me and tried to force me in the back seat of his blue sedan. I stabbed him in the left side of his neck just under his lower jaw. I was yelling, managed to pull up my jeans and got out as fast as I could, ran for about half a block, hid behind a BFI bin so I could tuck in my shirt and do up *my jeans. He drove around the block a couple of times then disappeared. I wandered through Polo Park to calm down until the mall closed and caught the Glenway bus to go home.*

Relane transferred to John Henderson and I was alone. Since I wasn't interested in floor hockey, the guys began to torment me. Grade 8 was just as bad as Grade 7. I even contemplated suicide and had one unsuccessful attempt. A teacher name Murray was concerned and came to visit me at Concordia Hospital.

Izzy had her own problems. She was constantly comparing herself to Ann (Daddy's little Princess) and was on boyfriend number 5. I lost count after Ken Reeve. We had some pretty wicked fights. I bitch slapped her a couple of times.

Dan (I believe I've already told you about the accountant Henry in the exchange district, Richard, and me throwing a knife at Izzy when she locked herself in mother's bedroom.)

*   *   *   *   *

Dan,

I HAVE CAREFULLY SELECTED A NUMBER OF FAMOUS QUOTES THAT I WANT TO GO WITH *certain chapters, at the beginning of each one.*

In regards to my adoptive parents:

Quote: "Children begin by loving their parents; as they grow older they judge them; sometimes they forgive them." (Oscar Wilde)

In regards to the chapter on Robin Greene:

"To perceive is to suffer." (Aristotle)

In regards to the chapter of my trial and preliminaries:

"Disloyalty, treachery, are the worst crimes, and deserve the severest punishment." (Diana Rigg, as Helena Vessey in "Mother Love")

On a single page after the book dedication:

"Sometimes I go about pitying myself, and all the time I am being carried on great winds across the sky." (Ojibway)

EARLY 90s — ABBOTT MANSIONS/LIFE WITH MICHELLE (MARK)

I FIRST ENCOUNTERED MICHELLE IN THE ABBOTT LOBBY, COMING HOME FROM NATIVE Youth Job Corps.

We did the usual introduction. I lived on the third floor beside the elevator, Michelle and Lorraine (Leroy), another Tranny, lived on the fourth floor. They turned tricks on Vancouver's lower eastside to feed their cocaine habit. The streets of Vancouver's eastside (Main and Hastings) can be a very unfriendly place if one gets acquainted with the wrong crowd.

I partied with Michelle and Lorraine. We'd go across the street to Chuck's Pub, a neighborhood gay bar, shoot some pool, and watch the Drag Shows on Friday nights. Other times, I brought a bottle of whiskey and mix home and Michelle and I would sometimes talk for hours. Michelle (Mark) didn't have an easy life growing up. A lot of us didn't.

I've met street hookers, male and female from poor or rich backgrounds (abuse does not discriminate). Other times, I'd be piss drunk up at Michelle's place, drinking, keeping him/her company while she shot up. It wasn't long before I started to inject the white powder into my arm.

Michelle and Lorraine had a falling out and Michelle needed a place to stay. He/she moved into my suite in exchange for free dope. Nothing in this world is free. I was lucky if I got to shoot up once a day. She'd come up with all these excuses. We had our fights.

I had gone to Boys Town every now and then when cash was running low to feed my new crack addiction. After some problems with building management, we moved farther up the eastside near the shipyards. Another ghetto-style cocaine-infested cesspool. My friendship with Michelle became tumultuous. I had done a couple of practicum and had applied to the Native Education Centre and King Ed. Campus. Michelle was getting jealous. She started volunteering at the Tranny Centre but that didn't last long. I sold my tuition fee check to get high and used a friend's bankcard to keep the supply coming in.

Dan, do not let anyone else read this; it goes directly into the book.

Vancouver mid-90s — Mr. Berry

> "Knowing that such a man is perverted and is sinning, being self-condemned."
>
> Titus 3:11

A LOST MEMBER OF THE ADDAMS FAMILY, I ACQUAINTED MYSELF WITH WILLIAM SEAN Berry at A Kettle of Fish. We both worked in the kitchen. I looked after the appetizers and dessert part of the menu; Berry was the saucier (broiler cook, sauces, main course). He was about as tall as Lurch and reminded me of someone from Texas Chainsaw Massacre. I'd watch him cut meat; at home I'd fantasize about Berry doing that to me. We started hanging out after work; Ravi, Kyle, Phillipe, Berry and I, played darts and shot the shit like all fellow employees do.

After I left Meera, I lived in a dump, one room suite on Granville for about four months. My coke habit took off like a British Airways Concorde. I was getting high or bingeing every payday. Somehow, I managed to pay my rent. Berry took me to a Goth Nightclub. I was amused by my new surroundings. I knew people from my S&M crowd and ran into Noxema a couple of times. There was a fetish night. I wondered how I would go about that. On fetish night you brought your fetish. How could I possibly bring 3,000 pairs of men's used underwear into a nightclub?

Berry may have gotten into my scene but it was mostly men and transsexuals. A piss party is like any other party except it's in a secret location (sometimes at a residence, which is rare), it's dark, and there is loud music. Men are scantily dressed in jock straps or latex. You can be pissed on directly or someone will shower you in piss from a watering can. I enjoyed having it rubbed all over while having sex. I'd have two or three men stand around and urinate on my sex partners and me, or there would be an old bathtub filled with piss and one could bathe in it.

In Vancouver

In my quest for the perfect male specimen I discovered sadomasochism. I found pleasure in perverse sexual pain, being bound and forced to perform oral pleasures on my masters (they slapped me, pissed on me; soaking me in it, I was spit on, humiliated verbally; I'd lick their leather boots, rimming them was a personal favorite, just the thought of having a man's naked hairy ass in my face, I became helpless, I wanted more, I never wanted the rimming to end), society would say this sort of lovemaking is torture or sick, I found it passionate, my masters were always good to me.

We would go to private "piss parties", a horde of gay men into their fetishes, dirty underwear and piss. A massive orgy of men fucking, sucking, eating ass, we'd rub piss all over each other. It became a frenzy of climatic homosexual love for one another.

*   *   *   *   *

We argued a few times. I mean space was limited. Our lifestyles were opposite. I have what I call dirty sex. I carefully choose some native drunk, coerce him to come home with me, bathe him and give him some pills to knock him out, then I have my way with him. Berry would entertain his partners and would want to be done with them. A couple of times I had come home to him partying with some chick. I'd leave and come back a couple of hours later.

Ewen had left a bottle of Wisers. I drank it, got into one of my drunken stupors. I shaved my head in the bathroom. I was talking to myself. I got all dressed up, danced around the living room. I thought I was waltzing with mother. Then the voices came. I popped some pills, sat on the couch and held a conversation with her. She was wearing her purple dress and bolero jacket. We danced suddenly I was alone. I began shedding my clothes. I don't know how I got to Stanley Park. I had my knapsack with me. I was walking through the bush in a pair of light blue briefs I tore open in the front exposing my genitals. Some old man liked what I had on. I let him molest me. He took off my undies and kept them. More gays appeared out of nowhere. It was dark and it was the peak hours of the cruising scene in that area of the park. My head ached from snorting too many poppers. I was all fucked out of my mind. This was turning out to be an orgy, an all-out fag-fest of balls and ass and fucking. I fucked two guys one after the other.

There was a cook at the restaurant that sold coke and rock to the staff. Yeah, I thought now I don't have to go all the way into Vancouver. It was a real pain. I'd have to take two buses, the sky train and another bus to get to my crack dealer. That's two hours just to get there. Again, my coke habit took off like a Broadway Chorus Line. I ended up going to Surrey Memorial three times. The third time was a mild heart attack. I was given NITROGLYCERINE in case of an emergency. Within a couple of weeks, I was back to my old self.

On several occasions I would fondle Ewen when he was passed out; another time, the voice inside my head told me to get the saw Berry left in the closet. I stood over Ewen for what seemed like an eternity, looking at his partially nude figure; I got to my knees, had the saw in my right hand. I heard Berry get up to use the washroom; I put the saw under the couch and continued drinking. (Mother was sitting on the couch smoking menthol cigarettes and shaking her head).

Berry had this friend named Murray. He was tall, skinny, and a bit odd. He'd come over and they would write music together. Berry told me one day that Murray liked me; he even phoned me a couple of times when I was alone. I thought he was kind of cute in a perverse way. I had sexual fantasies that Murray kept me captive as his sex slave. He'd keep me tied up in a coffin that he and Berry built. Then Murray would rape me every night.

"There is nothing stronger in the world than gentleness."

Han Suyin

After completing Native Youth Job Corps, I decided to further my education at the Native Education Centre. I had missed a class to undergo a biopsy to remove a lump in my armpit. The following day, Lori introduced herself; she needed a partner for a class project.

Lori had a tumultuous childhood, had eventually lived with her grandmother, now she was on her own, and trying to make a life for herself and her daughter Sarah. I could see Lori was struggling. She had no support from anyone; she basically had to do everything on her own. Her daughter Sarah was comfortable with me and we became family. They first lived in a rough blue-collar, East Van neighborhood, and then moved into my condo complex on 10Sth in Mount Pleasant.

We were very close. Some nights we'd sit on the patio on Sarah's little chairs, talk for hours smoking menthols. It felt like I knew her from a past life experience. I knew everything about her. I could tell Lori things I never told anyone else.

We couldn't live together because welfare would cut her off.

Most people spend a couple of hours at the beach. For us, it was the highlight of the week, although we took it a step further; everything but the kitchen sink.

I would spot for Lori and Hez when they'd work the streets in East Van near Pender. There'd be a freak show of trannys in latex, crack hoes, gender benders and renegades. Some nights, I'd stay home and watch Sarah. We'd rent movies or color and I'd read to her. Lori would come home around 6 a.m., have a long hot bath and I would sit in the living room and smoke crack. On the living room floor we would fuck while she told me what some of the Johns looked like or what they did to her. It turned me on, just the thought of all those pervs getting off. We fucked hard in a crack-induced frenzy. There were also the regulars. I'd hide in the bedroom closet and watch while some John did his thing. If anything were to go wrong, I'd be ready to jump out holding a butcher knife.

Pay the baby sitter, smoke crack in the bathroom. Lori would come back a couple of hours later, then I'd pass out on the couch. Another time, I didn't go home. We went to the hospital instead because I overdosed.

Catherine had this sick idea that her nigger daughter, Devonne, and Sarah would grow up together, go to some school. Her own mother was afraid of her.

Devonne was the ugliest little nigger I have ever seen. I hated that kid and so did Lori. We never fed her when we babysat her.

They spent a weekend at Lori's. I took Catherine's Big Daddy Kane cassette and pulled out the tape, gave it to Devonne, wrapped it around her arms and said, "Go show Mommy." All happy, Devonne shows Catherine, we hear a bunch of swearing and a big slap. Devonne screams. Lori and I are laughing in the living room, rolling on the floor.

I watched the girls while Catherine and Lori pulled tricks down by Quebec Avenue. Sarah had a nice hot bath and played with her Barbie's. Devonne got a nice ice cold bath.

I left Devonne on the bathroom floor wrapped in a wet towel and asked Sarah what we should do. She said to turn off the light and shut the door, so we did. We had ice cream and colored in her coloring books for an hour out on the patio. The very sight of that nigger disgusted Lori and I. I taught Sarah how to say nigger and insult Devonne. The sad part was Catherine didn't even know who the father was.

One year, I hung all her Barbie dolls heads on the Christmas tree. Sarah got up the next morning, I could hear her mumble "Dummy," and then she kicked me and hid in the bathroom while Lori was on the toilet.

Lori had gone to Ontario to visit Sarah's grandparents. (Sarah's father just disappeared one day.) I frequented the gay bars, to a gay home every now and then. When Lori first got pregnant, we had an abortion, a pregnancy would ruin the extra income plus I had a coke habit to feed. Besides, my ex-girlfriend, Barb, wanted to take my son Leon back to the States. It was a very stressful time with my computer course and staying up late didn't help. Lori did get pregnant a second time, and then Catherine staged a fake robbery and claimed I did it. Impossible, I was away with friends Les and Toka. We were celebrating her friend Helen's birthday. Catherine caused a lot of grief for both Lori and me. She eventually moved out of the condo complex and I missed the birth of Alissia.

In New Westminster I completed my computer course. I had problems with my roommate Jocelyn. I wanted to get off the coke and her habit was interfering with my sobriety. We had some pretty intense arguments. I threw the kitchen table at her for getting high in front of her kids.

Her boyfriend, Shawn had stayed over, not paying rent. Whenever Jocelyn vanished on a three or four-day binge, I would rape Shawn. I knocked him out. He got mouthy on one of his drunks, so I dragged him into my bedroom and had my way with him. He came to, to find a black eye, his rectum bleeding all over my sheets. I was pretty mean towards him when I drank. I don't know how many times I'd pull him out of bed when Jocelyn was passed out, take him to my bed and fuck him silly.

I was getting my student loan in Vancouver South, on Broadway, when someone tapped me on the shoulder. There stood Lori with baby Alissia. I got to hold her. The last time I held a baby was my son Leon, now living in the Seattle area. We made our amends. Catherine was out of the picture. (Lori caught her stealing out of her purse.) We had gone for a walk along False Creek. I told Lori how hurt I was, we had a good cry and decided to be friends.

We sat on her patio and talked all night. She needed to go out to get some extra money and we talked about the pros and cons. Some psycho was killing hookers; I told her to be careful. A john at the Biltmore, about a year ago knifed Heather. So I'd watch the girls, Alissia peed on my leg, Sarah laughed at me. I had to wear Lori's pink track pants while I did some laundry.

Christmas was awesome. There was music, presents and we had a turkey. I got my student loan and would start my chef schooling in the spring. Again, things began to run smoothly for the next couple of months.

We celebrated Alissia's birthday over at Lori's aunt's new home. There were balloons, presents, cake; we even took pictures of Alissia sitting by the fireplace. She had on her new dress. She looked like a Squamish Princess, sang Happy Birthday. Alissia got to eat her own piece of cake, which ended up everywhere else except in her mouth. These are moments that we carry with us throughout our lifetime.

My life had certainly changed. I had health issues to deal with, and cooking school was about to commence. Like Tammy Wynette's song says, "I don't want to play house." I was 27; there were things I haven't done yet. I didn't want to be tied down. I was still young. I wasn't being selfish either. I wanted Lori to have a life too. Not even realizing, I was slowly killing myself every time I got high and I nearly did.

On that fateful day, I had gone out with friends to the Odyssey in Vancouver. I met a cokehead and we went back to my place in New West. I told him to give me a "Big Fix". He shot it up my arm. About a minute later, I realized I had overdosed, reached for the bedroom door, called my roommate Bill. The last thing I recall was falling toward the plush carpeting.

It was very peaceful, calm. A celestial being knelt beside me placed its hand on my heart. I gasped for air. I was in the back of an ambulance being rushed to Columbia Hospital. My heart had stopped. I remember starring at the fluorescent lighting on the hospital ceiling, two nurses looking down at me. I couldn't understand a word they said. There was a tube down my throat. I couldn't breath on my own. Within 48 hours I was on Main and East Hastings buying crack from Lorraine, a transsexual I knew from the clubs. I sold my watch to get some more rock my hands were all gray. I had dark circles under my eyes and I was really thin. Sitting in a back ally on Vancouver's east side dirt under my fingernails, looking at the surroundings, I thought, "This sucks."

So once again, I tried to pick up the pieces, get myself in order, and start that endless cycle of NORMAL. But what is normal? I had spent a lifetime trying to figure that one out. To me, NORMAL was a cycle on the washing machine. For the longest time, I kept thinking about that celestial being. It was not a hallucination. I knew this being from somewhere.

"Children begin by loving their parents; as they grow older they judge them; sometimes they forgive them."

Oscar Wilde

On a single page after the book dedication:

Hands adorned with her precious diamonds. Those diamonds had
    found it's way from South Africa, worn by Pels women in the
    Netherlands at the turn of last century, eventually finding their
    way to Foxdale and now they would belong to a new generation of
    Teerhuis women. She would take many secrets to the grave, secrets
    only mother and I shared, some things are better left unsaid.
"Oh mommy, mommy full of grace,
Pull down your panties and sit on my face,
A kiss is ideal, a kiss or two,
Oh mommy, mommy I long for you".
I loved my mother, I hated my mother, the bitch left me. I had to find
    my way without her. I've been abandoned by my soul mate, no
    woman can ever replace her, no male will ever give me ecstasy.

Dan, do not let anyone else read this; it goes directly into the book.

THE CLOWNS

WHILE IN VANCOUVER, I HAD MET PEOPLE FROM ALL WALKS OF LIFE. THE ONE THAT stands out the most is an East Indian male from Bangladesh. He owned a dry-cleaning shop on East Broadway called Betty Brite. We met in the men's washroom at Pacific Centre. He was about six feet tall, short black hair, glasses. He had a mole on his right cheek and was slightly heavy set. I was a lot thinner back then, about 190 pounds. When I met him I knew I had this feeling about him. This guy was really unusual.

We engaged in sex at the back of his shop. We'd both be naked among the hanging garments. I sat on a footstool while he sucked me off. Every time I came in the condom I was wearing, he'd pull it off and lick my penis clean. Then he tied the end of the condom and put it in this jacket pocket that lay on the sewing machine. I asked him one time, what he did with them. He said when he gets home he uses it. This time, when he pulled off the condom, he looked at me while he tied the end and said, "I'm going to eat it." He stood up then and said, "You have a good body," put his arms around me, he bit my left nipple and started biting my shoulder. He sucked real hard on my neck and whispered into my ear, "I wish I could eat you."

I asked, "What?? And he replied, "I want to eat you." So I turned and bent over. He held me against him, ran his fingers over my lips, his other hand all over my body.

"That's not what I meant," he replied. I turned towards him and asked, "You mean you want to eat my body?"

He said, "Yes." I asked, "You mean cannibalism?"

He said, "I want you."

I won't say what the two of us talked about. I did however, give him my consent that eventually, I would go home with him and he could have my body and cook it. We went out several times. I wanted him to get to know me and I told him the only way I'd go through with it is if he kept all my bones.

I got a job in Rocky Mountain House, Alberta, in 2000. Before I left, we bought a huge roasting pan from a commercial distributor and a pressure cooker. We had made plans that I would return to Vancouver in around Easter, 2001. I'd stay at his place for a month. I would get a prescription of sleeping pills and we'd prepare everything for the date we agreed on in May 2001.

The plan was on that day, we'd spend the whole day in bed having sex. Then I'd get intoxicated and down the pills. After I passed out, he would strangle me and make sure I was dead. We'd planned in advance what he would do with my body and that he'd boil my bones and keep them in a wooden trunk under his bed.

We kept in touch for a while, and then I moved to Edmonton. I called him and we tried to set another date for October 2001. Finally he said for me to just come and see him when I got back to Vancouver. Apparently, he told his brother and he wanted to partake in the dismembering process and eat my tongue.

I never did make it back to Vancouver and I lost his phone number. He was going back to India for a while, but didn't say when he would return. I still think about him every now and then, and hope that someday I will run into him so he can cook me. I did phone a former roommate, Bill Berry, while I was still in Edmonton. In case I wouldn't reunite with the East Indian, I said to Berry, "I have a proposition for you."

I told him I wanted him to dissect me. He asked if I was serious and I told him yes. Then Berry said, "It sounds like a good idea." I told him I would try to get there by spring and that I wanted him, Murray and Owen to be a part of it, all three of them taking turns dissecting me.

I ended up getting a good job in Edmonton and postponed my plan until I find the right man or men who'd be willing to have my body on their dinner table. I've even thought about putting my phone number and address at the Peep shows in Edmonton, hoping some perv would take me up on my offer. When I get out of jail, eventually, I will desperately look for any takers. I want to be eaten by another gay man or some all-male cult. Sometimes when I jerk off at night, I fantasize about the East Indian sautéing my cock and balls in red wine with garlic and fresh herbs or being slow roasted over a fire pit.

Other nights I lay in bed fantasizing about Berry, Murray or Ewen hacking my body to bits, taking my cock and tossing back and forth (playing catch with my dick). They're laughing and having a good time, or Berry boiling my skull and bones and making a headboard for his bed out of me. I then hope his friend Murray will eat my cock and balls and my brain. While Berry chops me up and rips out my guts, Ewen is videotaping it so they can watch it later. It sounds pretty fucked up, but that's how I want to end up, by being eaten.

*　　*　　*　　*　　*

Dan,

YOU MAY THINK I'M NUTS, BUT WHEN I GET OUT OF JAIL, THAT IS MY WISH. IN THE meantime, if you could put on the Internet somehow my wish, and have anyone who is interested write to me directly at Headingley. (Put some of the highlights, like the East Indian) I'm really hoping someone will respond. I do prefer to be eaten by Asian or East Indian men. I don't care how old they are either.

Thank you,

Do not let anyone read this; this is our little secret for now.

Sidney

9

The Dreaded Letters

OCTOBER 6/04

Dan,

I STILL NEED A LIST OF OFFSHORE BANKS IN THE BAHAMAS THAT ARE NOT AFFILIATED with the United States or Canada. I will have it set up so the check will go directly into the offshore account. If you do this appearance on CJOB with Charles Adler, I will give you an interview right after the preliminary hearing. If Adler asks you where you got your information just say a reliable source. Don't mention any names.

As for this book title "Drunken Defense", it's not eye-catching. I want something more dramatic, like Human Trophy or Room 309, or Murder at six-twenty p.m., the time of Greene's death, or Kill Time, (or use Greene's last words "Please don't kill me").

Type or write up what you have so far on the first chapter and send it to me, I need to get a sense of your style of writing. I'll proof read it, make any necessary adjustments and send it back to you, send it in a large brown envelope, along with another large brown envelope inside with your return address.

As for the book title Trophy Kill it sounds perfect except for the subtitle (The Sidney Teerhuis Story). I feel Trophy Kill, Murder in 309 would sound better, or Trophy Kill, the Murder of Robin Greene, or even something a little more shocking Trophy Kill, Slaughterhouse at the Albert. I'm even sure if you asked permission from Hollywood you could call it Trophy Kill, the Shall We Dance Murder. It's what Gere and Sarandon called it. Perhaps on the cover we could have a photo of me, Greene, the necklace center and the title.

ADLER

(Sidney refers to Corus Entertainment radio station CJOB talk show host Charles Adler, addressing the following letter to him)

AT ONE POINT TEERHUIS PARTIED WITH HOTEL STAFF IN THE ALBERT'S LOUNGE, smoking pot outside. Hotel staff said Sidney Teerhuis was always polite, quite, kept to himself, paid his rent on time.

After Greene was stabbed to death, Teerhuis dragged the body into the washroom, decapitated Greene and performed sex acts on the corpse. Greene was dismembered and a disemboweled human trophy.

The following day police entered suite 309 and found Greene in the tub dismembered and he was emasculated. The internal organs are still missing to this day. Teerhuis had intricately dissected certain parts of Greene's body, the left forearm, the eyes, and the penis. Greene's right nipple had been cut off. There were forty-seven stab wounds to the chest. Green had been drained of all his blood, very little blood was found at the crime scene.

Sidney

JANUARY 12/05

Mr. Zupanski,

YOU FEEL MY SITUATION IS SHOCKINGLY SIMILAR TO THE LIKES OF DENNIS NILSEN. *I find that interesting. Do you think Nilsen had any influence? I hadn't really looked at it that way. The only time I ever entertained the thought of Dahmer or Nilsen was when I sliced open Greene's abdomen. Seeing the intricate design and coils of the transparent intestines, only after playing with them did I want to experience what Dahmer and Nilsen did by inserting my arm deep inside Greene's chest cavity and exploring his insides.*

What fascinated me about Dennis was his first male victim, and the skinhead, I'd like to find out more about it. I would like to write to him. (I could send the letter to you, you send it to him, he would send a response to you and you send the response to me.) Nilsen may be in Brixton, Wandsworth or Strangeways penitentiaries in England.

You wanted a list of missing organs: lungs, part of the esophagus, epiglottis, digestive tract, heart, spleen, stomach, liver, pancreas, aorta, one of the eyes (the other was punctured).

They said there was little to no blood. There was no blood to be found in Greene's carcass.

Greene wasn't my ideal candidate, I could have picked anyone, I was looking for sex, this would have been no different from any other bar room sexual encounter. In the gay lifestyle you meet someone, have sex, and go your merry way.

Sidney Teerhuis

JANUARY 3/05

Dan,

WE HAVE COVERED A LOT. SOME OF YOUR QUESTIONS I CAN'T ANSWER SIMPLY BECAUSE *certain things haven't even crossed my mind. Greene fulfilled my sexual needs. I liked the way he sucked my cock. What makes it even more gratifying is that this was Greene's last sexual experience before his death. There's nothing more beautiful knowing Greene died sexually satisfied.*

When Greene took off his underwear and tossed them on the floor, it would be for the last time. His last erection his last ejaculation, his last blowjob. I was the last person to have sex with Greene. Little did Greene know he'd be dead in an hour-and-a-half, that he would no longer exist as I sucked him off.

Sex with Greene's dead body was intoxicating, the silence remembered as I drove myself in and out of him, the best sex I ever had! I can but vaguely analyze the complexity of my thoughts at that tender moment; I enjoyed the sex so much because he was dead, fucking Greene like a locomotive electrified me into a divine sexual vulgarity.

When you kill someone you experience a frenzy, a vehemence for what cannot be changed; the triumphs and trophies Greene's physical body had to offer when I carved him up, was like working on him like a trampe l'oeil, having sex with a dead body was more powerful than anything you could fathom. The poetry of Greene's viscera, the inexplicable beauty of his intestines elaborately coiled and folded, the rich aroma of fresh human meat, the sound of stainless steel cutting into bone, ripping out the lungs with my bare hands. When Greene was sawed in half, the shreds of flesh hung from his rib cage like colorless frond. Randomly stabbing his corpse, butchering him for the mere pleasure of it, because I can (when you cut off a human arm or leg, then hold it and admire it, you are overwhelmed with this ideology that the victim was ultimately sacrificed for the right reasons).

When I butchered Greene's body, watching the steel blade enter the body and the sensation of pulling it out again was beyond any moral connection. I treated the corpse like a side of beef, like Greene was a dead animal and portioned him like a giant turkey, cutting off the arms and legs.

Gutting him (scooping out the organs) was a lot of fun, I took my time. I made an evening of it slowly dismembering Greene's body, taking a break every now and then to admire my culinary and meat cutting skills. After Greene had been dismembered I held open the giant cut in his abdomen and took a nice deep breath of his empty chest cavity. It was like a sense of accomplishment. His flesh was starting to turn gray, his forearms were cold, the fingertips turned blue-black under the nails. What sort of haunts me is after I had Greene on the bathroom floor and began to slice into his neck, I think he was still alive. There was a deep ughh and a groan. (However sometimes when a body dies it twitches and makes noise). Even if he was alive I probably would have held him down and continued to chop his head off.

What was really sexually gratifying was having Greene's penis on my pillow beside my face while I masturbated, what a beautiful sight, knowing his body was cut to pieces in the next room.

Here's some food for thought, the next time you have a hard-on, I know what the inside of your penis looks and feels like, the different layers of skin, muscle tissue, the erectile tissue.

I want you to try something; the next time you shower or sit at the foot of your bed; look at your genitals; the shape and texture of the shaft; cup them in your hand; try to feel the weight; look at your own pubic hair; do you feel the sensations of yourself touching it? Then I want you to think of Robin Greene. In life he experienced those sensations. Stand in front of a mirror and look at your own nudity. Try to imagine what you would look like without your head. Place your hand on your chest; can you imagine someone scooping out your internal organs? If at all possible, lay on your bathroom floor naked for five minutes staring at the ceiling (your mind blank), this exercise I have given you may help you better understand what it was like to be Robin Greene after I killed him.

In your next letter I want your feedback on your feelings, what you experienced (in the exercise how did you feel being a murder victim?) Could you picture Sidney Teerhuis kneeling on top of you, dismembering you?

Do you feel compassion for Greene? Do you think what I did to Greene's body (dead) was an act of love for him in a macabre manner or was it lust for a dead body? Would you consider what I did to Greene's corpse a morals crime (charge); according to law after Greene died, legally he was no longer a person. Would it be safe to say I am guilty of doing indignities to a corpse? End of exercise –1:

I don't think I have told you anything about the actual last seconds of Greene's life, the actual murder, the stabbing, have I? At this point I wouldn't have anything to say to Greene's parents. Why the dissection of certain body parts? I don't think I was finished, I hadn't gotten a chance to smash Greene's skull and dissect his brain or dissect the hands or feet.

Do inmates treat me like a celebrity? No I don't get much fanfare, I'm yesterday's news; one inmate in particular, Barry Antil (the American bank robber) found the gruesome details of Greene's demise entertaining; said as he smiled in his American accent, "You're one sick fuck" and that I reminded him of Ted Bundy.

What made it erotic or sexy was the dead weight of his body. The sound of friction (Greene's flesh being dragged over the carpet), the way his head nodded from side to side, his arms dragging over his shoulders and bumping into things.

When I masturbate at night my sexual fantasies vary, when I fantasize about Greene it's when I'm sexing his headless corpse after he was decapitated (that's how I'd like to remember Greene as a naked headless corpse on my bathroom floor, before the dismemberment, disembowelment and emasculation. You seem to be so focused on the missing internal organs, so here is a little quiz: Only one of these statements are true:

What did I do with Robin Greene's internal organs? Were they?

    a) Flushed down the toilet

    b) Did I sell them to George for fifty dollars?

    c) Did I eat them in a cannibalistic ritual?

    d) Were they tossed in a BFI dumpster near H.S.C. (Health Sciences Centre)?

    e) Were some tossed in a vacant lot and a dumpster near H.S.C.?

    Only one of these statements is true, what do you personally think I did with Greene's organs? Be realistic.

2. Greene's murder is similar to who:

    a) Dahmer

    b) Zodiac Killer

    c) John Wayne Gacy

    d) Dennis Nilsen

3. Do you think I have the characteristics of a serial killer?

    [ ] Yes

    [ ] No

4. Do you think I enjoyed the entire event (the murder stabbing death of Greene and the necrophilia and dismemberment) from beginning to end?

    [ ] Yes

    [ ] No

    [ ] Not sure

I am amused by what the newspapers say. There are no post-killing photos. At the crime scene they speculated to reporters, just like they assumed the organs had been flushed. There are photos of the jazz festival, the Royal Crown, the Richardson Building, Greene modeling underwear, of Greene sitting on my lap, and Greene sitting on George's lap, and a photo of Greene posing his anus for the camera.

Dan,

I HOPE THIS DIAGRAM GIVES YOU A BETTER INSIGHT OF THE HOTEL SUITE AND WHERE I *chopped Greene up. I had left Greene's headless nude corpse on the bathroom floor for quite a while before chopping him up.*
Some of Greene's organs were tossed in a vacant lot in some tall grass. The rest of Greene's organs were tossed in a B.F.I. bin, near Health Sciences Center. I got a hard-on when I heard the plastic bag containing Greene's organs hit the bottom of the dumpster making a loud thud. After tossing the organs in the tall grass (in the vacant lot) I had to give my cock a good hard swipe, before I headed back to the Albert.
There is still a lot more on the earlier hours of the morning, I don't think I went into detail on cutting off the arms and legs. There are certain things I did to Greene's dead body that I'd never tell anyone (something happened right before Greene died that I'll never tell either, a sort of respect for the dead). When I see Kent Somers next, I'll try to smuggle a photo of Greene's mutilated corpse on the examining table, there are some really awesome pictures of Greene's body parts (you'll know what I meant when I described Greene as a side of beef). Do you need more details on Greene's last five minutes of life? Why do you find Greene's actual death so fascinating? Do you think there are people out there who are obsessed with Greene's murder and me? Why do people talk about me anyway? If Susan Sarandon's necklace weren't involved would this be just another Winnipeg homicide? Upon my release from jail, do you think I'll ever get to live a so-called "normal" life again?
Things have calmed down at Headingley for the moment, I have a government job doing laundry, a couple of projects on the side; I have my own group of "Bros", a new boyfriend, for the moment I'm quite happy in jail (I guess you could call it taking a break from society, we have playstation in every unit, a computer in every unit, air conditioning, satellite T.V., radios (headphones) three meals a day, the taxpayer covers all my escorts and expenses for medication, my treatment for Hep-C, we have a game room, play air hockey, ping-pong, AA meetings, artwork, drumming in the multi-purpose room, library, play bingo, have crib tournaments, play canasta, sweat lodge, we even have a sewing room and a garden to grow vegetables and flowers.
ALL PAYED BY TAXPAYER'S MONEY. HA HA HA HA HA HA HA.
The jokes on the legal system, if they decide to put me away for a long time, I'm going to milk the taxpayer for every cent they are worth and sooo much more. I'll demand they build me a special cell with my own shower and bathtub or send me to a Club Fed in beautiful British Columbia.

Write soon,
Sidney

*   *   *   *   *

Dan,

THIS CASE IS MORE SENSATIONAL THAN YOU CAN COMPREHEND. IF WE GO TO TRIAL I *have news that will shock the world. There is a lot that nobody knows, of what went on those early morning hours of July 2nd, 2003.*

After the preliminary I will send you a chapter in graphic detail on how Greene ended up in the tub. Until then don't say anything otherwise you won't possess privileged information. I'll make diagrams for that chapter of what happened to Greene and the shocking statement I said to Greene seconds before he died. As we get closer to the preliminary and trial this case will get more gruesome and bizarre and how the East Indian man relates to this crime of passion.

I'm not going to go into too much detail on Greene's death; the actual killing took less than three minutes. I felt Greene's body relax; his eyes became unfocused toward the ceiling. About a million thoughts and emotions went through my mind (perhaps someday I may go into great detail).

I got up off the bed, walked towards the window, lit up a cigarette. My hands caked with Greene's blood; they smelled of copper. I washed my hands in the sink (it reminded me of that scene from the Hunger at the beginning of the movie). I poured myself a drink, sat by the open window looking at Greene on the bed. I performed oral sex on Greene as he lay on the bed. Prior to that I pulled out the knife from his neck.

I rolled Greene's body off the bed, grabbed him by the ankles and dragged him into the bathroom. I had an erection, the idea of having sex with the corpse somehow aroused me, I lay Greene out on the tile floor, went back into the bedroom got the knife from the bed, finished my rye and coke and went into the bathroom, took off my underwear, hung them on the door knob.

At first I molested Greene's body, I had to make sure he was dead, picked up the knife with long cuts began slicing into his neck. It was like cutting a roast; the knife was so sharp. Blood began to ooze out; there was so much of it. I looked into Greene's eyes as I sliced into him. (It was kind of erotic). The spinal column was hard to cut. I had to feel inside the neck, the muscle tissue was warm, it made a squishy sound.

I felt a spot at the base of the skull, using my body weight began to saw into the bone. Greene's head nodded side to side, then turned to the right, I knew the head was no longer attached to the body. The stump of his spinal cord jutted out and some veins and his jugular. I picked up the head with both hands (I was amazed how heavy it was) stared at it then put it in the sink, turned on the tap to rinse the excess blood away.

I began to masturbate as I looked at Greene's headless body, lying on the bathroom floor. Put a condom on and had sex with his body. It felt good as my penis entered his rectum. The thought that even in death, Greene was still able to have sex excited me. I took my time fucking him, watching my cock slide in and out of his ass.

After I came, I washed up the floor and the blood splatter on the bedroom wall. I remember just looking at him, masturbating. I think that's all I'm going to say for now. I certainly don't need this information said to anyone.

(I do want you to write back ASAP on your thoughts, if you want to know every detail (e.g. what it felt like exploring the chest cavity with my bare hands, extracting the organs, what it was like cutting off the limbs) Do you want to know my thoughts, how it felt, what made me horny, do you want detail on the dissecting of certain organs.)

(Dismembering) I like to take care of my culinary tools; Greene was no exception. Placed my sharpening stone beside his bodice, cleaned the knives in the sink until they sparkled and began to sharpen them, anticipating the disembowelment. I was looking forward to it, cutting him open. By now the fireworks could be heard in the distance coming from the Forks. I loved the way Greene's body looked (diagram B). I thought he looked sexy in that state.

I felt the chest, wanting to make the incision just below the breastbone. I placed the paring knife in position, watching it pierce the flesh and go all the way in. I began to carefully slice the abdomen open. I liked the sound of the blade cutting the raw flesh and meat.

Greene's abdomen sliced open like a zipper, I was in awe at the sight of his intestines, I looked at them in amazement. The coils, the intricate folds, their transparency. (Now I know how serial killer Dennis Nilsen must have felt when he dissected his first male victim).

The pure beauty of Greene's viscera gave me an erection. I inserted my right hand into the mass of intestines. They were slippery, made squishy sounds as I stirred my hand around, squeezing them. I liked what I was doing. I then reached all the way into the chest cavity.

Greene's organs were still warm; he'd been dead for about four hours by now. I felt around exploring Green's insides with my hand. I could feel the curve and ripples of his inner rib cage. The spinal column was bigger than I thought; it had a thin layer of meat coating it. Its size gave the chest cavity two chambers. I ran my hand up and down its length feeling the organs glide over my hand. As I looked at Greene's chest, I couldn't believe my right arm was elbow deep inside of him. I kept feeling around trying to guess the different organs as I squeezed them. I grabbed onto something and pulled it out of the body. It was Greene's liver.

"Wow" I said slowly. I took the chef knife and disconnected it, holding the liver in the palm of my hand. I laid it on his chest and sliced it open like a butterfly to examine the inside. I felt it with my fingertips; some areas were smooth, others leather-like or rubbery (scar tissue). I tossed it aside, reached back in his chest and pulled out the stomach. It had a blue like tone; as soon as I cut it open a bunch of bile and fluid leaked out. It smelled really bad; it made a mess all over the floor.

I pulled out the large and small intestines and put them in the sink, rinsing them. I could see partially processed human waste in them. (I thought it was fascinating).

Dissecting Greene was a lot of work. It was a messy job; the intense odor of the intestinal gas and body fluids was intensified by the summer heat.

When I reached inside Greene, I pulled out the heart. It was kind of small, not what I expected. I severed the major arteries, the aorta, squeezed the heart and let the still warm blood drip all over me, smearing it all over my face and body. I then cut it open. I was intrigued by the hearts inner chambers, its ventricles, it's texture. I diced it up into little pieces and put it in the stomach on the floor.

The spleen was kind of neat. Greene's kidneys were shrunken; they looked almost black due to alcoholism and the kind of life he led.

I had trouble extracting his lungs so I had to rip them out. They were kind of transparent, I cut them open so I could feel the insides; I blew one up like a balloon. I then took the paring knife and scraped the hollow chest cavity to make sure everything was out. I peeled a thin layer of sinew from the inner ribs and examined it. It had the texture of Kleenex and transparent like tissue paper. I stretched open the gaping hole in Greene's abdomen and kept looking inside his empty chest cavity. He smelled of fresh meat like in a supermarket. I couldn't believe that I had just gutted a human being.

I scooped out Robin Greene's internal organs with my bare hands. Greene didn't seem human anymore; he had become an inanimate object. He was nothing but dead meat; I had dehumanized him. He was a sex toy, whenever I fucked him throughout the dismemberment process as the evening went on; I fucked his mutilated corpse for the mere pleasure of having gay sex. I loved having sex with his dead body; I was fulfilling my sexual fantasy of necrophilia. I was in love with his body (I fucked him slowly, enjoying him, knowing he was dead and still having sex; made me love him more. (Diagram A) I was actually jealous at one point.

I filled the tub and bathed with Greene's corpse (Diagram C) and dozed off for a while. After I got out of the tub and dried us both off, I wanted to remember Greene in a special way. At first I thought of hanging him from the ceiling or on the wall over the headboard from my bed. Then I came up with the idea of a human trophy. (Greene's mutilated body was my creation).

I enjoyed cutting him up, I displayed his body parts in different forms. I then sat and admired my creations. After cutting off Greene's penis and holding it in my hands and looking at him in pieces; I was glad he was dead; glad that I killed him. (Earlier that day, when I realized there was no turning back; seeing all that blood; I wanted him dead; I wanted it to be over for him; I didn't want him to suffer and he didn't). Killing him made me horny, yet I still couldn't believe what was happening.

I never intended to hurt or kill Greene. There was something about him I liked. He gave good head. He had a nice penis. After he died, I fell in love with his body. He died very quickly; he didn't suffer; if he felt any pain at all it was momentarily. It's what I did after that is disturbing.

Dan I'll leave it here for now; there's more, a lot more. I hope the diagrams give you an idea as the evening of July 1st 2003 progressed. The order of events are killing, sex, dragging body into the bathroom, sex, decapitation, sex, hanging, cutting off arms and legs, (I'll write about that later) cleaning body, sex, disembowelment, draining more blood, sex, admiration, playing with the parts, the trophy on the dresser, sawing body in half at the waistline, cutting off penis in sink, etc.

I'll leave you hanging for now. Remember at that time I wasn't in my right mind, today I'm saddened for Greene's family, I didn't enjoy what I did, (at the time July 1st 2003 I did) one thing led to another and I couldn't help myself or him. I'd like to see you in person soon.

C- ya
Sidney

April 1/05

Mr. Zupanski,

Haven't heard from you in a while, wonder why eh? I didn't find any article in the Winnipeg Sun pertaining to that law you claim that offenders or whatever can't cash in on their crimes or anything related.

I find it rather convenient that you suddenly said that over the phone, when you thought you had all your information, or how you thought you could butter me up with a $20 money order. I knew from the beginning that you were going to pull a stunt like this (only I was surprised you didn't wait until the last minute).

If you look back to all the false information I gave you about the necrophilia, Greene's death, if you put two and two together, I took excerpts from Dahmer, Gacy, Nilsen and Wournos and put them together and gave you a story (fiction). In your letters you say many things don't make sense, well of course not, you think I would tell you so voluntarily about July 1st 2003? I'm telling you this, at the very least, I don't want you to make a fool out of yourself, or spend money on a book of lies about July 1st 2003. Like everyone else you will have to wait until the trial or tribunal to find out what really happened. There was no East Indian, no grave digging, no necrophilia.

Everybody seems to be interested (including you) in some Hollywood drama or some macabre ritual or something. People are still convinced that it was Jennifer Lopez's necklace. People are always going to believe what they want to believe.

Please don't waste any more time on your project, you are only going to make yourself look stupid if you do. In my letters when I asked you to do something I know for a fact that you have not. I have also made Mr. Brodsky aware of who you are, I gave him your home address and phone number.

As for the drawings, I had gotten the basic drafts from textbooks from the jail library including a biology text on the human body. If you go to the Albert to room 309 you will see there is nothing in the bathroom to hang Greene from (the ceiling is 12 feet high) and I had nothing to hang the body with.

I don't know if you're anything like Don Abbott, after he told me how you wanted to "help" I had already became suspicious. Do you recall the fictional story about the bathtub murders in it? Sorry if I wasted your time.

Sidney

Figure 11: "Diagram 1." — *The Murder of Robin Greene,* by Sidney Teerhuis.

Figure 12: *Cell-Mates*, by Sidney Teerhuis.

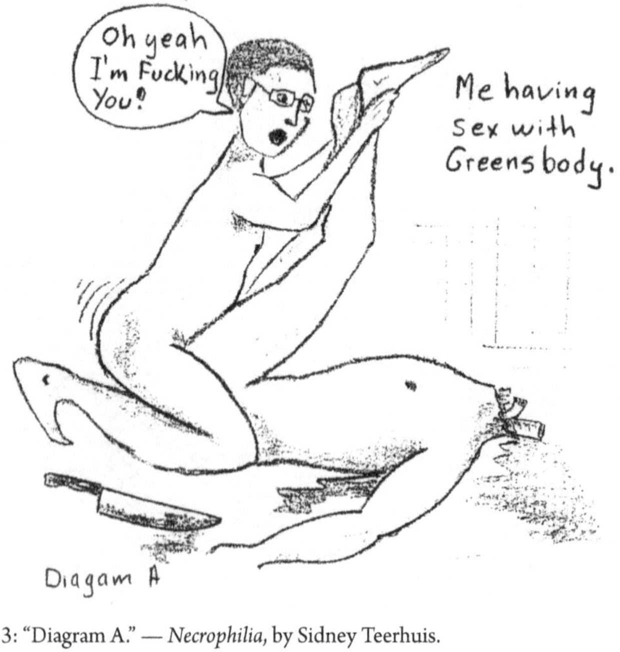

Figure 13: "Diagram A." — *Necrophilia*, by Sidney Teerhuis.

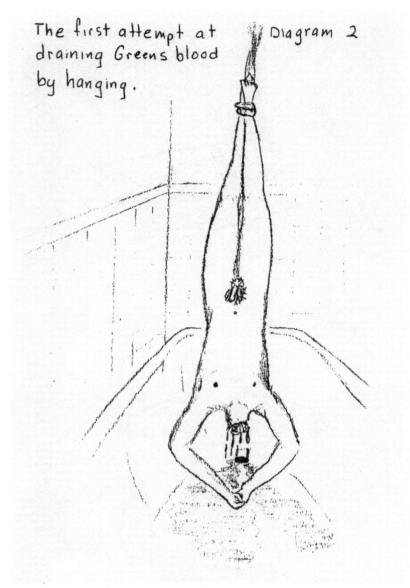

The first attempt at draining Greens blood by hanging.

Diagram 2

Figure 14: "Diagram 2." — *The Hanging*, by Sidney Teerhuis.

Figure 15: (Next page, top) "Diagram C." — *Bathing With The Corpse*, by Sidney Teerhuis.

Figure 16: (Next page, bottom) "Diagram B." — *Dismembered*, by Sidney Teerhuis.

Bathing with Robins Corpse, the water was red like tomato soup.

Diagram C.

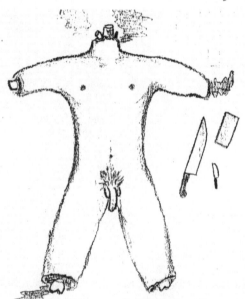

What Green looked like on the bathroom floor before I disembowelld him.

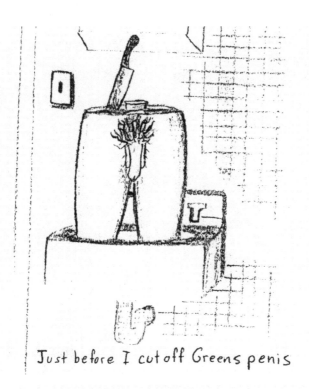

Just before I cut off Greens penis

Green as an art form

Diagram E

Figure 17: (top) "Diagram D." — *Sawn in Half*, by Sidney Teerhuis.

Figure 18: (bottom) "Diagram E." — *Greene as an Art Form*, by Sidney Teerhuis.

Green as my trophy, my creation, a work of art.

Diagram F

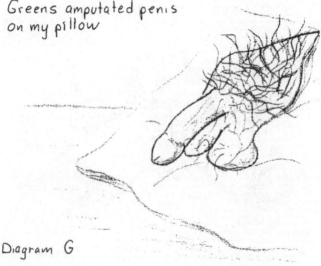

Greens amputated penis on my pillow

Diagram G

Figure 19: (top) "Diagram F." — *The Trophy*, by Sidney Teerhuis.

Figure 20: (bottom) "Diagram G." — *Castration*, by Sidney Teerhuis.

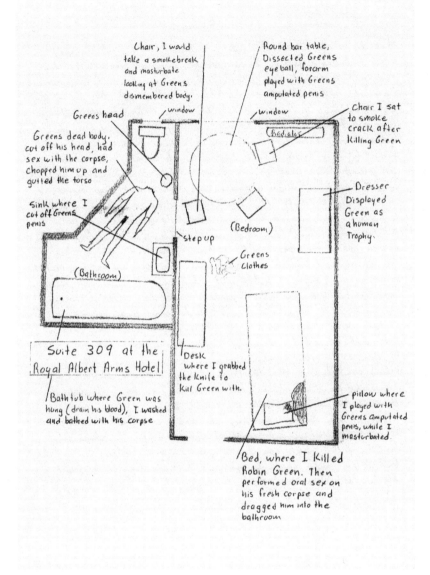

Figure 21: "Blueprint/room-layout" — Depiction of murder-scene, by Sidney Teerhuis.

that this victim was ultimately sacrificed for the right reasons.)
When I butchered Greens body, watching the steel blade enter his
body and the sensation of pulling it out again was beyond any moral
connection. I treated the corpse like a side of beef, like Green was
a dead animal and portioned him like a giant turkey cutting off the
arms and legs. Cutting him (scooping out the organs) was a lot of fun, I
took my time. I made an evening of it slowly dismembering Greens
body, taking a break every now and then to admire my culinary
and meat cutting skills. After Green had been disembowelled I held
open the giant cut in his abdomen and took a nice deep breath of
his empty chest cavity. It was like a sence of accomplishment.
His flesh was starting to turn grey, his fore arms were cold,
the finger tips turned blue black under the nails. - What sort of haunts
me is after I had Green on the bathroom floor and began to slice
into his neck, I think he was still alive. There was like a deep uhhh
and a groan. (however sometimes when a body dies it twitches and makes
noise.) Even if he was alive I probably would have held him down
and continued to chop his head off. - What was really sexually
gratifying was having Greens penis on my pillow beside my face while
I masturbated, what a beautiful sight, knowing his body was cut
to pieces in the next room.
(Here's some food for thought, the next time you have a hard-on I
know what the inside of your penis looks and feels like, the different
layers of skin, muscle tissue, the erectil tissue.
I want you to try something; the next time you shower or
sit at the foot of your bed, look at your genitals, the shape and
texture of the shaft, cup them in your hand try to "feel the weight
look at your pubic hair, do you feel the sensations of your self
touching it? Then I want you to think of Robin Green ⟶

Figure 22: "Letter 1/03/2005, page 2." — Extract from letter, written by Sidney Teerhuis.

his body. The sound of friction (Greens flesh being dragged over the carpet) the way his head nodded side to side, his arms dragging over his shoulders and bumping into things. When I masturbate at night my sexual fantasies vary, when I fantasize about Green it's when I'm sexing his headless corpse after he was decapitated (that's how I'd like to remember Green as a naked headless corpse on my bathroom floor before the dismemberment, disembowellment and emasculation. - You seem to be so focused on the missing internal organs, so here is a little quiz: Only one of these statements are true:

1. What did I do with Robin Greens internal organs?
   Were they; a) flushed down the toilet
             b) did I sell them to George for fifty dollars
             c) did I eat them in a cannibalistic ritual
             D) were they tossed in a BFI dumpster near H.S.C.
             E) were some tossed in a vacant lot and a
                dumpster near H.S.C.

   Only one of these statements are true, what do you personally think I did with Greens organs. Be realistic.

2. Greens murder is similar to who: A) Dalmer B) Zodiac Killer
   c) John Wayne Gacy D) Dennis Nielson

3. Do you think I have the characteristics of a seriall Killer? ☐yes ☐no

4. Do you think I enjoyed the entire event (the murder stabbing death of Green and the necrophilia and dismemberment) from begining to end? ☐yes ☐no ☐not sure

   - I am amused by what the newspapers say. There are no post killing photos. At the crime scene they speculated to reporters, just like they assumed the organs had been flushed. There are photos of the jazzy festival, the Royal Crown, the Richardson Building, Green modeling underwear, pictures of underwear, of Green sitting on my lap, and Green sitting on Georges lap, and a photo of Green posing his anus for the camera.

Figure 23: "Letter 1/03/2005, page 4." — Extract from letter, written by Sidney Teerhuis.

The coroner or autopsy report concluded that the accused must have had same knowledge of human anatomy. The left forearm had been dissected and cut in such a way that the accused may have been curious or interested of the content of the forearm.

Even the way the penis pubic area and testicles had been sliced off all in one piece they concluded the accused must have had knowledge of the genital area.

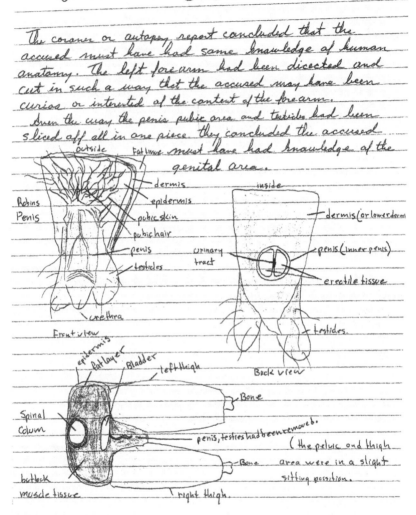

Figure 24: "Letter 3: Autopsy" — Extract from letter, written and illustrated by Sidney Teerhuis.

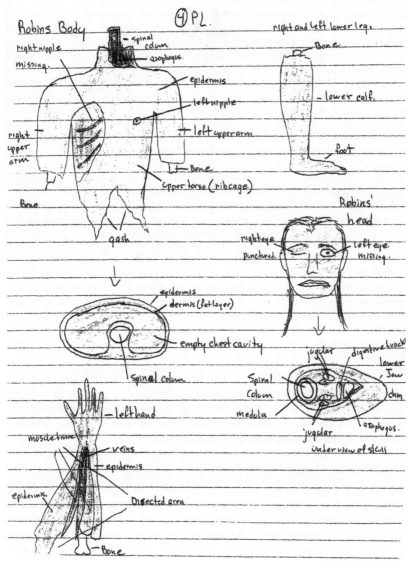

Figure 25: "Letter 4: Autopsy" — Extract from letter, written and illustrated by Sidney Teerhuis.

10

First Contact

I
T WAS DURING WORK THAT I CALLED THE CROWN ATTORNEY'S OFFICE on the morning of April 24th. I had asked if I could speak to the Crown Attorney in charge of the Sidney Teerhuis murder trial. The woman that answered the phone told me that Liz Thomson was the prosecutor on the case. I asked if I could leave a message on her voice mail. In the message I stated my name, and that I had information in my possession about the Sidney Teerhuis case that would be considered evidence.

April 25/05

THE NEXT DAY, IN THE MORNING I RECEIVED A CALL FROM ROSS READ, A WINNIPEG Homicide Detective. He asked me what I was referring to in the message I had left for Liz Thomson. I explained how I had become involved with corresponding with Teerhuis and that through that correspondence I had obtained information that would be regarded as important evidence to the case.

Ross said that the normal procedure was to set up a meeting so they (the police) could determine if I did indeed have what would amount to evidence in this case. He had mentioned that there was someone else who had come forward with information as well. I expressed surprise and Ross said he would tell me about it when we would meet later that week.

I told him about Teerhuis' reaction to my informing him of a recent provincial law not allowing criminals to be able to profit from their crimes any longer, and the letter Sidney sent me as a result. During our conversation, Ross said, "*We both just want to see this guy behind bars as long as possible.*" I told him, "*Teerhuis won't be in jail forever, and I'm risking my neck by giving you this evidence against him.*" Ross acknowledged that point and said that it would be very seriously taken into consideration.

He told me to bring all the letters in question with me to the meeting. We agreed to meet the next day at 3:00 p.m. I asked Ross to meet me at the Shopper's Drug Mart on Main and Redwood Avenue. I requested that they pick me up there, as I wanted to complete the photocopying of all the letters and the diagrams.

April 26/05

Ross Read and his partner Dale McMillan arrived around 3:00 p.m. in an unmarked brown Crown Victoria, a typical plain looking police vehicle. I opened the passenger side back door and got in.

Once I was in the vehicle and had closed the door, Ross introduced himself and extended his hand to shake. Ross introduced his partner as Dale McMillan. Ross was driving and we proceeded to the Public Safety Building, which was only about 7 or 8 minutes away. During the ride, through our conversation, I found out that Ross was the lead Homicide Investigator on the case. Some small talk ensued, and then the three of us arrived at the Public Safety Building. As we left the car and entered the police station, I commented to Dale, "*Homicide must be a tough job.*" He replied, "*It's just a job.*" I was at the time surprised but in thinking about it later at home I realized that was an appropriate response. What was he going to say to a stranger about his chosen profession?

Once inside the police station we went to an interview room. Ross asked if I wanted anything, some water or a coffee. I had water with me but decided that I could use a coffee to stay alert during the interview.

Ross is tall and thin, about 6' 1, maybe 180 lbs. He has curly, light brown colored hair and a fair complexion. He came across as an easy-going cop, bright and very serious. He didn't seem to fit the stereotypical image of a homicide detective; that being said the image I did have is primarily based on television and movies. His partner Dale is heavier in build, about 5'9 and about 200 lbs. Dale is quite dark in complexion and he had dark stubble on his face. Both officers looked maybe 45 years old.

The interview room was a bit intimidating. The room was a cold, drab room about 8 x 10 ft. there was a thick gray metal table on the left-hand side of the room with two heavy wooden chairs on either side. Another smaller metal table was on the right-hand side of the room.

Ross sat directly across from me and Dale sat at the other table. Ross handled all the questioning and wrote down all that I was telling him on a small notepad. He asked me how I came to meet Sidney and I explained how I knew Don Abbott and how I came to correspond with Sidney. Ross seemed to be very careful to include all that I was saying, making sure to record it essentially verbatim. Whenever Ross was taking considerable time to write down what I had said, I happened to look over at Dale. Every time I did, Dale was staring very intently at me. He had a notepad for taking notes but it seemed that he was there to observe me and not as much to write about what I was saying. Dale's face did not reveal much emotion when I recounted many of the things Sidney had revealed to me through our correspondence.

Ross painstakingly continued to write down what I was saying, he asked questions about the chronological order of events. He asked about when I first visited Sidney, about the phone conversations Sidney and I had. I told him about some of the contents of the letters and how I offered Sidney a share of the proposed book's profit in order to gain his cooperation. I told Ross and Dale that Sidney had revealed to me intimate details of the murder, dismemberment and location of the missing internal organs. Ross then asked if I had brought all the letters in question. I handed him the letters in a manila envelope. I told him that I had brought all the letters that contained references that pertained to the killing. He then told me that he wanted to see all of the letters and all the correspondence between Sidney and I. He stated that they (the police) wanted all of the material, as they would determine what of that correspondence they would utilize in the prosecution of the case. He said that we would meet again in a few days so that I could hand over the rest of the letters.

After about an hour the interview was completed. Ross said that he and Dale would be back in a little while and they locked me inside the room.

I occupied my time by reading a newspaper I had, and after about 20 minutes or so Ross and Dale returned to the room. They told me that they had met with their supervisor and they had determined that they would like me to make a Video Statement. Ross instructed me to basically re-iterate what I had just previously told him, while the interview was being videotaped. He told me that the Video Statement would be utilized in court during the trial.

THE VIDEO STATEMENT — 4:41 P.M.

Detective Sgt. Read: Now what I'd like to do here for the most part, Dan is I'd like you to carry the bulk of the conversation. Dale and I will have--definitely we'll have some questions for you, regarding the information you provide. But we'll try to hold those off as best we can. So if you can, be as specific as possible regarding the information, and as candid as possible. We'll go through how it is that you became knowledgeable of this investigation, the person you spoke to regarding what that information was, bringing us up to today. Is that fair?
Me: Yes
Detective Sgt. Read: So we'll kind of start off with how was it you became aware of this investigation, and what persons were involved.
Me: I was in Thunder Bay, I guess for, during July 1st, July 2nd, when this crime apparently happened. When I came back from Thunder Bay, I happened to see the Winnipeg Sun, front page, describing the article concerning the alleged murder at the Royal Albert Hotel. I had read the article and I cut out the clipping, out of the paper. In subsequent days, there were follow-up stories as well and I cut out those articles and just put them in a pile with the other clippings. They were interesting--it was an interesting story to me, by virtue of the facts that were relayed in the stories that appeared in the newspaper. I didn't think anything of it; I just collected subsequent clippings that appeared in the newspaper concerning this case.

A person that I had originally met back in 1976 in Thunder Bay, I had visited with him in the summer. In the fall of 2003, he was charged and incarcerated, and called me on the telephone after he was charged and asked if he could call me.

Detective Sgt. Read: Okay. Who is that person?

Me: That person's name is Don Abbott. Don had called me to ask if he could correspond with me and to also address the charges that he was alleged to have committed. Subsequently, I listened to his explanation for the charges he was charged for and I believed that he would be eventually cleared, and decided on letting him call me, and so we corresponded by telephone.

While he was in the institution, he had called me numerous times. One of those times, he asked me, "Listen, guess who is the jail range with me?" I said, "Who?" He said, "The guy that cut up that guy at the Royal Albert, Sidney Teerhuis." In fact, he had mentioned Sidney Teerhuis' name first. Sidney Teerhuis, I didn't recognize the name initially. When he said, "Oh, the guy that chopped up the guy at the Albert." I immediately knew whom he was referring to. I remembered the case because it had been so dramatic, we'll say, or so controversial a case.

I have done a regular radio program on the University of Manitoba since 2000, March of 2000. In this one-hour weekly talk show, interview-style program, I handle many issues. A particular interest to me were cases where I felt there was some inherent problem in the judicial system handling very serious cases involving violence.

A couple of years into doing my radio program, I was made aware of a group called People for Justice. I joined the group; it was formed by a victim's father. In subsequent meetings, I was voted the Media and Policy Affairs Chairman. I did that from 2002 to 2003, approximately a year. I am no longer associated with the group, officially.

Detective Sgt Read: Okay.

Me: With Don's revelation that Sidney Teerhuis was in his range, I immediately thought, because I was interested in the case, that I would ask Don if this Sidney Teerhuis would be interested, at some point in being interviewed. Don called me within a couple of days, I believe, to tell me that yes, Sidney was interested.

I expressed to Don that I was very interested in this project. I thought because of the celebrity connection, and what I felt was the alleged killer's craving for celebrity, by my surmising of the case; that I thought that there would be some potential for this story being-- that I should be involved with this story in some capacity. Within a short period of time, I re-thought my original idea and thought that it based on the potential that it might certainly make for an interesting book.

Detective Sgt. Read: Okay.

Me: I believed that there would be possibly an ability for me to be able to write this book, and that there would be some potential profit in writing the book.

Detective Sgt. Read: Okay.

Me: I Asked Don to request to share a cell with Sidney to gain more information. I was not privy to what Don had said to Sidney Teerhuis to convince him that certainly I would be a good person to write the story, no matter what. I did have conversations with Don to express that I was certainly willing to offer a financial split between the three of us for this story.

Detective Sgt. Read: What were the terms of that?

Me: Thirty percent each of the profit of the book itself.

Detective Sgt. Read: Would go to whom?

Me: Don, Sidney and myself.

Detective Sgt. Read: So now you're talking about--you obviously see financial gain through a book that you've offered to...

Me: I see...

Detective Sgt. Read: A potential...

Me: I see financial gain, but I actually--my main primary motive was because I saw a clear, in my mind, a clear demonstration that this case would provide. In the end, I thought that there were enough ingredients; to indicate to me that this case would clearly demonstrate the kind of thing I was already at odds with, that I had problems with, that I certainly didn't agree with.

Detective Sgt. Read: So those are your issues with the judicial system?

Me: Yes. That these are the kind of things that I had spoken about, that the inherent difficulties of the judicial system, with changes to certain laws over the last few years. And just the kinds of things that I had seen in cases like murder. I was very concerned with those things and aware of some of the--again, I say what I believe to be inherent problems with trying to convict someone of a serious crime like murder.

Detective Sgt. Read: Okay. So you've spoken to Don. Don has approached Sidney. You're talking about potentially a book being written and splitting a, you know, a thirty percent profit. Is there any reaction at all that you became aware of from Sidney back to Don? Is he for this, against it?

Me: Sidney expressed his full cooperation. I start this officially by asking for Sidney's complete background. I believe this is the best approach to be able to--because I had expressed fascination about the entire crime. I saw early on that Sidney Teerhuis believed that I was interested in every facet of his life from birth. I did not discourage this. I felt that this was a very effective way of building a bonding--of creating some kind of bond between us, some sort of, at least a trust, in as far as that person that would completely try to understand him and his case. And I felt it was important to start with flattering him, that I was indeed very, very interested in every facet of his life, his past, and that's the way I proceeded.

Detective Sgt. Read: This is purely your doing. Certainly not at the direction of the police, or the Crown's office, or anyone like that. This is your own belief, your own doing.

Me: This is totally my interest.

Detective Sgt. Read: Okay. I'll let you continue.

Me: I had spoken to Don while he was incarcerated, briefly, and we both spoke about what we felt was the absurdity of the claim that Sidney Teerhuis, despite killing this person and cutting up this person; according to the newspaper; cutting him into eight pieces; and taking photos of the body after the killing, according to the newspaper. I don't know if that's accurate. But everything that had to be involved with the dismemberment, disposal of the organs, and the actual forty-seven stab wounds; I found it absurd. And everyone I spoke to--but especially Don, that in fact it was an absurd contention that he could not remember any of the killing whatsoever.

Detective Sgt. Read: Okay. Now those details you just spoke of with respect to dismemberment, the number of stab wounds, that he couldn't remember, where are you getting that information?

Me: From the newspaper, Winnipeg Sun, and the Winnipeg Free Press, primarily the Winnipeg Sun.

Detective Sgt. Read: Any other sources other than those two?

Me: No.

Detective Sgt. Read: So the number of stab wounds, for example, forty-seven mentioned, you believe that's from the newspaper?

Me: Yes.

Detective Sgt. Read: It is definitely?

Me: Absolutely.

Detective Sgt. Read: And the dismemberment, the lack of memory?

Me: All those details were from the original story and his claim of not remembering and in fact being intoxicated, and then actually disposing of the organs in a manner that the police couldn't find them. So he did dispose of those organs effectively. That he would have cut the body into eight pieces. It was just absurd to me. So both of us spoke of how we thought it was fairly certain that we could get him to certainly admit that indeed, he did remember some aspect of this, negating his contention that he could not remember any of the killing. And that was based on what Don--it just seemed that Sidney was very, very cooperative and very talkative. And very forthcoming and very trustworthy--he found us--Don especially, and subsequently speaking on behalf of me to be trustworthy.

Detective Sgt. Read: Okay. Now you're just anticipating that because, I mean, that's something for Don to say, but that's just your perception of the relationship that Mr. Teerhuis and Don had established based upon Don's conversations with you?

Me: Yes.

Detective Sgt. Read: Okay. And then we'll get into some contact that you had which would lead you to feel that way. Is that fair?

Me: Yes.

Detective Sgt. Read: Okay. So I'll let you continue. Obviously there's a rapport being established.

Me: What happened is that Don shares a cell with him. He makes the request to share a cell with him. They start documenting—Don is employed, basically. He's trying to see if he can find, like just through conversation, find anything that really will signify that indeed, he does remember certain aspects of this crime. Sidney was employed, instead of Don doing it; it was up to Sidney to document his life; and for all the details from his adoption, right up.

Detective Sgt. Read: That's what he was asked to do?

Me: That's what he was asked.

Detective Sgt. Read: So now, you've got this first bit of correspondence with him by way of phone.

Me: Right.

Detective Sgt. Read: Okay. Had you met with him in person?

Me: I believe that I met him after I had spoken to him on the phone, after he had sent me the letter requesting for me to see if I'd like to visit him. And then subsequently, I went to visit him.

Detective Sgt. Read: And when was that?

Me: That was in March of 2004.

Detective Sgt. Read: Okay. Let's talk a little bit about that.

Me: He was very forthcoming. He had expressed, I believe at the first interview, if not the second interview at the Remand Centre, that he believed it would be more likely that they would listen in on phone conversations during those visits. But since he knew the law, or believed the law to be that it was only in rare cases that they would read and censor letters that were outgoing and incoming, that it would be better for him to answer some of the questions I had asked him and began to ask him, via letters.

That first interview was just to meet and to establish more of a rapport. He seemed very forthcoming, considering we were strangers. He seemed to trust me. He didn't seem to have any trepidation or apprehension. He wasn't guarded, in how he spoke to me. That was my impression. It was a good indication to me that I thought we could do something, as far as I could get some answers from him, certainly.

Detective Sgt. Read: Answers regarding what?

Me: The crime itself. I felt optimistic, just by virtue of that. Not being concrete on exactly why. I had no idea what I'd be getting, but I just felt confident that this relationship would garner some of the facts.

Detective Sgt. Read: Based on his demeanor in meeting you the first time?

Me: Yes

Detective Sgt. Read: Now to this point in time, you had talked about March of 2004. Have you discussed, be it in that first letter or phone call, or this first meeting, any

96

details regarding this homicide at that point in time, that you recall, or...?

Me: I had always spoken about details of the homicide. But there were many details of the homicide that he could verify without actually revealing anything regarding his guilt. So I always asked some question. Of course I proceeded cautiously. I felt that I would have to do that. So there were always questions, somewhat related, we'll say, for example, even if I asked a question about, something—later on I'd ask, "What about the police investigation? What about the questioning?" I was and I am still interested in every aspect of this. So I may ask him a question about post-killing during the interrogation. But that doesn't mean that was a specific question about the killing itself. That's just an example. There were things related to the crime itself that weren't necessarily details of the killing that I was still interested in. And went about it in the peripheral of, and slowly tried to gain his trust, and be more probing with questions.

Detective Sgt. Read: So is it fair to say that was your mindset initially; was just to get comfortable with each other before getting into more specific questions? Or am I kind of jumping the gun there? It sounds...

Me: I wanted to just proceed slowly. And also give him the impression that I was interested in his entire story. So obviously he felt that I was interested in all of his story. His primary focus was his life—what he stated as his sexual abuse, his personal sexual history; his life according to him, the teenage male prostitute, his work-related brushes like with celebrity Ivana Trump. So every aspect of his life, I felt that I just should let him go and exhaust all this that he certainly wanted to tell me.

Detective Sgt. Read: Okay. So over the course of the next year...

Me: Over the course of the next year, starting sometime in the summer, he gave me much more details. Let me go backwards a bit. One of the first things that happened is that—and this is where I determined his craving for celebrity. Is that he said that, he started asking me questions about the prospective book, and how it could be sold, and what he had read about Susan Sarandon's comments. And about that people were calling it the "Shall We Dance murder." And you know, "Could Marilyn Manson write a song about this?" And, "I would like you to sell t-shirts outside the courthouse." And...

Detective Sgt. Read: That was his suggestion?

Me: Yes.

Detective Sgt. Read: So your opinion is he definitely was enthralled in enjoying whatever celebrity status may come from this?

Me: Yes. In my estimation, it's pretty evident by everything that I saw, heard and read, that he craves celebrity. That he really wanted to be in the company of some of the serial killers that he admired and was very interested in their stories. His fascination with other serial murderers when, it was strange to me in that he knew the victim's names of Jeffrey Dahmer, even for people that are familiar with the story like myself. I found it odd that he knew details like the names of the victims of Jeffrey Dahmer. Again, he talked a lot about celebrity. He talked about the t-shirt, he talked--and then he'd start talking about the title of the book. And he'd call the book; at first it was 'Constantly Abiding', and explaining the reasons for that. Just in the release form was a tentative title of the book project and film project, which was "Drunken Defense." He said, "I don't like that." And then he sent me another one, he said, "You know what? Why don't we go with Trophy Kill?"

Detective Sgt. Read: Whose suggestion was that?

Me: Sidney. And then he wrote that in a letter. "Why don't we go with Trophy Kill? Or Murder in Room 309? Or Death at 6:20?" So there are a few examples that he wrote.

Detective Sgt. Read: And these are all documented letters?

Me: Yes.

Detective Sgt. Read: And you actually turned over a number of these letters to Dale and I earlier? Do you remember how many letters you turned over to me?

Me: The original bundle of letters is fourteen.

Detective Sgt. Read: Okay. And as well you turned over some documents.

Me: Four letters. Four letters that I had sent him. Four phone interviews...

Detective Sgt. Read: Kind of notes...

Me: Documentation.

Detective Sgt. Read: Are they (the letters) hand written? Typed?

Me: Hand written. And including hand written drawings.

Detective Sgt. Read: Okay. Who is the author of the writings and the drawings?

Me: Sidney Teerhuis.

Detective Sgt. Read: All of them.

Me: Yes.

Detective Sgt. Read: And in fact, I mean you also--with these letters; you've had numerous phone conversations?

Me: Yes, numerous.

Detective Sgt. Read: Okay. How many phone conversations would you say?

Me: I'd say approximately fifty.

Detective Sgt. Read: Okay. And in addition to these fourteen letters, you've received other writings as well? Is that accurate? Other writings regarding--you mentioned that the fourteen letters you have are with respect, or what you feel is directly linked to this homicide investigation?

Me: To where the other ones are, they have no information other than his background.

Detective Sgt. Read: Okay. And I've asked you, and you have indicated that you weren't aware of that today, but

those are letters that you are going to turn over to us?
Me: Absolutely.

Detective Sgt. Read: These conversations, do they correspond with the letters? Like I mean, you're getting lots of specific letters regarding this, we'll say, investigation, without getting into the details. Do the phone conversations correspond to the letters at all?

Me: In the phone calls, I would express one of two sentiments: "Please respond to each of the questions in order because that will make this easier," especially after the New Year, in 2005, after I came back after Christmas, specifically I had also spoken to him, "Please don't exaggerate. Be real with me here. You know, I really can't use stuff that can't be really--that has no foundation that could be embellishment on your part. So lets keep it real."

Detective Sgt. Read: Is that stuff you would tell him? Or is that stuff in letters you would write to him?
Me: Both.

Detective Sgt. Read: And for the most part, without getting into the details of the letters, the response that you got back in the correspondence, do you believe it to be just that? Is it consistent and accurate as you know it, I mean, it's all in your perspective, but...?

Me: Everything was very believable about the details of the killing, except the grave digging, and death by cannibalism. To me it made no sense, and I told him so in letters and in phone calls. I said, "It makes no sense." So I said, "I'm not saying that you're a liar, I'm saying that it doesn't make any sense." And that's what I would say to him about those things. Everything else, you know, subsequently as I continue to re-iterate, overlap, take stuff from one bit of the interview with him, or the letters and build from that, as far as--say for example, I was very, very determined to find where the internal organs went to. What he did with those internal organs. So I asked many questions about those internal organs. On the telephone, I would follow that up with, for example, at the end I had asked him, "how did you get those...?" This was on the telephone, "How did you get those internal organs to the Health Sciences Centre, where you planned to dump them in a BFI can and in a vacant lot, in two places?" I asked him, "What organs went to the vacant lot? What went into the BFI bin? How did you transport those?" He said, "Well, you know, that's in the letters." I said, "It's not in there." He said, "I used shopping bags."

Detective Sgt. Read: So that's a conversation you had with him over the phone?

Me: And so he said he doubled up shopping bags, and he had a bunch of shopping bags, and he took the organs there. I tried to ask him if it was two trips, one trip, and anything else you know. He said, "I can't quite remember, I don't know which organs went where or why, but..." And so those are the kind of questions that for example, were built from one letter to another letter to the point where he got, and said, "Listen,

99

I'll give you a multiple choice. You're so concerned with these organs, A, B, C, or D." And he said, "Be realistic. What do you think?" And I just kept probing. Because it doesn't matter what I think, it matters what he says.

Detective Sgt. Read: Absolutely.

Me: So I got him finally down to narrow it down to "I disposed..." He said, "I disposed of the organs in the BFI and some at the vacant lot." And then he wrote about that. I told him, "Write that down."

Detective Sgt. Read: Through the conversations you had with him, do you recall when you talked about the organs, what other specific details do you recall him saying to you over the phone regarding this homicide?

Me: He said he shut the eyes, because I asked him about the eyes. He said he took one out and dissected it. I had asked him about the dissection of the eyeball. And he said, "Well one was collapsed." So I said, "You didn't take both eyes?" "No, one was collapsed and I took one out and dissected it." So I said, "When the cop came in there and looked in the bathtub, did he see the guy's eyes open?" He goes, "No". He didn't see the eyes poked out. I closed the eye lids." I said, "Okay." And then I also asked him on the telephone, "If you could send me a diagram of what the room looked like, where the bathroom was? What he (police officer) may have seen as he came in?" So he sent me a detailed drawing of the room where the body was. I had also asked him, oh, the details: "Was he lying on his right side?"

Detective Sgt. Read: So is this stuff he told you over the phone or did you respond in letter about that?

Me: I asked him to send me a drawing, we'll say, on the phone.

Detective Sgt. Read: Did you receive a drawing?

Me: Yes I did. So then when I spoke to him again on the phone; February, I said, "it would be nice if you drew me a picture of him in the bathtub." That was my last request, just a drawing of him in the bathtub. Also I believe I asked him to give me maybe a map of exactly where--those are the kind of questions I asked him: Where exactly was the BFI can? Does he remember what street? You know just...

Detective Sgt, Read: Did he give you a landmark where the BFI bin was by, any particular buildings?

Me: No, he couldn't do that. That's just some of the things I was trying to get on the telephone after, you know...

Detective Sgt. Read: But does he tell you where?

Me: He couldn't really be specific. He wasn't sure exactly what street. All he knows is it's very close to Health Sciences Centre, and there was a vacant lot next door. So I said, "Well you know I haven't been down there." But if it's true, then it should be fairly easy to find a vacant lot and the BFI can so--it's not hard to do that.

Detective Sgt. Read: Again, what sort of specific details will we get from the letters? And I mean, of course we're

going to take (the letters) and they'll be reviewed and things like that. What details did you learn from the writings that you hadn't learned from the newspaper?
Me: That the victim was killed at 6:20 p.m. on July the 1st. Details of Robin Greene trying to sell a piece of jewelry in the Woodbine Hotel. Details of where that jewelry was in the crime scene, despite the tabloids' representation that it was J. Lo's necklace found in a pool of blood. So I learned, according to Sidney, what those details were. I've learned that he claimed that he went downstairs, previous to the killing, went downstairs to have a few drinks while the victim slept. When he came up he tried to arouse the person from the sleep, and he said that the person was urinating, pissing the bed. I asked, "What time was that?" He said, "6:00 o'clock." And also, in his letters he offers an explanation of why this happened. There's really no explanation, but he tries to offer an explanation. He says that one thing led to another. I asked him in subsequent letters but I never got a response about that one thing that led to the other thing was. He told me how he enjoyed the sex with the corpse, the dismemberment, the dissection, and the dragging the head into the washroom, the draining of the blood, the castration, and the desecration. Masturbating with the genitals cut from the body on his pillow. Him being sexually excited throwing the organs in a BFI bin, his utter lack of remorse. In fact, he talks about certain jokes with all kinds of bad puns about the victim. He talks in his letters, an incredible amount of things. He talks about how he would like to be judged by an Aboriginal Tribunal, because he's an aboriginal and the other person is an aboriginal. He believes that it should be handled by an Aboriginal Tribunal Court.
Detective Sgt. Read: Did he get into at all with respect to witnesses regarding this matter?
Me: Yes, in fact he spoke of person named George that apparently they all—the three of them drank together and George apparently was present when photos were taken of Robin Greene in sexual poses.
Detective Sgt. Read: George was present during that?
Me: That's what he claims. This gentleman named George.
Detective Sgt. Read: Does he say how he met George? Is he a friend of his?
Me: I believe he met George at the Woodbine. Again it's a stranger. He goes on to say that himself and Robin Greene go to a park and some homosexual had, you know, sex with Robin Greene while he watches. Apparently George met them outside the Woodbine and they go for drinks at the Royal Albert where Teerhuis has a room. Then George leaves and then Greene says, "What a wonderful day. Let's go by the Assiniboine, and have some drinks." Greene puts Susan Sarandon's necklace around Sidney's neck and he thought it was a sweet gesture. They talked about how they should get a room or that they should share a room and move in with each other. They go to pick up some more beer, go back to the room. This is around 4:00 o'clock. Apparently

101

George comes back because he forgot his six-pack of beer. Picks up his six-pack. They (Sidney and Greene) have sex again. Teerhuis says that Greene said, "Hey, I'd like to get some sleep." He (Teerhuis) says, "Oh that's okay." He goes downstairs, he says hello to the bartender. He has a couple of drinks, maybe smokes a joint, I'm not quite sure about that. Anyway, an hour or so ensued. After an hour and a half, he comes back, almost at 6:00 o'clock. He figures, "Hey, I'll you know, party on." He tries to wake up Robin Greene and Robin was urinating in the bed.

Detective Sgt. Read: Okay, so based upon what you've just told me, and I want to clarify: You mentioned 6:20 as the time of this murder.

Me: According to Sidney Teerhuis.

Detective Sgt. Read: Is that in the evening or the morning?

Me: Evening.

Detective Sgt. Read: Okay. I just wanted to clarify that.

Me: He said that he was dead at 6:20, and he said that the guy was urinating in the bed at 6:00 o'clock. Now, I also asked him questions about the knives. Because the very first thing in this was—I just asked a couple of people, a butcher. What kind of knife would they have to use to cut through bone? Cut the guy in half? And he says, "Well all chefs, even though this guys' a pastry chef, dessert chef; they all travel, they all have in their possession a full set, including a cleaver and all kinds of very, very sharp knives." I did ask him on the telephone about the knives. I said, and this is later on, he (Sidney) said he had lost his full knife set (in Edmonton), or they were stolen, "While I was a chef there." I said, "Did you report it to the police?" He said, "No." So he said that just before—just when he came back to Winnipeg, he had purchased two knives, I said, "The whole set?" "No, just two knives." Two knives that for some reason, he felt he still needed, even despite not having a full set of proper knives. Despite being in a hotel room, he needed these chef knives. And that's the kind of question I asked him on the telephone, it was about the knives.

Detective Sgt. Read: Did he indicate if he still had them? Had he gotten rid of them?

Me: He had those knives in the murder. They were used in the killing and the dismemberment. Those knives, he admitted, that they were used in the killing.

Detective Sgt. Read: Okay. Did he mention—had he gotten to dispose of them? Were they still around, didn't say?

Me: I didn't ask. As far as I know, he had never spoke of disposing of the weapons themselves.

Detective Sgt. Read: Did he speak whether this act was premeditated or was it spur of the moment?

Me: He actually has indicated that—like I will restate, that he had said that one thing led to another. He uses statements like, "I couldn't help myself or him. He was a reasonable sacrifice." That's not the actual quote, but the guy died for a good cause, in his actual words, that the sacrifice was worthwhile. He talks about how beautiful he was in bed. How he was happy that this was the last orgasm this guy had. And it was interesting to believe that this was the last sexual experience that this Greene would have. He didn't really suffer. He talks about in there how supposedly, I guess he compares it to animals; if they're killed really quickly, then there's no trauma in their flesh. In the letters he talks like a butcher. And he talks about slaughtering, butchering, gutting...

Detective Sgt. Read: So all these details that we're talking about right now, these are all documented in the letters you've turned over to us?

Me: Yes.

Detective Sgt. Read: Okay. Now, you mentioned first meeting him in March of last year, and this carried on essentially for a year. When does this correspondence terminate?

Me: In--it's now April, so I spoke to him in March. After the three letters, I sent him identical letters three times, he claimed to not receive the letter with the release. It seemed to me, it was an important letter I felt, I sent it again. I copied it and I sent it again. I sent it three times. He claimed to not get it. The last time I spoke to him on the phone, we talked about him not getting these letters, seemed kind of unusual. He said, "I sent you a letter. Haven't you gotten it?" I said, "No." And I said, "By the way, did you read the Winnipeg Sun today?" He said, "About what?" So I said, "About the law actually being passed, that criminals can't profit from their crimes." And I think he said, "No." And he hung up.

Detective Sgt. Read: Okay.

Me: So I did write him, he wrote me a letter, it was dated April 4th, so I got it about you know, April 10th or something. And it said, you know, "I haven't heard from you in a while, I wonder why?" And, "I'm not surprised. I never heard anything about the Winnipeg Sun and criminals not being able to profit from their crime. So I think you're full of it, and I never read anything. And it's--how convenient for you to say this at this time. I thought you might do something like this, but certainly not at this time. I thought you'd wait till the very end. You thought you could butter me up with a twenty-dollar money order. You shouldn't waste your time with this. This is fiction. I've taken four stories from four serial killers and created a story. Of course it doesn't make sense, because it's a combination of four different stories."

Detective Sgt. Read: So at the time now that he feels cut off by you, now he's retracting?

Me: Yes. He's retracting, what he said specifically was that Greene was not hung from the ceiling at the Royal Albert. He had nothing to hang him with, and he certainly didn't. He also said there was no grave digging, which he documents in his letters to me which I didn't believe and told him so. And he also said this East Indian, which he spoke about his fantasy

103

of being eaten, suicide by cannibalism, and this East Indian having similar--being a full participant in this bizarre sex death fantasy, that indeed, that there was no East Indian whatsoever. He said, "Did you really believe that I would be giving you intimate details of Greene's death?" He posed that sort of as a question. He also said that I shouldn't waste my time, because I would look like a fool, and that he had given Mr. Brodsky my phone number and address and told him who I was. And so he basically said, "I'm sorry for wasting your time. Please do not pursue this. You will look stupid. Remember, I told you about the story that I was working on about..." There's a fictional story apparently, when I first started talking to him, he had something in his property. Well, a fictional story that Don had read where bodies end up in the bathtub, people dead in the bathtub. I just kept asking him for a copy of that fictional story to see if he could get it out of his property. And he told me, "Remember the stories about the dead people in the bathtub?" he said, "That was fiction, and that's what you have here is total fiction."

Detective Sgt. Read: But this is only after?

Me: Absolutely.

Detective Sgt. Read: Up to that point he's been giving you details regarding this investigation?

Me: Yes.

Detective Sgt. Read: Or this murder?

Me: Yes.

Detective Sgt. Read: And only in the end does he try to retract it once he feels you've cut him off financially?

Me: Yes, and I mean, he has, if you think about it, he has the ability to retract in entirety everything that he felt was not true. And I felt that he knew it was not true. And this--it's telling, I believe, in that this is his only retraction.

Detective Sgt. Read: Okay. And I guess the other question we have is, you know, this has been going on for quite some time. What is it that's brought you to bring this to, you know, our attention now?

Me: I as of about December, started inquiring what my responsibility would be, because I felt concerned that, I knew I had evidence. I knew this. No one had to tell me that this was stuff that can amount to evidence, material evidence. And I asked a journalist, a couple of journalists actually, with experience. And I said--because I really didn't trust speaking to too many people. I thought, like many writers I have found out now, that you're paranoid about someone stealing your opportunity. It might sound crass, but I'm a volunteer journalist. I've done everything for no financial gain whatsoever. More importantly, it's not even a matter of financial gain. I would like to be regarded as a writer. Especially given the work and the research that I've done in that capacity.

Detective Sgt. Read: Okay.

Me: So why I brought you this was to do the right thing, that's the first primary motivation, to do the right thing. And the advice I got was that you should certainly do this. The second reason is that these people felt it was my responsibility. So that's the second thing, I certainly didn't want to break the law. I certainly didn't want to have any, even a chance of me being charged with anything. That would be very, you know, non-productive. It would be bad for me, I would say. And so I came forward because it's the right thing to do. I believe that without this evidence, certainly his excuse that he could not remember anything might work in court. Now, I'm not trying to affect an outcome of a court case, that's not my purpose. And it wasn't my purpose in the first place when I gathered information. As a journalist, my goal is to determine the truth. And I don't believe that the judicial system's main primary goal, to the exclusion of everything else; is to find the truth necessarily, the way it's set up. So I have a responsibility that will be to tell the truth. Where as far as I know, the defense lawyer, even if he was given the same information, and according to Sidney Teerhuis, we had almost the identical information—that his legal obligation is not to do anything with that information, not telling anybody about 'the truth', about what really happened. So the only person that has the responsibility and the opportunity is myself. So I felt without my participation in this, this person would receive a sentence that would not reflect the truth.

Detective Sgt. Read: So these details that you provided, Dan, these aren't details that you've heard from someone else? And you're saying that Sidney told you these specific things that you've learned through conversations with Sidney, through your writings with Sidney Teerhuis, and then earlier on through some conversations that you had with Don?

Me: Yes.

Detective Sgt. Read: Okay. Dale, do you have any questions?

Detective Sgt. McMillan: None.

Detective Sgt. Read: Okay. We're going to conclude this statement then, Dan. It's three minutes to 6:00. You can follow Dale out of the room please.

Me: Okay.

Detective Sgt. Read: I appreciate that.

ROSS THANKED ME FOR MY COOPERATION AND SEEMED TO EXPRESS AN APPRECIATION of what exactly I had been able to uncover through my efforts. I left the Public Safety Building and headed home. Being interviewed by the police had been a very interesting experience, and as interesting experiences go, this I felt was just the beginning.

MONDAY, MAY 2/05

I RECEIVED A CALL FROM ROSS READ THIS MORNING ASKING WHEN WE COULD meet so I could give him the rest of the letters that I had. I agreed to meet the next afternoon and said I would be bringing him the rest of the letters.

As well I am going to give him the People for Justice Literature so the police and the Crown will understand that part of my background so as not to leave them off guard from this information coming out via Greg Brodsky at the trial. They also asked about the whereabouts of Don Abbott. I told them I didn't know how to contact him.

When I checked my messages in the afternoon, Don had called and was anxious to talk to me as the police were looking to speak to him about Sidney Teerhuis.

Thursday, May 5/05

I MET ROSS READ AFTER WORK AND GAVE HIM ALL THE REST OF THE CORRESPONDENCE including the notebooks (2) in that Don had interviewed Sidney, his letters to me, and some loose (tan-colored) pages. Despite Don calling me to inquire as to how the police became aware of and how they came to be in possession of Sidney's letters; I still have not actually spoken to Don. I have no idea as to how to contact him however the Police seemed to locate him quite quickly to question him about the letters and the relationship he developed with Teerhuis. Ross Read stated that the information they received from Don was pretty well consistent with what I had told them.

I asked when it would be likely that the Crown Attorney would be speaking to me regarding the letters that I had provided to the police and was told that the Crown would be probably contacting me about two weeks before the preliminary hearing on July 11th. I also asked when they thought that Greg Brodsky would be given the letters, and Ross stated that the letters had just been given to the Crown Attorney and that she would have to go over them thoroughly and then let Brodsky look at the letters. Ross said that could take a couple of weeks or so before Brodsky would be notified of this very new development in this murder trial.

I had handed Ross the People for Justice literature but Ross said that I should give the literature to the Crown Attorney when I meet with her. Because I had so many copies of a P.F.J. leaflets that were left over from one of our leafleting campaigns, I used the blank backside of them to write questions and/or take notes when speaking to Sidney. The notes were turned in to the police. The subject of People for Justice will definitely come up in this trial.

11
Reaching Out

I CONTACTED FORMER CROWN ATTORNEY AGNEW JOHNSTON ON SUNDAY and spoke to him briefly. I wanted to know where I stood legally concerning the interview I had conducted with Greg Brodsky on March 7th. Agnew said that Brodsky would not even mention the interview to the Crown because "*he would be unwilling to enter the forum, he won't want to mention the interview lest he becomes a witness.*"

He said that Brodsky would "*treat me at arms length*" and not want to be a witness where he would be obliged to testify and in a situation where there was a conflict of interest, end his participation in the trial.

WEDNESDAY, MAY 18/05

I HAVE SPOKEN TO AGNEW ON SUNDAY AND THEN AGAIN MONDAY. I ASKED HIM about the defense attorney's responsibility in determining the truthfulness of their client's story. He said that the lawyer has to decide the truthfulness of the story and as long as the lawyer is not advancing a known lie then they are okay. Agnew stated that there was no critical standard applied to the client saying, "*A defense attorney can clean up a client's evidence. It is possible to put words in a client's mouth; there are ways and means to do that.*"

JUNE 9/05

LIZ THOMSON CALLED ME AT WORK ON THURSDAY JUNE 9TH, RETURNING MY PHONE call that I had made to her office the week before. Liz Thomson is the Crown Attorney prosecuting this case. I had called to find out details regarding my appearance at the preliminary trial. Liz said that they had not yet decided as to whether they wanted me to testify at the preliminary or what date that might be.

The preliminary trial was to run from July 11th to July 22nd. Liz Thomson proceeded to tell me that the Crown's office would have proceeded with the second-degree murder prosecution regardless of the information that I had provided.

I couldn't understand why she was speaking to me the way she was. I knew they had laid a second-degree murder charge and would be proceeding accordingly—I would hope so. It was unnerving though to not have Ms. Thomson even acknowledge the important evidence I had been able to uncover and it was disturbing to sense that the Crown was not very appreciative of my participation in this trial.

WEDNESDAY, JUNE 17/05

I RECEIVED A CALL FROM ROSS READ FROM THE WINNIPEG HOMICIDE DIVISION and he was inquiring about whether I knew how to contact Don Abbott. He told me that he had been informed that Don had moved to Calgary. I had not spoken to Don since January, after having moved out of my place in December.

Because Don was the original contact person for Sidney and I, his testimony is also of importance to this murder trial. Don shared a cell with Sidney to facilitate the writing of the book but he did gain very little actual incriminating information as a result of speaking to him during that time period.

MONDAY, JUNE 26/05

I SPOKE TO ROSS READ AND HE SAID THAT THEY HAD CONTACTED DON AND THAT he was still committed to testifying for the Crown. Ross also mentioned that he spoke to Liz Thomson about my perception that she really had not expressed the importance of the evidence that I had brought forward. Ross stated that she did regard the evidence as well as my future testimony as of vital importance.

I asked him about the likelihood that I would be testifying at the preliminary trial and he said that it was unlikely. He told me that the Prosecution needed only minimal evidence to be able to proceed to actual trial. I asked about the possibility of finding out in general what had transpired at the preliminary and Ross said it would be mundane stuff with all the minor details of the trial process having to be dealt with.

TUESDAY, JUNE 27/05

I RECEIVED A PHONE CALL FROM THE CROWN ATTORNEY'S ASSISTANT REKHA Maliveri. She seemed very pleasant and had called to tell me that the Crown's office had decided that they would not be requiring me to testify at the preliminary.

MONDAY, JULY 11/05

GEORGE JACUB IS A 30-YEAR VETERAN JOURNALIST WITH 13 YEARS IN NEWSPAPERS and 16 in television news and current events that last worked for the C.B.C. I had met him when he was a guest on my program. I called George and he had said that up until about ten years ago Greg Brodsky had not lost a murder case in Winnipeg. He did not gain acquittals in each of those cases, however he did obtain significant reductions to the original charges, which would be considered as actual trial victories.

George had said that while working at C.B.C. he had proposed to his employers that they do a story on the inordinate amount of legal judgments involving an 'insanity defense' that Greg Brodsky along with psychiatrist Dr. Fred Shane had put forth successfully many times. The C.B.C. passed on George's proposal. I asked him about the actual murder trials that he had sat through as a court reporter involving Greg Brodsky. George told me he had attended at least a half dozen trials where Dr. Fred Shane used the exact same psychiatric assessment, and in those cases George found the eventual insanity verdict to be unwarranted. George pointed out that the admissions of guilt contained in the letters Sidney had sent me could be rife with certain embellishment.

George said that there were three things now to consider: what he originally said, the lie that had now been established, and the actual truth. Did he kill him or did he just desecrate the body? If they have the murder weapon, it may just be consistent with the type of weapon that could be used in this murder. The defense never has to tell how they may choose to proceed, they get to hear the entire evidence that the Crown Attorney has and they can modify their defense as they proceed.

George said that once it is established that Sidney has embellished the story whatsoever, Brodsky would point to that fact as proof that nothing Sidney has said is necessarily true. The fact that I offered an equal share of potential book or film profits to Sidney for his cooperation in writing this book will be interpreted as the motivation for any of this information to be revealed. It may be seen as, that crucial and incriminating information only surfaced as a result of the financial offer I had made to Sidney. He had commented that Brodsky and many other defense attorneys look at court as a game. He said given that Brodsky is in the last few years of his legal career, the only aspiration he has left professionally is to see if he can establish another precedent setting case.

George said that Brodsky's reputation is that he is very thorough and he argues the facts of a case and he does not typically resort to personal attacks on witnesses.

I asked what would happen at the preliminary trial. He said that no one in the media is really interested in the preliminary trial, he stated that he would not sit through a preliminary, there would be little or no benefit as it is, and would be mind-numbingly boring.

There was a very brief mention of Sidney Teerhuis' preliminary trial in the Winnipeg Sun simply stating that there was a publication ban in effect. The story included a brief outline of the crime, which included a mention of the Royal Albert Hotel and the date of the murder.

FRIDAY, JULY 15/05

IN THE WINNIPEG SUN TODAY APPEARED A LITTLE ARTICLE TITLED "MURDER TRIAL ordered by judge". The story re-iterates the basic facts, Sidney's present age, which is 35, the crime and the date and basic details about police finding the victim Robin Greene dismembered and mutilated in the bathtub of room 309 at the Royal Albert Arms Hotel. It stated in the article that details of the preliminary hearing couldn't be published. It also said that the hearing was to determine whether there was cause to proceed to trial. Provincial Judge Fred Sandhu ordered Teerhuis to stand trial for second-degree murder. He next appears August 10th to set a trial date.

Greg Brodsky did not call any witnesses. The pathologist testified and arresting officers also testified at the preliminary.

WEDNESDAY, AUGUST 31/05

I HAD CALLED CARY CASTAGNA OF THE WINNIPEG SUN TO FIND OUT INFORMATION regarding the next trial date that was to be set on August 10th. I read the papers on the 11th and following days and I did not read any mention of what had transpired on the 10th in court.

Cary Castagna was the police reporter on this case and he had the opportunity to interview Sidney at least twice for the Sun. His stories were my main sources of information about this murder case. The Free Press did not bother to use the information the Sun had obtained and while this story made the front page of the Sun, a version of the story was featured in the "B Section" of the Free Press, City and Regional news with the headline, "*Man slashed pretty good*". I thought that was an understatement if there ever was one.

I had met Cary at the Provincial Courthouse last year when I had attended another trial. At that time I had told him that I was working on a book about Sidney's trial. He said that Sidney had sent him some 'crazy' letters.

Cary explained that he was not covering the story but that Natalie Pona was. He told me that Sidney's next court date would be October 12th of this year. I asked him why there was a delay and Cary said that he didn't know but stated that most likely it was simply a scheduling conflict between Brodsky and the Crown Attorney.

Cary couldn't recall our meeting last year but asked basic questions as to how I came to correspond with Sidney. We also spoke of the story regarding Sidney's views regarding being ultimately tried by an Aboriginal Tribunal as opposed to regular court. Cary commented that, "Sidney knew he had done something wrong, that was why he was saying all these things, to come up with reasons for what he did."

Cary told me that Robin Greene's family had sent numerous E-mails to the Sun threatening to sue the newspaper if the paper continued mentioning their family member.

TUESDAY, OCTOBER 25/05

I HAD CALLED CARY CASTAGNA LAST WEEK IN EDMONTON. CARY HAD RECENTLY moved there and was working for the Edmonton Sun. I told Cary that I was interested in interviewing him for my book, as he was the only person beside myself that had spoken to Sidney. Cary seemed to be somewhat disappointed once discovering what I wanted from him. I felt that he thought that I might have something new to add to the Teerhuis story.

Eventually we got around to discussing the fact that Sidney had previously lived in Edmonton for quite some years. Cary soon after said that he had to cut our conversation short and attend to some work. Before we ended our conversation I asked when Cary might be available to be interviewed. He replied that he would "get back to me."

NOVEMBER 1/05

I OPENED THE WINNIPEG SUN THAT MORNING AND WAS VERY SURPRISED TO SEE A photo of Sidney and the accompanying story with the headline "*No Murderer, Says Ex-Chef—Accused of grisly killing*".

```
From Edmonton - Cary Castagna - He's accused of beheading,
disemboweling and castrating a man in one of Winnipeg's
grisliest murders. But Sydney Teerhuis, a former Edmonton
chef who claims to have once cooked for ex-mayor Bill Smith,
has a message for his old coworkers and friends in Edmonton.
```

> "They're just allegations," Teerhuis, 37, told Sun Media in
> a phone interview from the Winnipeg Remand Center. "It's not
> over until it's over."

The article continued with Sidney intimating that there might have been another person present in the room and after passing out he awoke to a horror spectacle that he wishes not to discuss.

He described himself as "*a rising star in Edmonton's culinary industry*" and had worked at a restaurant that was located in the West Edmonton Mall.

> "I made a lot of friends in Edmonton and I haven't heard
> anything from them. I don't know exactly what they are
> thinking (of me) right now."

The article mentioned that in the fall of 2002, while still living in Edmonton, Sidney spent an extended 42-day stay at a treatment center near St. Albert for alcoholism and an addiction to painkillers.

In mid-2003, he accepted a position in Kenora, Ontario working at a summer resort, but drinking got him fired from his job. He had planned to venture back to Edmonton, but he ended up in Winnipeg after running out of money.

> Not much has changed since his arrest more than two
> years ago, he commented. "Every day is July 3rd for me. I
> haven't moved forwards or backwards or anything", adding
> he has found a method to get through the long pre-trial
> wait. "I just don't think about the outside world. It's
> a waste of energy."

Obviously my conversation with Cary Castagna spurred him to contact Sidney. The more coverage this story receives the better chances are that this murder trial will spark interest by other media, and help to make this story more well known. The article appeared 'out of the blue' without any announcement regarding Sidney's trial date, the setting of that date being postponed twice so far. The trial date was to be set October 12th and that date was postponed without notice.

WEDNESDAY, NOVEMBER 9/05

I CALLED ROSS READ TO FIND OUT IF HE KNEW WHEN SIDNEY'S TRIAL WAS SET FOR. He said he didn't know but that he would call the Crown and find out. He told me to call back the next day.

THURSDAY, NOVEMBER 10/05

I CALLED ROSS IN THE MORNING AND HE SAID THAT THE CROWN, LIZ THOMSON did not have an actual date but she said that the trial would commence sometime next fall.

I mentioned the article that appeared In the Winnipeg Sun November 1st. Ross commented, "*Ah, more bullshit from Sidney is all it is.*" I said, "*It is interesting though, don't you think given that Sidney and Brodsky have all the letters that are to be used, and yet they seem to be proceeding with the original story in that he claimed to not remember anything. Despite all the damaging evidence in the letters, he is sticking to his first story. It is very interesting."* Ross then said, *"That's the beauty of it."* I asked him what he meant and he told me, *"His own words will be used to convict him."* I agreed with him and thanked him for the information regarding the trial date.

I appreciated the response that I received from Ross in our phone call. Of all the players that I have been personally involved with, in this case, Ross seems to be the most willing to help and certainly the most understanding regarding my efforts to write a book about this case and trial. Ross has stated that once it is legally permissible, he will provide me with all the pertinent information that I require from him and his department.

NOVEMBER 17/05

I WANTED TO ASK SOME QUESTIONS OF ROSS, MOST OF THE QUESTIONS I DIDN'T expect that Ross would be willing to answer. He said that he would not respond to those questions that might compromise the case or that may influence my testimony. He used an example of information he might tell me that later, under cross-examination, that I would be asked to tell where and how I came to learn about this information. If the courts determined that I received the information from the police, the case would be in jeopardy as a result.

I asked why a warrant to take a D.N.A. sample from Sidney was taken on August 19th of this year? Ross said that he could not confirm that. He told me that he would answer questions that pertained to our relationship only.

I asked, *"Could Sidney have been shown post-murder and autopsy photos of Greene's body by his attorney Greg Brodsky?"* Ross stated that all the evidence was given to Brodsky and that he was legally able to show all and any evidence to his client.

This admission surprised me somewhat. George Jacub had said that Brodsky would claim that Sidney only became aware of certain details surrounding the killing as a result of police and media reports rather than witnessing them firsthand.

I asked Ross *"How much input do you and your department have in assessing the information that was provided, as evidence to be potentially used?"* Ross said, *"We work hand in hand with the Crown's office. We strategize with the Crown, assessing the information, and discussing all the relevant points to consider. Our department and myself prepare an overview of the information that you provided and then assess points such as Sidney's revelations concerning motive, time of death and details regarding the missing organs."* Ross also stated that their department would be responsible for conducting follow-up interviews and any new interviews that needed to be done.

*   *   *   *   *

APRIL 2/06

I CALLED ROSS READ TO SEE IF I COULD FERRET OUT SOME BIT OF INFORMATION by employing a certain tactic. I stated that I understood that he could not discuss any investigation that was ongoing or otherwise, *"I just wanted to state for the record that based on all the information that I have studied, Sidney Teerhuis is a serial killer."*

Ross said, "That possibility certainly crossed my mind. You're not the first person to have said that and certainly we (the Police and the Crown) have explored that possibility." He went on to say, "I can appreciate what you are saying, but it's one thing to believe something and another to prove it."

He informed me that Liz Thomson, the Crown Attorney assigned to prosecute the case had been transferred to another unit and another attorney had been assigned the case. I asked what the reason might be and Ross said he didn't know of any specific reason for the change.

The last week of March I finally sent George Jacub a copy of the interview I had done with Greg Brodsky. I asked if he had listened to the interview and he told me he hadn't finished listening to the entire interview as of yet.

I proceeded to tell him about Sidney not wanting to talk to Fred Shane, the psychiatrist and instead was going to cooperate with a provincial psychologist named Kent Somers. George stated that he was not familiar with the name. I asked if the fact that Sidney wouldn't cooperate with Dr. Shane and that Brodsky seemed determined to have Dr. Somers, a psychologist and not a psychiatrist aid in the defense; would be detrimental to their case. He said that a psychologist would be better than a psychiatrist in court because he would testify the behavior exhibited in the commission of this murder and post-murder was part of a mental disorder, at that time. He said that the next psychiatrist to examine Sidney would be for the Crown and he would have to agree with the psychologist that it was a disease of the mind. He continued, there needs to be no consistency with the psychologist. Bang on the head, confirmed by an M.R.I., artery bypassed, or blood flow restricted to the brain. He said that the defense was looking for the right interview to ultimately use; all they need is reasonable doubt. Of course the defendant would definitely respond favorably to long-term psychiatric treatment. George said finally, "This is how the legal profession misuses psychiatry to get dangerous offenders off."

April 12/06

I HAD CALLED ROSS AT THE END OF HIS SHIFT THE DAY BEFORE AND TODAY HE called back. He apologized for not calling back the day before. I wanted to fish for more information, I felt a bit pushy but determined nevertheless. I asked if Ross had five minutes and he said he had three. In our brief conversation Ross did say, "If there was no documented proof of your conversations, the defense would have a heyday with you on the stand." He went on, "Lets face it, he's (Brodsky) going to go after your motive in writing this book; no doubt about it. What course of action could he use? You created a sensationalistic story just to sell some books! He could maybe challenge Teerhuis' mental state, we'll have to see during the trial." Ross said, "I have to go." I thanked him for his help and said goodbye.

April 13/06

THE NEW CROWN ATTORNEY FOR THE TRIAL, SHEILA LEINBURD CALLED. SHE ASKED for a Mr. Zaparski and as a result of that mangling of my last name's pronunciation I at first thought she was a telemarketer. After she had introduced herself she didn't say anything else, so as to give me an opportunity to explain why I had called requesting that she contact me.

I said "*As a witness involved with this case and responsible for evidence to be used in the trial, I want to make you aware that I am writing a book about this case, however it was only because of this book project that was I was able to discover the evidence that I have.*"

Surprisingly there was no response from her and so I continued, telling her about my work with People for Justice, protesting the Bryan Larsen case outside the Law Courts (he had been convicted of possession of child pornography and sexual assault).

She couldn't have acted more indifferent, barely acknowledging what I was actually saying. How I had spoke and the substance of what I had said warranted some form of response but none was forthcoming.

I reverted to simply asking her when the trial would be taking place. She said it would most likely be taking place in September. However, she said that the trial date could be moved. I asked if the actual trial date would be announced in the newspapers. She coldly said, "*Our office doesn't notify the press, if they are there in court fine, otherwise no.*" She told me that their office would send me a subpoena notifying me as to the actual trial date.

I asked how long before the trial began would that happen and she informed that it might be a month to six weeks before the trial. I asked how long the trial might last and she couldn't say but did say, "*The proceedings may be shortened if the Defense were to agree to certain evidence.*" I thought that she may have been referring to a possible plea bargain offer and said, "*Are you talking about a plea bargain?*" "*No*" she said, "*And I wouldn't discuss a plea bargain with you*". I said, "*I understand.*" She explained, "*There are other witnesses you know and if the defense agrees we can eliminate the need to have them testify.*" I asked, "*Is that likely?*" She responded, "*Not likely.*"

Sheila also spoke of the defense possibly challenging the 'array'. I asked what an array was. She said that an array was a jury.

In concluding our conversation I asked about my eventual meeting with her and her assistant. I said, "*Regarding our first meeting, how many weeks before the trial will you call me?*" She replied, "*About two weeks.*" I was surprised by what she was saying, she continued, "*We will meet with you about a week before.*" I was incredulous, "*A week before?*" She answered, "*Yes.*" I also asked, "*And how many times will we be meeting to prepare me for direct and cross examination?*" She responded, "*Just once.*" I again asked incredulously, "*Once?*" She said, "*Yes.*" I thanked her for her time and said goodbye. I felt that our conversation was not very reassuring at all.

April 18/06

I called George Jacub again today; I needed to get his take on my conversation with the Crown Attorney Sheila Leinburd. I repeated essentially what had transpired and he asked, "*How long has it been since the killer was first arrested?*"

I replied, "*July 2nd, 2003.*"

"*Oh,*" he said, "*And who is the victim?*" He answered himself, "*Nobody, and no one important."* He went on, *"Were you following the case where the drug dealers killed their former friend and then were convicted of second-degree murder?"*

I replied, *"Yes I noticed that at least three of those guys were convicted on the second-degree charge."*

George said, *"That young guy's father and his family have been on that case; talking to the media, demanding the courts prosecute their son's killers to the full extent of the law."*

I replied, *"And that made the case high profile?"*

He said, *"They made the case high profile."*

George stated that it had been over three years with this case and the Crown would be anxious to accept a plea bargain as a result. I didn't want to believe what he was saying; that the Crown would recommend accepting a plea bargain for a conviction of manslaughter, despite having those letters as evidence, despite having read those letters and having seen those drawings, despite the fact they will all know that Sidney is a psychopathic killer, despite the fact he would be out walking the streets in 2007 or early 2008.

April 30/06

I called Agnew Johnston today; I hadn't spoken to him for nine or ten months. I wanted to ask a Crown Attorney if there was any valid reason for the Crown in this case to want to accept a manslaughter plea bargain. He said, "If the family doesn't make any noise then the court will quietly do what they want. The families of the victim are very important. If the case winds up with the family making a stink, the Crown will cater to the family. They will 'run with it', even though it may very well be manslaughter and let someone else decide the verdict" (the judge and jury rather than the Defense and Crown).

Agnew cited an example where a Grand Chief's family member was slain and he as a Crown 'ran with it' because they were an important family. He then said, "There will be a *voir dire*, where the Crown and the defense will argue in the absence of the jury, how much, if any of the information from the letters will be deemed admissible." He continued, "When the plea is entered in court Brodsky will say, 'On behalf of my client; not guilty of second-degree murder, but rather manslaughter.' Whether he is criminally responsible or not, he will admit his client killed the victim and then that's not an issue anymore—it's whether he had the intent to kill the victim. All the correspondence becomes irrelevant if he admits to the killing." Agnew continued, "The killer will say that everything he wrote was just some jailhouse bullshit, he wanted to make you think that you were going to become some best-selling serial-killer writer."

I could sense that Agnew felt that I was naïve about how things actually worked, but I thought he could only relate to his past experiences and I was pretty sure he had never seen anything like the letters and the drawings.

12

A Former Prosecutor Provides Information

MAY 30/06

I HAD CALLED GORDON SINCLAIR JR. AT THE WINNIPEG FREE PRESS YESTERDAY. I spoke with him briefly, and he told me that he had a deadline to meet, he was busy but he gave me his cell phone number, and asked if I could call him about the same time today. Gordon Sinclair is a long time regular columnist for the Free Press and the award-winning author of *Cowboys and Indians—The Shooting of J.J. Harper.* I had interviewed Gordon on my radio program a few years back.

Because he was good enough to appear on my program, as well as the fact that his book dealt heavily with racism and the judicial system, I felt that Gordon might be the right journalist to take my story to. I thought he would provide a sympathetic ear and potentially regard this as a much more important story once I had given him vital information in this case that he could not possibly have known otherwise.

Gordon was very friendly and polite and we spoke for more than half-an-hour. At the beginning of our conversation I had asked if he was aware of the Teerhuis case and he said he was. I then went on to explain how I came to be involved with the killer and then with the trial as a witness. He seemed to understand what I was saying but at some point he said, "Why are you calling me?" I could understand that was a reasonable question and I was prepared, "I'm calling you because the Free Press didn't really cover this story, Mike McIntyre was busy working on the Brian Sands case at the time and the Sun covered the story. Cary Castagna from the Winnipeg Sun, now Edmonton Sun, interviewed Teerhuis." Sinclair replied, "Who?" He sounded like he'd never heard of the fellow journalist and I told him, "Cary Castagna from the Sun." Sinclair responded, "What did Teerhuis say to him?" I said, "That he couldn't remember the murder; that he was not a monster; that he was no Jeffrey Dahmer." I said, "The Free Press had run a story with the headline, "Man slashed pretty good."

I continued answering his original question saying, that despite the incredible evidence I had been able to provide, there was still a really good chance that this evidently psychopathic killer's second-degree murder charge could be plea bargained down to a manslaughter charge.

Gordon asked why I believed that might happen. I answered, "He has Brodsky as his lawyer and he'll challenge the admissibility of the letters or certain portions of them, he will question my credibility, my motivation; and the Crown may want to agree to certain things in the letters not being allowed purely to expedite the process; plus the fact that I have been very critical of the courts. I've protested at the Law Courts against Bryan Larsen, I've told the Crown about my criticism. I've been told from a former Crown attorney from Thunder Bay, Agnew Johnston that this is what will happen and why." Gordon replied, "Why does he think that the manslaughter charge will be offered by the Crown?" I said, "As he told me, that if it's no one of any prominence as a victim, and or if the family of the victim doesn't make a stink, or if the story is not considered 'high profile' by the media, then the Crown will be anxious to agree to the lesser charge plea bargain."

As an example I said, "Take the case of T.J. Wiebe. His family has made a stink and appealed to the media and their son's killers were subsequently convicted of second-degree murder—despite the fact that their son was a drug dealer and typically as a result the Crown would have opted for the reduced charge. Gordon then incredibly asked, "How did Teerhuis get caught?" I didn't react as I would have, which would have been me admonishing him for stating that he was aware of the details of the case, but somehow was not aware of the basic known facts, like how the killer came to be apprehended. I explained to Gordon how Sidney had turned himself in at the Remand Center, thinking it was the police station and how he had only told the police that he had found a dead body in the bathtub, not preparing the police for the spectacle they ultimately found. Gordon asked, "Does Teerhuis have a criminal record?" I replied, "No he's never been in trouble before." I went on to explain that despite not having a record that he had told me of strikingly similar murders that had occurred in Alberta and British Columbia, that he had been questioned about. I told him that the killer had written to me about this questioning, and that he had also referred me to Ann Rule who had exclusively covered serial killers, starting with Ted Bundy. I also told Gordon regarding the serial killer possibility, that one police officer involved had told me that despite everything it was much harder to prove murder than to make the allegation, but the police had seriously looked at the possibility of other murders.

Gordon asked the question again, "Why are you calling me?" He was asking the question again and so I answered, "Imagine if the person found murdered in the bathtub was an eighteen-year old white woman with no criminal background, found stabbed forty-seven times, cut into eight pieces with her sex organs surgically removed along with all her internal organs which were, and are still missing. Do you think that this story would be more important then?" I heard him audibly acknowledge what I had just said, and then he asked, "So you think this is a case of institutional racism?"

I was both surprised and disappointed at this question and I responded, "No. It's much bigger than that. It seems no one really cares about this murder, this aboriginal man, this victim!" In retrospect I should have said, "It seemed that the very newspaper he was working for was not interested in this story, because the crime did not involve a white woman without a criminal background, so no it's not a case of institutional racism, but a blanket non interest in the case because the victim is aboriginal, male, a suspected petty thief and a likely homosexual."

I went on, "The killer instructed me to reveal the information he had sent me after the trial was finished. But the former Crown I had been speaking with urged me to contact the Crown in this case as soon as possible regarding the evidence I possessed.

"I promised to split the proceeds of the book between the cell-mate, myself and Teerhuis." I continued, "During one of our phone conversations I mentioned to Teerhuis that the law concerning criminals not being able to profit from their crimes had been passed, and immediately he hung up on me."

Gordon asked, "When did the law get passed?"

I said, "I believe March 2005."

Gordon asked if in effect I had broken the agreement, reneging on the contract. I told him, "When I negotiated the agreement in 2004 there was no law in place. When I mentioned it again to Teerhuis in March 2005, it had been passed as law in the province of Manitoba."

Gordon asked again, "But why call me?" Now this was the third time and I couldn't believe that he still felt it necessary to pose the same question. He stated, "I think this is the most gruesome crime in Winnipeg history!" I thought that was an interesting statement given that he wasn't aware of very much about the most gruesome crime in Winnipeg history, including not being aware of how Teerhuis was even arrested; and yet he was asking me why I was calling him. I replied, "I am testifying against a psychopathic killer! If he gets a manslaughter charge instead of murder he will be out in 2008!"

Our conversation was interrupted by another phone call that Gordon said he had to take, and I could hear Gordon speaking, and he told the caller that he was almost finished, and he would call him back shortly. I realized that Gordon would want to be wrapping up, and so I said, "I wanted to inform you about this case and my involvement, and I appreciate you listening to what I had to say." I hadn't gotten the kind of reaction that I would have liked, or even I think expected from the conversation so far, but I thought Gordon would certainly give me some good advice, or hopefully tell me that he would be interested in finding out more about the murder trial and the entire story. After all he had seemed to be listening, he had been good enough to give me adequate time to explain most things involved in this story.

Gordon replied, "Well Dan, hang in there. Keep in touch." I was almost speechless but nevertheless spilled out, "Thank you Gordon, goodbye."

August 2/06

I received a call from Sheila Leinburd this afternoon. Her tone seemed to be different than the first time we had spoken in April; she seemed friendly and very positive. She simply asked, "Did you give all of the correspondence you had received from Teerhuis to police?" I responded, "Yes I did, including copies of notes made during phone conversations." Sheila asked if we could meet on Wednesday the 9th of August. I said that date would be fine. I quickly realized that I was to be in Thunder Bay as of the 7th and asked if we could set another date. She asked if Friday the 4th was okay. I asked if we could re-schedule for when I got back to Winnipeg on the 14th. The meeting was set for Tuesday August 15th at 3:00 p.m. I would have the opportunity to interview Agnew Johnston on Tuesday the 8th, and be much more prepared to fully comprehend the entire murder trial process and to be able to ask some serious questions about how the Crown would be proceeding with the trial. I thought that the fact that the Crown had decided to contact me so many weeks before the trial (almost 5 weeks) bode well for a more positive outcome than I had been expecting might happen. This was coupled with just the impression I got from the tone of her voice that she may have had a chance to read the letters in question finally, and perhaps she now had a much different view regarding my participation in this trial. That's what I hoped for.

August 8/06

I HAD SENT AGNEW AS MUCH INFORMATION TO READ ABOUT THIS CASE BEFORE I was to interview him, so as to prepare him to give a fair, informed assessment of how the Crown would likely assess the information and proceed with the case.

I met Agnew at the Superior Court of Justice on Camelot Street at 11:00 a.m. We had never met before despite having spoken numerous times on the phone and via E-mails. Agnew was dressed in an opened gray tweed jacket with a light blue denim shirt, belt and jeans with brown casual dress shoes. He was about 5'9, a bit overweight but healthy looking, with a lot of color in his face. He had a neatly trimmed, pure white beard and mustache. Agnew smiled and his eyes seemed to convey a happy, confidant and respectful man. We shook hands and I thanked him for agreeing to do our interview on camera.

THE AGNEW JOHNSTON INTERVIEW — THUNDER BAY

Me: It's August 8th, 2006, maybe you can introduce yourself please.

Agnew: My name is Agnew Johnston. I am a resident of Thunder Bay. I was a practicing lawyer both as defense counsel, and an Assistant Crown Attorney.

Me: I've asked you to do, somewhat of an overview of this case, providing information to you, some of the information that the court in the trial of Sidney Teerhuis will be hopefully seeing as well. Initially you told me that this looked like a typical manslaughter case. Can you tell us why you believed initially that this looked like a manslaughter case? What about it looked like a typical manslaughter case rather than a second-degree murder?

Agnew: It wouldn't be the first time in my life I had gone out on a limb with too little information. And when we first spoke I was giving an 'off the cuff' opinion based on the fact that we were dealing with two street people, two gay street people, involving the consumption of alcohol, and a flophouse in Winnipeg, and an initial statement from the accused that he could not remember, because of intoxication, what had happened, and it sounded, once again, 'off the cuff' like a manslaughter to me. Whether they charged him with first-degree murder or second-degree murder, I could see it shaking out as manslaughter. The more information I received from you, particularly copies of letters, or a letter that the accused had written to you, made me change my mind drastically.

Me: What was it, in or about that one letter that made you have such a dramatic reversal in your prediction of what would happen in the murder trial?

Agnew: The letter describes in almost a cavalier way the horrific dismemberment and abuse of a human body, and it is crystal clear in it's detail, it almost wallows in the horrific nature of it, and should that information, even though it's post-homicide information; should that work it's way to a jury, it would be hard for a jury to find this gentleman guilty of anything other than murder.

Me: Now talking about the murder trial, which is to begin September 5th and continue till September 29th, walk us through the process from the preliminary trial, what will happen before the trial is going to commence on September 5th?

Agnew: There has been a preliminary enquiry, which is where a provincial judge would listen to evidence to determine whether or not a jury properly instructed, and acting reasonably could convict. That's a fairly low threshold, based on a case called Shepherd. So the matter has gone through that and is now proceeding to trial. What will happen is that a jury panel will be assembled, people will get jury notices, and will show up at the courts and they will be brought forward, one after the other as their names are called. Their names are drawn out of a drum and they will come forward, and the Crown and the defense have a certain number of peremptory challenges, in which they can get rid of jurors because they don't like the looks of them, or because of their job, or because of their age, they can get rid of jurors. I don't know in this case if defense counsel will seek to challenge for cause; based upon the fact that these two gentlemen were homosexual, or native or a combination of the two. I don't know that. It's possible to ask the judge to put questions to the jurors but I don't know if that's going to be the case. In any event a jury will be selected, then a judge will ask the Crown and the defense if they have any issues that should be dealt with in the absence of the jury? This is called a Voir Dire, and it may involve statements made by the accused, letters to you Mr. Zupansky, particularly, that could be part of the evidentiary train here. Whether they should be placed before the jury, and so the jury will be excused to some, next morning, or two days later, and they will re-assemble while these issues are dealt with.

In those *Voir Dires*, which are done in the absence of any witnesses that are called, most likely yourself; these *Voir Dires* will potentially call evidence, maybe not, depends on what is admitted by either side, but a lot of the evidentiary framework will be settled right there, so the trial can proceed smoothly and seamlessly from there on.

Whenever the jury is recalled then the Crown will, most likely, call the nuts and bolts evidence first, the pathologist, the descriptors of the death, the state of the body, and the location. Photographs will be entered from the identification officers, and I would imagine your part in the proceedings would occur after that, after they established there was a homicide, that the accused had something to do with the homicide, and any initial contact with police. But the jury will have seen the physical evidence and then it will become an issue of intent.

Me: Okay, we're talking about intent maybe you can explain that. What do you mean by "it will all come down to intent?"

Agnew: Not every homicide is a crime.

Me: How's that?

Agnew: Well there are homicides that are committed by accident. In order for there to be criminal homicide there must be an intent to commit homicide, and then it becomes whether it is a first-degree murder or a second-degree murder, or manslaughter.

Me: Now you talk about intent, and, and it comes down to what the intention of the offender was at the moment of the death, to explain this somewhat, there was forty-seven stab wounds, so the first part of the crime was that initial stabbing to death of the victim. When you talk about the intent at the time of the actual murder are we talking about that first or second, or one of those fatal knife wounds, is that what we are talking about, his state of mind at that time?

Agnew: Assuming here you can take first-degree murder out of the picture, which involves planning and deliberation, then second-degree murder is done on the spur of the moment; now you have one fatal stab wound or forty-seven; if it's a frenzy then forty-seven stab wounds is certainly not unheard of, even if the first one is a fatal one. The issue then becomes whether it's second-degree murder or manslaughter, and manslaughter involves either provocation or some external factor that the defence must raise, either in cross-examination or by direct evidence to take it out of the murder category. Provocation reduces murder to manslaughter. Here I understand the only provocation that I am aware of is the deceased wetting the bed, and I doubt that would meet the bar.

Me: When you talk about other factors that can possibly reduce a murder charge to a manslaughter charge, and one of those is intoxication, why is intoxication not going to be a major factor in possibly reducing this from a murder to manslaughter?

Agnew: Once again I'm operating on the information that you have given me. I understand there is some evidence of drinking but the mere fact that the accused claims not to remember the incident does not mean he does not have an operating mind at the time of the killing. I think it's almost a matter of rote in criminal courts to say, "you don't remember", it doesn't mean you weren't functioning at the time. I don't know if the police took a blood-alcohol sample but he had to have some considerable time after the event, with the body, in any event, so it may not be relevant, but to get anywhere into that territory, you have to provide evidence, either through cross-examination or your own testimony, or external testimony that you were clearly not mentally functioning at the time of the killing.

Me: You talk about clearly mentally functioning; are you looking at clearly mentally functioning because of some of the things he did, including surgically removing this person's sex organs, surgically removing the rest of the organs, and just the dissection and dismemberment itself, or the fact you've seen his own words regarding the events, before the killing, during the killing and after. Which one are you saying that clearly demonstrates this functioning mind, the nature of the crime as described, or you having seen this other information indicating that he was cognizant of what he was doing?

Agnew: I have seen two letters, one describing what happened before the homicide, and one describing what happened after the homicide. It stretches my ability to believe that any human being, short of pretty amazing psychiatric testimony, could be that lucid up to and that lucid thereafter, to have that kind of clear memory, and almost clinical descriptors on either end of the incident, and then to have no memory of it.

Me: But your determination comes from, as a result of the correspondence, some of the stuff you have read?

Agnew: Yes.

Me: You would not be able to, honestly make that estimation without seeing this kind of information?

Agnew: Absolutely. If this man had walked into the police station, and said, "There was a bunch of body parts in my bathtub, and I have no idea how it happened", and left it at that. I think he would be in a lot better shape than he is.

Me: How good a shape would he be in? He went with the story that he was drinking, he passed out with his acquaintance, when he woke up in the morning he went to the washroom and found this person disemboweled and dismembered into eight pieces, with all the internal organs missing, nowhere to be found, to this day. Given that fact...

Agnew: If I were Mr. Brodsky I would be far happier if my client had left it at that. The information that the accused has given you for whatever reason, and once again assuming it's true, has created great complications for his case.

Me: Greg Brodsky is a forty-seven year legal veteran, a well-known criminal defence lawyer, one of the most effective murder trial lawyers in Canada. Given the years of experience that he has, given what you've seen with this case, what do you think about this case and what may be his strategy?

Agnew: I am a very big fan of Greg Brodsky. He is a great fan of Abraham Lincoln. So am I. I would direct initially his attention to having the letters that were sent to you excluded from evidence, on the basis of information that the client may have received that allowed him in his delusional state to recreate events that never occurred. Clearly you can't dispute the dismemberment, but some of the gory details may have been embellished, and they go to the issue of doing an indignity to a corpse, as opposed to doing a homicide. So I would imagine that Greg will direct his energies to attempting to exclude any of the post-homicide information from the evidentiary train here, and the Crown will of course argue that it is a global picture that has to be looked at, and as I said earlier, you've got a letter dealing with the up to, and a letter dealing with the thereafter. So the Crown will argue that it goes to show he's pretty well boxed in here. The accused can't say, "Whoops, I can't remember those two or three minutes, but I remember everything else." So that will be where, I think, the battle will be fought, lost and won.

Me: When you talk about Greg Brodsky's strategy, to be able to render this correspondence, some two hundred pages, including ten pages of drawings of the killing and post-killing; to have that deemed inadmissible in court, and judging the information, as either prejudicial or of any probative value. How else will Greg Brodsky be able to approach this in terms of getting that material deemed inadmissible?

Agnew: I would think that Greg will go after you. That he will try to portray this as an atmosphere that you have created in your desire to make money from a book, and he will say that you have drawn his client into a series of, as I said earlier, embellished tales of fantasy to make you happy and to make him famous, like Jeffrey Dahmer. That is more than likely, I think.

Me: I will tell you, he probably has no evidence to prove that. That being said, how much evidence will he have to bring forward to be able to potentially persuade a jury or a judge that indeed this has no probative value.

Agnew: It certainly has probative value. It will be up to a judge to determine, whether descriptors of the mutilation of the corpse after the death is relevant to the death. I believe from having read it, and the judge will read it, that it is, because it shows that this gentleman is very intelligent, and very capable of description, and the two letters that I've read show him remembering all sorts of details, right up to the room and right up to afterwards.

And as Crown I would argue that this is fundamental to show the jury the overall picture of what happened. That is where Greg will go I'm sure, is to try to get that particularly damning letter out, the one describing the dismemberment.

Me: In a potential *Voir Dire* to look at the admissibility of this correspondence, is there some effort to separate certain potentially prejudicial parts of that correspondence, and remain with only a fraction of the correspondence that has been deemed admissible? Is that also a potential strategy for Greg, will that help him by diminishing how much of those references, those revelations of the killer himself?

Agnew: It will be looked at. Each letter will be looked at individually, and they can be edited, parts can be left out. A judge will be obliged to see what portions are of clear evidentiary value and are clearly relevant to the issue of intent at the time of the homicide. So it will be a potentially lengthy process, going through all of those pages.

Me: Potentially, if Greg Brodsky puts forth the notion that this person has a certain part of fantasy involved with these letters, and a certain amount of fabrication based on seeing the police report, seeing the autopsy reports and speaking to his counsel about all the evidence in the trial; can Greg Brodsky reasonably raise the notion that potentially his client fabricated, if not the entire thing, but the important things in this, and as a result, because he may be able to raise some evidence of some fabrication, he will be able to point to that. Does that negate the entire correspondence?

Agnew: It will certainly undermine it. If he is successful in projecting the fact that this gentleman was playing to what he thought Dan Zupansky, what he wanted to hear. He is a man with no prospects, a troubled life and simply just wanted to be famous, and gave Dan Zupansky what he wanted to hear. None of it is true except what is supported by the physical evidence. Then it will certainly go to the weight, and the judge will have to caution the jury about how much weight to put on that particular evidence, and that will be part of the charge to the jury at the end of the trial.

Me: Why given everything that happened, everything that he has said, the way he has described this; with utter joy and glee in butchering this human being, and doing other indignities to the corpse after the fact, his reveling in this. Why is he not insane in your mind?

Agnew: The term they use in the law is not criminally responsible. Most murders, except for contract killing, involve some degree of emotion or mental deviance, and most killing is done in a blur of alcohol, drugs or anger. All of that is, to use the colloquial, crazy. What the law has to determine if there was intent to kill, and whether the accused appreciated the nature and consequences of his act. And that; if you consider that most murders are conducted in a haze of alcohol, drugs or emotion, it's not a very high bar to meet. If the accused is operating under some psychosis, if voices tell him to do things, or if he is in some altered state because of some chemical imbalance, then that takes murder off the table. Here from my reading of the letters that you've shown me, he's clearly lucid, very intelligent, and like you said he revels in the detail, and that's going to be his difficulty. Those letters are into evidence. I think, his goose, regardless of the competence of his counsel is pretty well cooked.

Me: Greg Brodsky has said in an interview, stated unequivocally that he dislikes the Not Criminally Responsible designation because of the difference between a penitentiary term and a mental facility term, in terms of advantages, privileges, and what he calls freedom, Greg Brodsky's best bet, what will that be?

Agnew: Having not seen the police report once again, and I'm in no position to give legal advice here, but I would say that Not Criminally Responsible is so highly unlikely, that it's better to focus on other things.

Keep in mind that in the criminal justice system, we are not talking about innocence; we're talking whether or not the Crown can prove that you are guilty, beyond a reasonable doubt. You're never found innocent, you're found not guilty, and the letters, if I were Greg, I would focus on the letters. I would try to reduce it to what the Crown can prove. I would try to eliminate any statements that the accused may have given police, and I don't know if he's given any other than, "I don't remember", and I would focus on trying to keep the letters out. And then it becomes having a dead body, and coming into the police station and saying, "I don't remember, it was just there", and seeing what the Crown can make out of that.

Me: You've called this a beautiful case to look at, tell me why this is a beautiful case to look at?

Agnew: Beautiful may be the wrong word. It's certainly a fascinating case. It has enough elements of ah blood and gore, and a very intelligent accused. It is almost the stuff that crime novels are made of. It has elements of psychiatric testimony, but also tactics that both Crown and defence, would, maybe enjoy is not the right word, would...

Me: Appreciate?

Agnew: Would grow to appreciate certainly, because of the tactics, because you would have to anticipate the other person's moves, and a murder trial is very much, besides the human element of the jury and the judge; is planning your case and being prepared for twists and turns as they come, and so it's very much a chess game, and this case has all those elements.

Me: Now you spoke after you had read one letter I had sent to you, and at that time, you had a complete reversal in your prediction of what would happen in this case. You also stated that this is the kind of case that law students will be looking at for years to come. Why is this case potentially one that students might be looking at in law schools?

Agnew: It will relate to external information provided by the accused to an author. In my experience, I've never come across anything like this. It will relate to issues of privilege, what information the accused had before he made those statements to you, and the use or misuse of disclosure. It will be an evidence case, as opposed to procedure. It will be an evidence case, and most of the rulings will stem from whatever Voir Dires are held prior to the trial.

Me: Now there is a term called Burden of Proof. If, for example, Greg Brodsky wanted to raise the issue of intoxication, or provocation, there's the issue of Burden of Proof. Can you explain what Burden of proof is, and who has the Burden of Proof, and how it may work in this trial specifically?

Agnew: The Crown carries the Burden of Proof throughout, and that burden is beyond a reasonable doubt. If you are going to raise a positive defense like provocation, you can do that through cross-examination. It's always dangerous to call your client as a witness, but sometimes it's necessary to establish the provocation that would reduce murder to manslaughter. There are all sorts of externals that can be brought out through cross-examination, such as the degree of intoxication of one or both parties, and the "spur of the moment" nature of the homicide. The other factors such as the accused's state of mind will be a matter of dueling psychiatrists probably. It may be necessary to call the accused as a witness, but as I say, that's a very dangerous proposition. Depending on the sympathetic nature of the accused, here you have a very intelligent man, but put somebody in the witness box, you never know what you are going to get.

Me: Given that Sidney Teerhuis can be seen as a loose cannon by his own defense team, what's the likelihood of putting him on the stand?

Agnew: Generally if you have nothing to lose, and if your client is halfway sympathetic, then you have nothing to lose by calling your client as a witness. You're not going to dig his hole any deeper. And if he is able to connect with the jury, in terms of his childhood abuse, his substance abuse, if he is able to present as a sympathetic character then you have nothing to lose by calling him. As opposed to without these letters, sitting back and saying to the Crown, "Prove it. All I did was cut up a dead body, so just put me away for a year."

Me: So it's not out of the realm of possibility, even though it's unusual to put a client accused of a murder on the stand, with Greg Brodsky with nothing to lose, and only a challenge in front of him, and with Sidney Teerhuis with nothing to lose except to have this information deemed inadmissible. Is there a likelihood that this may happen, this scenario we've discussed?

Agnew: It's possible, I've called an accused when I was defence counsel in a murder trial to the stand, because I felt we had done interviews, very much like this, where we had interviewed him with another lawyer from the firm, and cross-examined him, and he was great. Then he got onto the witness stand and finished himself off in short order, so you never know, it's a risk.

Me: You have said that the jury would not be sympathetic to this killer, especially given if they get to hear these revelations; regardless of whether they get to hear the entire revelations, which do chronicle, according to him, his abuse by, from his own family, and his adoption from a reserve into a white family, a Dutch family in Winnipeg. That being said, the Crown Attorney will have the ability, and will have the desire to present this information to the jury. How can Greg Brodsky approach the fact, if that is the fact, that this information is going to be admitted in, how will that factor into Greg Brodsky's strategy then? If all these things are to go forward, what will what will be his course of action, likely?

Agnew: If you know something bad, something harmful is going to come out, whether you're Crown or defense, the best thing is to own it, to bring it out yourself and try to control it, rather than look like you're trying to hide from something. If you have an Achilles' heel somewhere, it is better to bring it out, show the jury, show the judge, and try to control it, and admit it, own it, and diffuse it if you can.

Me: Let's talk about Greg Brodsky's strategy with his client. And again, keep in mind the information that you already know. In your experience, let's talk about the nitty-gritty; what exactly, kind of conversations are spoken in the room with Greg Brodsky, the defense, or any murder trial lawyer and his client? What kinds of conversations, are actually spoken? Give us an example.

Agnew: This is an unusual case, and as I say, maybe an evidence case, down the line in some law school casebook. Because you've got, as you say, a loose cannon, whose spouting off all over the place, where he shouldn't have. My practice when I was counsel was always to say, "Don't tell me anything. I'm going to show you what the Crown is going to try to prove, you can comment on it." That way you don't have a client saying, "This is what happened, but this is what I'm going to say in court." And you can't as counsel let your client perjure him or herself. So it makes imminent good sense to put the disclosure to the client, first, and say, "Okay what have you got to say about that?" If your client, no matter what the truth is, if your client is halfway smart, he will move to what the Crown has and try to explain it, as opposed to telling you some fairy tale that you can't work with. Here, unfortunately for the accused, he has given you the fairy tale, and how much of it is true I don't know. Maybe all of it, maybe some of it, but it is out there and that's what complicates this thing for Mr. Brodsky greatly. Instead of being able to control this case, his client has put material out there that is going to complicate Greg's defence greatly.

Me: Now given the considerable ego Greg Brodsky may have, could that possibly interfere with his execution of this court case? Will he be able to put that aside and see this just as another challenge, or will his ego come into play because of his client's disloyalty, or disservice? Can Greg Brodsky defend this person to the best of his ability, and put his ego aside?

Agnew: You wouldn't be trial counsel if you didn't have an ego of some sort, and you won't be a good one unless you have plenty. Greg Brodsky is the second best trial lawyer that I have seen next to Alfred A. Petrone from Thunder Bay. When you have nothing to lose, and here I sense that is the case, then the pressure is off and I think Greg will do his damnedest, but without worrying about making some

127

little error that will screw the case up. And if the client is convicted, you can turn around and say, "Look you idiot, you're the guy that did this." So I think it will be a fun trial to watch, I might even go to Winnipeg to do that.

Me: I have been frustrated with this case, at the face of it in Winnipeg, and across Canada when talking about it; it seems very evident to me, that if the victim happened to be a non-aboriginal person, a white woman with no criminal background, not to say this victim had a criminal background, but just to say, to create a scenario where there was a white woman, say for example twenty years old, that the police report said had met a man, and they went up to a hotel room, had drinks, he passed out, and when he woke up he found her cut into eight pieces, and all her internal organs missing, and this person claimed to have had consensual sex with this woman. Given that description of the crime, rather than the actual description; do you think this would be a much, much bigger story? And how on earth can it not be a bigger story just because the victim happens to be gay, drunk and aboriginal? How does that work?

Agnew: That I'm afraid is the kind of society we have created for ourselves, and whether Winnipeg is better or worse than Thunder Bay, I don't know, I suspect it's roughly the same, but if you have street people, living in flophouses, and if one is killed, more or less society moves on; whereas if you have someone from a high profile, rich neighborhood, something that affects the tourist industry, that certainly would get a lot more attention, whether it's in Toronto, Winnipeg or Thunder Bay. Here you have two people on the fringes of society, whether it's alcohol, sex, whatever; society tends to put that in a little side bar in the newspaper and move on.

Me: Lets talk about the victims for a second. The family of this Robin Robert Greene is from Shoal Lake, a small reserve near the Ontario border. Apparently the parents of Robin Greene are Elders, on this reserve, this community. The only information I have about the response of the victim's family comes from the Winnipeg Sun, which has featured some sensationalistic stories about this murder. The paper was asked to cease and desist from portraying their family in the way they felt the paper was portraying the family in the stories. Now they didn't take that request, to heart, and continued with their reports in their newspaper. You talked about what makes a high profile case, and we just spoke about how if this were a white woman with no criminal background, from a wealthy family, it would be a different outcome; or would be considered high profile, since this case isn't high profile. That being said, how would this family make this case more high profile, is there a way of having the Crown Attorney treat this case as if it were a more high profile case? How can that happen?

Agnew: Depends on the nature of the parents and the family. In Thunder Bay, in the not so distant past, the son of the grand chief, of the Anishkanabe Aske nation was killed. A young fellow who was very upwardly mobile was charged and it became a highly charged case, and every moment of it was covered intensely by the media. So it's got nothing to do with whether you're native or not, it has to do with where you are on society's radar screen, and if these parents, like some parents; if that were my son or daughter I don't think I would want all that attention, I think I would rather move on, would rather accept the grief and move on. If you, however are on a mission, you can make the Crown Attorney's life hell by calling every day, by camping outside his or her office, and getting their attention by persistence. That has happened to me, where mothers have been on a mission, and certainly you can't ignore that and have to accept that. Some parents not. So, it depends on what they want, they can make this more high profile, or less, and that's their call.

Me: Now when I go to my meeting with the Crown Attorney, Sheila Leinburd from Winnipeg, the prosecutor on this case, what am I entitled to ask for, because there is some possibility of this killer receiving a manslaughter conviction rather than a murder conviction? If we were to take the 2006 mathematics model, and truth in sentencing, that if he were to get a sentence in the typical range of ten to twelve years for manslaughter, given that he has done over three years in pre-trial custody, that would count automatically as twice as much time. We're talking about having this person walking the streets in approximately two years if the manslaughter conviction would be obtained. Given that, am I entitled to ask if the evidence that I have brought forward will most likely be able to create a second-degree murder conviction? Am I entitled to ask for those assurances in this case? I realize this is an unusual case with extraordinary circumstances but I think it calls for extraordinary provisions to be considered. What am I entitled to, given everything you know, in terms of asking about manslaughter versus murder, and my own protection as a result of this person, walking the streets in two or three years, after I have testified against him.

Agnew: Essentially you are entitled to nothing. You can ask and you'll be given something. The Crown needs to know or it needs to appreciate that you have gone out on a limb here, when you could have, like Pontias Pilate, washed your hands and put it on the backburner, and written your book. But you have a stake in these proceedings; the Crown needs to appreciate that, and she will, I'm sure, appreciate your concerns. And it will be easy enough for any Crown to pat you on the back and say, "There, there Mr. Zupansky, don't worry". It's important that you connect with her, let her know that you have a child, and that you want this gentleman to receive what is his due. She will no doubt say, "Don't worry Mr. Zupansky, we will do our level best", and I'm sure she will, but to a large extent it is out of her hands and in the hands of twelve people. So as long as she appreciates that you have a stake in the game, and that you are concerned, I'm afraid that is the best you can do. She will be cautious about sharing information because you are an author. And she is not going to be a pawn, she will tell you what your position is, which is a witness, and that's about it, but you certainly can express your concerns, and make sure she appreciates it.

Me: Now you talked about, after this person gets sentenced to whatever term he gets sentenced to, that it would be in my best interest to attend the parole hearings, despite the fact that I am not a victim, per se. Do you believe, these letters, and my involvement in the parole hearings will be successful in restricting when he may be released on parole?

Agnew: I am not familiar with parole hearings and their rules, but I would be astounded if you cannot claim status and ask to appear. I base that on no legal knowledge, but I would be astounded if you cannot appear and express your concern. And that's simply reading the newspaper to seeing who attended at Karla Homolka's hearings. You are as much a victim, in some ways, as anybody, Mr. Zupansky, except perhaps the deceased, because you have gone out on a limb, and you have done the honorable thing, and how any system could deny you the right to participate would be beyond me.

13

The Meeting

I MET WITH CROWN ATTORNEY SHEILA LEINBURD AND HER ASSISTANT Rehka Maliveri at 3:00 p.m. at the Woodsworth Building, on the corner of Broadway and Kennedy Streets, just across from the Supreme Court. I went up the elevator to the fifth floor, I signed in and shortly after I was told to venture up to the 6th floor. Once there I met Sheila and Rehka and they ushered me into a comfortable, spacious room. Sheila opened by telling me that she wanted to ask me some questions first, and then discuss where the case was at this point, and then I would be able to ask questions after that. She said early on in the meeting, "I will discuss the facts with you but not the law."

Sheila was a reasonably attractive woman, around fifty years old, well dressed in a blouse with jacket and skirt and heels. She had medium brown shoulder-length hair, parted in the middle. She had a youthful but distinguished look and spoke with a quite serious tone.

Rehka was younger, tall and tanned, with a dark complexion. She had on a blue and white light summer dress with a floral design. I sat directly across from Sheila, while Rehka sat about eight feet away, to my right side. I spoke almost entirely to Sheila.

She had asked in our previous phone call, two weeks before, and she asked again; "Did you give police all the correspondence you had with Teerhuis?" I said, "Yes, including my notes made during phone interviews." I explained that if something was said during the phone call that I felt was significant then I would request that he refer to it specifically in his letters to me.

Sheila asked why I did not give all the correspondence to the police immediately? I told her that I had only given them those letters that specifically referred to the murder and post-murder, some 14 letters in total. She asked what my reason was for doing that, and I told her that I felt that the police would want to see the letters that were relevant to the case itself, at least at first. She also asked why it took a few days for the rest of the correspondence to be given to the police and I told her that I had not finished photocopying all the correspondence. She asked if there was any reason to be holding back any of the information and I told her, "No." She then asked why I didn't contact police sooner, when I realized that I had evidence why did I not contact police then? I answered, "I had been in contact with two veteran journalists and I had asked their advise as to when I should contact authorities with what I had, and they both advised that I contact police after the preliminary had been conducted but before the actual trial. "Oh " she said, "What are the names of these journalists?" I said, "George Jacub, ex-C.B.C and John Webb, C.B.C." She said, "I'll get their names from you at a later date." I added, "I also was in contact with a former Crown Attorney named Agnew Johnston and a law professor and author named Alan Young, who both told me that I should contact police as soon as possible. Soon after this, Sidney sent me the last letter and discontinued correspondence completely. "To answer your question as well I still didn't know what the motive was, and I knew how valuable that would be, and I thought I could get that crucial bit of information with just a bit more time."

Sheila had commented, "These are, in the thirty years I have been working in Manitoba, the most horrendous facts I've ever seen."

I asked if there was any chance that she would accept a plea-bargain, and she answered bluntly, "There will be no plea-bargain." That's exactly what I had needed most to hear right then and it has been what I needed to hear from the very beginning of this ordeal.

I wanted to know when I would likely be called to testify, stating that I realized that the various people that had been called at the preliminary to testify would testify again. Sheila told me that I would testify last, and so that would mean I wouldn't testify till the last week of the trial. I asked how many days I might expect to be in court to testify and she said that it would be three or four days maximum. I had already been informed that I could not attend the hearings until after I had testified.

I asked whether Brodsky could say that Sidney had confabulated the story; reconstructed a memory about the murder from reading the police reports given to him by the defense, along with Sidney seeing the autopsy photos and the photos that Sidney took himself of the victim after the murder and dismemberment. Sheila answered, "You can't suck and blow." I laughed out loud at that statement understanding what she meant was that simply you can't have it both ways, showing him the evidence and then stating that is the only reason that Sidney knows details of this murder; "There has to be an air of reality present", she said.

I asked Sheila if provocation could be used as a defense in this case, provocation being a reason for a murder charge to be reduced to a manslaughter charge. She said that there was no mention of provocation in any of the letters, and I agreed. I asked about the issue of the burden of proof, knowing that the burden was on the Crown to disprove provocation. She stated that the burden was on the Crown, however if the defense were to raise the defense then the only way to do that would be by having Sidney testify. She explained since there were no other witnesses then there was but one choice and that is to have Sidney testify. I asked if Brodsky would want that and Sheila told me that he would strongly advise not taking the stand but if Sidney wanted to testify then he would have to allow him or otherwise he would have to resign from the case. I asked if she knew of any time Brodsky had quit a case and she said no. She said quickly, "Oh no, I did see him quit one case". I said, "Well Sidney's a loose cannon and he's going to perform". Sheila answered, "He's going to perform in the prisoner's box, he's going to perform on the witness stand, he's going to perform in this trial!" Sheila said something else I thought odd, "Brodsky will go out of his way to impress Sidney."

We discussed the issue of admissibility, whether certain evidence such as the drawings would be included in the trial and ultimately seen by the jury. Sheila explained that the evidence would have to be measured in terms of its probative value versus its prejudicial effect. I understood what she was speaking about as Agnew Johnston had explained the concept just the week before at the courthouse. She continued, saying, "For example, the photos taken at the crime scene would be so shocking and therefore bias a jury potentially so they couldn't look at all the evidence objectively." The drawings also could be determined to be prejudicial and many of the drawings could be excluded from the trial.

Far along in our meeting there was a comfortable exchange between us and Sheila was very open. I wanted to make certain that I explain that my criticism of the judicial system lay not with the prosecutors but with the actual law, for example the fact that in Canada a multiple murderer couldn't receive a consecutive sentence like they would in the U.S. She responded that she wished it were like the U.S. where you could give someone a sentence of a hundred years. We discussed what might happen in terms of setting a minimum amount of years before Sidney could even apply for parole. She did say something somewhat surprising and that was that Sidney would have a life sentence no matter what by way of a lifetime of mandatory supervision. Needless to say, I didn't feel re-assured by her statement; how could any kind of supervision actually prevent Sidney from killing again?

I asked if I could get the opportunity to review my video statement. Sheila said, "Absolutely. I can let you watch the video statement here or I can make a copy of the transcript for you to take home". We discussed that the video statement's transcript would be used in the trial only to refute potentially contradictory statements later made while testifying on the witness stand. I asked for a transcript of the video statement and Sheila left the room to get a copy for me.

Sheila told me that the jury was to be picked on August 31st, that it might take one or two days, and then motions would be made by September 4th, the day before the trial was to begin.

We talked about meeting again several times to aptly prepare me for direct examination and for the difficult cross-examination. She said she would provide me with a list of questions she would be asking of me in direct examination. She spoke of answering questions directly so as to not give Brodsky any opportunity to draw me into areas where I would not have been prepared to answer questions. Sheila commented that Brodsky was a man of his word, and very forthright, in as far as his professional dealings with her, an experienced Crown Prosecutor. She said that he would not attack me personally on the witness stand.

Far along in the meeting I felt that I should disclose the fact that I had interviewed Greg Brodsky on my radio program. She informed me that Brodsky had told her. I was surprised and relieved, as I wasn't sure how that revelation would be received. It seemingly was not a big deal to anyone involved; the overall impression I got from Sheila was that

Brodsky would not take anything that happens in this trial personally. She talked about when I was to be on the witness stand, and she said, "Don't get angry."

I asked about the defense of intoxication and if the surgical precision demonstrated in this crime could refute the claim of intoxication? She said, "It does to me!" She added that we would see when the coroner takes the stand. She essentially said that despite evidence of drunkenness, the facts are for the jury, and she seemed confident that intoxication was not going to be a viable defense. That being said Sheila wanted to stress that juries are unpredictable.

She spoke of the Nexus. A nexus is a connection to a group or series by definition. Nexus would apply to explaining the connection from Don Abbott to myself, and then from Don to Sidney and then Sidney to me via the correspondence.

We discussed the Cross-Examination process a little bit. She said, "The whole testimony is about credibility. Fraud, perjury, public mischief, impersonation; those are the kinds of charges that would affect credibility. You were as I see it simply a conduit. The story is sensationalistic you didn't make it sensationalistic! The defense could possibly persuade a jury of that."

I mentioned that I had contacted Cary Castagna at the Edmonton Sun and I had told him that Sidney had lived in Edmonton for a few years and that he had been questioned about similar murders in Alberta and B.C. Sheila quickly interrupted me to say, "Don't even suggest Sidney is a serial killer, don't mention his past questioning, don't mention the questioning, it will kill this case!"

I spoke about eventually contacting someone from the family for an interview. I told her that no matter that I had a book to write I didn't want to further traumatize these people by asking questions. Sheila said that it had been a wise choice to wait as I had, and that Rehka was in contact with the victim/witness representative, an aboriginal worker assigned to the family for this trial. The appropriate way to approach any member of their family would be via this route, after the trial has ended.

I had made sure that I had brought along to the meeting the People for Justice literature, the two-pages that I wrote for the group. I gave that to Sheila along with a copy of a photo of myself and other PFJ members that appeared in the Winnipeg Sun regarding the protest at the law courts over the Bryan Larsen, child pornography/sexual assault case.

People For Justice Inc.
lawreform@canadianjustice.ca
www.canadianjustice.ca

Did you know that in 1996, the reigning Liberal government enacted Conditional Sentencing as an alternative to incarceration? Conditional Sentences were sentences to be served in the community, which means in the offender's own home. Conditional Sentences were designed to deal with those convicted of less serious, non-violent crimes.

Since 1996, however, Conditional Sentences have been applied to cases involving violence and even death. Violent crime convictions that had Conditional Sentences apply include manslaughter, sexual assault and child molestation.

The Liberal government enacted these new laws; defense attorneys, prosecuting attorneys and judges have used these new laws to enable violent criminals to do no jail time for their violent offenses. (We are always talking, by the way, about violent crime, the most serious crimes committed in our community, those that impact the victims and their families and the whole community, the most.)

Conditional Sentences are very problematic in other crucial areas. A Conditional Sentence is not regarded like an actual first offence when an offender is re-charged, even for the same type of crime. For example, when a sex offender completes their Conditional Sentence, and is re-charged for the same offence, the first conviction does not affect the sentencing on the offender's actual second offence. Information gained by the investigation of the first offence cannot be used in the investigation of a "second" offence.

The mandatory requirement for a D.N.A. sample from the violent offender, to assist police in a second similar offence investigation, is not automatic. Police must petition the court to be able to obtain a D.N.A. sample from the offender. For these reasons, police do not like or agree with Conditional Sentences for any violent crime.

People for Justice believes that Conditional Sentences are a reasonable alternative to incarceration for many offenses. However, our group, like the police, does not believe in the application of Conditional Sentences for any violent crime.

Leniency for violent crime is unnerving. When did we as Canadians agree on this degree of leniency regarding violent crime?

The Liberal government has enacted legislation called the Faint Hope Clause, dealing with murder convictions. Initially the new legislation applied to those convicted even of more than one murder, (take the case of Stony Mountain double murderer Fred Bleitch) and was designed to give an opportunity for a convicted killer to be paroled much sooner than originally possible. For example, a convicted cold-blooded double murderer has the opportunity to be released in seven years. Why? Is our government simply expressing Canadian's desire for tolerance and leniency towards violent crime? People for Justice does not believe so.

Murder convictions are down statistically. However, what was once considered murder is now considered manslaughter, by virtue of our judicial system's interpretation of Charter Law. When alcohol is involved, murder in the first-degree convictions (pre-meditated murder) and murder in the second degree are difficult to prosecute, hence the reduction of the murder charge to manslaughter. Manslaughter does not have a minimum sentence but it can carry a maximum of a life sentence.

People for Justice have seen a murder conviction reduced to a manslaughter conviction, and then regardless of circumstances, the offender is given an inappropriate, very short sentence. For example, a seven-year sentence is given

135

to a curb stomping, murdering gang member. The sentence is deemed appropriate because it follows the precedent set in another court. Lower and lower precedents are set each day and the courts are forced to follow these lenient inappropriate sentences. A seven year sentence means anywhere from one year to four years in actual time to be served, and if these gangs operate in jail (and they do), then we have a murdering gang member back in our community in a few short years; worse of all, that gang member is still a threat to society, a definite threat to public safety. Whose fault is this, is it ours, is it the victim's fault? No, it is our courts fault for not protecting us to the best of their ability.

Why should murderers necessarily get out of jail, let alone in a few years without proof of rehabilitation? Can these murderers be rehabilitated, should we take the chance? The same mentality applies for rapists and child molesters. Do we take a chance on them re-offending? Will their behavior escalate like police have described, what is the sexual offender capable of?

The number one right for all citizens is that of the right to public safety. We pay for it dearly, and we should expect it. When violent offenders have proven that they are a threat to public safety, then we must, as citizens demand much more from our courts than excuses and arrogance. We must expect much more from our politicians to understand what is going on in our courts as far as sentencing is concerned, and to respond to the public's need for appropriate sentencing to ensure public safety.

Protest is one of the most important and effective ways in which to achieve many short term and long term objectives. Criminal cases which are highly publicized and that especially demonstrate certain things that People for Justice know to be true, can be used to point out certain things to the public and to the media, via media coverage. When we do a good job resonating with the public and the media with what we as a group have to say via these protests, the protests have nothing but positive effect.

The Bryan Larsen child-porn/child-molestation case was our group's first demonstration and we were effective in gaining positive press coverage from C.B.C., Global, CKY, A Channel, C.J.O.B., and the Winnipeg Sun. Although there are admittedly more serious crimes, such as murder, we felt that given the very serious sex offences he was to be sentenced for, and the very inappropriate sentence he would surely receive, we had decided by committee to use the Larsen case as a demonstration case, and to therefore organize a protest at the Law Courts at his sentencing dates.

The media was very receptive and cooperative; it was by all means successful. We thank the media and commend them for their concerns on public safety.

I FINALLY DECIDED TO CALL ONE OF THE PEOPLE WHO SIDNEY HAD RECOMMENDED that I contact, a former junior-high schoolteacher named Murray Lampert. This teacher had also visited Sidney three times since he had been incarcerated in 2003. I told Murray who I was and my involvement in this trial, I was completely forthright.

Murray told me that he was Sidney's social studies teacher when Sidney was 14 or 15 years old. Murray said that there had been a few incidents in school where he was taunted and constantly tagged by fellow students because he was so unabashedly effeminate. Murray stated that Sidney's sexual orientation was the issue that was most troublesome for him. Murray said, "The system just worked against him. I read his file, he had been given basically all the tests, and everyone had spoken to him. Yet, not one of them concluded that his struggle was with his sexual orientation; despite how effeminate he was, not one (professional) could see it". Sidney was the most flamboyant and obvious gay person that he had ever seen, and he said, "Often Sidney brought attention to himself just to get a reaction."

Murray said that he felt a lot of sympathy for Sidney and he had taken him out for a hamburger a couple of times, just to talk. Sidney felt he could confide in Murray somewhat; when Sidney had been out of town working, over the years, he had sent a few postcards, to stay in touch.

Murray said he had visited Sidney at the Remand Center on three separate occasions but Murray told Sidney, "I'm not interested in the crime or any details about it—I'm just interested in you!" Sidney told Murray that he had been instructed not to speak to anyone regarding the case. Murray told me that he brought Sidney a few books that he had requested, a few novels. I asked if the novels had anything to do with this type of crime and he quickly said, "no, not at all." They were just regular novels written by an aboriginal author.

I asked Murray if Sidney had spoken to him about his adopted parents and their treatment of Sidney. Murray said that he had once spoken to Mrs. Teerhuis, in person, one time only, but had come away with the distinct impression that she was very authoritarian and very strict. I asked if Sidney had spoken of physical abuse at the hands of his father, and Murray indicated that he had not. I then asked if Sidney had spoken at all of any sexual abuse by a family member or any sexual relationship with his mother. He told me that Sidney had not ever mentioned any sexual abuse whatsoever involving anyone.

Murray wanted me to understand that despite being a friend to Sidney, he expressed strongly that, "We can't have people threatening society, and even though I feel sympathetic to Sidney's situation, I want to you to know I have no sympathy for this crime!"

I believe I understood his position and I told him that I admired his dedication to Sidney as a friend; especially since the murder charges had been laid. I asked if he would submit to a full interview, possibly on camera. He stated that he wanted to check on the legality of him speaking about a former student of his by contacting the

Teacher's Society. He said that he wanted to visit Sidney in the near future and ask him if he would approve the interview. I told him that I fully understood his position, and I encouraged him to contact Sidney as to ask his permission to interview him further. I wanted Murray to tell Sidney what we had spoken about—I had spoken to Sidney's chosen contact and asked about the alleged sexual abuse at the hands of his family members, along with a teacher; and this confidant was not told about this seemingly important information. I had gotten the information I was looking for however, with that short phone call.

AUGUST 20/06

A STORY APPEARED IN THE WINNIPEG SUN TODAY TITLED, " 'I ACT FOR THE UN-represented' – Sex case raises Brodsky profile". It featured an interview with Greg Brodsky's eldest son, Defense lawyer Daniel Brodsky, about his involvement in serial pedophile sex offender Peter Whitmore's case, who had gotten the attention of the Canadian public with a brazen child abduction. In this article, Brodsky's son utilized the same kind of pre-trial grandstanding as his father is known for, which amounts to making unqualified statements that are at best irresponsible and inappropriate.

Brodsky spoke of 'knowing' Whitmore since 1999, and in this case said the issue at hand was the monitoring of high-risk offenders, and how the system fails society miserably. "To put it bluntly, we don't supervise people very well. That has to change. Someone has to wake up and pay attention." He continued, "I don't keep track of my cases, but my dad can tell you right now that he has defended 640 murder cases—a record in the English-speaking world." I clipped out the article and shook my head.

AUGUST 24/06

A STORY APPEARED ON THE FRONT PAGE OF THE WINNIPEG FREE Press TODAY. " 'Jury System Put On Trial' – A man accused of killing and dismembering a victim in a Winnipeg hotel room has launched a legal challenge of the way juries are selected, delaying his own trial indefinitely." On page 3, "TOP NEWS", the story ran with a 12x8 photo of Sidney with the headline, "Jury system 'doesn't work' lawyer says—Accused killer wants rules changed to allow native jurors with records." by Mike McIntyre.

The story stated that Sidney had filed a legal challenge claiming that aboriginal people are being discriminated against because a large number have criminal records and as result cannot serve as jurors.

"There are a large number of aboriginal people being excluded from jury selection based on that rule. It does affect the representativeness of the jury," argued defense lawyer Kathleen Fotheringham.

Sidney said that because of this the jury selected isn't a true representation of the public and is therefore a violation of his rights.

Sidney has demanded what he sees as a 'jury of his peers', that being a primarily aboriginal jury to hear his high-profile case.

Greg Brodsky claimed, "The courts have created a system where the only people picked as jurors are the elderly and the unemployed. You may be getting a jury, which is unbiased, those 70 year-old unemployed people and homemakers, but you're not going to get a jury that is representative of the community. The process just doesn't work."

The story stated that about 1,600 jury notices were sent out and that more than 1,400 who received notice were excused for such reasons as health issues, work responsibilities and other responsibilities that could negatively affect them financially. Of the 189 left, 13 were disqualified because of criminal records. 12 jurors would then be selected from the remaining 176.

Brodsky stated that, "The threshold to get off a jury panel is far too low," taking issue that jury officials didn't require written declarations for the reasons that they could not perform jury duty and simply had to take people at their word. Brodsky continued, "That gives the impression justice isn't being done and we don't have procedural fairness."

Queens Bench Chief Justice Mark Monnin presided over the motion and has reserved his decision, which has created an indefinite delay of Teerhuis' trial.

"He doesn't care if his trial is delayed. He wants a fair trial before a representative jury. If he has to sit and wait for it, he will," said Brodsky.

He claims the motion is unique in Canada and would have far reaching implications about the way juries are selected if successful.

Monnin said Teerhuis isn't allowed to handpick a jury of his pleasing.

"He's entitled to have a jury chosen randomly from a group the community as a whole. That doesn't mean the end result has to be exactly how the community is compromised," he said.

The Jury Act also prohibits other certain individuals from being jurors, including MPs and MLAs, judges, police officers, lawyers and other court officials, correctional and probation officers or persons afflicted with a mental or physical infirmity that makes if difficult to perform the duties of a juror.

Potential jurors may also be excused if the length of the trial could create a financial hardship on the individual or his or her family.

Friday, August 25/06

I called Crown Attorney Sheila Leinburd to talk about the latest development in the trial. She explained that the case had been adjourned and that the presiding judge was not ready to render a decision regarding the motion brought forward by Brodsky on behalf of Sidney Teerhuis. Sheila said that the judge would deliver his decision sometime in September. She told me that the Crown had argued the motion unsuccessfully. She stated, "Sidney has the right to challenge the jury selection."

I asked what this decision would mean in terms of time till the trial would commence. I understood that jury pools are selected twice a year, and so I assumed that this trial could definitely be postponed till sometime in early spring. Sheila responded by saying that the trial could be delayed by a year or longer.

I asked why the trial wouldn't be able to proceed at the next available jury selection. Sheila told me that Greg Brodsky's schedule didn't allow him to be available at that time. I asked if she was surprised by this development in this trial. Sheila told me that she wasn't surprised, but she did wish there had been a different response by the judge. I did my best to hold back my anger regarding this delay, and I asked, "Why would Sidney and Brodsky want this delay other than to accumulate the two-for-one credit towards his end sentence?" She replied, "That double time concept doesn't work for murder, it's just regular time." I immediately felt that at least that was some good news. Sheila ended by saying, "Go on with your life Mr. Zupansky."

∗   ∗   ∗   ∗   ∗

Wednesday, July 4/07

IN THE WINNIPEG FREE PRESS A STORY APPEARED:

> WINNIPEG – A man accused of a dismemberment killing has lost a unique legal challenge of Manitoba's jury system in which he claimed the right to be tried by a jury composed mostly of natives like himself.
>
> Queen's Bench Chief Justice Marc Monnin handed down a decision Wednesday, ruling Sydney Teerhuis' rights are not being violated by the current system.

I was relieved that the jury challenge had been dismissed. I believed it would be, as I had read all the other very similar challenges, some 7 or 8 of them and why they had been eventually dismissed. In fact Marc Monnin's father Alfred Monnin had also been employed to rule on a very similar jury challenge, which ended up being dismissed also.

There was absolutely no merit to the jury composition challenge because the definition of the word 'peer' merely means a person of the same age, status, or ability as another specified person. So an accused is entitled to a 'jury of their peers', which does not include however having a jury made up of any one race, color or creed.

January 9/08

I ROUTINELY GOOGLED SIDNEY'S NAME IN CASE THERE WAS ANY INFORMATION I could obtain from new stories appearing on line. I found an article that Mike McIntyre had posted on his website but that had not appeared in the Free Press.

In the article it stated that Sidney had been arrested, charged with threatening to kill a fellow inmate's family members. He had been arrested a few days before at Headingley Correctional Centre for allegedly making phone calls to two people resulting in two charges of uttering threats.

In the news article it mentioned something that I was much more interested in reading, which was that Sidney's trial was to occur sometime in December of 2008.

An interesting point is that there was no announcement of the trial date or mention of Sidney's new charges by any media. I guess it just wasn't newsworthy enough.

I was relieved to finally have word of a new trial date—after all by the time the trial commences it will have been almost 4 years since I first contacted police with the evidence against Sidney.

Canada
Province of Manitoba

COURT OF QUEEN'S BENCH
Winnipeg Centre

SUBPOENA

Manitoba

Canada
Province de Manitoba

COUR DU BANC DE LA REINE
Centre de Winnipeg

ASSIGNATION

TO / À:

DANNY MITCHAEL ZUPANSKY
##########
############################
NOT IN SERVICE

PERSONAL SERVICE ONLY

Witness Instructions / Directives au témoin
To contact Victim/Witness Services (Mon-Fri 10 a.m. - 4 p.m.) at
945-3594
To report to courtroom 400.

WHEREAS/ATTENDU QUE

SYDNEY TEERHUIS

has been charged with/   **SECOND DEGREE MURDER**
a été inculpé d'avoir

and it has been made to appear that you are likely to give
material evidence for the prosecution.

THIS IS THEREFORE to command you to attend before the COURT
OF QUEEN'S BENCH, 408 YORK Avenue (Old Law Courts),
Winnipeg, Manitoba on

et qu'on a donné à entendre que vous êtes probablement en état
de rendre un témoignage essentiel pour la poursuite.

À CES CAUSES, les présentes ont pour objet de vous enjoindre
de comparaître devant COUR DU BANC DE LA REINE, 408 YORK
Avenue (Old Law Courts), Winnipeg, Manitoba, le

Tuesday, SEP 05, 2006 to Friday, SEP 29, 2006 at/à 9:00AM /heure

COURTROOM   **QB**

To give evidence concerning the said charge.
And to bring with you anything in your possession or under your
control that relates to the said charge(s).

SALLE D'AUDIENCE   **QB**

Pour témoigner dans cette affaire.
Et d'apporter avec vous toutes choses en votre possession ou
sous votre contrôle qui se rattachent à l'inculpation.

Dated/Daté   AUG 03 2006   , at/à Winnipeg, Manitoba

Trial Unit #1: Jbihun
Issued Date: Jul 28, 2006 10:55:35
Incident Number: 03/139622

Clerk of Court/Greffier(e) de la Cour
in and for the Province of Manitoba
dans et pour la province du Manitoba

Figure 26: Subpoena issued to Dan Zupansky by Court of Queen's Bench (Winnipeg Centre)
for the September 5th, 2006 trial of Sidney Teerhuis. Due to objections over the jury selection
process raised by the accused, the trial was postponed indefinitely.

14
Getting Prepared to Testify

Tuesday, October 20/08
Phone Call from Crown Attorney Sheila Leinburd

I received a phone call from Crown Attorney Sheila Leinburd. She seemed very friendly, almost warm in her tone. She asked if I were available for October 27th and the 28th? I replied that I would be in town and available. She said there was to be a *voir dire* near or on those dates to determine the admissibility of the letters and the drawings that Sidney had sent me. She stated that the *voir dire* was not part of the actual trial and that the trial would be December 1st till the 19th. She asked if I was available to meet her the coming Friday at 10:00 a.m. and I said that I was.

She asked if I had been in contact with Don Abbott and I said that I hadn't. She asked if Don had been employed to write about what Sidney had said and I replied that he was but that Sidney ended up writing everything himself and Sidney did not impart to him anything of relevance. She asserted that Sidney had imparted to me the vast majority of information rather than Don and I agreed. She asked me to bring to our meeting all of the correspondence and I asked if that included the diagrams and she said, "Yes."

October 24/08 — Meeting with Sheila Leinburd

As soon as I walked through the doors of the Woodsworth Building I saw Greg Brodsky in a heated either debate or negotiation with two others. I walked by and glanced at Greg as I turned and walked to the elevators. He looked pretty good for his age, I thought but his yellowish/red hair was long so as to necessitate him using the long hair to cover his bald areas.

I ventured into the elevator and up to the fifth floor. The receptionist asked my name and I told her whom I was there to see and she requested that I sign in the log. I asked about the washroom and I was told that there were public washrooms on the third and first floors. I headed to the third floor and the washroom and afterwards traveling back up to the fifth floor, low and behold, Greg Brodsky walked into the elevator. I immediately introduced myself, "Hello Mr. Brodsky. My name is Dan Zupansky." He replied, "Yes I understand you may be a witness in the trial." "Yes", I said, "I'm just going to speak with Miss Leinburd." He replied, "I will be seeing her starting next week a lot myself." Brodsky then nodded as he got out at his floor.

I got off on the fifth floor and the receptionist gave me a clip-on 'Crown visitors pass' and told me to now go to the sixth floor. I went upstairs and had to bang on the locked glass door with the sign overhead Criminal Prosecutions Branch. Eventually someone came to the door and I told him whom I was there to see and he let me in and directed me to a conference-type room. The room was called 'The Dangerfield Meeting Room' named after the lately discredited retired Crown prosecutor George Dangerfield.

Sheila and her assistant (this was not the former assistant Rehka Malivari) walked into the room and said, "Hello Mr. Zupansky", and directed me to sit across from her and her assistant. Sheila introduced me to Deanne Sahulka. She soon took out a smaller writing pad and began to take notes and observe. Deanne was somewhat overweight, pleasant looking and she seemed quite friendly, smiling a fair bit. She was attentive and took extensive notes as the meeting progressed.

Sheila was dressed in a form fitting black dress, more suited I thought for evening-wear or a wedding than day attire.

She started off asking me if I had given the police the H.P. Lovecraft novel that was sitting in plain view on top of all the correspondence that I had provided to police. (As I discovered later that H.P. Lovecraft is a famous horror/science fiction writer whose work was first published in the fifties). I was confused and told her that I had not given police the Lovecraft novel.

She asked when and how I had met Don Abbott. I told her that I had met him in Thunder Bay in 1976. She asked how I came to communicate with Don in jail and I explained that since he had called and asked me, that I had decided to let him call me from jail.

I told her that Sidney had no idea where I stood in all of this, and I felt that Sidney believed that I was 'an ally'. I told Sheila that Don was gregarious and outgoing and had likely spoke highly of me as a journalist. I stated that despite Sidney being seemingly quite intelligent and articulate, it didn't mean he wasn't foolish. She asked when the correspondence began and I told her that it began in February 2004.

We spoke of the interview that I had done with Greg Brodsky in March 2005 and she asked if Greg Brodsky was aware that I had been corresponding with his client. I told her that he was not. She asked what questions I had asked Greg. I said, "if he is not to use perjured testimony, to have his client lie or for him to lie on his client's behalf, then how would he determine the truth?" She then asked what he had said in response? I replied, "This is not a church—I don't care about the truth!" He went on to tell me that often his client would offer four different stories as to what really happened and I kept asking him the same question for 15 minutes, and he kept repeating that he didn't care about the truth. I told her that very much like a politician Brodsky would try avoiding my questions. Sheila asked if I had asked any questions about Sidney's case and I said that I had not. She asked how long the interview had been and I stated that it had lasted for one hour.

I told her that Brodsky was not concerned as he said with the truth and that she wasn't either (I said it as an actual dig) but as a journalist, I was. I felt a fair amount of animosity towards her as she had asked me to be prepared and I had spent a lot of hours organizing it so I could reference anything for her quickly, and I felt she had obviously not been prepared. Based on her questions, asking me to clarify things that we had 2 years previously already covered, I did not think that she had read the material, at least recently, in it's entirety, or carefully and as a result asked me questions that confirmed that to me—hence the sarcasm and lack of respect.

I said to Sheila that Brodsky would focus on false information provided by Sidney and try to say all of the information might be false. I stated, " Brodsky will try anything and throw in everything including the kitchen sink." Sheila responded, "And that's his job."

She at one point said, "You sat on this information for quite a while." I replied emphatically, "No. I didn't. I asked two veteran C.B.C. journalists what I should do and they advised that I contact you after the preliminary but I took the legal advice of Alan Young a law professor at Queens University and a former Crown Agnew Johnston and turned the material in after I couldn't get any more information." I told her that I wanted to get information regarding the motive, as the actual motive Sidney provided I felt was suspect.

Sheila showed me two letters written to Sidney and asked if I had written them. The handwriting was not even similar to mine and thought it surprising that she could not figure that out just from the opening sentences, which spoke of, 'a wife and kids...' I quickly stated that the letters were from Sidney's high school guidance teacher, whom I had spoken to and I knew was possibly the only person writing to Sidney since he had been in jail. I told her that I had spoken to him and had asked about Sidney and his life during high school.

I told her that I had asked him if Sidney had told him of any physical abuse at the hands of his family and he had said, "No." I asked then if he had spoke of any sexual abuse and he said, "No."

In the letter I had just began to read, Murray explained to Sidney that he felt it best not to divulge any particulars of the murder to him. He didn't want to be involved and he didn't want to know any details.

Amazing, I thought was the next thing she asked me, "How do you know that Sidney didn't confess?" I excitedly answered, "It was in the paper!" Assuming that she also had not seen the actual stories in the newspaper she would have likely read which would have been the Free Press, I told her that Mike McIntyre was out of town covering the Dennis Sand trial and with the police media relations intimating in their on-line press release that Sidney had basically confessed combined with McIntyre not following up by speaking to the actual officer as Alex Reid from NewWinnipeg.com had done, the Winnipeg Free Press had dropped the ball.

I told her of Free Press editor Bob Cox continuing with running the story with the incorrect information despite being informed otherwise by myself while the Winnipeg Sun ran the exclusive interview where Sidney explains his story about telling police that he had passed out and when he awoke he had found the man dead in the bathtub. She then asked, "How do you know he was cut into eight pieces?" Again I strongly stated, "I read it in the papers." I continued, "The story about the missing organs was in the papers as well as well as the statement by police that

Sidney had taken photos of the victim post-murder." She expressed surprise at that statement and then I added that she had let that fact slip last time we had met in 2006. She immediately denied saying it but I said that I took very detailed notes of our conversation and that I was sure of what she had said. She repeated that she did not make such a statement.

She then asked me a question that floored me. "How do you know that Sidney didn't, like he had said in his last letter that he simply took four separate serial killer stories and put them together?" Sidney had written, "I took excerpts from Dahmer, Gacy, Nilsen and Wournos and put them together to give you a story-fiction." I replied, "First off I've read all of those cases and there is nothing in those stories that even relates to his story whatsoever." I was very firm regarding that. For example I said that Sidney had stated that he killed Greene at 6:20 on that evening in question and why would I not believe him. I said that the extent of the organ removal had not even been done by Jack-the-Ripper himself and that no one I had ever read about had actually ever turned themselves in and then went on to claim that they could not remember the crime or that they had done it.

I said that the unique aspects of the murder made me believe that it would be of interest to publishers. She then asked, "So you are still planning to write a book?" I replied, "I wouldn't do all of this otherwise!" She went on to ask if I had finished the book already and I said, "No. I can't finish the book till the trial is over." I went on to explain that rather than writing that Sidney had said this and that—I would want to have published what he actually had said. I told her about famous true crime writer Jack Olson's last book, 'I—The Creation of a Serial Killer' and how he just let his book's subject speak, that the book was almost autobiographical and that I had planned to present my book in a similar way.

I also told her of the status of the book and that Kensington Press had requested my proposal and that an agent from New York was considering my proposal presently.

Despite knowing the answer already I asked again if I would be permitted to attend the trial and she explained that the rule prevented my testimony from being tainted. I asked, "What is stopping me from reading the papers?" She replied, "The press is incomplete and inaccurate."

She stated that she didn't think that intoxication was an acceptable defense and grounds for a manslaughter conviction, but that's what Brodsky will attempt. I replied, "Of course. But the surgical butchering would prove otherwise." She agreed. We went over the concept of provocation, as a defense and that there seemed to be no evidence to support any such claim. Sidney had offered only a highly implausible motive where he claimed that the victim was 'pissing the bed' while asleep and Sidney couldn't awaken him. I stated that I believed that Sidney stabbed him while attempting to rape him—as he had, according to his own writings—drugged and raped other unconscious victims. I believe that Robin Greene either refused or reacted to Sidney's attempt to rape him. I also told her that I was certain that Sidney knew Greene had stolen the jewelry from the set of 'Shall We Dance'. I informed her that the Woodbine Hotel where Sidney and Greene had met was right next door to the Ted Matoyka Dance Studio where Richard Gere had been coming regularly to put in as many hours of rehearsal time as possible since the movie had begun shooting in Winnipeg. I also mentioned that according to Sidney, he and Greene had walked to Assiniboine Avenue, to a park there while at the same time the 'Shall We Dance' crew was set up just down the street. I stated that they must have had a conversation about the jewelry and where it came from, and even though he may have thought that it was costume jewelry (as he stated in his letter to me), he must have known it was quite valuable. Sidney definitely knew about the movie being filmed in Winnipeg, and he knew that the jewelry ensured certain fame for him. Sheila did listen very intently to that idea.

I went on to tell her that I could recognize that he was psychopathic and wanted to be famous, and that he likely had killed before based on all the research I had done. I immediately followed with, "But I won't be saying that in court" and I smiled, alluding to her admonishment 2 years previous when I mentioned that Sidney had been questioned about other murders, she loudly proclaimed that I was not to reveal that he had been questioned about other murders and that any mention of it would sink the case!

Sheila said she would contact me on the following Monday, October 27th to let me know if I was needed to testify at the *Voir Dire*. She explained that the *voir dire* would be equivalent to another preliminary for the sole purpose of determining the admissibility of the evidence provided by the correspondence and the gruesome diagrams.

The meeting had lasted about an hour and a quarter. I felt it was a bit rushed. At the end of our meeting Sheila said, "Thank you Mr. Zupansky." I replied, "It's been my pleasure."

I walked out into the bright sunshine of an unseasonably warm day, confident that I had done all that I could and had managed to impart all that I had intended.

MONDAY, OCTOBER 27

SHEILA LEINBURD CALLED TO TELL ME THAT I WOULD NOT BE NEEDED TO TESTIFY at the *voir dire*. I asked if she would notify me as to whether the letters and drawings were deemed admissible. She told me that she would.

NOVEMBER 24 — PHONE CALL TO SHEILA LEINBURD

I MADE A PHONE CALL TO CROWN ATTORNEY SHEILA LEINBURD. WE EXCHANGED pleasantries and then I proceeded to ask if the evidence that I had provided was deemed admissible at the *voir dire*. She responded that the *voir dire* had just concluded the week of November 16-21 (I was somewhat confused as to whether she was referring to the voir dire as also including the juror selection, as she had said that the admissibility hearing would last only two days).

She informed me that half of the letters that Sidney had sent to me and half of the letters I had sent to Sidney 'were in'. I asked if the diagrams also had also been deemed admissible and she said that they were. She immediately and very matter-of-factly stated emphatically, "You are not permitted to disclose anything that has gone on at the *voir dire*. Do you understand me Mr. Zupansky?" I replied, "Yes."

Canada
Province of Manitoba
COURT OF QUEEN'S BENCH
Winnipeg Centre

SUBPOENA

Manitoba

Canada
Province de Manitoba
COUR DU BANC DE LA REINE
Centre de Winnipeg

ASSIGNATION

TO / À:

PERSONAL SERVICE ONLY

DANNY MITCHAEL ZUPANSKY
###########
###########
###########################

Witness Instructions / Directives au témoin
To contact Crown Attorney SHEILLA LEINBURD at 945-8017 for inquiries

WHEREAS/ATTENDU QUE

SYDNEY TEERHUIS

has been charged with/   **SECOND DEGREE MURDER**
a été inculpé d'avoir

and it has been made to appear that you are likely to give material evidence for the prosecution.

THIS IS THEREFORE to command you to attend before the COURT OF QUEEN'S BENCH, 408 YORK Avenue (Old Law Courts), Winnipeg, Manitoba on

et qu'on a donné à entendre que vous êtes probablement en état de rendre un témoignage essentiel pour la poursuite.

À CES CAUSES, les présentes ont pour object de vous enjoindre de comparaître devant COUR DU BANC DE LA REINE, 408 YORK Avenue (Old Law Courts), Winnipeg, Manitoba, le

Monday, OCT 27, 2008 to Tuesday, OCT 28, 2008   at/à   9:00AM /heure

COURTROOM   **QB**

To give evidence concerning the said charge.
And to bring with you anything in your possession or under your control that relates to the said charge(s).

SALLE D'AUDIENCE   **QB**

Pour témoigner dans cette affaire.
Et d'apporter avec vous toutes choses en votre possession ou sous votre contrôle qui se rattachent à l'inculpation.

Dated/Daté   OCT 21 2008   , at/à Winnipeg, Manitoba

General Prosecutions: pcreighton
Issued Date: Oct 20, 2008 14:03:15
Incident Number: 03/139622

Clerk of Court/Greffier(e) de la Cour
in and for the Province of Manitoba
dans et pour la province du Manitoba

Figure 27: Subpoena issued by Court of Queen's Bench (Winnipeg Centre) to appear at *voire dire* for trial of Sidney Teerhuis, October 27th, 2008.

She continued. "I know that there has been some activity on your part and that you are not to post anything on a website either Mr. Zupansky." It seemed to me that she was referring to the TrophyKill website but it was hard to believe then she would not have mentioned it and the contents specifically, including the film clip. Her tone was very stern and dead serious but I didn't feel that I was in any serious trouble—but I definitely had been warned.

She informed me that I would be appearing in the second week of the three week trial, appearing in court to testify between the 8th and the 12th of December. I then asked if she were planning to meet with me to prepare me for direct and cross-examination. She replied that she would be contacting me later that week.

She didn't call.

Not so suddenly, the trial was set to begin.

15

The Trial Begins

DECEMBER 1/08

(JURY SELECTED BEFORE THE HONOURABLE MR. JUSTICE JOYAL ON NOVEMBER 27, 2008)

(JURY IN AT 10:11 A.M.)

THE CLERK: My Lord, this is the case of The Queen versus Sydney Teerhuis-Moar and, for the record, the accused has not been put in charge of the jury, and all 12 jurors are present

THE CLERK: Can you please stand? Members of the jury, the accused stands charged by the name of Sydney Teerhuis-Moar. Sydney is spelled both S-y-d-n-e-y and s-i-d-n-e-y. You are Sydney Teerhuis-Moar?

THE ACCUSED: Yes.

THE CLERK: Sidney Teerhuis-Moar, stands charged that he, the said Sidney Teerhuis-Moar, on or about the 1st day of July 2003, at the City of Winnipeg, in the Province of Manitoba, did unlawfully kill Robin Robert Greene, and did thereby commit murder in the second degree. And upon these charges he has been arraigned, and upon his arraignment he has pled not guilty. Your charge, therefore, is to inquire whether he is guilty or not guilty and hearken to the evidence. You may be seated.

THE COURT: Ladies and gentlemen, Crown and defence counsel have chosen you as the jury to decide this case. It is your job to decide from the evidence that you will see and hear in this courtroom what the facts are in this case. You are the only persons who decide the facts. To decide what the facts are in this case, you may consider only the evidence that you hear and see in this courtroom. The evidence includes what each witness says in response to the questions asked. It is the answers that are the evidence. The evidence also includes any things that may be made exhibits. When you go to your jury room to decide this case, the exhibits will go with you. The charge that you heard read out a moment ago is not evidence. What the lawyers and I say when we speak to you during the trial is not evidence. Only the exhibits and the things witnesses say are evidence. Radio, television, newspaper, and Internet reports, or anything that you may have heard from anyone else about this case or the persons or places involved in it, are not evidence. You should ignore them completely. Consider the evidence with an open mind. Make your decision without sympathy, prejudice, or fear. Do not be influenced by public opinion or the comments of others about this case or how it should be decided. Punishment has nothing to do with your task. Your task is to determine whether the Crown has proven the guilt of Mr. Teerhuis-Moar beyond a reasonable doubt. If you find Mr. Teerhuis-Moar guilty of an offence, it is my job, not yours, to decide what punishment is appropriate. Finally, in this case, you are to be judges of the facts. To help you understand what will happen in this trial, I will explain to you briefly the procedure that we will follow.

Crown counsel is Ms. Sheila Leinburd and Ms. Deanne Sahulka. They will prosecute this case. Defence counsel is Mr. Brodsky, perhaps sometimes joined by Ms. Buset. They represent Mr. Teerhuis-Moar, the accused on trial. In a trial, each side has a chance to present its case. Crown counsel goes first because she has the job of proving the charge. It is not Mr. Teerhuis's job to prove that he is innocent.

After her opening address, Crown counsel, Ms. Leinburd, will call witnesses to the witness box. She may also file various things as exhibits. Because accused persons are not required to prove their innocence, they are not obliged to testify or to present evidence. It is Crown counsel's job to prove the charge beyond a reasonable doubt. This rule never changes. When lawyers ask questions, questions of witnesses, they have to follow certain rules. One set of rules applies when they're asking questions of witnesses they have called; these questions are called examination in chief. Another set of rules applies when lawyers are questioning witnesses that the other side has called; these questions, as you know, are called cross-examination.

Although the testimony of every witness has been recorded by a court clerk monitor, we will not have a written transcript of the evidence available for your review when you go to the jury room to discuss your decision in this case. If you need help to recall any parts of the evidence, I will be available to assist you.

After the evidence is finished, Crown and defence counsel will address you. They will tell you their positions and refer to some of the evidence that they say you should rely on to reach the conclusion they suggest at the end of the case. What counsel say about the evidence is only their memory of some parts of the evidence that was given at trial. It is your memory of the evidence, all of the evidence that you must follow in deciding this case.

You should always remember, however, that the only memory of the evidence that counts in this case is yours, not mine, nor that of counsel. It is also your job to consider all, all of the evidence, not just the parts of the evidence that I will mention.

When you watch and listen to testimony, and later when you go to your jury room to decide the case, you use and must use the same common sense that you use every day in deciding whether people know what they are talking about and whether they are telling the truth. There is no magic formula for deciding how much or how little to believe of a witness' testimony. Nor is there a magic formula to decide how much or how little of a witness's testimony you wish to rely on in deciding this case. But let me give you a few questions that I propose you might want to keep in mind as the trial proceeds.

Does the witness seem honest? Is there any particular reason why the witness would not be telling the truth or that his or her evidence would not be reliable?

Does the witness have an interest in the outcome of the case or any reason to give evidence that is more favorable to one side or the other?

Mr. Teerhuis has pled not guilty. He is presumed to be innocent of the crime charged. The presumption of innocence also means that Mr. Teerhuis-Moar does not have to testify, present evidence, or prove anything in this case. It is Crown counsel who must prove the guilt of Mr. Teerhuis-Moar beyond a reasonable doubt, not Mr. Teerhuis who must prove his innocence. You must find Mr. Teerhuis not guilty of the offence unless Crown counsel satisfies you beyond a reasonable doubt that he is guilty of it.

The phrase 'beyond a reasonable doubt' is a very important part of our criminal justice system. A reasonable doubt is not a farfetched or frivolous doubt. It is not a doubt based on sympathy or prejudice. It is a doubt based on reason and common sense. It is a doubt that logically arises from the evidence or the lack of evidence.

The Crown is required to prove each of these essential elements beyond a reasonable doubt. In this case, the offence charged is second-degree murder. The charge in the indictment reads: That he, the said Sydney Teerhuis-Moar, on or about the 1st day of July, 2003, at the City of Winnipeg, in the Province of Manitoba, did unlawfully kill Robin Robert Greene, and did thereby commit murder in the second degree.

For you to find Mr. Teerhuis-Moar guilty of second degree murder, Crown counsel must prove each of the following essential elements beyond a reasonable doubt: first, that Mr. Teerhuis-Moar caused Robert Greene's death; second, that Mr. Teerhuis-Moar caused Mr. Greene's death unlawfully; and third and finally, that Mr. Teerhuis-Moar had the state of mind required for murder.

MS. LEINBURD: Thank you. Good morning. My Lord, ladies and gentlemen of the jury, my name is Sheila Leinburd, my colleague is Deanne Sahulka, and as His Lordship has already told you, we are the Crown prosecutors in this case. At this point in time in my opening address, I will be giving you an outline of the evidence that I expect that you will hear in support of the charge of second-degree murder against the accused, Sydney Teerhuis-Moar.

On July the 1st, 2003, the deceased, Robin Greene, who had just arrived in Winnipeg the previous day, was befriended by the accused, the man in the prisoner's box. He and the deceased had a few drinks at the Woodbine Hotel. The accused and Robin Greene then returned to the accused's suite at Room 309 of the Royal Albert Hotel in Winnipeg, Manitoba. In that room, the accused brutally and senselessly killed Robin Greene.

I apologize to you in advance and forewarn you that the pictures that you are about to see and that the evidence that you are about to hear is graphic and very disturbing. I urge you to remain dispassionate in this regard.

Robin Greene was stabbed to death. He was stabbed a total of 68 times. His body was decapitated; it was dismembered into eight separate pieces. He was eviscerated, he was mutilated, and he was left in the bathtub. All of his organs were removed and they have never been found.

After the killing, the accused left the decapitated and dismembered body of Robin Greene in the bathtub, and he walked to

151

the Winnipeg Remand Centre. That's the building just across the street here, on the corner of York and Kennedy. Sydney Teerhuis-Moar, that accused, arrived at the Remand Centre at approximately 9:22 in the morning. He walked in calmly and he plainly told the duty officer, Donald Steenson--and you will hear from him--that there was a chopped up body in his bathtub. The police were phoned immediately and the accused told the 911 operator that he had killed someone yesterday and that the person was chopped up and in the bathroom of Suite 309, 48 Albert Street, his address. He also told the 911 operator that he'd used a knife to kill Robin Greene and that the knife was still on the bathroom floor. The police ultimately found this knife exactly where the accused told them it would be: on the bathroom floor in Suite 309 at 48 Albert Street.

The police arrived at the Remand Centre and they spoke to the accused. And when the police asked him why he went to the Remand Centre, calmly and directly he told the police: I thought it was a police station. I came to turn myself in because I killed someone.

The accused took the police to his suite at 309-48 Albert Street, where they unlocked the door and they walked in. There they found the decapitated and eviscerated body of Robin Greene, in eight pieces, lying neatly stacked in the bathtub. The knife, as I say, that he told the police he had killed the deceased with, was found under the bathroom sink. The accused was arrested for the murder of Robin Greene.

In the bedroom, they found a blood-soaked bed, a blood-soaked mattress with knife cuts through it, and a blood-soaked blanket and pillow. In the bathroom, they found several bloodstained towels near the deceased's body and they found two knives, one a large knife covered in blood. Robin Greene's DNA was in that blood. They also found a smaller knife on the top of the medicine cabinet, and the plastic sheath that covered that knife had the accused's name, Sidney Teerhuis, printed on it.

In searching the accused's room, the police also found three disposable cameras, and when they developed the photographs from those cameras, they noted that Robin Greene's picture had been taken inside the accused's suite. These photographs were taken shortly before his death.

After the police arrested the accused, they took him to the Public Safety Building, where he was photographed and fingerprinted, and you will see these photographs as well. You will see blood on the accused's head and on his foot, and the DNA on the accused's foot was Robin Greene's DNA. Robin Greene's DNA was also found on the shirt and the sock that the accused was wearing on the day that he was arrested.

I anticipate that the evidence will also disclose that after killing Robin Greene, that the accused wrote letters about that killing to Tom Pomplum, an American publisher, and also to Dan Zupansky, a Canadian journalist. In those letters, the accused described how he killed Robin Greene, in detail. He even drew diagrams depicting the killing itself.

There will be testimony from witnesses such as police officers or experts, and the first witness that you will hear from in this trial is Constable Chris McLean. He is a City of Winnipeg police identification officer. He's an expert in photographs and fingerprints. He took the photographs in this case with brother officers and he, in fact, analyzed fingerprints in this case. He attended the scene, he photographed the scene and he seized the exhibits from the scene. You will see his photographs and you will see the exhibits. They will be marked as evidence in this case.

Another expert whom the Crown will call is Dr. Charles Littman. He is a medical doctor and he's a forensic pathologist for the Province of Manitoba. He will tell you the cause of Robin Greene's death and he will refer you to pictures that were taken at the autopsy. Again, these photographs are very graphic and disturbing. This will help Dr. Littman to explain to you and you to understand how Robin Greene died and how he suffered his injuries.

There will also be civilian witnesses called, who will tell you that they saw the accused and the deceased, Robin Greene, having drinks together at the bar at the Royal Albert Hotel the day that Robin Greene was killed.

Lastly, I will call the witnesses, Tom Pomplum and Dan Zupansky, the author and the journalist to whom I referred. I anticipate that they will tell you about the letters that they wrote to and received from the accused respecting this murder.

As this trial now starts, I ask you to carefully consider the evidence as it unfolds and I thank you for your kind attention this morning. Thank you.

THE COURT: Mr. Brodsky?

MR. BRODSKY: My Lord, as you indicated to the jury, it's appropriate for the defence to make admissions in order to save the proof of those things that are admitted. And it is at this time that I would like to advise the court and members of the jury that we have some admissions to make.

The first is we agree that Sydney Teerhuis-Moar, the accused in the prisoner's dock, is the killer. Crown need not spend time proving that. We admit that.

Insofar as the dismemberment of the body is concerned, as my learned friend described it, we are not disputing at all the dismemberment. We are not disputing the fact that it was dismembered in the fashion to be described by Constable McLean or Dr. Littman who did the autopsy or anyone else, so that I'm hoping that the agreement that the body was dismembered in precisely the fashion that my learned friend wishes to put to the jury will save us from having to have this proved over and over again or proved by photographs. I make the admission as clearly as I can on the record.

Your Lordship indicated that the issues in the case are cause of death; we agree to that. My learned friend knows and I make the admission for the record again that the accused caused the death—he is the killer.

Two, Your Lordship indicated that the second point was whether or not the death was caused unlawfully. We agree that the death was caused unlawfully.

The third point was that Your Lordship put to the jury that the Crown had to prove beyond a reasonable doubt the state of mind of the accused at the time of the death of Mr. Teerhuis. We agree that that is the primary issue for the Crown to prove in this case, his state of mind. And when I say, so there's no misunderstanding here, that the accused agrees that the body was dismembered in precisely the fashion the Crown is alleging, we are not agreeing that he knew how that took place. We are agreeing to that fact. The how he came to know remains an issue in dispute and to be proved beyond a reasonable doubt. That is, as Your Lordship put, the state of the mind of the accused at the time of the death is a factor to be proved beyond a reasonable doubt by the Crown, and we say that that is a matter in issue.

THE COURT: All right. Thank you very much, Mr. Brodsky. All the exhibits were listed, 83 in total, which included: One vial of blood taken from Robin Greene; a blood swab from toe of Sidney Teerhuis; a blood swab from the head of Sidney Teerhuis; a plastic knife sleeve with bloodstains; a sharpening stone; 3 disposable Fuji cameras; an unwrapped Durex condom; a yellow blanket with bloodstains; a blood-soaked pillow case; a portion of the blood soaked mattress that had been cut out and analyzed; various pairs of underwear, many with bloodstains; various beer bottles; a Seagram's Five Star Whisky bottle, a blue-striped dress shirt found stuffed into the bathroom vent; a black-handled butcher knife from underneath the sink with bloodstains; a paring knife found on the medicine cabinet; a letter from Sidney to American publisher Tom Pomplum dated September 7, 2004; letters from Sidney to journalist Dan Zupansky dated April 13, October 6, November 27 and December 10, 2004; January 3, January 12, January 31 and February 7, 2005 and 2 undated letters, 'Galatians 5:19' and 'The Clowns' (which referred to cannibalism); 3 letters from Dan Zupansky to Sidney dated September 6, September 16, 2004 and February 14, 2005 and 2 Appearance Releases from Bright Eyes and Ears Film Inc.; a gold necklace and bracelet found on the desk; a copy of Profits of Criminal Notoriety Act; a booklet with 110 photographs; Robin Greene's identification and toiletries found under the bathtub; a piece of biological tissue found underneath the tub, near the drain and another piece of biological material from the tub drain itself and a crumpled Greyhound bus ticket in Robin Greene's name dated June 30, 2003.

THE COURT: Do you want to call your first witness, Ms. Leinburd?

MS. LEINBURD: Yes, Constable McLean, please. And I wonder if the booklets that have been marked as Exhibit Number 82 could be distributed to the jury, please.

THE CLERK: Constable Chris McLean, courtroom 117.

MR. BRODSKY: With respect, My Lord, I'm very concerned about the effect the photographs, if they're just distributed to the jury without a word of caution by you; I mean, I made the agreement. I'm concerned that they are very graphic. I wonder if Your Lordship would either caution the jury, or maybe indicate that we might have a recess after they look at them, or...

THE COURT: Well, I'm going to suggest, actually, we have our-- maybe I'm going to excuse the jury just for a moment. I'll hear your comments a little bit further, Mr. Brodsky, and then we can take our morning break and we'll start with the first witness.

(JURY OUT AT 11:06 A.M.)

THE COURT: Why don't you be a little bit more clear, Mr. Brodsky, what it is...

MR. BRODSKY: Yes.

154

THE COURT: ...you'd like me to do? I thought we had turned the page on this issue, not in the sense that we have minimized it. You're not particularly happy with the ruling, I appreciate that, but my ruling is my ruling.

MR. BRODSKY: I'm not challenging your ruling, but...

THE COURT: I know that.

MR. BRODSKY: As I indicated when I was trying to keep the when I was concerned about the effect the photographs would have, I still am concerned about the effect the photographs will have. My suggestion is that when they look at the photographs, because I don't think they're going to be paying attention to any evidence that comes out soon after that, their minds will be so fixed on those photographs, that it may be not inappropriate for you to ask them if they need a time-out at that point.

THE COURT: So is your concern about potential prejudice or just potential discomfort and distraction, just so I'm clear?

MR. BRODSKY: I'm not arguing, obviously I already argued the potential prejudice.

MS. LEINBURD: They are the photos that have, in fact, been ruled admissible. I see Mr. Brodsky's interjection at this point as nothing more than a tactical move. I mean, clearly the jury will, in fact, be forewarned about the photographs as we go through them and I don't believe that it was necessary for Mr. Brodsky to take the position that he did, in fact take. If something does happen in the jury box, clearly Your Lordship will address that issue if and when it occurs, and if Your Lordship sees that a recess is, in fact, necessary, then I'm sure that Your Honour will call one.

THE COURT: And I think Ms. Leinburd is right, if I see or if you see or if anybody sees any witness reacting in a way that obviously ought to concern us, either with respect to their being unsettled to the point where they're not able to pay attention or, as importantly, that they're actually on the verge of perhaps being ill or something, I'll be advised and you can make your intervention and Ms. Leinburd will do the same. But at this point, beyond that, I don't want to say much more. I warned the panel, Ms. Leinburd warned the jury this morning and you indirectly did that just now. Anything more, I think, is almost going to be a self-fulfilling prophecy. So why don't we take 10 minutes, no more than that? Thanks.

THE CLERK: Order, all rise. Court's in recess.

(BRIEF RECESS)

THE CLERK: Court is re-opened, please be seated. Are you ready for the jury?

THE COURT: Yes, please. Thank you.

(JURY IN AT 11:24 A.M.)

THE CLERK: My Lord, all 12 jurors are present.

THE COURT: Thank you. Ms. Leinburd?

MS. LEINBURD: Thank you. Your Lordship, this is Constable Chris McLean. I'd ask that he be sworn, please.

THE CLERK: State and spell your full name for the record.

155

THE WITNESS: Constable Chris, c-h-r-i-s, McLean, m-c-l-e-a-n.
THE CLERK: Thank you.
Direct examination by MS. LEINBURD:
Sir, I understand that you're a member of the City of Winnipeg police department; is that correct?
A Yes, that's correct.
Q And how long have you been a police officer, sir?
A Seventeen years.
Q I understand that you are now assigned to the identification office of the Winnipeg Police; is that correct?
A Yes, that's correct.
Q And how long have you been an identification officer, sir?
A Eight and a half years.
Q On July the 2nd of 2003, I understand that you and your brother officers, Constable Timchuk and Constable Weiss, now retired, became involved in this particular murder investigation; is that correct?
A Yes, that's correct.
Q And I understand that you and your fellow officers attended to the Royal Albert Hotel; is that correct?
A Yes.
Q And specifically, you were directed to Suite 309; is that correct?
A Yes.
Q Your function, as I understand it, was to photograph the scene?
A My function was exhibits. Basically what happens is that for major crime scenes like homicides, a team of three officers go out, in the capacity of the identification unit and for forensic evidence gathering. A team of three officers goes out, you have usually one sergeant who acts as the scene supervisor and two constables that act, one does exhibits and the other one does scene description and photography. So in this specific incident, Sergeant Weiss was the scene supervisor, I was in charge of exhibits, and Constable Timchuk was in charge of photography and scene description. And in Winnipeg in the ident unit, we are fingerprint experts so we do the fingerprint examinations ourselves, and that involves the different examinations for fingerprints. As well, we do footwear, we do tire tracks and we do photography. But when it comes to DNA, we seize the exhibit, package it properly, and then forward it to the RCMP crime lab, where they have people that work in their DNA lab that will do the actual examination for DNA.
Q Now, I understand as well that this morning in your testimony you're going to be covering the work that you did as well as the work done by Constable Weiss and Sergeant Timchuk; is that correct?
A Yes.
Q Now, you arrived at the scene at 309-48 Albert Street at approximately 11:07 a.m. on July the 2nd of 2003; is that correct?
A Yes
Q And prior to going further into the suite, am I correct that during the course of your exhibit seizing and photography, that Joanne Abbott from the pathologist's office attended; is that correct?
A Yes.
Q And pronounced the death of Robin Greene; is that correct?
A Yes.
Q He was identified further on in the day, and subsequent to Joanne Abbott's attendance, Dr. Littman, the pathologist in this case,

156

and Dr. Balachandra also attended at approximately 1:45 and they also viewed the deceased's body. And as I understand it, in that pile of items found behind the chair near the radiator was Exhibit 20, which is the Greyhound ticket that Robin Greene had purchased on June the 30th of '03. It was crumpled up and found by you?

A Yes

Q And if one proceeds to photograph number 18. That is the jewelry that was reported stolen from the set of Shall We Dance, a film that was being filmed in Winnipeg at the time of this particular murder. It's alleged to have belonged to Susan Sarandon; that is correct?

A Yes.

Q And it was reported stolen on July the 1st of 2003; is that correct?

A Yes.

Q And that was found right on the top of the desk, upon your entrance into the hotel suite; is that correct, sir?

A Yes. If the jury looks at photograph 16, the lower right-hand corner, you can just see the necklace on top of the desk. That's where it was found.

Q Photographs 19 and 20--and we're going to be dealing with more graphic photographs from this point onward.

Luminal is a chemical substance that will assist the police in a presumptive test. It doesn't conclusively prove it's blood, but it's a presumptive test that will help us visualize what may not be immediately apparent. We use it to try and find blood if we think there's been a clean-up, we also use it to try to visualize faint blood, and what it does is, it's a chemical substance, you spray it on a surface, and if--the room has to be dark, but there's a chemical luminescence reaction so the surface will glow like a whitish-green and then we will photograph that and use that as part of our observations.

Q And one sees a very dark stain of blood adjacent to the baseboard; is that correct?

A Yes, just in the carpet.

Q And above it appear to be blood drops and blood dropping onto the carpet; is that correct?

A Yes. It's hard to see in photograph 22, but the area we circled "A" looked like a big "Z" wipe. It was very faint. It was obvious to us that it was blood and it was very faint on the wall.

Q So a wipe mark through the blood?

A Well, it was a wipe, it was a wipe of blood that was in the shape of a 'Z' roughly.

Q Continuing on, then, sir, with photograph number 21, that is the bed that the jury has seen depicted in the previous photographs, but the bedding, the linen, has been taken off so we're left with just the mattress *per se*.

A Yes.

Q And it appears to be blood-soaked; is that correct, sir?

A Yes.

Q And those are slices or cuts into the mattress cover itself.

A Yes.

MS. LEINBURD: Thank you. I'm wondering if this might not be an appropriate time at which to recess. It's now 12:15, and prior to getting into the remaining photographs, this might be an opportune time to take the noon hour break.

THE COURT: Mr. Brodsky?

MR. BRODSKY: Whatever.

THE CLERK: Order, all rise. This court's in recess.

(LUNCHEON RECESS)

THE CLERK: Court is reopened, please be seated.

(JURY IN AT 2:08 P.M.)

THE CLERK: My Lord, all 12 jurors are present.

THE COURT: Good afternoon. Ms. Leinburd?

MS. LEINBURD: Thank you.

Chris McLean, previously sworn.

Direct examination continued by MS. LEINBURD:

Q And the next photograph, photograph number 32, shows a more focused view of that particular entryway into the bathroom and there appears to be blood on the left-hand portion of the door frame; is that correct, sir?

A Then there was blood on the east wall behind the tub. There was also blood on the east bathroom wall. There was blood near the tub taps. Again, a different area of the east bathroom wall. We had the south edge of the bathtub; we had the bathroom floor just south of the radiator. You'll see the radiator in some pictures coming up. One area of the bathroom floor, we had the southwest bathtub leg, we had the side of the bathtub, the floor under the tub, the west bathroom wall, north bathroom wall, the top of the toilet lid, the toilet bowl base, another area of the north bathroom wall, two different areas of the east bathroom wall, and then two other areas in picture 33, in the lower right corner, there's a wall that we refer to as a diagonal wall because directly we didn't know how to refer to it, but there was blood swabs off that wall as well.

Q Proceeding to turn the page to photograph number 35, that is a picture of the toilet area and there appears to be a blue cloth stuffed into a vent; is that correct, sir?

A Yes.

Q Can you comment on that? That's Exhibit 46, which is a dress shirt.

A Yes. Photograph 35, if you look upper right centre of the frame, there's a vent up there and you can just see it sort of looks like a blue rag. That's a blue button-down shirt and it was stuffed into an air vent there.

Q You had indicated it was a very hot day.

A It was very, very hot in that building. We laid a thermometer out that day and I think we measured; it was 38 or 39 degrees. It was really hot in that hotel. I surmised at the time that that shirt had been stuffed in the air vent as some form of effort to prevent odor from spreading.

Q Is that the knife you found under the sink, sir?

A Yes, that's the same knife that's pictured on the floor under the sink, photograph 38. Well, the knife, this butcher knife has approximately a 12-inch long blade. It's about four inches wide at the widest part. The handle itself is about five inches. And the paring knife has about a four-inch blade. The width of the blade

158

itself is about three-quarters of an inch and the handle is about four to five inches.

Q Now, if we might return to photographs 52 and 53, sir, 53 appears to be a sharpening stone; is that correct?

A Yes.

Q And what are sharpening stones used for, sir?

A Sharpening stones are used to sharpen knives.

Q And this was found in a dresser drawer, as I understand it, as well, Exhibit 8?

A Yes.

Q The sharpening stone. And the cloth in which it was wrapped, that is Exhibit 6, and Exhibit 8, the sharpening stone.

A Yes. So this is Exhibit 8, the sharpening stone. This is the cloth that the stone was wrapped in. Photograph 52 depicts the condition that I found the cloth and the sharpening stone in the dresser. The stone was wrapped in the cloth, just like you see in photograph 52.

Q Thank you, sir. If we might now proceed to the photographs of the deceased's body, and they're depicted in photographs 39 through to 42. Is that the condition in which you found the body in the bathtub, sir? Yes, we were at the point where you had just discovered Robin Greene's body in the bathtub. Did you find any internal organs?

A No. There was, there was absolutely--his entire torso was emptied out.

Q And how many pieces was the body chopped into?

A Eight. You can see in photograph 42 the body had been cut into the head; the torso up to his elbows; his legs including pelvis and top of his legs, quadriceps type area; his feet and calves both, from both legs; and arms from the elbow to his hands. As well, his penis and testicles had been removed. So that makes eight pieces, and they were in the bathtub.

Q And they were stacked as they are depicted in these photographs?

A Yes.

Q Now, in terms of the organs, we spoke of those a moment ago. They were not found. Did you do a search of the toilet itself?

A Yes. We used a toilet snake. We were trying to--because one of our theories was that different body parts had been flushed, perhaps cut up to some small sizes and flushed. So we used a toilet snake and plumbed the entire toilet and didn't find anything.

Q Now, I understand that a search was done of the immediate area surrounding the hotel and the hotel itself, and you were, in fact, looking for organs. Were any discovered?

A No.

Q You searched the dumpsters outside the hotel as well. Were there any organs discovered in the dumpsters outside of the hotel?

A No.

Q In examining the body, sir, can you comment on whether or not there was very much blood?

A There was very little blood. Maybe the pathologist wants to speak to this, but basically, without getting into there was hardly any blood.

Q Photograph number 42, almost a yellow circular portion. What is that, sir?

A The victim's right nipple had been cut off.

Q In terms of the eyes of the deceased, did you make any notes about the right eye of the deceased?

A Both of the victim's eyes had been cut. One eye had been removed and the other eye had been punctured and deflated.

Q I'm going to ask you, if I could, for a moment, to look at photograph number 107, towards the latter part of the booklet. There appears to be a hand and a forearm, sir; is that correct?

A Yes.

Q And the forearm seems to be dissected; am I correct?

A Yes.

Q And is that the state in which you found it in that bathtub?

A Yes.

Q There appears to be a white pair of underwear in the bathtub as well. Was that found under the body?

A Yes.

Q And if one looks at photograph number 45, there appears to be some biological matter that is caught in the drain, is that correct, sir?

A Yes.

Q Exhibit 32, what was it, sir?

A A piece of biological matter that we surmised to have come off the victim.

Q Was there any other biological matter found?

A Yes, there was another chunk of biological matter found under the bathtub, on the floor.

MS. LEINBURD: Perhaps we could have a recess.

THE COURT: Could we have a break?

(JURY OUT AT 2:39 P.M.)

(BRIEF RECESS)

THE CLERK: Court is re-opened, you may be seated.

(JURY IN AT 2:54 P.M.)

THE CLERK: My Lord, all 12 jurors are present.

THE COURT: Okay, Ms. Leinburd.

MS. LEINBURD: Thank you.

By MS. LEINBURD:

Q Now, proceeding to the photographs. And they're going to be numbered as photographs 70 through 89. There were three disposable cameras found in the accused's room. They were found inside the top drawer; is that correct?

A Yes.

Q In referring to photograph number 77, the deceased appears to be wearing a pair of Sportsman navy blue shorts; is that correct? And these were pictures that were in the disposable cameras that were found in the accused's room.

A Yes. Appear to be underwear hanging, displayed on doorknobs, displayed on dresser drawers and displayed on the bed, on the floor, on the tables. And number 85 is an interesting photo. It appears to be a pair of white underwear on a man's head, the man is wearing glasses and he has black hair.

160

Q I'm now going to ask you to reference two letters. They are Exhibit 64 and Exhibit 68. Each of them are letters from Mr. Teerhuis to Mr. Zupansky. Begin with Exhibit 68, sir. It's a letter from the accused, Sydney Teerhuis-Moar to Dan Zupansky dated February 7th of 2005, with a diagram attached to that particular letter; is that fair to say?

A Yes.

Q I want you to examine that diagram, sir. What did it appear to be a diagram of?

A This appears to be a diagram of the suite and bathroom in Suite 309.

Q And is this an accurate depiction of Suite 309, the bathroom and the bedroom, sir?

A Yes.

Q Does it actually accurately position the bed, the dresser, the tables, the chairs, the bathrooms, the toilet and the bathtub?

A Yes. There's a radiator drawn in here as well.

Q Now if you might reference Exhibit Number 64, sir. Again that's a letter from the accused, Teerhuis-Moar to Mr. Zupansky. There appear to be a set of diagrams; is that correct?

A Yes.

Q Now, in terms of those diagrams, if you might reference diagram B for the jury, please?

A Diagram B, yes.

Q That depicts a body with no lower arms below the elbow and no legs beneath the knees; is that correct?

A Yes.

Q Does that accurately depict the deceased's body as you saw it?

A A portion of it, yes.

Q Yes. And then continuing on to the next diagram, if one looks at diagram number D, reference that for the jury, that is the bottom portion of the body dismembered; is that correct?

A Yes.

Q As was the deceased, Robin Greene.

A Yes.

Q Proceeding to diagram G, it depicts a penis and testicles, is that correct, pubic area; is that correct?

A Yes.

Q And is that similar to the mutilated body of the deceased, Robin Greene, sir?

A Yes.

Q Proceeding to diagram F, sir, reference that for the jury. It appears to be a torso sliced down the middle; is that correct?

A Yes.

Q With the depiction of a leg and a foot, an arm and a hand, is that correct?

A Yes.

Q That was similar to the way in which the deceased's body was found, that is, absent the leg and foot, hand and arm detached?

A Yes.

Q Now, I'm going to direct you, if I could for a moment, to diagram B, the decapitated torso.

A Yes.

Q There appears to be a drawing, if you might show it to the jury, of a large knife, a small knife, and a square that resembles a sharpening stone.

A Yes.

Q They're Exhibits 34, 45, and 8. Do those accurately depict those exhibits, in your view, sir?

A Yes.

MS. LEINBURD: Thank you, sir. Those are all my questions.

THE COURT: Mr. Brodsky?

Cross-examination by MR. BRODSKY:

Q Realistically speaking, would it be fair to say that the diagrams not only depict the body as you saw it, they depict the photographs that you told us about and the jury has, as distributed to the jury. Would that not be fair, that what you saw, the body's condition is shown in the photographs? Would that be fair?

A How do you mean? Do you mean that my photographs resemble his diagrams and vice versa?

Q Yes.

A Yes.

Q And the diagrams were sent or dated when?

A Diagrams, just a moment. I don't know when they're dated. 2005. Would be some time in 2005? It just says the last letter of '04, December 10th.

Q December 10th, '04. All right. Would it be fair--so you understand where I'm headed with this, would it be fair to say that the photographs had already been prepared by that December date of '04?

A Had they already been disclosed to the Crown and defence?

Q Yeah.

A Yes, they would have been, yeah.

Q And the defense would have had the opportunity of disclosing them to the client, Mr. Teerhuis?

A If the defense did, I don't know that.

Q But that would be his duty, wouldn't it?

A It would be normal for the defense to do that, yeah.

Q So you don't know whether or not the diagrams that you see are diagrams of what's portrayed in the photographs or memory of an incident. You can't say one or the other.

A I can't say for sure, no.

Q Now, you made a search for the internal organs in this case. Who, who was actually in charge of checking for the internal organs?

A It was Sergeant Frank Weiss. And on that day, Sergeant Weiss and Craig Boan also searched the area. The following day Sergeant Weiss and another ident Constable Russell, searched the entire, it's blocks. The area we're talking about is blocks. They didn't just search a dumpster at the back or a garbage can or only the garbage can in the hotel. They searched whole blocks, every garbage can and dumpster within blocks. Was that area searched? Yes. Were organs found? No.

Q So you don't know how far the organs were taken. If they were not in the Suite 309, you don't know how far away they went?

A No. We searched an area that included blocks around the Royal Albert. If they were taken beyond that area, they could have been, we never found the organs. Now, the question is where do you stop? It's physically impossible for us to check every dumpster and sewer and everything in the whole City of Winnipeg. But within, you know, blocks, we did that, and our search was negative.

Q Did you look for bloody, bloody footprints; too, I take it, outside the Royal Albert Hotel?

A No, there was no bloody footprints observed outside the Royal Albert.

Q Would it be fair to say that you cannot prove or disprove that Mr. Teerhuis awoke to a horrible scene and tried to cover it up? That is, wash away blood?

A Well...

MS. LEINBURD: Objection. He can't speak to what Mr. Teerhuis can or can't do.

THE COURT: Mr. Brodsky, that question's almost self-evident. I mean this witness described himself as being the witness, who arrived on the scene, took pictures, took certain swabs and took other samples. He's not in a position to answer that.

Q Would it be fair to say that when you got to the scene, you saw that there was a good amount of blood on the floor, on the bed, on the mattress, on the wall, beside the bed, dripping down as seen in photograph 16. There's still a lot of blood quite visible to you.

A Yes.

Q Insofar as photograph 36 is concerned, that pipe that's on the ceiling over the, the dresser, and appears to be again in 37, that's a fire...

A It's for the sprinkler system in the hotel room. It's like a water pipe that the sprinkler systems in the hotel room come off of.

Q And I'd be correct, would I, in suggesting to you that it wouldn't take much weight before it came crashing down. That be fair?

A I wouldn't expect it to be that strong. I don't know how much weight it would take, but it's...

Q I want to be very specific here. I want to ensure that there is nothing that would allow a body the size of the victim here to be suspended over the bathtub, including that sprinkler system. Nothing was there to allow that to happen; would that be fair?

A I can't say conclusively because...

Q Well, you...

A I didn't hang on it, but again it would be my guess. My guess would be that I don't know. A body would be pretty heavy and that pipe wouldn't last that long, but I don't know that for sure.

Q Well, did anybody do any check to confirm what appears to be your best guess that you couldn't hang a body from there without it come crashing down? And so again, and I know I'm being repetitious but I just want to make sure you understand my suggestion. You cannot hang a body or suspend a body from anything in that bathroom, from the ceiling. There's nothing there that will allow the body to be hung or suspended, including that bar that's in photographs 36 and 37.

A I know you...

Q That's your best guess, is that?

A I know what you want me to say and all I can tell us is what I've already guessed. I didn't test it, I didn't hang myself from it, to see what kind of weight it would support, so I don't know for sure. To my knowledge, no one has checked that. However, it's possible that Constable Timchuk may have. If she did, I never talked to her about it. I don't know, but my guess would be that a body's not going to hang long from that pipe, but I can't conclusively give you your answer yes, no. I don't know for sure.

Q The top of the pine dresser that you see in photograph 13 and photograph 12, would it be fair to say that there was nothing that

163

showed that the torso of the deceased had ever been placed on that dresser.

A Yes, there's no, there's no blood on the top of that pine dresser.

Q And there was, in fact, dust and those articles that we see displayed there now, to show that it doesn't seem to have had anything disturb those items.

A I don't believe there was dust, but there's nothing, you know, those items looked like they had been there, you know, and they were not bloodstained or anything like that.

MR. BRODSKY: Those are the questions I have, My Lord.

THE COURT: Thank you, Mr. Brodsky. Ms. Leinburd, any re-examination?

MS. LEINBURD: No, thank you.

THE COURT: All right. Thank you very much, Officer. Appreciate your help.

(WITNESS EXCUSED)

THE COURT: Ms. Leinburd?

MS. LEINBURD: That completes the evidence for today.

THE COURT: Okay, ladies and gentlemen. It was the first day for you, so maybe it's a good opportunity for you to go home and rest, and come back fresh tomorrow morning. Thank you very much.

(JURY OUT AT 4:04 P.M.)

THE CLERK: Order, all rise. This court is adjourned till 10:00 a.m. tomorrow.

16

The Trial - Day 2

DECEMBER 2/08

A HEADLINE THIS MORNING APPEARED FRONT-PAGE IN THE WINNIPEG Free Press and in the National Post: "*Accused in mutilation murder says he can't recall killing*" by Mike McIntyre. The article stated that Sidney did not deny killing and dismembering Robin Greene. He wanted a jury to find him not guilty of second-degree murder because he doesn't have any memory of the killing that made "headlines around the world because of the gruesome details—and a strange link to a Hollywood movie that was shooting in the city at the time."

It went on to tell of Brodsky's address to jurors stating that the sole issue in the trial is whether his client "had the intent to kill."

The article quoted Sheila Leinburd's address, "This is a tragic story of the brutal killing of a 38-year old man." She also warned the jury about the graphic evidence they were going to see and hear during the three-week long trial.

The story reiterated the basic facts as they had already been reported but focused very much on the more lurid and gory details of the murder itself.

The article quoted heavily from Constable Chris McLean throughout his testimony recalling seeing the dismembered body and later searching toilets, sewers and garbage bins looking for the missing organs.

Members of Greene's family broke down and left the courtroom in tears as McLean gave his evidence.

The Free Press told of Winnipeg Police recovering the gold necklace, which the article stated had been stolen days earlier from the set of *Shall We Dance* when in fact it had been stolen only the day before it was found at the Royal Albert.

The Free press went on to mention that it was Sarandon's jewelry and that Jennifer Lopez, Richard Gere and Sarandon were starring in the movie. They claimed that Sidney was not accused of stealing the jewelry and details regarding how and why it was in the room were not provided.

The article mentioned the three disposable cameras and the nude photos of Robin Greene that were taken a while before his death. It also told of Sidney appearing at the Remand Centre to direct police to the body of Robin Greene announcing, "I came to turn myself in because I killed someone."

The article ended with Brodsky's statement that his client may have "awoken to a horrendous scene" and then tried to cover it up to some extent.

Dean Pritchard and the Winnipeg Sun did not mention the jewelry whatsoever in their article about the previous day's trial. They said, "Sitting in the prisoner's box dressed in a natty black blazer and sporting a shaved head and neatly trimmed moustache, Teerhuis-Moar appeared bored and uninterested for much of the day's testimony." Jurors heard graphic and disturbing details of Greene's killing, prompting one family member to break down in uncontrolled sobs.

*　*　*　*　*

R.C.M.P SERGEANT GEOFFREY ELLIS WAS THE FIRST WITNESS TO TESTIFY ON December 2nd. He was with the R.C.M.P. for 19 years and the last nine years a forensic identification specialist, and since 2005 a bloodstain pattern analyst.

In this case he had done an analysis based on reviewing crime scene photographs. He had told the court that blood patterns are divided into several categories with three main categories being passive, projected and transfer bloodstains.

Sheila Leinburd almost from the start began to utilize drawings made by Sidney to question Sgt. Ellis.

Q I'm going to direct your attention to diagram 1. I gather you've seen that diagram previously?
A I have.
Q And in terms of that diagram, it depicts an individual lying on the bed, another individual stabbing him with a knife.
A Yes.
Q Now, thank you, sir. In terms of that particular diagram, you used the word 'bloodletting'. What does that mean, sir?
A Any instance where blood is released from the body through an action.
Q And given the blood staining that you found on the bed, and I'm going to ask you to refer to the different type of blood staining momentarily, but given the blood staining and the blood pattern that you describe on the bed, coupled with the diagram that you've examined, are the actions on that diagram consistent with the blood patterning that is exhibited in photographs 19 and 20?
A In the diagram, it shows a person lying on a bed. The position of the head on the bed would be similar to where it would be in this drawing. He's also drawn it looks like blood coming out from the head. That is consistent with what a pool stain is, a blood source bleeding on or above the surface.
Q Now, in terms of the scenario that's depicted in the diagram that the accused drew and is before the jury as Exhibit 64, is it consistent with those actions, sir, that is, stabbing?
A That would be one possibility for some of those stains, yes. What he's drawn here would be considered cast-off stains.
Q Now, if we might proceed to the next grouping of photographs, and those are the photographs of the door jamb and the door itself on the inside of the bathroom and on the outside of the bathroom

door. So those would be photographs 32, 31, in particular. So if, for example, sir, there was a blood source such as a bloody stabbed body that was being dragged into the bathroom, if, in fact, that body came into contact with the door frame, that would be an impact source; is that correct?

A That would be a transfer stain. The transfer stains on the door frame are consistent with any bloodstained object, and I can't exclude that it could be a bloody body coming into contact with the door frame so there's actual direct contact. Those projected stains near the floor are not from direct contact with the blood source; it's from there been force applied to a blood source, causing those stains to take flight and they were moving out into the bedroom.

Q So if, for example, the blood source or the bloody body were dropped, would that cause that kind of pattern?

A Any situation where you'd have a blood source and a force applied to it, so that could be one scenario that could have created those.

Q If one examines Exhibit 68, sir, which is again a diagram drawn by the accused, it depicts Room 309, the bathtub, the toilet. There's a picture of a body without a head lying on the floor.

A Yes.

Q So if, in fact, a source such as a knife had been taken to the bloody body, which is the blood source, and it had been decapitated in that particular area, would you expect projected stains to appear?

A These stains had a north to south directionality, which means they were travelling, according to the diagram, away from the centre of the bathroom, and so that's consistent with their origin being somewhere in the bathroom.

Q So if, for example--and you have seen the placing of the body in the bathtub?

A Yes.

Q If a body were, in fact, dismembered and chopped up in the bathtub, would you expect that type of staining on that wall?

A That's consistent with those actions, yes.

SHEILA LEINBURD CONTINUED TO ELICIT TESTIMONY FROM SGT. ELLIS TO SUPPORT her claims that what Sidney had said in his letters and made drawings regarding, was by and large accurate.

It was then Greg Brodsky's turn to attempt to make some salient points while cross-examining the officer to counter what Sidney had written and drawn diagrams regarding.

Regarding the conclusions he was asked to make during his cross-examination by Brodsky he responded: "In this case, bloodstain pattern analysis doesn't have enough information to provide all the answers to the who, what, when, where, and why of this case."

Q Not just the bloodstain pattern analyst, but also someone looking at the photographs would have difficulty in determining, in reconstructing what happened.

A I agree. And part of our job, we're not reconstructionists. We don't profess to be able to come to a scene and reconstruct the scene, so I agree.

Q For instance, in photograph 13, there's a dresser there with a clock on it and a photograph, what appears to be a photograph. Were you provided with a photograph of the top of that dresser?
A I was not provided any photographs that would show me the top of that dresser in detail.
Q So you're not able to say, wait a minute let me back up. There's absolutely nothing to suggest that the torso was ever placed on that dresser.
A I have no information to base that on because I was not provided a photograph where I could even comment on that. So either way, I can't say, without looking at a good photograph of the top of that dresser, what or what did not happen.
Q But again, going back to your earlier testimony, you would have expected that had there been even the suggestion of bloodletting on the top of that dresser, that you would have been provided with a photograph of it or a description of it and asked to comment on it insofar as your expertise is concerned?
A It's my assumption going into this case, as with all photographs, examinations I do from photographs, that I'm provided with photographs of what they've observed where the bloodstain evidence is. So based on if they did not provide me a photograph, I assume that they did not observe any bloodstains on top of that dresser.
Q Now let's look at the other diagram. Did you find insofar as the draining of the blood, did you find any evidence of blood on the floor in the bathroom, showing a suspended body being drained of blood?
A No, I did not.
Q Did you find anything, anything whatsoever, to verify or support or give corroboration to the fact that there was a, quote, first attempt at draining Greene's blood by hanging? I'm again, My Lord, referring to Exhibit 64, and it says here, Diagram 2.
A No.
Q Did you find anything, anything whatsoever to support that, in fact, that depiction is a depiction of an actual event that occurred?
A No, I did not see anything in the photographs that would lend me to come to that conclusion, that any of those stains in the bathroom originated from specifically a body being hung upside-down and drained in the bathtub.
Q Did you find anything to show that the body was taken into the bathroom and the blood drained in the bathroom? This photograph obviously shows...
A Can I see that photograph, please?
Q Sure. This diagram shows, diagram 2 of exhibit shows a body, a torso being...
A The same photograph we just...
Q The same diagram, not a photograph.
A Sorry, the same diagram. No, I did not see anything that would cause me to come to any sort of opinion that this was what took place in the bathroom.
Q In fact, there's no head on that torso.
A On this drawing, yes, there is no head.
Q So that would indicate to you, I take it, that you should find

168

some evidence of draining blood because that's certainly a heck of a wound, a dramatic wound, to have no head.

A Again, I don't deal in "should have found something." I did not see anything that would lend me to come to a conclusion that there was a body hung upside-down in the tub.

Q And this shows blood draining out of the body.

A It shows a representation of blood draining out of the body.

Q Yeah. Did you find, and you would expect, I take it, that if somebody had have suspended a body in the fashion that's in this diagram 2, that would take some effort. The body would have to be moved around and there would be blood on the floor and all on the walls and on the toilet and in the small, enclosed space called the bathroom?

A Again, I try to not expect anything when I either go to the scene or look at the photographs. But from that representation--I have no experience in moving decapitated bodies around, but I would think it would probably take some effort to accomplish that.

Q And that is by "some effort," you mean the body would have to move here and there?

A Well, it's obviously, in the diagram, it's strung up, so I don't know what weight we're talking about, but probably enough that it would cause some effort to exert to create that situation.

Q What I'm suggesting is that this is fictional. It's not a representation of a true event, it's a imagined event, and that had it not been fictional, you'd have found some blood or blood splatter or pooling or whatever to support some part of the accuracy of that diagram 2 being real, a real event.

A I really am not comfortable commenting on a cartoon that there is no indication either way that I observed that that event took place or didn't take place. So I can't really comment either way.

MR. BRODSKY: With Your Lordship's permission. This is going to be diagram A, and for the jury's benefit, they will have it in the jury room so they can take their time looking at it, if they want to, at a later time.

Q Now, that shows blood on the floor, on the floor.

A Are we diagram A?

Q Yes.

A Yes, a representation of blood that he's drawn.

Q Did you find any place from any photograph, blood on the floor showing that this is a depiction of a real event as opposed to an imagined, fictitious event?

A If I'm reading his interpretation correctly, what I think he's trying to draw is a pool stain where the head was, and in my report I commented on two pool stains, one on the bed and then one that overflowed onto a floor. That's all I can comment on the pool stains. I did not find any information that would support what I'm viewing in that photograph.

Q But when looking at this, not photograph, diagram.

A Diagram, sorry.

Q When you're looking at this diagram, it doesn't show a bed, doesn't show the edge of a bed. It shows what clearly looks like a floor; would that be right?

A Well, again, you know, I'm looking at a cartoon and you're asking me if it shows clearly something. I think it's kind of ambiguous on exactly where that takes place. Again, there's nothing from what I observed anywhere in that residence that I could say that the event that's depicted in this cartoon actually happened.

Q So in diagram C of the same exhibit, that shows a head on the floor in the bathroom beside the tub. We don't have to guess whether it's the floor, it is the floor.

A That's what he's drawn, yes.

Q All right. And it shows a large amount of blood or some pool of blood under the head.

A That's correct.

Q You didn't find, in any photograph, any support to show that this is a depiction, this diagram C, of an event that actually happened.

A Specifically in the bathroom, there were no pool stains that I observed in the photographs, in the bathroom.

Q Or any sign of a wiping, I think you called it a wipe stain or transfer stain or anything to show that the head was in the place where it's shown in diagram C of this exhibit. You never saw any support to show that this was a real, as opposed to an imagined, event.

A That's correct. I didn't see anything in the photographs I looked at that could either support or disprove that event that is drawn in that cartoon.

Q Well, disproof is the fact that you didn't find the blood that's shown in the diagram.

A But the lack of blood does not necessarily mean it wasn't there.

Q Well, did you find any wipe stain?

A I found diluted stains throughout the bathroom, so that's why I'm not commenting on, there was no pool stain there, but I didn't comment on what could have--the absence of the blood, why there was an absence of blood.

Q Did you find, next to the tub, a pool stain as depicted in diagram C from this Exhibit 64?

A No, I did not.

Q But that's what it shows in the diagram.

A In diagram C, it shows...

Q Yes.

A He's drawn a decapitated head with dark stains under it, which I assume is supposed to be blood coming out of the head, yes.

Q By the leg of the tub?

A That's correct.

Q The head of the tub. Or at the end of the tub.

A At one end of the tub, yes.

Q Did you find any evidence whatsoever that the decapitation took place in the bathroom?

A No, I...

Q Any support for the decapitation having taken place in the bathroom?

A No, I did not.

Q But you were advised that he wrote in Exhibit 64 that the decapitation took place in the bathroom.

A I've seen some of the letters. Specifically that one, I don't know if I read that one specifically.

Q That's the one attached to the diagram. The order of events are...

MR. BRODSKY: And I'm looking at the back of Exhibit 64, My Lord, at a page that's entitled or circled '8'.

Q It says, order of events are killing, sex, dragging body into bathroom, sex, decapitation, sex, hanging, and then cutting off arms and legs. Do you see that?

A Um-hum.

Q Did you find any support to show that the decapitation took place in the bathroom?

A No, I did not.

Q All right. Now, we've talked about the dresser. I want to be absolutely clear that we're talking about the dresser and not the table, and I want the jury to be clear about the fact that we're talking about the dresser, which has the clock on it and the photograph and all the rest of it. He's talking about playing with the parts, the trophy on the dresser, which I take to be the body because he's talked about that body as a trophy many times. Did you find any support that the trophy, that part of the torso or part of the body ever was on top of the dresser as he says in this letter?

A I wasn't provided with a photograph of the top of the dresser, so no, I did not see any evidence because I wasn't provided with the photographs to do an analysis of that dresser.

Q When you looked at the sink that's shown in photograph 38, were you able to ascertain whether any large body parts were ever in that sink, bled into that sink?

A No, I was unable to determine anything of that nature.

Q But you know that in diagram D that he shows that a large portion of the body was...

MR. BRODSKY: And I'm referring again to the same exhibit, 64, My Lord.

Q ...Large portion of the body is in the sink.

A Yes, I see that.

MR. BRODSKY: I'm showing the jury.

Q You didn't see any draining of blood that would show that this was a representation of an actual as opposed to a fictional event, did you?

A In the photographs provided to me, I did not see anything that would support a torso in the sink.

Q Did you ever find any support insofar as diagram F is concerned, which is the major portion of the body being placed on top of the dresser? Any support?

A No, I did not.

MR. BRODSKY: With Your Lordship's permission, I'll show the jury the same exhibit number.

Q So there's an arm, a leg, and most of the body on top of the dresser in this diagram.

A It appears to be, yes.

Q You found no support whatsoever that anything had been moved on top of the dresser; would that be fair?

A I didn't have anything in terms of photographs presented to me that would support that diagram.

Q So this is fictional, is that your conclusion, fictional?

MS. LEINBURD: Objection. He can't speak to whether it's fictional.

THE COURT: Mr. Brodsky, I think on this subject, in fact, we're revisiting the dresser for a second time. I think the witness was more than clear the first time, and I don't know that we have to spend too much more time on that.

MR. BRODSKY: I have no further questions, My Lord.

THE COURT: Thank you, Mr. Brodsky. Ms. Leinburd.

MS. LEINBURD: Yes, I just have a few questions on re-direct. They will be very brief.

Re-examination by MS. LEINBURD:

Q Mr. Brodsky has spent most of his cross-examination showing diagrams to you and then suggesting that there is no support found for various diagrams; is that correct?

A Yes.

Q Because you found no support doesn't mean it didn't happen.

A I can't comment. That's why I didn't comment in my conclusions either way. There wasn't evidence, from my bloodstain analyst point of view, to support certain situations. If a hypothetical situation is presented to me, I can say if those events possibly could have created those stains because I've seen the stains, I know that, provided certain things happen, those stains will be created, but whether it was specifically this event and this event only, or event B and event only, there wasn't sufficient evidence there for me to go either way.

Q So what that means is because there is no evidence, doesn't mean that it didn't happen.

A I think the term that we use is, it's been put to me that the absence of evidence is not evidence of absence, and that sort of sums it up.

Q That's right. So Mr. Brodsky's questions that you didn't find any evidence in support, you also didn't find any evidence denying that those things happened.

MR. BRODSKY: This is not, in my respectful submission, I would ask Your Lordship to have my learned friend restrict herself to a specific thing that I said, as opposed to in general. For instance, when I was talking about the top of the dresser, it shows the diagram, a clean top to the dresser. The photographs don't show that. It doesn't show any blood. He's already testified to that. So that's what she's referring to, then I would ask that she let us know what it is when we're talking about evidence in support, absence of evidence. It shouldn't be in general.

THE COURT: All right. Let me give Ms. Leinburd one last chance maybe to...

MS. LEINBURD: I'll happily...

THE COURT: ...Rephrase the question.

MS. LEINBURD: ...Deal with it in detail, My Lord.

Q Mr. Brodsky spent a lot of time showing you the photograph of the man on the bed being stabbed; is that correct?

A Yes.

Q And he also showed you a photograph of a body being drained of blood.

A Yes.

Q Those are obvious in the drawings. Now, you cannot say, in the drawing related to the hanging of the body over the bathtub, that that did not occur because you did not find evidence to support it.

A My training in bloodstain pattern analysis and from what I was provided does not, I can't support or not support any of those situations. It's not something that's within the realm of what I can do.

Q So the bottom line is you can't tell us whether or not that happened because there was no evidence documenting the hanging of the body.

A That's correct, I can't comment either way on those.

Q The same is true of the stabbing of the body on the bed. Because there isn't any evidence there to support a certain manner of killing doesn't mean it didn't happen in that way does it?

A It's a theory and I can't support it or I can't disprove it with what my training allows me to say and what I was provided with for photographs.

Q Going to go to diagram number C, the head. I'm just looking here to see a copy of it for the jury. But diagram C, Mr. Brodsky spent a great deal of time saying that there was a decapitated head and blood on the floor next to the bathtub.

A Yes, that's correct.

Q Because you didn't find support of that doesn't mean that there was not a head on the floor in the bathroom, does it?

MR. BRODSKY: That's not what I said, with respect, My Lord. I was pointing at the blood that's depicted in the diagram and I was talking specifically about the blood at the bottom of the head at the leg of the tub. I was not talking about the head.

THE COURT: All right. Ms. Leinburd, do you want to just rephrase the question, please?

MS. LEINBURD: Yes, we could ask two questions then.

Q My learned friend, Mr. Brodsky, pointed to both diagrams, diagram A where there appears to be a pool of blood...

A Um-hum.

Q ...And because you found no evidence of that pool of blood does not mean that that pool of blood was not there at one time, does it?

A That's correct.

Q Again let's go to what Mr. Brodsky referred you to in diagram number C, the head of the body laying on the floor. Because you didn't find any evidence of that does not mean that at one point in time there was no head lying on the floor, does it?

A That's correct.

Q The dresser that my learned friend is so apt to refer you to with the body on it, diagram F for the benefit of the jury, because you found no evidence of it does not mean that at one point in time this torso could not have been on that dresser, does it, sir?

A That's correct, I can't comment on that.

Q And all this presupposes that this scene was not cleaned up doesn't it? So if, for example, I had this torso on the dresser at one point in time and I cleaned the dresser, there would be an absence of evidence of this torso being on the dresser, wouldn't there?

MR. BRODSKY: I'm objecting to, with respect. We can only deal with the evidence and we're into so speculative, hypothetical silliness in my... I apologize. Speculation. To assume that somebody could have taken the objects off the top of the dresser, put a torso there, and then cleaned up the top of the dresser and then put the clock back and the picture back, is speculation that should not be allowed.

THE COURT: Right. The witness has already given what I think was a permissible answer about clean up. The jury has it. The jury will do with it, as they want on the basis of their examination of the whole of the evidence and the arguments in due course. Next question, Ms. Leinburd?

Q This entire scenario that you commented on presupposes that there was not a major clean up, doesn't it?

A I agree.

MS. LEINBURD: Thank you, sir. Those are my questions.

THE COURT: Thank you very much, Sergeant. Appreciate your help.

THE WITNESS: Thank you.

THE COURT: You're free to go.

THE NEXT WITNESS TO TESTIFY WAS THE OFFICER AT THE WINNIPEG REMAND Centre, Donald Steenson, who was the man who first spoke with Sidney:

Q I understand that you were on duty at approximately 9:22 a.m., that an individual walked into the Remand Centre; is that correct?

A That is correct.

Q Can you tell the jury what happened, sir?

A A man who I'd never seen before walked into the jail. I'd just come from a morning meeting. I was coming out of the radio room after checking some batteries. He approached me and asked me if he could speak to somebody in private. I asked him what about. He didn't say anything. I motioned him to my office. As we entered the office, I offered him a seat. He looked at me and said he went out drinking the day before, when he woke up he had a dead body chopped up in his bathtub.

I indicated to him that he should not be giving me this information, that he needed, this was a police matter, he needed to speak to the police.

Q And what did you do to facilitate his calling the police?

A I gave him my phone and I told him the number to call, which he did.

Q And you were present when he had a conversation with a person on the other end of the phone.

A Yes, I was.

Q And what do you recall of that conversation, sir?

A I recall he indicated to them, as he'd indicated to me, that he'd gone drinking the day before, that he had blacked out and woke up with a body chopped up in his bathtub.

Q Now, in terms of what occurred after he had called the police and again gave the information that he had just killed someone, what did you do then?

A After he finished speaking to the police, I told him to take a seat in the lobby as he was waiting for the police to arrive.

Q Did he do that?

A Yes, he did.

Q And how long a time do you anticipate he waited before the police came?

A It was under 20 minutes, I remember, by my watch. I first was broached by him at 9:22.

Q Yes.

A I believe he left the building at 9:40 with three police officers.

Q Did you ask him any further questions once he was seated in the lobby?

A The only thing I asked him after he was off the phone was whether he had any weapons in his possession, and I asked him if he'd just tell me what the number that he'd given them as to the address of the building. Other than that, I don't remember asking him any other questions.

SHEILA PROCEEDED TO ASK STEENSON WHETHER HE SAW ANY SIGNS OF IMPAIRMENT being displayed by Sidney or if he did detect any smell of alcohol on his person. Steenson indicated that he did not.

The cross-examination by Brodsky was very brief with the only real point that he wanted to make with the questioning was that Sidney didn't try to escape and didn't provide any reasons for what he had done.

The third person to testify that day was Robyn Sabanski, who since 2003 had married and changed her name to McIntyre. She was a civilian employee of the Winnipeg Police Department working as a 'casual complaint handler' with her task when answering calls to determine whether a call was an emergency or non-emergency.

SHEILA LEINBURD CONDUCTED HER DIRECT EXAMINATION OF ROBYN:

Q I want you to tell the court what you heard that day.

A Well, I answered the phone and I said, Winnipeg Police, how can I help you? And there was a gentleman on the other end of the phone and he said, "I killed someone yesterday."

Q Did he say anything else?

A I asked him how he did it, and he said that he chopped up this person and he put him in the bathtub. And I asked him what he used, and he said that he used a knife. And then I asked him where the knife was, and he said that the knife was still on the floor in the bathroom. And I also asked him where he was calling from; he said he was calling from the Remand Centre, he was not at the location where the body was.

Q So you actually transcribed what he was saying as he was saying it.

A Yes.

Q Now, I want you to tell the court about Mr. Teerhuis's voice. Was there anything in his voice that, to you, would indicate that he was drunk or had been drinking?

A Nothing at all. He was very calm when he spoke. He was, he was polite, he answered any questions that I would ask him and he just seemed to get to the point. It didn't feel to me like he was saying anything out of the ordinary. He was just telling his story and he had requested that police come down and see him.

Q So was his speech slurred at all?

A Not at all.

Q You termed him as calm.

A Very calm.

IT WAS NOW BRODSKY'S TURN:

Q So I don't want to interpret his words, but he didn't say to you, I put the person in the bathtub. He never said that?

A No.

Q He never said, I chopped him up and then put him in the bathtub. He never said that?

A No. He said he chopped him up, though.

Q He said, when he found the person dead is when he woke up. That's what he said to you. Right?

A Yes.

Q He didn't try to justify in any way his actions.

A No.

Q He didn't say, I was acting in self-defence, or the fellow was mean to me, or anything like that.

A No.

Q He never tried to say that somebody else did it?

A No.

MR. BRODSKY: Thank you.

THE COURT: Thank you very much, Ms. McIntyre. Appreciate your help.

THE WITNESS: Thank you.

(WITNESS EXCUSED)

MS. LEINBURD: We have no witnesses scheduled for Friday if we manage to finish them by Thursday.

THE COURT: Let's...

MS. LEINBURD: So that may be an opportune time to take the day off.

THE COURT: Yeah.

MS. LEINBURD: Because Mr. Pomplum has to be flown in to the city.

THE COURT: Right.

MS. LEINBURD: He didn't want to stay for longer than overnight. The only way I could accommodate that was a Sunday flight.

MR. BRODSKY: So Mr. Pomplum is on Monday?

MS. LEINBURD: Yes.

MR. BRODSKY: And Mr. Abbott is on Tuesday?

MS. LEINBURD: I didn't say Mr. Abbott. I said Mr. Zupansky.

MR. BRODSKY: Zupansky?

MS. LEINBURD: And the DNA officer, depending on whether I can alternate those two.

MR. BRODSKY: I wonder if I could ask, is Mr. Abbott being called?

MS. LEINBURD: At this point, no.

MR. BRODSKY: I may want to think about addressing Your Lordship on the letters and all of that.

THE COURT: If you could, earlier than later so Ms. Leinburd can govern herself accordingly and we don't waste too much time on that argument or getting bogged down and trying to get him here if he has to be called at some point.

MR. BRODSKY: Well, I was under the impression he was going to be called. I think Your Lordship was under the same impression.

THE COURT: He's on the witness list. I mean, that doesn't necessarily mean that all witnesses, as I told the jury, will be called.

MR. BRODSKY: No, I'm not just talking about the witness list; I'm talking about all the argument we had on...

THE COURT: Well, I'm not sure...

MR. BRODSKY: Post-offence conduct...

MS. LEINBURD: None of the letters that were sent to Mr. Abbott have been tendered.

THE COURT: So your concern is the fact that Mr. Abbott may not be called. If you have a concern about that, Mr. Brodsky, raise and all the rest of that.

THE COURT: Who is Mr. Abbott?

MS. LEINBURD: Mr. Abbott's name was never raised nor...

THE COURT: Who is Mr. Abbott?

MS. LEINBURD: He's an individual who spent some time in the cell with the accused.

THE COURT: Right.

MS. LEINBURD: And who, in fact, took down conversation that was had between the two of them. There was no argument made *vis-à-vis* Mr. Abbott, no evidence led in respect of Mr. Abbott, so...

MR. BRODSKY: My...

MS. LEINBURD: There is nothing tendered, Mr. Brodsky.

MR. BRODSKY: My submission is or was that Mr. Zupansky was asking questions that were proposed by Mr. Abbott.

176

MS. LEINBURD: No, it's the other way around, Mr. Brodsky, and the reality is Mr. Zupansky can tell you what he wants to tell you. You're not going to get Abbott's information through Zupansky and you're not going to get Zupansky's information through Abbott.

THE COURT: And you're intending to call Mr. Zupansky at the end, I take it; is that right?

MS. LEINBURD: Well, not at the end, towards the tail end of the case, yes.

THE COURT: I ask that only because it sounds to me like you need some clarification what Mr. Zupansky can tell you.

MR. BRODSKY: Yes.

MS. LEINBURD: Mr. Brodsky has all of the particulars respecting Mr. Zupansky, and has had for years. I don't know how that impacts anything that Mr. Abbott has to say, quite frankly.

THE COURT: Let's just leave it at this: If Mr. Abbott is not going to be called, Mr. Brodsky, Ms. Leinburd, I'm sure, will provide you notice as early as she makes that determination If you want to deal with that by way of a motion, we'll deal with it when you make the motion. Okay? So tomorrow morning, ten o'clock?

MS. LEINBURD: Yes, thank you.

THE CLERK: Order, all rise. This court's adjourned till 10:00 a.m.

17

The Pathologist Speaks

DECEMBER 3/08

(JURY IN AT 10:06 A.M.)

THE CLERK: My Lord, all 12 jurors are present.
THE COURT: Good morning, ladies and gentlemen.
JURORS: Good morning, My Lord.
MS. LEINBURD: Good morning. This is Dr. Charles Littman. I wonder if he might be sworn.
THE CLERK: Do you wish to be affirmed?
THE WITNESS: Yes.
THE CLERK: Please state and spell your full name for the record.
THE WITNESS: Charles David Littman, C-H-A-R-L-E-S, D-A-V-I-D, L-I-T-T-M-A-N.
THE CLERK: Thank you. Please have a seat.

DIRECT EXAMINATION BY MS. LEINBURD:
Q Dr. Littman, I have a copy of both your curriculum vitae and a copy of the autopsy report that you prepared in respect of Robin Greene.
THE COURT: Exhibit 86, no objection, Mr. Brodsky?
MR. BRODSKY: Not only is there no objection, but Dr. Littman is a well respected, well practiced, certified forensic pathologist who is eminently qualified to give opinion evidence in my respectful submission.
THE COURT: And a nice man.
MS. LEINBURD: Yes.
MR. BRODSKY: He has a nice dog, too.
BY MS. LEINBURD:
Q Dr. Littman, you graduated medical school, and received your medical degree as I understand it in 1973?
A Yes.
Q And subsequent to that you received your specializations in pathology and forensic pathology?
A Yes.
Q And you're presently practising at the Health Sciences Centre, and you are in fact a provincial pathologist for the Department of Medicine; is that correct?
A A pathologist and medical examiner, yes.

178

Q In terms of this particular matter, sir, it's my understanding that you in fact performed an autopsy on Robin Greene on July the 3rd, of 2003, at approximately 9:35; is that correct?

A Yes.

Q I wonder, sir, if we might then proceed to deal with your autopsy findings. I understand that Robin Greene was a 38 year old male; is that correct?

A Yes.

Q He showed no signs of any disease upon your observation of him?

A No.

Q Okay. And I wonder if you might indicate to the jury what your autopsy findings were, sir.

A The autopsy findings were listed in the front of the report, and the body had been dismembered --

Q What does that mean, Doctor?

A The limbs had been severed from the body. The body had been decapitated.

Q And what does that mean, Doctor?

A The head had been cut from the body. The body had been disembowelled, which means that the intestines had been removed from the body. The body had been eviscerated, which means that the internal organs, as well as the intestines had also been removed. The body had been mutilated, which in my opinion there were incisions indicating that there was some degree of lack of respect for the human body. One of the nipples had been, had been cut off, the, the penis and testicles had been cut off, one eye had been removed, the other eyeball had been punctured, and there were also multiple stab wounds to the body, and toxicology and alcohol testing showed that there was acute alcohol intoxication to the deceased.

Q And we'll turn to some of those findings further on into your evidence, Doctor. Can you tell the jury the body parts that the deceased presented in when he was in fact delivered to you for autopsy?

A Yes, when the body was brought to the morgue there were eight separate body parts. These comprised the head; the trunk and the upper arms, which were attached; the right forearm; the left forearm; the pelvis and the thighs, the right lower leg; the left lower leg, and the penis and scrotum.

Q Now, Doctor, we were at the point where we had in fact described the body parts that were unfortunately delivered to you. I wonder if you can indicate, Doctor, the cause of death pursuant to your findings.

A Well cause of death I determined to be multiple stab wounds, however, that, that is qualified by the fact that none of the internal organs were present, however, the injuries on the body were multiple stab wounds, which were not compatible with life, so therefore that was given as the cause of death.

They were almost symmetrical, 28 on one side, 27 on the other side, and many of these stab wounds entered the chest cavity.

Q So by my accounting that is 68 stab wounds in total; is that correct, Doctor?

A Yes. On the head itself there was an abrasion on the right side of the forehead in the hairline with some bruising underlying.

Q There seems to be an abrasion and bruising on the upper forehead, very close to the hairline; is that what you're speaking of, Doctor?

179

A Yes.

Q And there also is some bruising on the face, as I understand it, Doctor?

A Yes, there's some bruising over the cheekbone on the right side of the face, just above the number 12 in the, the ruler in photograph number 93.

Q Now, in terms of the eyes of the deceased if one looks at photograph number 94 and 95 those are unfortunately close-up photographs of the deceased's eyes. In photograph number 4 the eyeball itself appears to be missing; is that correct, sir?

A Yes, the right eye had been enucleated, had been removed from the head.

Q And the left eye seems to be deflated; is that correct?

A Yes, the left eye there had been a puncture wound into the eyeball and the actual eyeball had collapsed, and the puncture wound can be seen just below the forceps that is holding the eyeball. There's a small puncture wound in the eyeball itself.

Q Now, it's my understanding, sir, that you were shown two knives by the City of Winnipeg Police; is that correct, sir?

A Yes.

Q And they've been marked in this courtroom as exhibits, and I'm going to show them to you. They are Exhibits 45 and 34, Doctor. Thirty-four is a large butcher knife, 45 is a smaller paring knife, each of which appear to be stained with blood and hair.

A Yes.

Q Now, Doctor, I want to talk for a moment about defensive wounds. Defensive wounds are the kinds of wounds that people suffer when they're trying to defend themselves from an attack; is that correct?

A Yes.

Q So if for example I was being stabbed the normal reaction that you see in your practice is that there is wounding on the inside of the arms or the hands generally to protect themselves; is that correct?

A That's correct.

Q Did you see any defensive wounds on the body of the deceased?

A No.

Q None?

A None.

Q Thank you, Doctor. If we might now proceed to the dismemberment or disarticulation of the forearm in photograph 107.

A Yes.

Q Not only has the forearm been removed from the body, but it has in fact been dissected, if I could term it that way?

A Yes.

Q What does that mean, Doctor?

A Well, dissection to me means that the muscles have been carefully separated. The muscles in the forearm, each of the muscles controls the, the movement of the, the fingers and the hand, and although the muscles in the forearm are in a bundle they can be separated with dissection by carefully separating the, the muscles from each other. This would require some time, and it requires some degree of expertise. If there's no knowledge of this and then you would find a knife slicing through several of the muscles at once, but each of these muscles can be dissected off each other in an, in an individual manner, and as you can see from photograph number 107 this has been done.

180

Q Now, would you term this dissection precise?
A Yes.
Q Neat?
A Yes.
Q Surgical?
A Surgical-like, yes.
Q So this would not, from your observations of this dissection, amount to slashing or chaotic cutting of that particular arm?
A No.
Q Thank you, Doctor. In terms of the degree of dexterity and coordination, Doctor, can you comment on that?
A Well, it would require some degree of manual dexterity and coordination, yes.
Q Proceeding to the pelvis and the thighs, Doctor, as depicted in photograph number 91, please. Can you comment on that section, Doctor?
A Well, again, there seems to be one incision around the lower end of the abdomen to disarticulate or to, to remove the, the pelvis from the abdominal wall. The knife in fact passed through the spine itself, it didn't pass between the vertebrae, it passed through the body of I believe it was L5, which is the lumbar vertebrae number 5.
Q So it actually cut through the bone?
A Actually cut through bone. The bone of the spine is a spongy type of bone. It is bone, however, and requires a fair degree of force to cut through, so combined force and a very sharp knife it's possible to cut through bone. Generally speaking in the autopsy room if we were removing a portion of vertebras as we do to examine under the microscope the bone marrow, we would use a saw, but if we had a heavy, a very sharp knife, a guillotine type knife then you certainly could chop through bone directly.
Q Okay. And the knife that you have before you, if it was sharpened and sharpened up that it could do the same thing, is that possible?
A Yes, it's a heavy, heavy blade, yes.
Q The cutting the body in half you say is circular?
A Yes, appears to be.
Q And it's quite concise and precise as well?
A Yes, and then of course the excision or the incision extends down onto the thighs and around the genitalia and it's almost surgical like the way the penis and testicles have been removed from the pelvis.
Q So, again, when you use the word 'surgical' nothing chaotic about this dissection about the penis and testicles?
A No, this was a very precise excision.
Q Thank you, Doctor. In terms of the back I understand that there was some abrasion in the lower part of the back area; is that correct, Doctor?
A Yes.
Q Where would that be?
A I believe that's depicted in...
Q 108, Doctor.
A Yes, over the, the top of the buttock you can see there are two abrasions on the back. Abrasions is where the skin surface has been scraped off, it's the lay term for an abrasion is a scrape.
Q What kind of movement would cause this kind of scrape, Doctor?
A Well abrasions can be caused either by pressure, or a pressure type

181

abrasion where the skin surface is crushed or by a scrape abrasion, a friction abrasion where the, the skin is rubbed across a surface.

Q So if his body were dragged on a carpet and on a tile floor would that be the kind of injury that you would find?

A Yes, that could cause a friction abrasion, yes.

Q Thank you, Doctor. Now, in terms of the legs and the knees, Doctor, photographs 110 and 111.

A Yes.

Q The joints, Doctor, they appear to me to be precisely cut; is that a fair observation?

A Yes, the disarticulation has gone directly through the joints, rather than chopping through bone itself, and so this requires again some knowledge of the anatomy of a joint, and as you can see from photographs 109 and 110 there are some knife marks on the actual surface of the joints, the articulate surface.

Q Now, if we might return to the head for a moment, Doctor as depicted in photograph number 90.

A Yes.

Q There appears to be in the neck area some sort of a horn or a greater horny area that's been sliced through. Can you describe that, Doctor?

A Well, what you see is the actual upper end of the spine that's protruding from the trunk.

Q I want to deal with the issue of blood loss, Doctor. In terms of the human body how many litres of blood does the average human body hold?

A About five litres.

Q Five litres?

A Yes.

Q And when this particular body was presented to you, Doctor, can you estimate how much blood was left in it?

A There was very little blood left. In fact we had quite a difficult time collecting some blood for the toxicology and alcohol analysis. There was some blood left in the muscles of the legs, and we managed to massage enough blood out that the analysis could be performed.

Q Now, given the wounds that this deceased in fact suffered, particularly if you look at photograph number 99, 27 stab wounds to one side of the chest, 28 stab wounds to the other side of the chest, if the deceased were in fact lying down and were stabbed as the deceased Robin Greene was, where would you expect the blood loss to go into?

A Well, the bleeding would be into the chest, the chest cavity.

Q So that means the blood loss, rather than spraying out would go into the body, and the chest cavity would hold all of that blood?

A Yes.

Q I'm going to show you a photograph of the body as it was found by the police. You can direct your attention, Doctor, to photograph number 42.

A Yes.

Q There doesn't appear to be any blood?

A No.

Q Is that what you would expect with a body that was decapitated, dismembered, eviscerated and mutilated?

A No, I would expect to see blood.

Q So in terms of the body that you see is it fair to say that it is clean?

182

A Yes.

Q Okay. Is that consistent with it having been washed or cleansed in some fashion?

A Yes.

Q In terms of the organs that had been removed, Doctor.

A Yes.

Q Can you indicate those for the jury?

A Well, in the chest cavity the heart had been removed.

Q The heart?

A Yes.

Q Um-hum.

A Both lungs had been removed. In the abdominal cavity the entire intestinal tract had been removed, all the way from the stomach down to the colon. The liver had been removed, and that includes the gall bladder. The spleen had been removed, the pancreas had been removed, both kidneys had been removed, and in the neck the thyroid gland had also been removed. Oh, and I should add that in addition to the kidneys the adrenal glands, which sit just above the kidneys, had also been removed.

Q Now, in terms of the length of time that this dismemberment, and disembowelment, and evisceration would have taken, Doctor, can you comment on that? I appreciate that you're an expert and you've done hundreds of autopsies in your lifetime, but how long would an autopsy generally take if you had done it, and then comment upon what was done to this body, Doctor.

A Well, a straightforward autopsy being performed to determine cause of death with no surprises on the way generally from start to finish takes in the region of one to two hours. The type of dismemberment, mutilation, evisceration and so on that was performed on the deceased in my opinion, even with some previous expertise in working with animals or some such thing, I still think it would take probably several hours to perform, and when I say several hours I think that two to three hours, but that would be a baseline, it could take much longer. For instance, the careful dissection of the forearm, depending on how intrigued one is with the muscles, may take some time, could have lingered over that for an hour or so.

Q And in terms of the physical work required is there manual effort required to cut through bone, and saw off arms and legs?

A Oh, yes, there's physical exertion required, plus the body had to be moved obviously from the bed and all the parts placed in the tub, plus all the organs that were found or were not found from the body had to be disposed of, so yes it would be physical exertion.

Q Now, Doctor, you've described the cuts that were occasioned to Robin Greene's body as surgical, precise, neat, defined; would that type of cutting up of Robin Greene's body have required some degree of manual dexterity and coordination?

A Yes.

Q And does alcohol intake impact on that coordination, Doctor?

A Yes. As I said earlier coordination is certainly impaired by alcohol.

Q Now, Doctor, I'm going to refer you to several exhibits that are now before the court, particularly Exhibit 64 and 63, 65 and 66, Doctor. These are all letters that the accused, Mr. Teerhuis, wrote to Mr. Zupansky. I'm going to refer you to Exhibit 64, Doctor. I'm just referencing a copy of it. I'm going to ask you to turn to page 5 of Exhibit 64, Doctor. I'm just going to read it to you, and then I am going to ask you for your commentary, Doctor.

"Greene's abdomen was sliced open like a zipper. I was in awe at the sight of his intestines. I looked at them in amazement. The coils, the intricate folds, the transparency."

Q Now, Doctor, with your expertise, if one has a sharp knife, is it possible to cut an abdomen or stomach open like a zipper?
A Yes.
Q The site of the intestines, Doctor, are intestines coiled and intricate?
A Yes.
Q And are they transparent, Doctor?
A Yes.
Q I proceed on.

Now I know how the serial killer Dennis Nilsen must have felt when he dissected his first male victim. The pure beauty of Greene's viscera gave me an erection. I inserted my right hand into the mass of intestines. They were slippery.

Q Would intestines be slippery, Doctor?
A Yes.
Q Made squishy sounds. Would intestines make squishy sounds, Doctor?
A Yes.
Q Continuing on.

Then I reached all the way into his chest cavity. Greene's organs were still warm.

Q How long does a body stay warm for, Doctor?
A Oh, the internal organs would stay warm for several hours after death, up to--it would depend also on the temperature in the room, and how much body fat there was, but even with no body fat the organs would stay warm for several hours.
Q The accused goes on to write.

He'd been dead for about four hours by now.

Q So that's consistent with what you've just said, Doctor.
A Yes.

I felt around exploring Greene's insides with my hand. I could feel the curve and ripple of his inner rib cage.

Q Is it fair to describe the rib cage as rippled and curved, Doctor?
A Yes. The feeling between the ribs and the intercostal spaces would have that type of feel.

184

Q The accused goes on to write in his letter:

The spinal column was bigger than I thought. It had a thin layer of meat coating it.

Q Does the spinal column or spinal cord have anything coating it, Doctor?
A There are some Para spinal muscles, yes.
Q Does the human body have two chambers in its chest cavity, Doctor?
A Yeah, the chest is divided into right and a left chest cavity.
Q "*I ran my hand up and down its length feeling the organs glide over my hand. As I looked at Greene's chest I couldn't believe my right arm was elbow deep inside of him. I kept feeling around trying to guess the different organs.*" In order to remove the organs is it fair to say, Doctor, that a human hand would have to be at least elbow deep into the body to remove them?
A Yes.
Q Proceeding on to page 6 of the accused's letter that he wrote to Mr. Zupansky. He goes on to say:

I grabbed onto something and pulled it out of the body. It was Greene's liver. Wow I said slowly. Took the chef knife and disconnected it holding it in the palm of my hand. I laid it on his chest and sliced it open like a butterfly to examine the inside. I felt with my fingertips some areas were smooth, others leathery, like a rubbery scar.

Q In terms of the human liver, Doctor, is it fair to describe parts of it as smooth and parts of it as not smooth?
A Well, most of its smooth. It may be that what he's referring to is the hilum of the liver, where all the vessels enter the liver-- there are some, some increase in fibrous tissue there, and that may feel firmer or leathery like.
Q He goes on to say:

I tossed it aside, reached back in his chest and pulled out the stomach. It had a blue tinge. As soon as I cut it open a bunch of bile and fluids leaked out.

Q Does the human stomach contain bile and fluids, Doctor?
A Well, it contains fluids, and maybe bile stain because the bile duct empties bile into the duodenum, which is just distal to the stomach, but some of it comes back into the stomach itself.
Q "*It smelled really bad.*" Would it smell bad if you cut into a human stomach, Doctor?
A It smells like vomit.
Q "*It made a mess all over the floor.*" The contents are in fact liquid, as I understand it, or semi-liquid?
A Depending what's been eaten, and what's been drunk, yes.
Q "*I pulled out the large and small intestines, and put them in the sink rinsing them. I could see partly processed human waste in them.*" Is that accurate, Doctor, that if you look at intestines you find human waste in them?
A Yes.

185

Q *"I thought it was fascinating. Dissecting Greene was a lot of work, it was a messy job. The intense odor of intestinal gas and body fluids was intensified by the summer heat."* When one in fact cuts into intestines, or removes them, is there a smell of intestinal gas, Doctor?
A Yes.
Q *"I pulled out the heart, it was kind of small, not what I expected. I severed the major arteries, the aorta."* And what is the major artery that connects the heart in the body, Doctor?
A Well, the major artery that exits the heart is the aorta, and then the secondary one is the pulmonary artery.
Q *"I squeezed the heart and let the still warm blood drip all over me."* If one squeezes a human heart will it bleed, Doctor?
A Yes.
Q *"I was intrigued by the heart's inner chambers, its ventricles."* Does a heart have ventricles, Doctor?
A Yes.
Q And are those the inner chambers of a heart, Doctor?
A It's two of the four chambers, yes.
Q *"I had trouble extracting his lungs so I had to rip them out. They were kind of transparent."* Is that an apt description of what a human lung is like, Doctor?
A It's transparent and spongy, yes.
Q And he goes on to indicate that: *"I blew up the lung like a balloon."* And is it possible to blow up a human lung like a balloon, Doctor?
A It's possible I guess, yes.
Q And then he goes on to say:

> Then I took the paring knife and scraped the hollow chest cavity to make sure everything was out. I peeled a thin layer of sinew from the inner ribs and examined it.

Q Are the inner ribs covered with a sinew type material, Doctor?
A Well, they're covered with a lining called the pleura, the parietal pleura lines the inner surface of the ribs.
Q And he goes on to say: *"It had the texture of Kleenex, and it was transparent like tissue paper."* Is that a fair characterization, Doctor?
A Yes.
Q Okay. He goes on to say in the bottom portion of page number 7: *"I filled the tub and bathed with Greene's corpse, diagram C, and dosed off for a while."* You had indicated in your earlier testimony that it was your view that the body had in fact been washed; is that correct, Doctor?
A Yes.
Q I'm going to direct you to Exhibit 63, Doctor, which is also a letter that the accused wrote to Mr. Zupansky. Beginning in the upper portion of that particular letter that the accused wrote:

> At first I molested Greene's body. I had to make sure he was dead. Picked up the knife and with long cuts began slicing into his neck.

Q What is necrophilia, Doctor?

186

A Necrophilia is having sexual acts with a dead body.

Q Thank you.

> *It was like cutting a roast the knife was so sharp.*
> *Blood began to ooze out, there was so much of it, I*
> *looked into Greene's eyes as I sliced into him. It was*
> *kind of erotic. The spinal column was hard to cut.*

Q You described that in your testimony as well, Doctor. If one cuts through the bone it is rather difficult, is it not?

A Yes.

Q *"I had to feel inside the neck, the muscle tissue was warm."* And you say it would be, Doctor?

A Yes.

Q *"And it made a squishy sound."* Is that an accurate characterization, Doctor?

A Yes.

Q *"The stump of his spinal cord jutted out."* And you had in your observations of the photographs, Doctor, particularly photograph number 90, indicated that the stump of the spinal column was in fact jutting out right underneath the chin of the deceased, is that correct, that's photograph number 90, Doctor?

A Yes.

Q Okay. He goes on to say: *"The stump of the spinal cord jutted out and some veins and jugular."* And is the jugular in the neck itself, Doctor?

A Yes.

Q Okay. *"I picked up the head with both hands; I was amazed at how heavy it was."* You've indicted that it's one of the heavier organs weighing between six and eight pounds, Doctor?

A About seven to ten pounds I think I said.

Q Okay. Referring to Exhibit 65 now, another letter that this accused wrote to Mr. Zupansky. It starts with:

> *The poetry of Greene's viscera. The inexplicable beauty*
> *of his intestines elaborately coiled and folded. The*
> *rich aroma of fresh human meat. The sound of stainless*
> *steel cutting into bone.*

Q Doctor, you've already described the intestines as coiled and folded; is that an accurate description?

A Yes.

Q The stainless steel cutting into bone would make a sound; would it not, Doctor?

A Yes.

Q *"When Greene was sawed in half the shreds of flesh that hung from his rib cage like colorless frond."* I'm going to refer you to a particular photograph, particularly photograph 99, Doctor. Taking out the use of the word 'frond' but it is a colorless section of flesh that is hanging directly underneath the rib cage in photograph 99 to the bottom portion of the photograph; is that correct; Doctor?

A Yes, there are portions of fatty tissue that are hanging down, I presume that's what he's referring to.

Q Lastly, Doctor, I'm going to refer to Exhibit 66, another letter

187

written by this accused to Mr. Zupansky. Top portion, again he says:

> The only time I ever entertained the thought of Dahmer
> or Nilson was when I sliced open Greene's abdomen seeing
> the intricate design and coils of the transparent
> intestines.

Q Again you would agree with that description, Doctor?
A Yes.
Q Going down to the middle portion of that particular page,
Doctor, the accused writes:

> You wanted a list of missing organs, lungs, part of the
> oesophagus, epiglottis, digestive tract, heart, spleen,
> stomach, liver, pancreas, aorta and one of the eyes, the
> other was punctured.

Q In your view of the body is that a correct listing of the organs,
Doctor?
A Yes.
Q And you had actually not listed the missing organs per se in your
autopsy report; had you, Doctor?
A No.
Q And, lastly, Doctor, over the course of years as a doctor and
a pathologist I understand you've probably read many books of
anatomy; is that correct, Doctor?
A Yes.
Q And in any of those books, according to your recollection, is
there any indication as to the smell or the squishy feeling of
organs that you have read, Doctor?
A Not in the medical texts, no.
MS. LEINBURD: Thank you, Doctor. Those are my questions.
THE COURT: Before we start cross-examination maybe we can take a
morning break.

(JURY OUT AT 11:04 A.M.)

THE CLERK: Order, all rise. This court's in recess.

(BRIEF RECESS)

THE CLERK: Court is re-opened. Please be seated.

(JURY IN AT 11:21 A.M.)

THE CLERK: My Lord, all 12 jurors are present.
THE COURT: Thank you. Mr. Brodsky.
CROSS-EXAMINATION BY MR. BRODSKY:
Q Okay. Are you able to say how tolerant this person was to
alcohol?
A No.
Q Whether he was a chronic alcoholic or not?
A No.
Q And what difference does tolerance to alcohol make on a person,
to a person?

A Well tolerance as I said earlier, an individual who's tolerant to alcohol can still function. We have indications that I'm sure you're aware that people who drive impaired some of the impaired levels have been in excess of four or five hundred milligrams. At that kind of level if someone was not tolerant not only would they not be able to drive a vehicle they probably would be passed out, they wouldn't be able to walk so tolerance does allow an individual with a high level of alcohol to perform some functions, however, even with tolerance reaction times and coordination are impaired, and that's why a drunken driver, as long as there's no hazard or no untoward circumstance that occurs on the road on the way home may drive from the bar back to his house with nothing happening, but if something unexpected happening such a child runs out into the road, or a vehicle, or a cyclist comes out then the reaction time and the ability to avoid that collision will be impaired, and so even with tolerance coordination and judgment and are impaired.

Q So a person can drive from point A to point B whether it is a mile or five miles, and be precise, and drive straight, as long as there's no unexpected things that have to be reacted to there's not necessarily going to be an accident?

A That's correct.

Q Well, supposing we had a chef now dissecting or cutting up whatever he prepares in his kitchen are we talking about the same thing, his method of preparation, as long as nothing unexpected and startling happens, would be absolutely appropriate?

A Oh, I'm sure in some instances there are people who prepare food who may be intoxicated, and nothing untoward happens, yes.

Q Let's assume now that Mr. Greene, the deceased in this case, was in a hotel room at the time he met his unfortunate end, and let's assume there was no interruption, and the person who did all of this had time, and no startling event or any interruption I take it all of these dissections, and bisections, and eviscerations could all be done in the fashion that you saw?

A Yeah, that's possible, yes.

Q Even though his judgment would be extraordinarily impaired because of the level of alcohol he had?

A Yes.

Q Even though he would be, his judgment and his ability to make decisions, and to understand the consequences of his actions would be extraordinarily impaired he still could do all of the incisions, and cuts, and things that happened unfortunately to Mr. Greene?

MS. LEINBURD: First of all, the doctor can't speak to anyone else's understanding of consequences of actions, or anything like that. That's a legal term that he's putting to the doctor, and I object to that, and, frankly, his question isn't particularly well articulated, and I'm not sure what it is he's actually asking.

MR. BRODSKY: I'm not asking whether the person did weigh the consequences. That would be an inappropriate question. I'm saying generally someone who is intoxicated with a high level doesn't weigh consequences.

THE COURT: Well, this is a medical doctor, Mr. Brodsky, not a moralist. I'm not sure what this doctor can offer in that regard. I understand what you're trying to get out. Why don't you rephrase the question, in fairness to you, and see what Ms. Leinburd has to say?

Q Insofar as an intoxicated person, whose judgment is considerably impaired by alcohol, you would agree that all of these cuts and slices, and actions that were described to you, either by letter or by your observation at autopsy, they could be done in the fashion that you found them; would that be fair? Could be?

A If someone's judgment is impaired by alcohol it's still possible that their motor skills would be such that many of these incisions could be made, yes.

Q All right. I'm not talking about why you would hide the internal organs, and take them away, and leave a chopped up body in a bathtub, and think you're accomplishing something or hiding it in a bathtub, a body in a bathtub. I'm not talking about that kind of judgment. I'm talking about the ability to make a straight line cut could be done by a person whose judgment was considerably impaired by alcohol; would that be fair? He could still make the straight line cut?

A Well, the effects of alcohol on the body, and weird judgment, and severely impaired judgment, how severely that would impair the coordination to perform surgical skills I don't think that I can really give an honest opinion on that. That's not my area of expertise.

Q And when someone has a large amount of alcohol to drink is blacking out one of the symptoms that you see from time to time?

A Well, it's recognized that blackouts occur in alcoholics. In other words a blackout would be a period of time that the drunk in becoming sober can't account for. How long these blackouts last and what can be performed during that blackout again is not an area of my expertise. I believe that would be someone who works in the addictions area would be a better person in answering that question.

Q So you're not saying then, so that I understand you clearly, that a person in an alcoholic blackout couldn't perform that dismemberment, and disembowelment, and emasculation that you saw?

THE COURT: He's offering no opinion...

THE WITNESS: No, I'm...

THE COURT: ...at all, Mr. Brodsky, on that point. I want to be clear that the witness has indicated that he's not comfortable offering an opinion with respect to that question.

MR. BRODSKY: Yes, I expect him to say, I can't tell you whether he could do that or not in an alcoholic blackout. That's what I expect him to say, he may say something else.

Q Would that be fair that you can't say that a person in an alcoholic blackout could or couldn't do what you found at autopsy?

A My answer was going to be I don't know.

Q And just because you can drive your car while you're really drunk doesn't mean, and not get into an accident, it doesn't mean you're not really drunk?

A That's correct.

Q Now, I just want to make sure I understand. When you say that the abdomen sliced open like a zipper, or the intestines were coiled, that doesn't mean for humans only, that means any animal; would that be fair?

A Any animal with a similar digestive tract, yes.

Q Are the digestive tract in terms of restaurants we all know--I'm not--I don't want, I mean we're near the lunch hour, I don't want to get into that too much, but that's a common phenomenon that a hunter would see, that a chef would see, that a butcher would see, that the coils of the intestines were folded, that they would be transparent, this is a common thing to all mammals; would that be fair?

A Well, in answering your question I don't think it would be a common sight for a chef or even a butcher because the intestines would be removed in the abattoir and they would be removed at the slaughterhouse. In fact that's the whole reason that we have to be very careful in eating meat because the intestines contain E. coli and I'm sure that you've read about the coliform infections, if the intestine is punctured in the process of slaughtering the animal then the meat can be contaminated with the coliform organisms. I would agree with you, however, the hunter in dressing a deer or some game would notice the intestines, but not in a restaurant.

Q That would obviously depend on the training the person got to be a chef or to be a butcher?

A If training for a chef, which I'm not familiar with, involves going to the slaughterhouse and seeing how the animals is slaughtered, yes, but I don't know if that's part of the expertise.

Q Right. Now, you said that the liver was smooth. In dealing with the liver being smooth and a fibrous issue at the entrance to the liver is that peculiar to humans, or is that normal?

A No, the, the pig liver, for instance, is, is quite similar to human liver.

Q Blowing up a lung like a balloon is that peculiar to humans, the ability to do that, or do all animals?

A No, I mean basically the lungs in all animals are organs that facilitate transfer of oxygen to the blood, and function really as a bag of air to allow this transfer from oxygen within the air to the bloodstream.

Q So if it was porous it wouldn't work as a lung?

A Right.

Q Did you see any physical signs that any necrophilia had taken place?

A No.

Q Now, there's no doubt that the eyes of the deceased are listed as being removed, and punctured in your autopsy report, and in the photographs?

A That's correct. One was removed and one was punctured, yes.

Q And in connection with the abrasion to the head are you able to say when in relation to the stabbing that took place?

A No. All I can say is that the abrasion certainly occurred during life. There was evidence of a vital reaction. There's some bleeding in the area, so that happened. It could have happened 24 hours earlier, it could have happened one hour earlier, or it could have happened at the time of the fatal incident.

Q And the drag marks, or what appear to be the abrasions on the back, are you able to say if they were before or after death?

A Again they have evidence of vital reaction, there's some bleeding in the area and so they're not post mortem appearing abrasions that we sometimes see.

Q They're not post mortem?

A They're not.

Q No. So they occurred during life, right?

A Yes.

Q Before the decapitation and evisceration, and all of that?

A Yes.

Q Did you see any signs that this body had been hung from the ceiling, from an object on the ceiling, any signs at all of any rubbing or marks, or indication, any sign that it had been hung from the ceiling before it was cut up like that?

A No.

Q The body would be pretty heavy, how much did this body weigh?

A Total weight was 59 kilograms, and I estimated the missing body organs, and the intestines, to be about 10 kilos, so I believe that the deceased would have been in the region of 69 kilos or 70 kilos, which is between 150 and 160 pounds.

Q So if he were hung upside down by his legs you would expect some indentation on the ankles or legs if he was hanging, and 150 pounds?

A I mean if he's, yeah, you would expect some mark from the ligature or whatever method was used to hang him, yes.

Q And a forensic pathologist would be someone trained to observe that kind of thing?

A Yes.

MR.BRODSKY: I have no further questions, my Lord.

THE COURT: Thank you, Mr. Brodsky. Ms. Leinburd.

RE-EXAMINATION BY MS. LEINBURD:

Q My learned friend, Mr. Brodsky, asked you if there was any evidence of necrophilia upon your examination of the body.

A Yes.

Q Is it fair to say that if the person that was having sex with the body was wearing a condom that you would find no evidence of semen?

A Yes.

Q Furthermore you said to my learned friend, Mr. Brodsky, that there were no signs of necrophilia, and I take it by that that you mean that unless the body had been ripped open you wouldn't find any signs of necrophilia? I mean there are no signs of sexual intercourse or anal intercourse that would be discerned by you unless there was trauma associated with it; isn't that correct, Doctor?

A Yes.

Q So unless there was some injury sustained you could not say whether or not sex had occurred?

A Yes.

MS. LEINBURD: Thank you very much, Doctor.

THE COURT: Thank you very much, Doctor. I appreciate your help, as always.

(JURY OUT AT 11:58 A.M.)

THE CLERK: Order, all rise. This court is in recess.

(LUNCHEON RECESS)

THE CLERK: Court is open. Please be seated.

(JURY IN AT 2:04 P.M.)

MR. BRODSKY: So far I have no motion, My Lord. As I indicated before I just want to alert you in case--because I was under the impression that Mr. Abbott, first of all, wasn't going to be called, then he was going to be called on November the 4th when my learned friend advised that he would, and I made that submission to you on the understanding that he would be called, and I can't oblige my learned friend to call any witness. She has to put in the case that she thinks she has.

MS. LEINBURD: Just to put Mr. Brodsky out of his obvious discomfort, if not misery, in terms of the Abbott issue, Mr. Abbott was in fact subpoenaed. It's funny Mr. Brodsky originally contested the fact that I was calling him, and now he's contesting the fact that I'm not calling him, but in any event we issued a subpoena for him, and simply put he can't be found. We think he's in another city. If he were available to me I would call him, he's not available to me, the police have told me they believe him to be in Edmonton. They've done due diligence in trying to serve him in Edmonton, and the subpoenas went out I believe the first week of November, if not the last week of October. They've been looking all this time. My information as of yesterday is that they could not find him, so it's not as if we're being coy or we're playing tactical games, we can't serve him. If I can't serve him I can't produce him.

MR. BRODSKY: But that's a big difference.

MS. LEINBURD: You should have asked.

MR. BRODSKY: If I can have an explanation.

MS. LEINBURD: You didn't ask Mr. Brodsky.

MR. BRODSKY: If I have an explanation I'm more comfortable.

MS. LEINBURD: And that's why I put you out of your misery.

THE COURT: Okay, so tomorrow at ten o'clock. Thanks.

THE CLERK: Order, all rise. Court is adjourned.

(PROCEEDINGS ADJOURNED TO DECEMBER 4, 2008)

18

The Arresting Officer and the Bartender

DECEMBER 4/08

(JURY IN AT 2:03 P.M.)

THE CLERK: My Lord, all 12 jurors are present.
THE COURT: Thank you. Good afternoon.
JURORS: Good afternoon.
THE COURT: Ms. Leinburd.
MS. LEINBURD: Good afternoon. This is Constable Schroeder. We could have her sworn in, please.
THE CLERK: Do you wish to be sworn on the Bible or affirm to tell the truth?
THE WITNESS: Swear on the Bible, please.
THE CLERK: Okay. Take the Bible in your right hand. Please state and spell your full name for the record.
THE WITNESS: My name is Sylvia Schroeder, S-Y-L-V-I-A, S-C-H-R-O-E-D-E-R.
THE CLERK: Thank you.

DIRECT EXAMINATION BY MS. LEINBURD:
Q Constable Schroeder, I understand that you're a City of Winnipeg police officer; is that correct?
A That's correct.
Q And how long have you been a police officer?
A Ten years.
Q And I understand that on July the 2nd of 2003, in company with your brother officer, Marin, that you were on duty; is that correct?
A That's correct.
Q And you were on general patrol?
A Yes, I was.
Q And I understand you were briefed about the theft of some jewelry from a movie set; is that correct?
A We were.
Q And it was jewelry that was stolen from the set of *Shall We Dance* as I understand it?
A That's correct, yes.
Q And it was Susan Sarandon's necklace and her bracelet?
A Yes.
Q And you were shown a photograph of it?

194

A Yeah, it was passed around in my briefing.

Q After that briefing, you go out on your general patrol, as I understand it?

A Yes.

Q And you received a radio message; is that correct?

A We did.

Q And your radio message directed you to the Winnipeg Remand Centre, which is the jail just across the street here?

A That's right.

Q What time would you have arrived at the Remand Centre, Ma'am?

A We would have arrived at 9:41 in the morning.

Q And once you arrived, what did you do, Ma'am?

A Well, after we arrived at the Remand Centre, my partner, Constable Marin, and I attended to the front doors, and in the front lobby area. And at that point a guard had pointed out a male to us that was sitting and waiting for our arrival.

Q And I understand that Constable Beach, who was a beat patrol officer, joined you in the foyer as well?

A That's right.

Q But he had nothing to do with this particular individual ultimately, that is, he didn't speak to him in your presence or arrest him or deal with him in any fashion?

A That's right.

Q What happened once you were pointed in the direction of this male by the guard at the Remand Centre?

A We approached this male and Constable Marin, I believe, began speaking to him. We identified him with his birth certificate and we identified him as Mr. Sydney Teerhuis with a date of birth of August 23rd, 1969. At that point, we walked with the male to our cruiser car, which was just parked outside the front, and Constable Marin searched him and he had a seat in the back of our cruiser car.

Q Continue, please. You search the accused.

A That's right. Then he was seated in the rear of our car. And at that point, Constable Marin and I got in the car as well and Constable Marin began a conversation with the male.

Q Yes. Go into the conversation, please.

A Okay. So at that point Constable Marin asked him, he said: *Why did you go to the Remand Centre?* And the male said: *I thought it was a police station. I came to turn myself in because I killed someone.* So at that point Constable Marin said to him, *okay, Sydney, because of what you're saying I have to inform you of your rights, okay.*

Q Continue.

A And Constable Marin said: *As of right now you're under arrest for murder or manslaughter or some similar offence. Do you understand?* And the male replied: *Yes.*

Then Constable Marin read him the 10(b) Charter rights and asked him if he understood that. Then Constable Marin asked him if he would like to call duty counsel or any other lawyer, and he replied: *Um, uh-uh, no.*

Then Constable Marin read him the police caution and asked him if he understood, and he replied: *Yes.* Constable Marin then asked him: *Where did this happen?* And he replied: *My Place.* And Constable Marin said: *Where is that?* And he said: *43 Albert, 309 at 43 Albert.* Constable Marin said: *Who is he?* And he replied:

195

I don't know. So at that point, I was no longer taking notes. I started driving to the location of 43 Albert. But Constable Marin's conversation with the male continued as I was driving.

Q And you could hear it?

A That's right...

Q Continue.

A So Constable Marin continued and asked him, he said: *What makes you think you killed him?* And he replied: *I blacked out.* And Constable Marin said: *So when you came to, you found him in your room?* And he replied: *In the bathtub. He was chopped up.* Constable Marin then said: *What did you chop him up with?* And he said: *A knife.* Constable Marin asked: *Did you change your clothes today?* And he replied: *I just put this on this morning.*

Constable Marin said: *Did you have blood on you?* And he said: *Yeah, I did yesterday.* At that point, we attended to the third floor and Constable Beach was also present with us. And the male pointed out suite number 309 as his suite, and he advised us that we could enter. So at that point Constable Marin opened the suite with the key that the male had given him. Constable Marin entered the suite and then I followed in after he did. At this point, Constable Beach remained with the male in the hallway and when we walked into the suite, that's when I observed blood on the bed, and so I walked in behind Constable Marin. There was a door on the left-hand side. Constable Marin went to the door and I walked past the bed, which was on my right, and kind of around the bed, and took a look there. At that point I looked at Constable Marin.

Q And you indicated that you went around the bed. Why did you go around the bed?

A Because the bed was pushed away from the wall a little bit. And typically, from what I've seen, what I've observed in the past is the bed is usually butted up against the wall. So in, in checking out this information, confirming it, I wanted to see what was between the bed and the wall, thinking that there may have been a body there. So I walked around, and that's when I looked in between the crack. I saw that bed sheet there, lying on the ground as it shows in the picture, covered in blood.

Q And it was what color when you saw?

A It was orange.

Q What happened then, Ma'am?

A At that point, I looked at Constable Marin and he had the bathroom door open at this point and had seen what was in the bathroom, and confirmed to me that this was a legitimate call. At that point, I looked at Constable Beach and told him: *It's legit.*

Q Now, Constable Beach never came into the room?

A No, he did not, no.

Q Neither did the accused come into the room?

A No. They remained in the hallway. He then handcuffed the male and we exited the room. Constable Marin locked the room up and handed the key to Constable Beach so that he could make sure the scene stayed secure. At that point, we walked with the male into the elevator and we escorted him back to the cruiser car. However, when we were in the elevator, Constable Marin said: *Did you want to call a lawyer?* And he said: *Um, yeah.*

Q You indicated that your partner took a cell phone and called the duty inspector. I understand you received instructions to transport this accused back to the police station?

A That's right, to the homicide unit.

Q So your function was transportation at that point in time. You were told to deliver him to the homicide detectives?

A That's correct.

Q Continue.

A So at that point, after Constable Marin notified our duty inspector, we waited for the assistance of other units. And shortly after that, members of our unit, which we call delta 109, they arrived on scene as well as our street supervisor, which we refer to as delta 161. He arrived on scene, as well. At that point, once they were there and able to take care of the matters that were left there, we transported the male to the Public Safety Building.

Q Continue.

A So then we just transported him to the Public Safety Building, to the second floor, which is where our homicide division is, and he was placed in holding room, which they all have numbers on them, so it was number three. Constable Marin then searched him again and filled out what we refer to as a prisoner log sheet. At that point, I observed like a drip of blood on the top of his head and I also observed numerous bruises on both of his legs.

Q And you described bruising on his legs from the knee down?

A That's right. From his knees to his ankles.

Q Yes, that's right.

A Yeah. Okay. At that point, we didn't have much further involvement with him once the prisoner log sheet was completed. We left him alone in the room. And at 10:30 in the morning, we had a briefing with the homicide detectives and turned care and control of the male over to them.

Q So homicide took over the investigation of this particular killing?

A That's right.

Q At that point. Now, in my calculation, you probably spent about an hour with the accused to this point in time?

A Yeah. Not quite an hour but...

Q Now, you had spent time with him in an enclosed space, the cruiser car?

A Yes.

Q You had stood next to him as he walked up to the suite 309. You'd escorted him to and from the cruiser car?

A Um-hum.

Q Four times, actually.

A Um-hum.

Q Once at the Remand Centre and back, once at the Public Safety Building. In your training as a police officer, are you taught to notice signs of intoxication?

A Yes, we are.

Q And that is basic training for you. I gather you've arrested impaired drivers during the course of your career?

A I have.

Q How many intoxicated or drunk people do you think you've come into contact with during the course of your 10 years as a police officer?

A I'd say hundreds.

Q Now, let's deal with this accused, Mr. Teerhuis-Moar.

A Okay.

Q In the time that you spent with him, did he stagger, fall down, stumble at all in any of the times you saw him walking?

A No.

Q You were in a confined space with him. Did his breath ever smell of liquor?
A No.
Q Did he ever smell of liquor?
A No, he did not.
Q When you asked him questions, was he responsive?
A Yes.
Q Did you understand what he was saying?
A Yes, I did.
Q And he clearly understood what you were saying?
A Yes, he did.
Q Did he, at any time, not understand a question and indicate that to you?
A No.
Q His speech was never slurred in the time you spoke with him?
A No, it wasn't.
Q What about his eyes, were they bloodshot, glossy?
A No, they appeared fine.
Q Was his face ever flushed?
A No.
Q Did he show you any signs of intoxication during that almost hour that you spent with him?
A No, he didn't.
Q And lastly, what was his demeanor?
A He was calm, very matter of fact, answered our questions as we asked them. Yeah.
MS. LEINBURD: Thank you very much, Ma'am.
THE WITNESS: Thank you.
THE COURT: Mr. Brodsky.

CROSS-EXAMINATION BY MR. BRODSKY:
Q First of all, let's deal with the last part first, just finished it. You were asked by my learned friend if you'd dealt with impaired drivers in the past.
A I have, yes.
Q Yes. And that's what you said before. I take it you're not dealing with an impaired driver in this case?
A That's right.
Q But if it were an impaired driver, you have a machine called a Breathalyzer, whatever the new machine is called, an alcohol test that shows how much alcohol there is in a person's blood?
A We do, we do have it, yeah, what's referred to as a Data Master, yes.
Q And that's what you use for impaired drivers?
A Once the arresting officers have formed the opinion that a person is impaired by alcohol.
Q Right.
A Then they will ask them to, to give a breath sample.
Q So you could have given this fellow a breath sample?
A If I had formed the opinion he was impaired and that he had been driving a motor vehicle I could have, but that...
Q We're talking about a homicide?
A Yes.
Q Right. Pretty grizzly one, right?
A Yes.

Q We're talking about someone who said he had blacked out, right?
A Um-hum.
Q The blackout seemed to be, according to what he said, from alcohol?
A At no time did he tell us it was from alcohol, sir.
Q All right. Did you ask him?
A I did not, no.
Q There was nothing stopping you from asking him a simple question like that if you had doubt in your mind?
A I didn't believe he was impaired.
Q No. He said at the time that he, the day before, he had blacked out. When he came to, he found the deceased in his bathtub, right? He was chopped up.
A So, yes. If you'll note, Constable Marin asks: *What makes you think you killed him*? And he replied: *I blacked out.*
Q Right.
A Then Constable Marin said: *So when you came to, you found him in your room*? And he replied: *In the bathtub. He was chopped up.*
Q Right.
A So at no point did he advise us that he had blacked out because of alcohol or because he had been drinking.
Q But you clearly could have asked him that if there was any doubt in your mind?
A There was no doubt in my mind. I did not feel that he was impaired or had been drinking.
Q No, I'm not talking about the time he was talking to you. I'm talking about the day before, when he blacked out. If you had a doubt in your mind as to the cause of, or his belief as to why he blacked out, you could have easily asked him. That be fair?
A I wouldn't have asked him that, sir.
Q Okay. Constable Marin could have asked him that, if Constable Marin was...
A I can't testify as to what Constable Marin could have or couldn't have asked him. I don't know what he would have done.
Q When the fellow says: *What makes you think you killed him*? Answer: *I blacked out. So when you came to, you found him in your room in the bathtub. He was chopped up.* It sounds like Constable Marin is asking questions and he's answering them?
A Um-hum. That's right.
Q And when Constable Marin, when he says he blacked out and Constable Marin said, *so when you came to*, it sounds like; tell me if I'm wrong, that he came to from an alcoholic blackout?
MS. LEINBURD: He's asking for a conclusion that this witness cannot give.
MR. BRODSKY: Let me ask in a different way. With this person who was, what you say, calm, responsive, able to walk and talk, there was no reason for you not to ask him, you could have asked him if you wanted to, to describe the blackout, couldn't you?
A I could have. I would imagine I could have asked him a lot of things. However, Constable Marin was the one doing the questioning. And typically, when you're in a jumper position, the driver sits back and allows the jumper, for lack of a better word, to handle the call.
Q And you could have, at the Public Safety Building, given him the Breathalyzer, the Data Master; that is a machine that registers the amount of alcohol in a person's blood. You could have done that. When I say "you", I mean you and your partner?

A That's not typically the way we would be doing things. We had no reason to believe that he was impaired and driving a vehicle at that time. We were dealing with what he had told us at the time, which was that he had killed somebody, and we needed to confirm what he was telling us was accurate.

Q Right. We're talking about the blackout.

A No. I'm talking about I have no reason to believe, in my dealings with this male, in the hour I spent with him, that he was impaired by alcohol or that he had been drinking. I didn't observe any signs of that.

Q When you stop impaired drivers, do they all show signs of impairment?

A I'm not sure I understand what you're asking.

Q I'm going to be suggesting to you that you stop people who look perfectly sober who turn out, after blowing in your ASD machine, to fail with a subsequent large amount of alcohol in their blood. That's the reason for the Breathalyzer, isn't it?

A My Lord, I'm not trained in the alcohol screening devices so I don't know when or how they are administered. I've never received training on one of them.

Q This would be a matter, in any event, as the exploration of his blackout and his coming to, all that, that's a matter for homicide?

A I don't know if homicide did look into that or not. I'm not sure. I had no further involvement with the male after we turned him over to the homicide unit.

Q The bruising that he had on his legs...

A Yes.

Q When you look at the photographs, if you look at photograph 57 and you look at photograph 58, there does appear to be bruising or dark marks that appear to be bruising on both of his lower legs?

A Okay.

Q Is that fair?

A I would say yes. Yes.

Q Did you count the bruises? Did you make any note of the bruises where they were, how many they were, size of them? Did you note the bruises at all?

A No, I did not. I noted, what I've written is: *Also observed numerous bruises on accused's legs from knees to ankles*.

Q So there must...

A I didn't make a notation or take the time to count them or notice their size.

Q Who, who would have done that? Who would count them and who would notice their size, and more importantly, who would observe them in such a fashion to say whether they were recent or not?

A Well, I would, I imagine that responsibility of photographing them would fall under our forensic identification unit. And with regard to saying how long bruises, I would, could only imagine that it would be a doctor who could say that.

Q So who takes them to a doctor to say, to age the bruises? Whose responsibility is that? Is that identification, or crime scene, or homicide detectives? Whose job is that?

A If the bruises are causing the male or the accused any hardship or issue and he requires medical attention, then he would be taken to a hospital for medical attention. However, if they were just bruises that seem to be not causing any issue for the person, then I wouldn't see any need for them to go to hospital. However, typically, if we have somebody in our custody and they notify us that they're having a medical problem or an issue, then arrangements are made with, usually, the crew that has custody of that person at the time is the same, are the same officers who would take them in for medical treatment.

Q I apologize, but I don't think we're on the same page at all.

A Oh, I'm sorry.

Q I'm talking about the investigation of a murder charge.

A Um-hum.

Q That's what I'm talking about.

A Right.

Q I'm talking about determining what part these bruises on this fellow's legs played in a murder, that is, whether he was assaulted or whether he was kicking somebody, how old they were? So how do we know how old those bruises were?

A I don't know, sir. I didn't ask him anything with regard to the bruises.

Q But whose responsibility would it be to have him seen by a doctor to age the bruises?

A I can't answer that. I don't know. I've never worked in homicide. I've never done that. That's why we have experts in this field and that's why we were given instruction to turn him over to the homicide unit because that falls beyond my scope.

Q Well, I note from your notebook that you thought it important enough in your investigation of the murder, his physical health; you were investigating a murder at that point, right?

A It's standard procedure for us, when we log somebody into a holding room, when we have them in our care, it's standard procedure for us to make notifications of their physical condition or if any medical attention has been administered or, or anything like that.

Q Because it might be relevant to the charge that you arrested him for, right?

A That's one possibility.

Q When you observed the bruises...

A Yes.

Q ...and thought it important enough to include it in your notes...

A Because that is what we typically do.

Q Wait, wait, wait, wait. I haven't asked the question yet.

A Oh, sorry.

Q When you observed the bruises...

A Yes.

Q ...and thought it was important enough to include in your notes, did you, at that time, ask him if he was having any discomfort with them?

A I did not.

Q Did you ask him and when I say "you", I mean you or your partner, whoever was with you when you...

A Okay.

Q ...observed them, did you ask him how he got them?

A I did not, and I don't recall if Constable Marin did or not.

Q Did you say to him, because you thought it important enough to mark in your notes, that there were numerous bruises...?

MS. LEINBURD: My learned friend has repeated that "important enough to note in your notebook." She's already indicated twice its standard procedure. It's not an importance or non-importance issue; it's their duty to record these items and she's indicated it twice. My learned friend keeps repeating the questions and getting the same answers.

Q The question is, did you ask him how he got them and when he got them?

A No, I did not.

MS. LEINBURD: Asked and answered twice, for the record.

Q Was he as cooperative at the time you were making these notes about the bruises on his legs as he was at earlier time?

A Yes, his demeanor with us didn't change.

Q Were you present when these photographs were taken?

A No, I wasn't.

Q You have in your notes that the jewelry from Susan Sarandon mentioned in the briefing was seen on the dresser. It's at page 80.

A Yes.

Q Did you ask him anything about that jewelry; where did you get it, how was it, why is it there? Did you ask him anything about that?

A I did not, no.

Q Did your partner?

A I don't recall if Constable Marin did.

Q Did you see any signs at all, ever, while you were in that suite, that a bleeding body had been dragged along the carpet or from the bed to the bathroom, or any place in that room? Did you see any sign whatsoever that a bleeding body had been dragged on, in that room?

A I don't recall seeing anything like that.

Q Now, it's clear that Mr. Teerhuis never said he chopped up the body in the bathtub?

A It's clear that he never said that?

Q Yes.

A Actually...

Q He never said he chopped up the body in the bathtub?

A His comment to Constable Marin, after Constable Marin asked, *so when you came to you found him in your room*, his response was: *In the bathtub. He was chopped up.*

Q Right. So what I said to you is clear. He never said, *I chopped him up*?

A His words were not, *I chopped him up*, no.

Q And when you're talking about your safety and trying to protect your safety, when you took Mr. Teerhuis to the Royal Albert Hotel, he never made any difficulty for you, he never tried to get away or yell at you or --

A No, he didn't.

Q ...say unkind things?

A No, he didn't.

Q And when you left him in the hallway, he didn't run away or try to run away?

A No.

Q No. Right. So he never gave you any indication that he was anything but cooperative?

A That's right.

Q He didn't look to you to be dangerous, based on what he was saying and doing, except for the scene in the suite?

A That's right. He was cooperative with us, yes.

Q Did he say, at any time, that he was not responsible for this killing, that somebody else was?

A Not to Constable Marin or myself.

Q Did he try to put the blame somewhere else in any--I'm not going to go through the whole, all the things he could have said.

A No, he didn't.

MR. BRODSKY: I have no further questions, My Lord.

THE COURT: Thank you, Mr. Brodsky. Ms. Leinburd, any re-examination?

MS. LEINBURD: No, thank you very much.

THE COURT: Thank you very much officer. Appreciate your help.

THE WITNESS: Thank you, My Lord.

THE COURT: Thank you.

(WITNESS EXCUSED)

MS. SAHULKA: Crown's next witness, My Lord, is Dianne Last. Wonder if she can please be paged.

THE CLERK: Dianne Last to courtroom 117. Dianne Last, courtroom 117, please. Would you like to be sworn on the Bible or affirm to tell the truth?

THE WITNESS: Affirm to tell the truth.

THE CLERK: Okay. Please state and spell your full name for the record.

THE WITNESS: Dianne Last. D-I-A-N-N-E, L-A-S-T.

DIANNE LAST, affirmed,

THE CLERK: Thank you. Please have a seat.

DIRECT EXAMINATION BY MS. SAHULKA:

Q Ms. Last, can you please tell us how old you are?

A Fifty-five.

Q Thank you. And you currently reside in Winnipeg?

A Yes.

Q All right. And I understand that you're currently employed as a bartender?

A Yes.

Q And that's with the Royal Albert Hotel at 48 Albert, here in Winnipeg?

A Yes.

Q Right. And I also understand that you've been employed at the Royal Albert Hotel for the last 23 years?

A Right.

Q And how many of those years have you been employed at the Royal Albert Hotel as a bartender?

A Since about '91.

Q '91. All right. And before that, I understand that you were a chambermaid; is that correct?

A No, I was a waitress.

Q Waitress. All right. And you would have been employed as a bartender at the Royal Albert Hotel on July 1st of 2003; is that correct?

A Yes.

Q Okay. And can you advise us what your duties as a bartender would be?

A I serve drinks, clean up glasses on tables, wipe the tables.

Q That's the extent of your duties?

A Yes.

203

Q And I understand that when the police interviewed you on July 2nd, their interest was with regards to the tenant in suite 309; is that correct?

A Yes.

Q Okay. And how many times would you have seen him from the time that he moved in to the date to the July 1st date?

A Couple of times.

Q Okay. And in what capacity?

A He came in the bar or walked, going upstairs to his room.

Q Did you see Sydney on July the 1st of 2003?

A Yes.

Q Okay. And can you tell us how it was that you saw him that day?

A He came into the bar for a beer.

Q Okay. What time did he come into the bar that day?

A About 2:30.

Q And that's in the morning or afternoon?

A Afternoon.

Q And do you recall if he was alone or was with anybody?

A He was alone.

Q Okay. And so when Sydney came into the bar at 2:30 in the afternoon, what did he do?

A He went to the side of the bar and ordered a beer.

Q Okay.

A And so I brought it to him and told him what the price was, two eighty-five.

Q Okay.

A And that was it. He sat there, drank his beer, and then Damien and Sherry came in the bar and sat at the high table. And he had a beer over there and I guess Sydney wanted to talk to somebody so he went over just to Damien and Sherry, talked with them for a little bit.

Q And prior to Sherry and Damien--we'll get to them in a minute-- coming in, what did Sydney do?

A Just sat at the bar and had his drink.

Q And how long did he sit at the bar for?

A Roughly about half an hour, I guess.

Q So except for the extent of him asking you for the beer, that was the only conversation you had with him?

A Yes.

Q Okay. You indicated that Damien and Sherry came in?

A Um-hum.

Q Okay. And how did you know this Damien and Sherry?

A Damien worked at the bar but at nighttime.

Q Okay. And Sherry was who?

A Apparently his girlfriend.

Q And do you remember what time they came into the bar?

A Close to three o'clock.

Q Three o'clock. All right.

A Yes. And they were sitting at the first one closest to the bar.

Q Okay. And you indicated that when they came in, Sid moved over to them?

A Yeah, he went over and talked with them.

Q Okay. And did you note any conversation taking place between Sid, Damien and Sherry?

A Yeah, they were talking, but I don't know what they were talking about.

Q Okay. Do you recall how long the three of them spoke for?

A No, I don't.

Q Okay. And what happened after that?

A They went out the exit door and went outside, had their cigarette and came back in.

Q Okay. And how long were they outside having a cigarette?

A About five minutes or so.

Q And they came back into the bar?

A Yes.

Q All right. And then what happened with Sydney?

A Sydney left shortly after that.

Q How shortly?

A Ten minutes after they came back in.

Q Okay. So when they came back in from the cigarette, you're saying it was 10 minutes until he left. What did he do through that 10-minute time?

A Well, finished his beer, then he left.

Q Okay. Did you see Sydney again that day?

A Yes.

Q What time did you see him at?

A Between 4:30 and 5:00.

Q And under what circumstances?

A He came back into the bar.

Q Okay. Was he alone at that time or with somebody?

A He was with somebody.

Q Who was this person he was with?

A Robin Greene, a native guy.

Q Okay. Did you know Robin Greene?

A No, I didn't.

Q Okay. So how do you know the name?

A Oh, saw it in the paper.

Q Okay. So you didn't know Robin Greene before you saw him on July the 1st of 2003?

A No.

Q First time you ever met him?

A Right.

Q Okay. Can you describe him for us?

A He's, well, native. He was maybe about 5'7, long hair.

Q What color hair?

A Brown, dark brown, I guess.

Q No. Okay. So you indicated that Sydney came back into the bar through the lounge door with this other individual.

A Yes.

Q And what happened when he came into the bar?

A Sydney introduced him as his cousin and asked me to keep an eye on him because he wanted to go downstairs to get some ice.

Q Okay. And you said Sydney introduced him as his cousin?

A Yes.

Q Did he give you a name?

A No.

Q Okay. And then Sydney said what to you?

A He asked me to watch him so he could go downstairs and get some ice.

Q Okay. And why is it necessary to enter the bar to get ice?

A Well, the ice machine is in the basement.

Q Okay. All right. So Sydney came and told you that he was going to the basement to get ice?

205

A Yes.

Q And what else did he say?

A That was it.

Q That was it?

A Yeah.

Q And what happened with the gentleman he was with?

A He stood at the entrance of the bar.

Q Okay. At the entrance to the bar?

A Well, right in front of the bar where I could see him.

Q And again, are we talking again the six feet away?

A Yes.

Q So he didn't move from that spot?

A No.

Q Okay. And at that point, what happened?

A Sydney went downstairs for the ice and then came up the elevator.

Q How long was Sydney gone?

A Couple of minutes.

Q Okay. And when he came back up, you said through the elevator, come back into the bar area?

A Yes.

Q And what did he do at that point?

A He took his buddy out and they left.

Q Did he say anything to you at that point?

A No.

Q Did he have ice with him that you could see?

A Yes, he did.

Q And the gentleman he was with, did he move at all from the spot that he was in?

A Well, not really. He was kind of swaying back and forth.

Q Okay. What do you mean 'swaying'? From side to side, Forward and backwards?

A Forward and backwards, yeah.

Q Okay. So Sydney came back and took him out?

A Yes.

Q And didn't say anything further?

A No.

Q And did you ever see either the man he was with or Sydney again?

A No.

Q Okay. We've spoken about you being a bartender for a fairly significant amount of time.

A Yes.

Q So obviously your duties include providing people with alcoholic beverages?

A Yes.

Q All right. Is it fair to say that over your years as a bartender you've seen your fair share of intoxicated individuals?

A Oh, yes.

Q Can you comment on the state of sobriety of the gentleman that Sydney was with?

A Not really.

Q No?

A I wasn't up close enough to him so I don't know.

Q Were there any indications that he was intoxicated in any way?

A No.

Q What about Sydney--and I'll direct you back to the time that he came into the bar at 2:30 in the afternoon.
A Yes.
Q Right. And you indicated that he had the one OV at that time?
A Yes.
Q So when Sydney came into the bar earlier in the afternoon at 2:30 again, were there any indications that he was intoxicated?
A No.
Q You never saw or when he spoke to you and asked you for the OV, did you have any difficulty understanding what he was asking?
A No, he was fine.
Q Didn't slur his speech?
A No.
Q When he walked up to the bar from the lobby, did you notice if he was unsteady on his feet in any way?
A No, he seemed quite fine.
Q What about later in the afternoon. You indicated when he came back between 4:30 and 5:00 with the gentleman, again were there any indications that Sydney was intoxicated at that time?
A No.
Q And again, he made the comment to you about going downstairs to get the ice. When he was speaking to you, did you notice that his speech was slurred in any way?
A No.
Q Did you get close enough to him to notice whether his eyes were red or glassy in any way?
A No.
MS. SAHULKA: Okay. Thank you. Those are my questions.
THE COURT: Mr. Brodsky.

CROSS-EXAMINATION BY MR. BRODSKY:
Q This is a stupendous case.
A Yeah.
Q And you know that because of what you saw on TV?
A Yes.
Q And it's been a lot in the paper and a lot on TV?
A Papers I've been missing, though.
Q Right. So your source of information about the case is from television?
A Yes.
Q Right. And it was on the television right after Sydney was in getting the beer, the OV?
A Yes.
Q And that day and the next day and the next day on a lot, right?
A Oh, on television. Yes.
Q And it has been for a number of years?
A Yes.
Q Right. And, too, it was a stupendous case because that kind of stuff, a chopped-up body in a bathtub, that's not usual for the Royal Albert or any other hotel?
A No.
Q And that happened right in the place where you work?
A I know. Scary.
Q Right. Now, would be fair to say that you didn't have enough time to tell if Sydney was drunk?

A No.

Q What you do know is that Sydney seemed to be in the same condition as the fellow he was with, however drunk or sober that was; they seemed to be the same. Would that be fair?

A I don't know.

Q So you can't tell us how drunken Sydney was?

A No. He looked fine to me.

Q When Sydney came the first time, and this is before you saw it in the paper, before you saw it on the television and before you knew that anything was going to go awry, your best recollection is that he ordered a beer, period? That's all he said?

A Yes.

Q And you remember if he said anything more than OV?

A No, that's all he ordered, OV.

Q And did he say anything more?

A No.

Q And then he went and sat with some other people?

A Yes.

Q So they were the people who were with him the longest?

A Yes.

Q And you didn't hear what they were saying to each other?

A That's right.

Q And it would be fair to say that when Sydney said that he was going to get the ice the second time he came back, do you remember exactly what words he used?

A He just said...

Q Watch him?

A Watch him, and I'm going to go get some ice.

Q Okay. Whether he was slurring or not, he didn't say enough words for you to tell?

A No.

Q And it was in the paper also about the jewelry?

A Yes, I read that.

Q What did you read about the jewelry?

A They stole it from somebody's trailer.

Q A movie star's trailer?

A Yeah.

Q Like Susan Sarandon?

A I can't recall the name.

Q And Richard Gere and that group were in to make a movie; that was in the paper you read?

A I can't remember.

MR. BRODSKY: I have no further questions.

THE COURT: Thank you, Mr. Brodsky. Ms. Leinburd, any re-examination? Thank you very much, Ms. Last, for your help. You can leave. Thank you.

(WITNESS EXCUSED)

THE COURT: Tomorrow we're not sitting, so we'll see you back on Monday morning at ten o'clock. As I say, I expect that we're going to move pretty quickly once next week rolls around, all right. Thanks again for your attention.

(JURY OUT AT 3:20 P.M.)

THE COURT: Self-defense--was that ever on the table or is it on the table?

MR. BRODSKY: There's no evidence of self-defense in this case.

THE COURT: That's what I thought.

MR. BRODSKY: I'm going on the evidence that we have.

THE COURT: Okay. I just...

MR. BRODSKY: So I'm not going to raise a defense that I can't prove.

THE COURT: All right. That's always refreshing to hear.

MR. BRODSKY: All right. Let me rephrase that. I'm not going to raise a defense that I can't establish a reasonable doubt on.

(BRIEF RECESS)

MS. LEINBURD: There is one issue I'd like to raise with the court. The accused has now had two outbursts, one of which I've not commented on when he approached my colleague and called her a foul name. I said to Mr. Brodsky that I wanted that issue dealt with and I believe he had spoken to his client. But worse than that, this afternoon, while a female police officer was testifying, I heard the accused, and I was busy at the time, so his tenor and the loudness of his commentary was heard by me and I was speaking. He called her a bitch. Nobody in this courtroom needs to abide by that kind of foul commentary by the accused person.

THE ACCUSED: "I won't tolerate somebody who's fucking lying in court."

THE COURT: Mr. Brodsky, I heard it as well.

MS. LEINBURD: The jury heard it, as I understand it, as well, from the clerk.

THE COURT: I didn't say anything. I was going to raise it actually with you. Two issues. I think in fairness to your client, and I try to bend over backwards to be fair in a case like this, I'd like you, as a counsel far more capable than most to try to restrain Mr. Teerhuis-Moar from prejudicing his own cause, and I'd also like you to tell me what you want me to do at this point, if anything. The jury has heard that outburst. It's unfortunate, but this sort of thing can't continue. It's going to complicate things for you and your client.

MR. BRODSKY: I will speak to him right after court. And I don't want you to do anything. I don't want you to do a single thing.

THE COURT: Okay.

MR. BRODSKY: Neither of the comments were threats. I told my learned friend I would speak to him. The first time; I did; and I will again, right after court.

THE COURT: I have no doubt that you will, and as I say, I'm confident because it is you. But on that second point, you want me to say nothing; I'll say nothing.

MR. BRODSKY: Yes. I do not want the jury to think that he is dangerous in any way. That's the reason why we have the jury excluded, so they don't see the shackles, and I don't want any comment. I want him to have a fair trial.

THE COURT: Fair enough. Okay. So, ten o'clock Monday morning? Yes.

THE CLERK: Order, all rise. Court is adjourned to Monday at 10:00.

19
The Days Just Before

FRIDAY, DECEMBER 5/08

ON FRIDAY, DECEMBER 5TH THERE WAS A DAY OFF FROM THE TRIAL AND THE FOLLOWING headline appeared in the Winnipeg Free Press: **Accused killer wanted to be cooked and eaten, court told.**

I discovered later the story had made headlines across Canada and the U.S., but more importantly it made its way to major newspapers in various places in the world and especially news agencies in India because Sidney had planned his death by cannibalism with an Indian man.

The article was derived from Sidney's one letter, which spoke of cannibalism, grave digging and necrophilia. The paper quoted Sidney as saying, *"I told him the only way I'd do it is if he kept all my bones in a trunk under his bed,"* and *"I still think about him every now and then and hope someday I will run into him so he can cook me."* Sidney continued, *"I will wait to find the right man or men who'd be willing to have me on their dinner table,"* and another quote, *"I would go to their graves. Only once did I dig a grave and open a coffin."*

The newspaper article stated, *"Teerhuis wrote the letters to Dan Zupansky, a freelance Winnipeg journalist who established contact with him following Greene's killing. Zupansky will be called by the Crown to testify next week."*

SATURDAY, DECEMBER 6/08

I OPENED THE WINNIPEG SUN AND THE HEADLINE READ: **DRUNKENNESS DEFENCE: An obstacle to justice?** By Joyanne Pursaga.

The story referred to Sidney's case as an example of a trial that the 'drunkenness defense' was being used to lessen the charge of murder to manslaughter. Joyanne wrote: *It seems impossible that a night of drinking could be enough to reduce the penalty for ending a life. That is why the excuse of a 'drunken blackout' may come as a shock to those horrified and frightened by the alleged details coming out of the ongoing Sidney Teerhuis trial.*

She cited other examples: Those members of a mob that beat a man outside the Maryland Hotel received sentences raging from 11 and a half months to 5 years. The Crown stated that the penalties were determined partly by each assailant's level of intoxication.

Marie Daniels in 2007 was sentenced to 4 years in prison for killing her common-law husband. Her defence was that she was too drunk to remember stabbing the man to death.

The Crown said they couldn't prove Daniels 'had the intent to kill' because of her intoxication. The second-degree murder was reduced to manslaughter.

Michael Cochrane pled guilty to manslaughter in 2006 and received a five-year sentence after he claimed to have been so drunk he couldn't remember beating an elderly homeless man to death in 2005. He was also originally charged with second-degree murder.

Joyanne wrote that these cases demonstrated that self-induced intoxication has been regarded as an obstacle to proving an accused's intent to kill, a key issue necessary to convict someone of murder.

Sunday, December 7/08

I met with Sheila Leinburd one day before I was to testify for the prosecution. We had agreed to meet at 11:00 a.m. at the Woodsworth Building. It was a cold, windy and blustery day and Sheila was a few minutes late arriving.

She let us into the building and we traveled up to the 6th floor to the Crown Attorney's office. She told me to have a seat and she would be back shortly. She returned with her assistant Deanne and they both sat across from me.

I had been of course following closely the trial by reading the two city newspapers and watching the C.T.V. television news broadcasts. The coverage had been extensive and the city's news agencies were treating the trial as a very important one.

I had also been monitoring the extent that the trial was being covered worldwide via the internet and I was relieved to see that the trial was being carried by so many news agencies and that the story seemed to interest a great many people. I was pleasantly surprised that the Prosecution had chosen to utilize the letters that I had provided so prominently in the trial right from the first day. I was pleased with how the trial was progressing and confident about my testifying the next day.

Sheila had, early in the meeting, stated that I was to only answer questions that Brodsky would put forth to me, explaining that if I were not to directly answer questions and instead decided to expand my answers that I would wind up in trouble on the stand.

She asked me a series of questions regarding the correspondence between Sidney and I, the kinds of questions that we had gone over previously. I assumed that they were the kinds of questions she would ask me in her direct examination and that Greg Brodsky might very well ask during his cross-examination of me.

Sheila didn't however point out what line of questioning that Brodsky might likely pursue—no questions specifically that I should anticipate and prepare for. She had at an earlier meeting told me that she would give me a list of questions that she would be asking me during direct examination. She did not provide me with any such list.

Sheila continued with her questions and I easily answered them with strong conviction, trying as hard as I could to just simply answer her questions and not elaborate.

Near the end of our meeting Sheila asked a very important question that we had covered in our previous meeting in October, and that being if I felt that there was any truth to Sidney's claim that he had taken 4 separate serial killer's stories and combined them to create the story about the murder of Robin Greene, resulting in a fictional account. Previously I had stated that as a result of my research for my book I had read and studied all four serial killer's stories and I had concluded that there was no truth to the claim whatsoever.

When asked again I proceeded to explain that the only similarities were that John Wayne Gacy, Jeffrey Dahmer and Dennis Nilsen were homosexuals and that their victims men and that they dismembered their victims. As soon as I had stated that she told me that when asked the same question by Brodsky that I was to agree that there were some similarities between Sidney's story of Greene's murder and three of the serial killer's stories. She said quite sarcastically, "*Do not think that you are smarter than you are Mr. Zupansky. Mr. Brodsky will turn you right around on the stand if you answer otherwise.*" I was taken aback and didn't like her insult at all but I held my tongue. Based on what she had just said I could only imagine that I should take her warning to heart—Brodsky would be a formidable opponent.

Right at the end of our meeting Sheila asked me something about my book and I realized that she wasn't actually so interested but I used the question as an opportunity to explain that I had publishers looking at my proposal, considering my book. I had not decided before the meeting if I was going to let her know that I had a website set up for the book and that there was a film clip posted on YouTube. I decided at the end of the meeting that I should tell her so as to not surprise her given that I was to testify the next day. I figured that since it was just a day before that she would have little time if any to view the website for herself, but at least when it most assuredly would be raised by Brodsky during my cross-examination, she would have been informed of it's existence.

The meeting was almost over when Sheila instructed me to be at the Law Courts at 8:30 the next morning. I thought that the time she wanted me there was quite early and I asked her if she wanted me there at that time so she could further prepare me for direct and cross-examination. Instead she surprised me by stating that she just wanted me there to ensure I would be there and on time. I told her that I would be there and bid her and Deanne goodbye.

Monday, December 8/08

After a restless sleep, I got up early so as to make it to the Law Courts for 8:30, some hour-and-a-half earlier than court was to start.

At about 8:10 I received a phone call from Sheila Leinburd informing me that I needn't be there for 8:30, because she was interviewing the other witness Tom Pomplum who was also to testify that morning. He had just arrived from a flight from Wisconsin the night before and my assumption was that she hadn't interviewed him as of yet.

I arrived at the Law Courts with my girlfriend at about 9:30 and in the hallway outside the courtroom Winnipeg Sun court reporter Dean Pritchard warmly introduced himself. Mike McIntyre was there from the Free Press and Kelly Dehn from C.T.V. television.

Tom Pomplum was called over the P.A. system and he entered the courtroom. He seemed very nervous and apprehensive—looking very much like he would rather be anywhere else right about then.

20

My Testimony

(PROCEEDINGS CONTINUED FROM DECEMBER 4, 2008)

THE CLERK: Court is open. Please be seated.
MS. LEINBURD: Just come forward, Mr. Pomplum.
THE CLERK: Do you wish to be sworn on the Bible or affirm to tell the truth? Okay. Please state and spell your full name for the record.
THE WITNESS: It's Thomas Gray Pomplum.
THE CLERK: Can you spell all those names.
THE WITNESS: Thomas, T-H-O-M-A-S.
THE CLERK: Um-hum.
THE WITNESS: Gray, G-R-A-Y, Pomplum, P-O-M-P-L-U-M.
THOMAS GRAY POMPLUM, affirmed,
THE CLERK: Thank you. Have a seat.

DIRECT EXAMINATION BY MS. LEINBURD:
Q Mr. Pomplum, where do you live, sir?
A I live in Wisconsin, in the country near a little town called Mount Horeb.
Q And what do you do for a living, sir?
A I'm a small publisher.
Q I understand that you are the publisher of a series of books called Graphic Classics; is that correct?
A Yes, it is.
Q And I have an example of one of your books. It's titled, Graphic Classics, and it has cartoon images in it; is that correct?
A Yes, it is.
Q Wonder if you might describe the kinds of books that you publish under that series, sir?
A It's a series of comics adaptations of classic literature: Poe, Mark Twain, including H.P. Lovecraft. There are those in the series at this point and more coming.
Q So you basically take the classics and have them interpreted by way of comic drawing?
A Yes.
Q I understand, sir, that you sell your particular line of books throughout Canada, North America, sometimes in Europe; is that correct?
A Yes. They're distributed in the United States and Canada.
Q Do you know whether or not you sell to prisons?

A I have sold some directly to prisons. Most of my books are sold through a distributor and my main customers are libraries and that includes school and public libraries as well as prison libraries.

Q Now, I understand, sir, that on September the 18th of 2004, that you received a letter; is that correct?

A Yes, I did.

Q And it's that letter that brings you from Wisconsin to this court?

A Yes.

Q And the return address is Headingley Correctional Centre; is that correct?

A Yes.

Q Now, in terms of that particular letter, you received it on September the 18th of '04, as I understand it; is that correct?

A Yes.

Q And I'm going to go through the first portion of that particular letter. I'm going to direct you to the full first paragraph, and I'm going to indicate the following:

> *My unfortunate claim to fame, across Canada, and as far away as England; was the death of Robin Greene... Greene was decapitated, I then performed sex acts on his headless corpse after he was chopped into pieces and the internal organs scooped out. Greene was then emasculated (cutting of the penis and testicles in one large piece).*

Q What is contained in the letter? And before we go much further in the letter, look to the last page, sir. Whose signature is on that letter?

A I read it as Sydney Teerhuis.

Q Okay. Now, let's proceed back to the first page of the letter, sir. When you initially began to read this letter and completed it, what response did you have to it?

A Well, I felt a little sick to my stomach. I get the letter and it was accompanied by a cartoon, as you know, that is not unusual for me. I, I'm a small publisher. I get submissions unsolicited all the time, and usually accompanied by a color letter. This one was a little exceptional in that it had little to do with his artistic ability and details that were rather unsettling.

Q We're going to continue through to the letter. I'll direct you to the bottom of the first page of the letter. Mr. Teerhuis goes on to say: "*I have news that will shock the world on what happened that July first in room three 'O' nine, at the Royal Albert Arms. I'm the only one who knows what really happened to Robin, I know his last words; I was the last person to have consensual sex with him, the last person to swallow his semen after oral sex. There are photos of him posing nude and modeling underwear hours before his death.*" Now, once you had read this information, what did you do?

A Well, I swallowed, then I wasn't sure this was something serious or if this was a sick joke, so I looked up the case on the internet.

Q And without going into much detail about what you found on the Internet, was it consistent with what was in the letter?

A Yes.

Q And once you had read about it on the Internet, what did you do?

A Well, then I realized that this was serious and a real case and then I called the Winnipeg Police.

Q And it's my understanding that ultimately a Winnipeg city detective went to Wisconsin to your home?

A Yes.

Q Prior to that, he had contacted you, telling you to copy the letter, correct?

A No. He told me to put the letter in plastic.

Q And then to copy it.

A And safe hold it for him.

Q Okay. And did he, in fact, come to your home? and take that original letter that's now marked as Exhibit 59?

A Took the original and my deposition, yes.

Q Now, in terms of the particular cartoon, if we can call it that, it's a one-page drawing of seven square boxes; is that correct?

A Yes.

Q And it's entitled "Life in the Big City by Sidney Teerhuis"; is that correct?

A Yes.

Q One sheet. Is it at all to your standard, sir?

A No, it's not the sort of thing that I would publish, by any means.

Q In terms of the latter portion of his letter, he goes on to indicate to you that, and this is on the last page, sir:

> *I give you my permission to set up a website in my name listing my particulars that I sent to you. I'm pretty well known here in Canada.*

Q He was giving you permission to set up a website?

A I--yes, he was, but I don't know why he would. I do have a website for my publishing house and I do have pages for each of the artists who actually publish in my books, but he obviously was not.

Q You never had any further contact or any contact, as a matter of fact, with this accused, did you?

A No, I didn't care to. I turned this over to the police, and this is the first I've heard of the case, actually, since.

MS. LEINBURD: Thank you very much, Mr. Pomplum.

THE COURT: Mr. Brodsky.

CROSS-EXAMINATION BY MR. BRODSKY:

Q Is what you publish fictional accounts based on a true story, at least a published story?

A Well, they're based on classic fiction, yes. And so--

Q So the underlying...

A Remains fiction.

Q The underlying premise is that the book that you're doing the take-off on, the cartoons on, is accurate and then you let your imagination...

A They're adaptations of fiction, in the same way that a movie or a treatment of a fiction book would be anything like that.

Q Right. So some parts are real and some parts are flights of your imagination that would be appealing to readers?

A Not my imagination. They would be the original imagination of the writers.

Q Right. You didn't write him back to say, send me the photos?

A No.

Q ...That he's talking about. You didn't write him back to, to call to say that he would like to speak to his lawyer who he names?

A I had no further contact with him; sent him no letters.

Q Did you know who he was talking about when he says that a third party was having sex with Greene, there are photos of that, the guy's name was George?

A No.

Q The photos are missing?

A Never heard of him other than in here.

Q Did the police talk to you about the photos and whether or not you knew anything about where they went?

A I don't recall that they did. I had no connection with those.

Q Had you had any prior communication with Mr. Teerhuis? By that name or any other name?

A No. This letter was the first thing I ever heard of him.

Q And there was nothing that you put out that asked for a response from him, this response from him, which you know of?

A No, other than that my name is printed in all my books and apparently that's how he got my name.

Q Is it common for people to write to you to tell you how many times a day they masturbate?

A It's common for readers to write to me. I have never gotten a letter like this.

Q When he's talking, in his letter, about Dennis Nilsen and Jeffrey Dahmer and Westley Allan Dodd and John Gacy and Aileen Wuornos, you knew who they were, I take it?

A Most of them I've heard of, yes.

Q Who are they?

A Mass murderers.

Q And when he writes that Dennis Nilsen: "...*Truly loved his victims by bathing their corpses and making love to them.*" Do you know that to be part of that histology?

A I have not heard of that person.

Q And where did you go to on the Internet to look up this, whatever it is you looked up?

A I just Googled his name.

Q Wasn't too hard to find stories?

A No. Actually, the first time I Googled him, his name is spelled S-I-D-N-E-Y in this letter and nothing came up.

Q Right.

A And then it occurred to me to try S-Y-D-N-E-Y and then a huge list of things came up.

Q With many hits on it?

A I don't know about hits. I mean, there was many articles listed, mostly having to do with the Hollywood connection.

Q Now, in the letter, it says Mr. Greene was decapitated. Never says at anytime that he was responsible for the killing; would that be fair?

A Are you asking for my opinion?

Q In the letter that you got. When you got the letter, it talks about what?

A It says that he was decapitated.

Q Right.

A But there were other places where he says he performs sex acts on the corpse directly.

Q Right.

A And there are other places where he strongly implies that he was the author of this.

THE COURT: When you say 'author'...

THE WITNESS: Or the creator of this mayhem.

THE COURT: Sorry?

THE WITNESS: The person behind this mayhem is what I got the impression from this.

Q I take it what he expected from you, based on your reading of the letter, because you never spoke to him directly, was that he wanted you to publish what he was telling you?

A No, not what he was telling me. I got the impression that he wanted me to publish either this cartoon that he had sent me or other of his works.

Q And the cartoon is a cartoon of--an awful cartoon, silly cartoon?

A Well I don't know how to characterize it. It's crude. I mean, it's crude both in subject matter and in execution, and neither is up to the standards of what I would publish.

Q Right. So when he has an axe, a picture of someone with an axe chopping off a portion of a person's body, that's not something, you would publish?

A No.

Q Even if it was on top of a note that says, "Munchie takes pride in his work." That doesn't make it more acceptable to your audience?

A It would not either--even if this was done well, it would not be the sort of thing I would publish because I only publish adaptations of classic literature.

Q He didn't seem to be denying that he was involved somehow in this unfortunate event?

A Not to me.

Q And with the exception of not saying that he was the killer, the rest of it is gross?

A Yes.

Q And he clearly gives you the idea that there are international headlines around the world on what happened about the remains of the unfortunate victim here?

A There are implications in the website articles that I read that said that there are missing things, and of course they implied that there was something, cannibalism, or something involved. I don't know what that was directly.

Q Well, he says in his letter that there is international headlines, it's outlined in the fact that his internal organs, the viscera are missing, and you found that to be so on your website check, on your internet check?

A Yes, I did. That was what made me think that this was an actual letter and I should turn it over to the police, because it did correspond to what I had found on the web.

Q And the Susan Sarandon necklace and the movie about "Shall We Dance" with Jennifer Lopez and Richard Gere, you found that also to be recorded in the Internet search that you made?

A Yes.

MR. BRODSKY: I have no further questions, My Lord.

THE COURT: Thank you, Mr. Brodsky. Ms. Leinburd, any re-examination?

MS. LEINBURD: No re-examination, thank you.

THE COURT: Thank you very much for your assistance, Mr. Pomplum.

(WITNESS EXCUSED)

MS. LEINBURD: Thank you, Mr. Pomplum. I wonder if we might have a brief recess at this point in time.

THE COURT: Sure.

THE CLERK: Order, all rise. Court is in...

MS. LEINBURD: No, I wanted to...

THE CLERK: Oh.

MS. LEINBURD: In terms of my learned friend's questions, I have not commented on this to this point in time, but Mr. Brodsky has admitted that his accused is the killer, plain and simple, and yet in every witness that he has questioned, he says, well, he didn't admit he was the killer. Now, I haven't risen to this point in time but I think that's inappropriate, given his admission. I think it may lead the jury to be confused about what it is that was admitted, and frankly, I don't understand the basis of his questions if, in fact, he knows full well that the accused admitted to killing Robin Greene.

THE COURT: Mr. Brodsky, did you want to respond?

MR. BRODSKY: I've already responded to this many times. I can say once more, clearly, as clearly as I can, that my client admits he's the killer. I could say it again to the jury if my learned friend would like it.

THE COURT: All right. But Mr...

MR. BRODSKY: But the fact of the matter is, he knew he was the killer because he was in a unconscious state, he woke up, found the remains in the bathtub, as he says, and knew what he had done. That's how he knows he's the killer.

THE COURT: But Ms. Leinburd's questions are mores. Leinburd's objection is more nuance. She's saying that irrespective of your admission, which you're repeating now, there's a question of propriety with respect to your cross-examination. You're posing questions, which notwithstanding your admissions, seem to suggest that at some point in every witness' contact with Mr. Teerhuis, either orally or in writing, he doesn't specifically admit to the killing. So the question is: Is there confusion and a potential contradiction that is not appropriate for cross-examination?

MR. BRODSKY: I'm going to say to the jury exactly what I've just said to Your Lordship. He is the killer. He admits he's the killer. He knows he is the killer because when he woke up from his blackout...

THE COURT: Okay, well let's...

MR. BRODSKY: He saw what he had done.

THE COURT: Well, then let me...

MR. BRODSKY: He was the killer.

THE COURT: Well, then let me push you to the next stage. Again, you haven't changed your position. That is the position that Ms. Leinburd has understood you to take, position I understood you to take, it's the position you're going to put to the jury. That begs the question: What is the justification for the questions you're posing which seem to suggest, at best, confusion concerning...

MR. BRODSKY: Okay. I want the jury to take out of the letter to Mr. Pomplum the fact that even here he doesn't say he knows what he did as a result of--that he was conscious at the time he did it. He knows what he did. He knows that prior to the killing he had consensual sex with the, with Mr. Greene. He knows what happened after the killing.

THE COURT: No, but the confusion I think, Mr. Brodsky, I understood, and again, you'll conduct the cross-examination that you want and I'll permit you to conduct, but I can see you, for instance, cross-examining in a way that would suggest that he doesn't know what happened to the body and how the body came to be as it was found. That's one thing. But to the extent that the questions you're posing still leave some doubt as to whether or not Mr. Teerhuis-Moar is admitting to the killing, that's where the confusion becomes potentially impermissible cross-examination. I haven't decided that but that's what I understand Ms. Leinburd's position to be.

MR. BRODSKY: I'm not saying that George was the killer or Sam or Pete.

THE COURT: No, you're misunderstanding me. I'm not suggesting you are saying that. But I'm saying that your questions are difficult to reconcile with the admission that you make. So insofar as your questions are suggestive of the fact that Mr. Teerhuis, at no point in his time, in his contact with any of these witnesses was able to tell you--or had confusion about how perhaps the body was chopped up, if you will, and that's not the argument that Ms. Leinburd is going to be making, she's going to suggest that he knew what he did and he--anyway, you know the position. But...

MR. BRODSKY: I think the argument is...

THE COURT: That's different from what you're doing.

MR. BRODSKY: The argument that my learned friend and I are having is my learned friend says he knew what he did while he was doing it and I say he knew what he did because of what he found when he woke up, he knew what he did.

THE COURT: Okay.

MR. BRODSKY: And we're not denying that he's the killer. I mean, I've said that umpteen times.

THE COURT: Then can I ask you, Mr. Brodsky, just because it seems to me it's of no moment to you, given what you want to argue, would you not then continue to pose questions that Ms. Leinburd is objecting to, which leaves doubt as to who it was that killed Mr. Greene. If you want to pose questions that leaves doubt with respect to whether your client knew how the body came to be in the state it was when it was discovered the next morning, that's one thing. But to ask questions that seem to continue to suggest that there is some doubt as to who the killer was is irreconcilable with your admission and, based on Ms. Leinburd's objections, not questioning she wants you to pursue. So given your response, it doesn't seem like it's of any moment to you anyway, so why would you want to push that envelope?

MR. BRODSKY: When the cross-examination of the next witness commences, I will say clearly to him, in the presence of the jury, that we are not denying that he's the killer. What he's doing is building a fictitious story based on that event, the killing. He knows he was the killer because nobody else was around. He knows he was the killer because he was the last person with him, as far as he knows. He knows he was the killer because it was in his apartment. How could have all of that gone on, that is, the decapitation and the evisceration, while he was in bed? Nobody else would be sneaking into his room to do that to leave the body. I mean, he knows that. That's why he knows he's the killer. Now I'm going to say to Mr. Pomplum--not Mr. Pomplum but to the next witness.

THE COURT: Right.

MR. BRODSKY: I'm going to say, when he's telling you the things that went on while he was in this unconscious state, he's imagining. That part is fictitious. He knows he did it.

THE COURT: Well, how can...

MR. BRODSKY: And he's just building on a--he's building a fictitious account on a real fact. The real fact is...

THE COURT: And I understand that part of the position you're arguing; but how can the witness respond to what is fictitious? That's ultimately determination for the jury to make. That's my point.

MR. BRODSKY: I wasn't going to except that if that helps anybody or has helped my learned friend in the jury's understanding, I'm prepared to say it out loud. It's not a secret.

THE COURT: Okay. I think we're no...

MR. BRODSKY: I wouldn't have done it otherwise to the--at the outset to the next witness, but...

THE COURT: I can see you arguing, Mr. Brodsky, that there are--Mr. Teerhuis' position, in some ways, to a given witness, was inconsistent with, with certain things they later came to know as true, and then you could say, all right, the entire, or some other portions of the document, the letter, for example, ought to be seen as less true because of that. But I still don't get the point you're making, so--and I'm obviously not being clear enough to you. So what we'll do is we'll just take it as it comes. And I think I have your position that you're not going to pursue the questions that Ms. Leinburd has asked you not to do, but...

MS. LEINBURD: If Mr. Brodsky persists in asking, he didn't admit he was the killer, suggesting that someone else was the killer, or leaving that impression, I will stand up and just remind the court that there is an admission that this man is the killer, because that's the only way to make it clear. And I agree, Mr. Brodsky doesn't understand what I'm objecting to nor is he taking direction from the court.

THE COURT: Well, I'm trying to give direction but I'm also trying to understand the point Mr. Brodsky is making because I want to be able to see if there's any possible justification for the way you're formulating the question. I don't see it just yet, but...

MR. BRODSKY: He read the newspapers, he watched the television, he saw the autopsy photos and he read the autopsy report. He did all of that so he knows the true facts, that is, the condition of the body. He then...

THE COURT: No, I know that.

MR. BRODSKY: Built a fictitious castle.

THE COURT: I know that, but that's got nothing to do, though, with the objection Ms. Leinburd is making. We'll just leave it because I don't think we're going to be able to necessarily preempt it with our exchange here. Did you want to take a break, Ms. Leinburd?

MS. LEINBURD: No. That was the only comment I wanted to make because, as I said, I've not raised it thus far and I wasn't prepared to raise it in front of the jury without at least forewarning my learned friend and explaining my position to the court. So if that question is asked, I'm going to say that there is an admission before the court.

THE COURT: Can I get one other thing clear, if you're able to provide it to me, Mr. Brodsky. Are you acknowledging that the letters were written by Mr. Teerhuis-Moar?

MR. BRODSKY: Yes.

THE COURT: Okay. So that's not an issue?

MS. LEINBURD: That has never been an issue, as I understand it.

THE COURT: Yeah, okay. Please.

THE USHER: We may need a minute, My Lord, to get them together.

THE COURT: Okay.

THE USHER: Okay.

(JURY IN AT 10:36 A.M.)

THE CLERK: My Lord, all 12 jurors are present.

THE COURT: Okay, thank you.

220

MS. LEINBURD: Thank you. Then Crown's next witness is Dan Zupansky. Just come forward, Mr. Zupansky. Right into the witness box, sir.

THE CLERK: Do you wish to be sworn on the Bible or affirm to tell the truth?

THE WITNESS: Just affirm to tell the truth.

THE CLERK: Would you please state and spell your full name for the record.

THE WITNESS: My name is Danny Mitchael Zupansky. That's D-A-N-N-Y, M-I-T-C-H-A-E-L, Zupansky, Z-U-P-A-N-S-K-Y.

DANNY MITCHAEL ZUPANSKY, affirmed,

THE CLERK: Thank you. You may be seated.

DIRECT EXAMINATION BY MS. LEINBURD:

Q Mr. Zupansky, what is your occupation, sir?

A I work for a company called Innovative Hydrogen Solutions out of Winnipeg. I'm a major shareholder and was involved in the start-up of this environmental technology company. I'm now not working in the office but I'm enlisted to raise money for funds for manufacturing of the units to go to the market in the near future.

Q I understand at one point that you were a broadcaster; is that correct?

A I was a volunteer journalist at the University of Manitoba from the year 2000 to approximately year 2006.

Q And so you would interview people on the air; is that correct?

A Had a weekly one-hour interview-style radio program at the University of Manitoba, usually live, but once a week at the university.

Q Now, in terms of your background, I understand that you want, in fact, to be a journalist; is that correct?

A Yes, that's my aspiration.

Q Okay. And what have you done to forward that intention?

A I worked at the University of Manitoba from 2000 to 2006 and in 2004, when this journalistic opportunity, as I call it, arose, then I began writing in earnest.

Q And when you talk about "this journalistic opportunity", I take it you mean the fact that the accused, Sydney Teerhuis, was charged with the murder of Robin Greene?

A Yes. I did not decide at that time, when he was charged initially in 2003, on July 2nd, I had not decided that I would specifically cover that trial and that case, but when the opportunity came to correspond with Sidney Teerhuis through a fateful turn of events, I decided to cover the trial completely.

Q Now, in terms of your interaction with Mr. Teerhuis, how did that come about?

A I had previously met a gentleman from Thunder Bay, where I'm originally from. His name is Don Abbott. And Don Abbott, in the fall of 2003, was incarcerated on, or charged; pardon me, with a couple of offences. He had called me shortly after and explained the more serious of the charges and I agreed, based on that explanation, to allow him to correspond by telephone with me while he was in jail since I had met with him maybe a couple of months before and we were, I won't say friends per se but, acquaintances.

Q And what did that have to do with Mr. Teerhuis?

A I corresponded with Mr. Abbott and shortly after Christmas, some time in January, when Mr. Abbott had called me on the telephone, he asked to guess who was in the same jail range as he was. And he mentioned Sydney

Teerhuis' name. I didn't initially recognize the name till he noted that it was the person that chopped up the guy at the Royal Albert. And so I recognized the name then and recognized the case as I had already been interested in the case, as many cases, and had cut out the clipping of the news article from the newspapers.

Q So you had an acquaintance, Mr. Abbott, who was in the same jail as the accused, Teerhuis?

A Yes.

Q And you then began your correspondence with Mr. Teerhuis, is that correct, initially through Mr. Abbott and then subsequently writing directly to the accused and he writing to you, is that correct?

A Yes. That's correct.

Q How many letters would you have written back and forth approximately, between yourself and Mr. Teerhuis?

A Well, I wrote very few letters. I just included numerous questions. Mr. Teerhuis would write me letters, and I guess based on not having the funds for more envelopes, he would include very much of his personal background dating right back to entirely everything he could recall, and so some-- many of those letters, a vast majority of them were multiple letters with numerous pages of his background and then, we'll say for example, talking about his present-day situation in, say, Headingley or when he was in Brandon. So there would be a combination of things in most letters.

Q Why did you want to write to Mr. Teerhuis?

A I was interested in the case itself. I have a keen interest in the law. Many of my programs that were on the University of Manitoba radio station program dealt with issues of the law. I had interviewed prominent law professors and, for example, a former Attorney General of British Columbia. So I thought this case--at that time I didn't know the full details, obviously, but I thought it would clearly demonstrate certain things that I was interested in.

Q What were you going to do with this information?

A I was going to initially just, I thought I would write a book about the trial itself, and I thought that based on my experience, that any information, inside information or personal information from Sydney Teerhuis would be part of what I would need to write the book in the end.

Q Did you want to write a book of fiction?

A Absolutely not.

Q Why not?

A I had never done anything with fiction whatsoever and my interest has always been non-fiction, not just true crime but non-fiction in general. That was my radio program at the time, and when I initially was in contact with Don Abbott and Sydney Teerhuis, I initially had asked him if Sydney Teerhuis would be interested in being interviewed on radio. So being a non-fiction program, interviewing people about true issues, the book would be a continuum of that. True crime is just like the title, true crime, and that's what I was interested in, a non-fiction book.

Q And true crime is a genre; is that correct?

A Yes.

Q It's a type of book?

A Yes, it is. It's just a type of non-fiction book.

Q Now, were you at all interested in Mr. Teerhuis providing you with fiction?

A Absolutely not. And I indicated to him several times whether via telephone or in letters, I cannot recall the specific references, but I had said to him that I wanted to keep it real. In fact, in some of the letters, I do question the sense of some of the things that he had said so I did not take everything he had said at face value. I questioned and wanted clarification of certain things that he did impart to me.

Q I'm going to direct you, sir, and I'm just holding a copy of the letter that Teerhuis sent to you, or you sent to him, sorry. I'm going to ask you to read this line. It's on the top portion of the second page. Could you read that to the jury, please?

THE COURT: What exhibit is that, Ms. Leinburd?

MS. LEINBURD: It's Exhibit 74.

THE COURT: Thank you.

THE WITNESS: "I do not want you to make up things or embellish anything, keep it realistic please!"

Q So you asked him to provide reality to you, not fiction?

A Yes.

Q And your reason for that was because of the kind of book that you wanted to write?

A Yes. And I was just really interested in the truth.

Q I'm going to go through several of those letters. And before we do, I understand that you also had many telephone conversations with this particular accused?

A Yes, that's correct.

Q There were obviously many, many letters written by the accused, Teerhuis, to you. There have been many marked as exhibits. And as I understand it, there were only three letters that you wrote back to Mr. Teerhuis; is that correct?

A I believe it's four.

Q Sorry. Exhibit Number 74, Exhibit Number 75, Exhibit Number 77 and then a handwritten exhibit as well, which I will show to you momentarily. Could you examine those exhibits?

A I want to make a correction, too. I am not certain that those are the only letters that I had sent to Mr. Teerhuis.

Q No. I wasn't suggesting they were the only letters.

A Okay.

Q I was saying that what we have before us are, in fact, the letters that were turned over by you to the police?

A Right.

Q And in terms of the letters that Mr. Teerhuis wrote and have been entered into exhibits, those are amongst the many letters he wrote to you?

A Yes.

Q I'm going to direct you specifically, if I could, to Exhibit Number 77, sir. They're marked with the orange tabs on the outside. Again, I'm referring to... If you could read--you're familiar with it? That's your letter, sir? And I'm going to refer you to the bottom portion of that particular document.

A Okay.

Q When you read out a moment ago, "*I would like to know a little more details about your case so hopefully we can talk in a few days,*" was he providing you details about the case at that point in time?

A He was not giving me details initially. Initially, he was instructed to give me some of his background so we didn't get into the details of the case. That specific reference is not--is while he was incarcerated he was charged for...

Q Let's not go into anything else.

A Okay.

Q But it was another matter altogether?

A That's what I meant to say.

Q The only interest I have is about this particular killing and your correspondence between him and you in that regard. Now, in terms of that particular...

MR. BRODSKY: I...

MS. LEINBURD: Sorry.

THE COURT: Ms. Leinburd, one moment. Mr. Brodsky, you want to...

MR. BRODSKY: I'd like to address the court.

THE COURT: All right. Ladies and gentlemen of the jury, could we just ask for your indulgence for a few moments. We just have to deal with one quick matter, all right? Thank you.

MS. LEINBURD: Yeah, perhaps...

(JURY OUT AT 10:51 A.M.)

THE COURT: Did you want Mr. Zupansky here?

MS. LEINBURD: No.

THE COURT: Mr. Zupansky, would you step outside for a moment, please.

(WITNESS ASIDE)

THE COURT: Mr. Brodsky.

MR. BRODSKY: With respect, this comment about another offence is offensive.

THE COURT: Probably a little bit.

MR. BRODSKY: It is not another killing; it is not anything remotely resembling this incident. It is a matter, I take it he's talking about a matter on which he was acquitted or another charge on which he was convicted in connection with a Veronica Jackson, a guard, a correctional officer, rather.

THE COURT: Right, so...

MR. BRODSKY: I hesitate to use the words 'small potatoes' but it's insignificant. And when we get into the letters that the jury has, when they talk about the police officers trying to decide if he was involved in killings of other people and digging up graves and all the rest of that, the jury is going to make more of this last conversation, comment than...

THE COURT: Do you want me to--I'm happy to instruct the jury that a passing reference was made to a charge with respect to Mr. Teerhuis-Moar, you're to disregard that entirely? Do you want me to say something like that?

MR. BRODSKY: No. That's not good enough.

THE COURT: What did you want me to say?

MR. BRODSKY: You have to say that it was a minor charge.

THE COURT: Well, I don't know what it is. Unless you're...

MR. BRODSKY: My learned friend knows what it is. It's a...

MS. LEINBURD: I wasn't leading evidence in that regard. The details that I was suggesting were the details that had to do with something completely different.

THE COURT: Okay. All right. All I heard and all the jury would have heard, because I listened to the response very carefully, was that this is when he was charged with. All right. That's all the jury heard.

224

MR. BRODSKY: There was a disturbance in the jail. You don't have to go to the exact charge.

THE COURT: All right. Well...

MR. BRODSKY: We specifically, in the letters, know it had to do with a correctional officer named Jackson.

THE COURT: All right. Well, write my script, let me take a moment to examine it and I'll tell you what I...

MR. BRODSKY: If you say, My Lord, the incident referred to was a disturbance in the jail, it didn't, did not involve bodily harm, we don't want you to misunderstand.

THE COURT: Well, wait a moment. Mr. Brodsky, there was nothing characterizing the offence at all. It was just characterized as an offence, period.

MR. BRODSKY: That's why I think they're going to think that it's another homicide or another dismemberment because it wasn't characterized. That's why I think you should characterize it.

THE COURT: All right.

MS. LEINBURD: I think it will just fuel the fire. If he's concerned about a fire, why on earth would you even suggest to the jury that there was another dismemberment?

MR. BRODSKY: Well, because the police investigated him on that.

THE COURT: So what was the...

MS. LEINBURD: But nobody knows that.

THE COURT: What was the charge, Mr. Brodsky?

MR. BRODSKY: The charge was assaulting a jail guard. And he was charged with a mischief at another point on which he was acquitted. I don't know which one this one is referring to, but the name "Jackson" appears in the correspondence and I take it that's what he's referring to. And that was he didn't move when he was supposed to and he was supposed to have hit a jail guard. There was no injury. It was in Brandon. That's all it was. The circumstances of this case, where he talks about significant other offences, interfering with dead bodies, the jury will have that, the necrophilia, the police, they investigate him and take his DNA because they want to ensure that he wasn't involved in any other murders. The jury is going to, is apt to extend this charge to what it is my learned friend was referring to. And I'm trying to avoid a mistrial here but...

THE COURT: Well, you're not going to get a mistrial for that.

MR. BRODSKY: I'm trying to avoid it, and I think the way to avoid it--I'm not asking for a mistrial, what I'm asking for is for Your Lordship to characterize the charge for what it was. I'm not trying-- that anybody should make something up; let's tell them the truth.

THE COURT: What about this, Mr. Brodsky, and I appreciate your point and I want to say something but it's just a question of what we're going to say. And I agree with Ms. Leinburd to some extent, that this is potentially incendiary for what I do say more than for what I don't, but what about this: The incident referred to, cryptically described as a charge relates to a disturbance in the jail which had no resemblance or similarity to the offence for which Mr. Teerhuis-Moar is currently under charge.

MR. BRODSKY: That's fine.

THE COURT: Is that acceptable?

MR. BRODSKY: Yes.

THE COURT: Okay.

MR. BRODSKY: Would you add; and did not involve injury, because it didn't?

THE COURT: Ms. Leinburd, do you have any objection to that?

MS. LEINBURD: I have no objection at all. This has all been edited out of the letters that the accused wrote, and it's not in the letters that Mr. Zupansky wrote. So there's no issue. I was never going to raise that, anything about Victoria Jackson has been edited out of the letters; it's not before the jury.

THE COURT: I think the problem doesn't arise from what you were going to raise. I think the problem just comes from the slip that Mr. Zupansky fell into there.

MS. LEINBURD: Yes.

THE COURT: Is that all right, Mr. Brodsky?

MR. BRODSKY: Yes.

THE COURT: All right. So that's what I intend to do. Let me just have a moment, please. Okay. Can we bring the jury back in, please.

(JURY IN AT 10:57 A.M.)

THE CLERK: My Lord, all 12 jurors are present.

THE COURT: Thank you. Ladies and gentlemen, a few moments ago, during the testimony of Mr. Zupansky, he cryptically referred to a charge that was facing Mr. Teerhuis-Moar. The incident referred to relate to a disturbance in the jail, which had no resemblance or similarity to the offence for which Mr. Teerhuis-Moar is currently under charge and it did not involve injury. All right? Ms. Leinburd.

MS. LEINBURD: Yes, could you recall Mr. Zupansky, please.

Q Mr. Zupansky, I was just at the stage where we were going through several of the letters that you had written to the accused. I'm going to show you Exhibit 75, of which I have a copy as well. I'm going to direct your attention to various portions of that particular exhibit. It is dated December 16th of 2004. It is typewritten. You sent this letter to the accused, Teerhuis?

A Yes.

Q Okay. In the second sentence of that particular letter, it says: "*I especially was interested in your last letter and all the details that you provided about the actual killing. Please provide all the details that you can about the killing...*" Why were you asking him that question, sir?

A I just felt that all the details were important. I didn't know what details might not be important so I wanted to include every single detail of everything that I possibly could think of that might be of interest.

Q And this letter clearly was in response to a letter that you received from him?

A Yes.

Q In it, you go on to say: "*What did you do with the organs?*" That's four sentences down from the top. Is that correct, sir?

A Yes.

Q Why were you asking him about what he'd done with the organs?

A I thought was that it was important to the case.

Q You go on to ask him: "*Why did you dissect certain body parts?*"

A Again, I felt it was an important detail.

Q You actually go to the point, sir, of asking him to, to indicate to you why he killed Mr. Greene; isn't that correct?

A Yes.

Q And why was that important to you, sir?

A I was interested in the motive that he might have for this killing.

Q And in terms of the information, you were getting the information from him; is that correct?

226

A Yes.

Q You didn't have any independent information about this killing?

A No, other than the newspapers and media.

Q I'm going to direct you to the mid-portion of that particular letter and I will point to it. Right there. Could you read that out loud, sir, that sentence beginning with the word "you". You mentioned:

A "You mentioned that Greene had pleaded with you not to kill him, why did he know that you were about to kill him, what made him think that?"

Q Continue.

A "What was your response to his plea for mercy? When at what point did you decide to kill him?"

Q Now, is that responsive to information that Teerhuis had written to you in a previous letter?

A Yes.

Q So you did not know yourself whether or not Mr. Greene had, in fact, pleaded for his life; that was information that the accused gave you?

A Yes.

Q And you were now just asking him to explain what he'd said to you in one of his previous letters; is that correct?

A Yes, that's correct.

Q Did you, at any time, provide the accused any information that you may have had, what limited information it was?

A Not that I'm aware of.

Q You go on to ask him, as I understand it, if you turn the page to the next page, sir, that will be page 2, top of the second page: *"It is very important. I would like you to respond to these questions in order because I will now keep all my letters to you in a file so please answer the questions as they appear and it will be more organized for the book and documentary."*

A Yes.

Q So you were asking him, at this point in time, to provide you further information and you've indicated to him that you were going to write a book. He understood that, I gather?

A Absolutely.

Q Okay. And you also said that you were going to collect this information that he was giving to you in the letters for a documentary?

A Yes.

Q As a matter of fact, you use the word 'documentary' twice in that letter, once towards the bottom of the page. Is that correct, sir?

A Yes.

Q What is a documentary, in your mind, sir?

A A documentary is a truthful account of any story outlining a certain subject focus that you may have for that documentary.

Q Is it fictional?

A No.

Q Is it factual?

A Yes, it is.

Q Again, you underscore, then, that you want information for a documentary and your book?

A Yes.

Q Now, to this point in time did you know whether or not the accused had had sex with the corpse of Robin Greene?

A No.

Q That was not something that was in the papers?

A No.

227

Q That you read about?

A No.

Q So the information about having sex with the corpse came from the accused?

A Yes, it did.

Q Okay. You had no independent knowledge prior to his letters to you?

A That's correct.

Q Proceeding down to the middle portion of that page, and you say to him: *"At what point did you make the decision to kill, what was the thing that made you decide to kill him? When, at what point did you decide to have sex with the corpse? Why did you use a condom?"* You wrote those words to the accused?

A Yes, I did.

Q And, the information that you have in these questions; was that provided to you by the accused, that is, that he had had sex with the corpse?

A Yes.

Q And that he had used a condom when having sex with the corpse?

A That's what he had told me.

Q And you go on to ask, because you say you didn't know anything about the sex and had it not been for the accused telling you that he had sex with the deceased, you wouldn't have known that, you go on to ask him: *"Do the police have any idea about the post-killing sex?"* Is that correct?

A Yes, I did ask him that question.

Q You, in fact, received a letter from the accused dealing with these issues, as I understand it. We'll refer to them later.

A Yes.

Q The last question that you asked in your particular letter, under the date of December the 16th of '04, *"So if you could please,"* and I'm reading from the last line of the fullest paragraph on page 2: *"So if you could respond to my questions and if there are questions that you do not wish to answer please let me know why you do not want to answer them."* So you basically were asking him for answers, if he was not prepared to give them to you, so be it?

A Yes.

Q Again, at the latter portion of that particular letter, you say: *"I will have to buckle down and focus on the material for this book and documentary in the New Year so please help me out by answering the questions that I have asked."* Is that correct?

A Yes.

Q So again, he is fully appraised by you of the fact that it's a documentary that you want to make?

A Yes.

Q Dealing with, if we might, for the moment, Exhibit Number 74, believe it's one of the exhibits that we have in front of you.

A Okay.

Q There seems to be a handwritten portion on the top of that document. Whose handwriting is that?

A That is mine.

Q Okay. And what does it say, sir?

A It says, written February, question mark, '05 and sent February 14th, '05 for TV release.

Q And that is, in fact, a letter that you again wrote to the accused; is that correct?

228

A That's correct.

Q Now, in terms of this particular letter, sir, you talked to the accused about the motivation for the killing; is that correct?

A Yes, I did.

Q Okay. And again, in that particular letter you ask him for details that he had expressed to you previously; is that correct?

A Yes, it is.

Q That is a letter in which you wrote to him: "*I do not want you to make up things or embellish anything, keep it realistic, please!*" Is that correct?

A Yes, it is.

Q Okay. Again, you question him about the organs, so is it fair to say that it was only after you'd written him several letters that you, in fact, got an answer from him about what he'd done with the organs?

A Yes. I asked him numerous times.

Q Now, in terms of your letter to him, I'm going to reference the middle portion of the second page, and it says the following: "*Do you now see this case as a challenge, where you are pitted against the judicial system with the incompetent and stupid police and if you stick to your official story you will ultimately win?*" What was the official story?

A Official story was that he had blacked out and when he awoke he found the body of the victim, Robin Greene, dismembered in the bathtub.

Q Okay. He had never denied killing Robin Greene to you in any of these letters, had he?

A Correct.

Q So you and he are, at this point, discussing the official story?

A Right.

Q And from your perspective, it's the blacking out version of events?

A Yes.

Q Now, he goes on to say, at the bottom portion of page 2, because this is the book that you're writing, the book is to be called Trophy Kill. That's what you say to him: "*...So I need to know why you consider Greene's body a trophy?*" Now, in terms of that particular Trophy Kill, is that a title that you suggested or that the accused suggested?

A The accused suggested it.

Q And is it fair to say that at certain times he even drew diagrams of what he wanted that book cover to look like?

A Yes, he did.

Q Can you look through the exhibits that you have. Exhibit Number 60. There is a drawing on the back portion of Exhibit 60. Can you tell the jury what that is a drawing of?

A That is two drawings of the book cover itself. It has the title of the book. Assorted family photos, it says, drops of blood. And I guess he gives the first title of the book. And he has suggestions for the current title, Sydney in his cell at Headingley, background of assorted men's underwear and sex toys, young Sydney at Anne Teerhuis' wedding in Tuxedo. So he has a first choice and a second choice for a book cover design.

Q Those were created by the accused, not by you?

A Yes, they were created by the accused.

Q And he wanted pictures of himself on the cover at one point, did he not?

A Yes.

Q And he wanted at least 10 pages of pictures in the book; is that correct?

A That's what he stated.

Q Okay. As a matter of fact, he indicated: *I want at least 10 pages devoted to photos. I want to have the last say on what photos are to be printed.* Is that correct?

A Yes, it is.

Q And he even indicated to you that he was thinking of having a photo of himself on the cover of the book; is that correct?

A Yes, it is correct.

Q Did it appear to you that he was very concerned about the book cover and the contents of this book?

A Yes, he was very, very concerned.

Q And in terms of Exhibit 67, Teerhuis wanted you actually to proofread. You have Exhibit 67?

A Yes.

Q And before we go into the proofreading, that's another example of his artwork, as I understand it. I'm just going to show the jury. Trophy Kill is the name Mr. Teerhuis drew on this particular drawing of the book cover. Correct?

A Yes.

Q There's a picture of the stolen necklace, the Shall We Dance murder. That was the name of the movie that was being shot in Winnipeg at the time of this killing; is that correct?

A Yes.

Q There's a photo of Teerhuis and a photo of Greene; is that correct?

A Yes.

Q And then he wanted Susan Sarandon, Lopez and Gere to be in his company on this cover; is that correct?

A That's correct.

Q Now, I'm going to ask you to reference the exhibit. If you go to page 3, the mid portion of page 3.

THE COURT: This is Exhibit 67?

MS. LEINBURD: Yes, that's correct.

THE WITNESS: Oh, okay.

Q Basically, it says that he wanted to proofread what you had written; is that correct?

A Yes.

Q Okay. And he even wanted to make corrections in what you had written; isn't that correct?

A That's correct.

Q And if anything was incorrect, he wanted you to have it corrected by way of his version of events?

A Yes, that's correct.

Q He wanted to make it clear that he didn't steal Susan Sarandon's necklace?

A Yes, he made that very clear.

Q As a matter of fact, he wanted you to go on Charles Adler's show to make sure that everybody understood that he wasn't the thief?

A Yes, that's correct.

Q Okay. He also gave you a list of other things that he wanted you to tell Mr. Adler when you went on the show; isn't that correct?

A That's correct.

230

Q And was that all the function of him wanting to set the record straight?

A As far as I know.

Q I want you to go to that Exhibit 77, sir, which I have a copy. And I will give you the original.

MR. BRODSKY: What exhibit number?

THE COURT: Exhibit 77.

MS. LEINBURD: 77.

Q You say, in the mid portion of the first page:

> *"According to the newspaper story, the police found disposable cameras at the... scene and stated that photos were taken before and after the killing."*

Q And then you go on to question him about how many photos were taken. Did you, in fact, know whether these photos had been taken before or after the killing?

A No, I had no idea.

Q So you were again querying him?

A Yes.

Q And did he respond to you?

A Yes.

Q About when those photos were taken?

A Yes.

Q What did he tell you, sir?

A He stated that despite my idea that there may have been photos after the killing, post-killing, that in fact he had stated that there were only photos of before the killing.

Q So he corrected your understanding?

A Yes.

Q You would have had no other way of discovering this, would you, sir?

A That's correct.

Q You talk in your letter, Exhibit 77, to Mr. Teerhuis about necrophilia--is that correct?

A Yes.

Q It's in the mid portion of the longest paragraph on the page. How did that topic come up, sir?

A It came up in response to him informing me or imparting the information to me that he engaged in necrophilia with the victim.

Q And he, in fact, wrote and gave you that information?

A That's correct.

Q Did you, at any time, raise the topic of necrophilia with him; that is, was it at your insistence that it was raised or was it also responsive?

A It was all responsive. I had no idea that it had occurred.

Q Now, this correspondence between you and the accused went on for some length of time, as I understand it?

A Yes, it did.

Q Okay. Ultimately, the accused did tell you what he'd done with the organs--is that correct?

A Yes. He had stated what he had done with the organs.

Q What did he tell you he had done with the organs?

A He said he took them to a BFI garbage can near the Health Sciences Centre and he threw some of the portions in the garbage can and some in a vacant lot near that garbage can.

Q He didn't give you that information at the outset, though?

A No, he didn't. He initially said I'd have to wait for that information. He had stated, quote: *"It's a little too early to go into that."*

Q Did you think you had gained his trust?

A Yes, I did.

Q And how did you do that, Mr. Zupansky?

A I first told him that I was interested in his case, I was interested in his story. And I was interested in his case and I was interested in his story as a journalist. I also had told him that despite not being homosexual or bisexual that I could empathize with homosexuals and bisexuals. I wanted to appear to relate to everything he said despite the disgusting nature of some of the information. I wanted to act like none of it shocked or concerned me.

Q In any event, Mr. Teerhuis gives you information about performing oral sex on the deceased--is that correct?

A Yes.

Q And in one of his letters he indicates to you, Exhibit 64 he says: *"As I performed oral sex on Greene, the fact that he was dead turned me on."* And he gives you a timeline. He says that, in Exhibit 64, that right after Greene died, that he performed oral sex on him--is that correct?

A Yes.

Q Further on in Exhibit 64, he again gives you a timeframe and he says, before the decapitation of Mr. Greene, he goes on to describe how he lay the body on the bathroom floor, caressing him and feeling every inch of his body and indicating that it was very erotic molesting Greene's corpse. Is that correct?

A Yes, that's correct.

Q Again, this is not information that you had prior to being delivered to you by the accused?

A That's correct.

Q In terms of the accused corresponding with you, is it fair to say that the longer you corresponded with him, the more information he gave you about the killings?

A Yes.

Q He actually drew diagrams in the letters that he sent to you; is that correct?

A That's correct.

Q He drew diagrams of where the corpse was in the bathroom, what he did to the corpse and how he dissected and decapitated the corpse--is that correct?

A Yes.

Q And what were your intentions in terms of dealing with that particular material?

A I just thought it was part of the, again, the non-fiction book. It was the truth as far as I knew it and it contained details that people that read true crime books might be interested in.

Q And frankly, you thought that this would be something that you could profit from in the sense that you might be able to make money from the writing of a book that was true?

A Well, I don't know about profit so much when you're talking about a few years of work, but I wanted to establish myself as a journalist, a book writer, a non-fiction book writer, so that was my main priority.

Q Now, in terms of your ongoing writing campaign with the accused, it's true that at one point you only knew that the heart and the intestines were missing—is that correct?

A Yes.

Q You knew of no other organs that had been missing. That was not available through the press—is that correct?

MR. BRODSKY: Were not available, pardon me?

MS. LEINBURD: Through the press.

THE WITNESS: The specific organs that were missing did not appear in the media, in the press.

Q Ultimately, the accused wrote to you in Exhibit 66 and actually gave you a listing of the organs and he writes: *"You wanted a list of missing organs."* And then he lists: The lungs, a part of the esophagus, the epiglottis, the digestive tract, heart, spleen, stomach, liver, pancreas, aorta and one of the eyes. Is that correct?

A That's correct.

Q You had none of that information prior to him writing to you except for the information about the heart and digestive system?

A Yes.

Q What ultimately happened to stop the letter writing between the two of you, sir?

A When we first began corresponding, in the press was talk of a law prohibiting criminals from profiting from their crime. When I last spoke to Sidney Teerhuis, the law had just passed in Manitoba, so I asked him, without any intention, I said, have you heard about, did you read about the law being passed that prohibits criminals from profiting from their crime. And he immediately hung up on me. From there, he subsequently sent me a letter, and that's the last letter he sent to me.

Q In terms of the law that you've referred to, sir, it's marked as Exhibit 81. It was assented to or passed on June the 10th, 2004 and it's called The Profits of Criminal Notoriety Act. And simply put, it's an Act that says you can't profit from your own bad doing. That is, if you happen to be a killer and you write a book, you're not going to make any money on that book?

A Right.

Q So what happened in your correspondence with Mr. Teerhuis?

A Mr. Teerhuis had said in the correspondence, in the letter to me that he had not read about this reference that I had mentioned and that he thought that this was a ploy on my part to rip him off.

Q Was it?

MR. BRODSKY: Well, that doesn't matter.

MS. LEINBURD: This witness can answer whether it was a ploy on his part or not.

THE WITNESS: It was simply a statement to tell him of the law that had passed, and that was it.

Q Mr. Teerhuis writes to you on April the 4th of '05 and he tries to retract the information he's given you, basically?

A He retracts certain information and then tells me overall that everything he has told me has been fiction.

Q Now, you write back to him, in Exhibit 76, and what do you tell him in that particular letter?

When we last spoke and you hung up, I was telling you only what I had read, that's it. You have overreacted completely. My goal is definitely not to rip you off.

233

A Rip off anyone.

Q Oh, sorry, rip off anyone. Continue:

A *"And that's why my reputation is sterling in that department, I can't say that for Don however."*

Q So basically, after the law passed saying he couldn't make any money from the book, Mr. Teerhuis writes you a letter saying what he told you was fiction?

A Yes.

Q Is that the first time he ever uses the word 'fiction' in the letters to you?

A Yes.

Q And you wrote back to him saying that you didn't want to rip him off that was just the law. And what were you going to do in any event, were you going to publish a book?

A I would still want to publish a book. However, based on the law, I knew that I was not myself going to break any law in the writing of this book.

Q So you could still make money from the writing of the book, according to your interpretation of the law, but he couldn't?

A Yes.

Q So now it became fiction, according to his letter?

A Yes, it did.

Q What did you do at that point?

A I wrote him this last letter and said that I wanted to still continue the correspondence and continue with the project itself. And I had said that I would rather have his cooperation than not and that I was going to continue with the book project with or without him or his involvement.

Q As a matter of fact, you sent him two releases--is that correct?

A Yes.

Q Exhibit 78 and 79?

A That's correct.

Q And the releases, where did you get them from and how were they worded?

A I have a documentary partner, Mr. Allan Smitty, and we got these releases and just modified them from standard releases that my associate, my friend, had used in other previous dealings when a release was needed to authorize releasing the material for use in a documentary.

Q So you expected that this was a legal document allowing him to release, or allowing you to release the information that he was giving to you?

A Yes.

Q And that's what it was intended to be, a legal document signed by Teerhuis?

A Yes.

Q The same is true of a film release--is that correct?

A Yes.

Q It's Exhibit 79.

A Yes.

Q So you were serious in your approach to him about the releases and you asked him several times about those releases and signing them?

A Yes.

Q Okay. Continue. What happened after the communication between the two of you broke down when the law passed?

A After I sent him the last letter, there was no more correspondence whatsoever, no more phone calls, no more letters.

Q What did you do ultimately with the information that you had received from the accused, Teerhuis?

A Shortly after, I contacted the police. Pardon me, I contacted the Crown Attorney's office and left a message that I had some information that may be regarded as evidence in the Sidney Teerhuis murder trial.

Q Now, that was, as I understand it, in April of 2004; is that correct?

A It's 2005.

Q Sorry, April of 2005. Now, why did you not disclose the information that you had about the crime prior to that date?

A I had always planned to contact the authorities with the information I had—however, given the flood, the virtual flood of information that was coming in quick succession from December, that I thought that if I had the opportunity to get more information about the motive, that's what I was interesting in gaining—that information I still didn't have, in my mind, and I wanted that information and felt it was important.

Q Did you seek anyone's advice on whether or not you should disclose the information that you received from the accused?

A Yes, I did.

Q Whose advice did you seek, sir?

A A gentleman, a law professor from Queen's University named Alan Young and a former Crown attorney from Thunder Bay, Ontario, named Agnew Johnston.

Q And?

A As well as two journalists.

Q And pursuant to their information, you disclosed this information?

A Yes. The journalists had said that I should contact the authorities after the preliminary, and the law professor and Crown Attorney said I should contact the authorities before the preliminary hearing.

Q And you did, in fact, contact the Crown attorney's office by way of speaking to a Crown attorney called Liz Thomson—is that correct?

A Yes.

Q And ultimately, the police came to your home and seized all of the letters that—or some of the letters that you had written to Mr. Teerhuis and that he'd written to you?

A I met with them and handed over the originals, drawings and all of the letters and the telephone interview documentation that I had.

MS. LEINBURD: Thank you very much.

THE COURT: Mr. Brodsky, we haven't had a break this morning. Could we take... it's 11:30, I take it you're going to be some time with this witness?

MR. BRODSKY: Yes.

THE COURT: Start at 1:30?

MR. BRODSKY: Sure.

THE COURT: Is that agreeable, ladies and gentlemen, if we left now and start at 1:30 rather than 2:00? Okay, why don't we do that?

(JURY OUT AT 11:32 A.M.)

THE COURT: Mr. Zupansky, you're about to start your cross-examination so I'd ask you not to discuss your evidence with anybody.

THE WITNESS: Right.

THE COURT: Prior your testimony this afternoon.

THE WITNESS: Yes.

THE COURT: Thank you. Okay.

THE CLERK: Order, all rise. Court is in recess until 1:30.

THE COURT: Sorry, just before we forget, Madam Clerk mark as Exhibit J1 the question that we received from the jury.

THE CLERK: Order. Court is in recess.

(LUNCHEON RECESS)

THE CLERK: Court is re-opened. Please be seated.

THE COURT: Mr. Zupansky, could I just ask you to wait outside for a moment, please. I want to address something with counsel.

THE WITNESS: Sure.

(WITNESS ASIDE)

THE COURT: Two things that were brought to my attention, counsel respecting the jury. First of all, we have one juror who's, who's ill. She seems to think, at this point, that she can continue. She was, she was ill this morning. I guess with the assistance of Pepto Bismol she thinks she can continue. She was asked a couple of times. So we'll see how that progresses.

The other matter of concern is a note that I received from the jury, from two jurors, I think. I don't know more than what I'm going to tell you but I'll bring it to your attention. The note reads: Gentleman sitting with witness at lunch playing with video camera. Light was on. At one point it was pointed in our direction (sitting on table). Not a camcorder but not a large TV camera. Fuzzy, dark hair, male, tall, black moustache. Camera looked like it had a small boom microphone.

The sign on the bottom says, number 6 and number 7. Presuming that that's jurors number six and seven. This was received by me. I'm going to do nothing more than simply tell them that they should not be talking about the case outside the jury room. Unless you have something you want to add, Ms. Leinburd or Mr. Brodsky.

MR. BRODSKY: I do.

THE COURT: Go ahead.

MR. BRODSKY: It's illegal. To take pictures of the jury is illegal and it's especially egregious in this case because in this case, this witness has been putting on a blog on his--what do you call it?

MS. BUSET: Website.

MR. BRODSKY: On his website reporting on the case, the facts of the case, the apprehension of Mr. Teerhuis, the trial and other things.

THE COURT: So what do you want me to do, Mr. Brodsky? I mean, apart from what I've...

MR. BRODSKY: I want you to conduct an investigation, determine who it was, determine what was taken and ensure that those pictures of jurors don't appear anywhere ever again. It's awful.

THE COURT: Well, first of all, we're not certain what happened. We won't...

MR. BRODSKY: But that's why I ask you to conduct some kind of an investigation.

THE COURT: All right. I'll see what I can find out. But in terms of my instruction to the jury upon receipt of this note, I've proposed what I wanted to say. Did you want to suggest anything else?

236

MR. BRODSKY: Yes. You should ask whoever it was what they took. There's a person in the courtroom now, for instance, and if they are, they should be asked by Your Lordship now to turn over whatever it is they took, and if they sent it some place, to advise you where they sent it. I'm repeating myself, but this gentleman, who is the witness, has a website and he's reporting on the incident, has reported on it, and advised on the website that he's going to continue to report on it and write a book. I don't want a picture of a juror in that news report. That would be an awful thing.

THE COURT: Ms. Leinburd, any comments?

MS. LEINBURD: I know nothing about the camera, et cetera, and Mr. Brodsky seems to know more about this apparent blog than I do.

MR. BRODSKY: Well, it's not a big secret because, according to my information, 7900 people have logged onto that blog and there's...

MS. LEINBURD: I'm not one of them, I can indicate to the court.

MR. BRODSKY: Well, I didn't go through who they were. It was not 7900 pardon me. There was 7552 as of May 29th, 2008 and there were 7596 as of December 8th, 2008. So we're not talking about an insignificant number.

THE COURT: The blog...

MR. BRODSKY: At this point, I'm not concerned about the witness because he's going to be here. I'm concerned about the jury and I wouldn't like their pictures to appear on this website. It's called, for your information, for the court's information, you can go, if you have access to Internet, look at Zupansky.ca. I found it on YouTube and on the Internet and I think it's on one other server. It's quite common. And it's the YouTube one that had the 7976. It's also on AOL video.com. Thirteen hundred and twelve hits on that one. It's all over the place.

THE COURT: So what exactly do you want me to ask the jury?

MR. BRODSKY: If they can identify who the person was, if he's in the courtroom. Then I would ask you to ask him, or ask a sheriff's officer, somebody, to ask him what's going on here.

THE COURT: Do you want me to make inquiries to who the witness was?

MR. BRODSKY: Who the person with the camera was or what I think was...

THE COURT: Well, there's a gentleman sitting with a witness. That's the assertion. Presumably it's Mr. Zupansky, according to your theory, but we'll find out.

MR. BRODSKY: I don't, I don't have a theory. I only know what Your Lordship tells me.

THE COURT: How do you propose, Mr. Brodsky, how did you want me to conduct the inquiry? Just have them provide me something in writing? Go ahead.

MR. BRODSKY: I'm open to suggestion.

THE COURT: My preference would frankly not be getting into a dialogue with the jury. I'll pose a couple of questions. They can get back to me in written form and then I can take whatever direction, whatever direction I want after that.

MR. BRODSKY: Maybe you can ask just the people in the courtroom now if they are one of them are the people, person who is being spoken of. Just a concern.

THE COURT: Your concern is principally for the, for the jury and...?

MR. BRODSKY: My concern is principally for the jury.

THE COURT: All right. So what I'm going to propose we do is this. I'll bring the jury back in. I'll read the note that I was given. I'll ask them whether they recognize the person about whom

237

they were speaking of in this courtroom. Is that person in the courtroom? If the person is, I'll ask the jury to...

MR. BRODSKY: Retire and tell the sheriff's officer.

THE COURT: Retire and tell the sheriff's officer, identify the person, we'll come back and we can deal with it as obviously I think we would have to. Okay?

MR. BRODSKY: Yes. I don't think it goes without saying, but you wouldn't want a jury with trepidation trying to decide this case.

THE COURT: I appreciate that Mr. Brodsky. I'm also going to ask who the witness was, if it's the Crown witness, just to find out.

MR. BRODSKY: Yes.

THE COURT: All right.

(JURY IN AT 1:42 P.M.)

THE CLERK: My Lord, all 12 jurors are present.

THE COURT: Thank you. Good afternoon, ladies and gentlemen. I received-- call it a note, because it's not a question, from perhaps some or all of you. I'm going to ask you, ladies and gentlemen, I'm not sure how many of you are part of this, this note to me. I'm going to ask you in a moment to retire and to advise me; first of all, how many were at the table. I'm also going to ask you to look around the courtroom, and I don't want you to tell me now, but you can tell me whether or not you see that person here. And then, when you retire, you can instruct the jury usher whether or not that person is present. All right? And I also would ask you to tell the jury usher, when you refer to a witness, whoever the two jurors are or however number of jurors are authoring this note, who that particular witness was. All right? I'll also remind you, ladies and gentlemen, that, as I mentioned at the beginning of the trial, you really ought not to be discussing this case outside the jury room. I know it's a difficult case and it's perhaps tempting to talk about it, but for reasons I think that I explained earlier on, it's best that the case not be discussed outside the jury room. All right? So I'll ask you to retire if you would, please, and provide that information to me, and we'll have you back here, hopefully very shortly. Okay.

(JURY OUT AT 1:44 P.M.)

(BRIEF RECESS)

THE CLERK: Court is re-opened. Please be seated.

THE COURT: Okay. I received a response from the jury. It reads as follows:

> In courtroom, last row, behind lady with pink hair. Nine jurors at lunch. With witness was Mr. Zupansky. We were not discussing case. More an odd coincidence--not a concern about our safety, more something prudent to ask.

Mr. Brodsky, here's what I propose to do. I'm going to make an inquiry of the gentleman I think they're referring to and I'm not going to start admonishing Mr. Zupansky just yet. I don't know what it is you're talking about when you're talking about a website. I don't propose to do more than that with Mr. Zupansky until he's--are you finishing with him today, do you suspect?

MR. BRODSKY: No.

THE COURT: Ms. Leinburd, any comments?

MS. LEINBURD: No.

238

THE COURT: Okay. Sir, in the back row, would you come forward, please, for a moment. Just step to the microphone if you would, please? Would you just state your name, please?

MR. SMITTY: Allan Smitty.

THE COURT: Smitty?

MR. SMITTY: Yes.

THE COURT: How do you spell your last name?

MR. SMITTY: S-M-I-T-T-Y.

THE COURT: All right. Were you sitting with Mr. Zupansky at lunch?

MR. SMITTY: Yes, I was.

THE COURT: Okay. Were you taking pictures of any of the jurors?

MR. SMITTY: No, just of Dan.

THE COURT: Were you taking any pictures of the jurors?

MR. SMITTY: No.

THE COURT: Did you have your sound recording on in the direction of the jurors?

MR. SMITTY: I don't believe so.

THE COURT: Well, did you have your sound recording on, yes or no?

MR. SMITTY: I don't think so. I have to check. The camera is available for you to look at or the sheriff. I could bring it in here. I could be escorted to my car with a sheriff, bring the camera here and show you.

THE COURT: All right. I'd like to have that camera seen by, or the contents of that camera seen by somebody. You understand, Mr. Smitty that you're not to in any way eavesdrop on the jurors?

MR. SMITTY: Absolutely.

THE COURT: You understand that you're not to take pictures of them?

MR. SMITTY: I do know that but I didn't plan to, so...

THE COURT: Well, did you knowingly or unknowingly take pictures of them?

MR. SMITTY: No. I don't know if I took them. I didn't recognize them so...

THE COURT: All right. Well...

MR. SMITTY: My camera was focused on Dan. I don't know who was in the background.

THE COURT: All right. We'll find out.

MR. SMITTY: Right.

THE COURT: You understand you're not to record them either by way of audio or by way of video, you're not to eavesdrop on their conversations. You understand that?

MR. SMITTY: I do.

THE COURT: All right. Would you be good enough perhaps to go outside-- are you available, sir? All right. Would you accompany, Mr. Smitty, please, just to his car and once you get the apparatus...

MR. SMITTY: I'll just give it to the sheriff and he could play it back. And it's maybe three...

THE COURT: Well, we'll deal with it. If we can avoid keeping it, sir, we'll do that. But out of an abundance of caution, understand that I'm not impugning your credibility right now, but this is, as one of the jurors would have said, a matter of prudence. All right?

MR. SMITTY: Sure, yeah.

THE COURT: All right. Thanks very much.

MR. SMITTY: Yeah.

THE COURT: Understand as well, sir, the reason I'm taking this step right now is because you're not able to say with certainty, and I appreciate your candor, whether or not you did or did not record or take pictures of the jury. Okay? It's actually as much for your own protection as anybody else. All right?

Why don't we do this, Mr. Smitty: Instead of coming back into the courtroom with the camera, I would like to start more or less right away, Ms. Leinburd, Mr. Brodsky, maybe you could just leave that with the sheriff and at a break we can address that question. If you want, you're certainly free to come back in but you do so maybe without the apparatus. You'll leave it with the sheriff, okay?

MR. SMITTY: Yes.

THE COURT: Thanks very much. Mr. Brodsky, did you want anything else stated on the record at this stage?

MR. BRODSKY: Just to assure the jury that they shouldn't be worried about their picture appearing anywhere. You've taken whatever steps, some steps to ensure that that doesn't happen.

THE COURT: Okay. Ms. Leinburd, anything?

MS. LEINBURD: No, I've no comment.

THE COURT: You can bring the jury in, please.

(JURY IN AT 2:00 P.M.)

THE COURT: Ladies and gentlemen, thank you for your note. I can advise you that after having spoken to counsel, can assure you that there'll be no pictures of you taken appearing anywhere else. We'll take whatever precautions to ensure that that doesn't happen. I'll simply again tell you what I told you a few moments ago. I appreciate that you weren't talking about the case, but it's always a good practice for me to remind you when and, if necessary, to not, as much a possible, to discuss the case outside the jury room. Okay? I appreciate you bringing that to my attention. Any other worries that you feel are valid, just pass them on to the jury usher and I'll get them in due course.

MS. LEINBURD: Could we bring in Mr. Zupansky again, please?

MR. BRODSKY:

Q Would it be fair to say that you have a website?

A Yes, I do have a website.

Q And it would be fair to say that in this particular case, you were concerned, or said to your viewers, that you were concerned that Mr. Teerhuis was going to be found not guilty of murder but guilty only of a charge of manslaughter?

A I believe so.

Q And that's because his recitation of what happened, as he couldn't recall anything whatever of the killing due to his intoxicated state, would mean that he inevitably would be convicted only of manslaughter. Would that be fair?

A Yes.

Q And it would be fair to say that because there were no eye witnesses to the story, no eye witnesses to the killing, rather, to use your words, that unless you jumped in and helped the police, he was going to just walk away with a conviction for manslaughter?

A Well, it's unfair. I never used those words "jumped in".

Q No.

A I never used those words whatsoever.

Q You didn't. But that's what you implied to your viewers, isn't it?

A No.

Q *"I felt the story that Sidney put forward about the killing would be the only story ever told. Right from the first time I read about*

240

Sidney and this case, it seemed absolutely absurd that anyone would accept that a person could do such an incredible act and not be cognizant of their actions. Because both alcohol and drugs could probably be proven to be involved in the crime, coupled with the fact that there was no eye witnesses the prosecution would not be able to successfully convict Teerhuis of murder and would have to settle for a manslaughter conviction." Is that what you said?

A That's correct.

Q So why didn't you go to the police?

A I did go to the police.

Q Why didn't you go to the police at the time you wrote the story? Why didn't you go to the police right away?

A I went to the police.

Q After how long?

A Shortly after the correspondence ended with Sidney Teerhuis.

Q So how long had you been corresponding with him before you went to the police?

A A little over a year.

Q A year? You didn't think the police could do their job?

A I didn't say that they couldn't do their job.

Q Okay. So why didn't you let them?

A I did.

Q Why didn't you let them do their job in the year that you were corresponding with Mr. Teerhuis and writing to him?

A Well, following your sense, your logic, then I would go to the police immediately after hearing any detail whatsoever that might be considered evidence. Since I'm not a police officer, I'm a journalist and I've never experienced this before, I gathered information. Since I knew the preliminary was well off in the distance, I talked to a law professor and a former Crown attorney, and I believe that I was not going to harm this case by gathering information.

Q Well, why didn't you keep the police informed as you went along at least?

A I had no experience in this type of thing. Some of the more profound information came to me just before Christmas, and then subsequently after Christmas it accelerated. So in a short period of time there was the bulk of the information, the damaging information, and in short order I went to the authorities well before I was advised by prominent journalists in Winnipeg, that I should come forward with the information. I was a journalist, but I didn't take the journalist's advice, I took the law professor and the Crown attorney's advice.

Q Well, he's not a Crown Attorney.

A He's a former Crown Attorney.

Q Do you know why he is a former Crown Attorney?

A I do know why he's a former Crown Attorney, yes.

Q Why is he a former Crown Attorney?

A He was disbarred.

Q Oh.

A But I took the advice of the law professor as well who was not disbarred.

Q If the police were involved, would it be fair to say that they would be expected to take careful notes of their interviews?

A If they were involved? You'd have to be more specific, if they're involved?

Q Sure. Involved in being an undercover agent or involved in trying to extract a confession or involved in trying to extract an explanation, they would either record or take notes of their interviews.

A I did take notes of the telephone interviews I had with him. I didn't have the ability to record them so I didn't. If I would have, I probably would have recorded those telephone interviews.

Q But don't you think the police would have the ability to record?

A Possibly, but I had no idea how the police work in undercover operations after the fact, after they've already charged an individual.

Q But you didn't ask them?

A No.

Q For over a year?

A I don't know any police officers personally to ask them any of these kinds of questions.

Q But just having a telephone, 411, you ask for the police and ask for homicide or major crime or anything you want to ask for and say, hey, I think I can help you. Didn't want to do that?

A I was probably not interested in becoming an undercover police officer and they probably wouldn't be interested in me being one either.

Q They wouldn't be interested, because you don't take notes and because you deal with dishonest people?

A No.

Q No.

A I didn't say that.

Q Well, you told the jury here that Mr. Teerhuis says that he has no memory of the events because he was drunk or, what was the word?

A Again, you have to be...

Q Had a blackout.

A You have to be specific of when I said this and in what context.

Q To the jury this morning.

A I didn't address the jury myself at all today.

Q Well, in answering the questions, isn't that what you told the jury that Mr. Teerhuis had been telling you?

A No. He wrote me details of the supposed crime that he is accused of, and I accepted those notes and asked him questions in response to the information he gave me.

Q At the beginning, when you first dealt with him, didn't he tell you and didn't you say on your website that he claimed to have no memory?

A Well, that's an audio book sample chapter. What that is, it's just like a book. A book can be out of context. That book expresses information before I became involved with the case at all. That's what I'm narrating in that book.

Q And you wanted to get from him flesh on the bones; is that a way of putting it?

A The truth.

Q You wanted to expand and you wanted to get him to have a memory; is that what you wanted?

A I believed that he remembered what he had done. That was just my opinion. I had no reason to believe that, but that was my opinion. And in that audio book sample chapter that was only meant basically to demonstrate to the publisher that I would, as per instructed--I'm supposed to have a website. I'm also supposed to submit chapter samples of my writing. I'm trying to persuade a publisher that it's an interesting story so I have to include something of interest.

242

Q Well, would it be fair to say that in order to induce, entice, bribe, whatever is the term that you're more comfortable with.
A I'm not comfortable with any of those terms.
Q In order to encourage Mr. Teerhuis to tell you some detail, you told him that you were going to make him wealthy?
A I never used the word "wealth". I said that I believed in my mind, based on the unique characteristics of this crime, and that's before I ever became involved, before he corresponded with me, that I thought there was enough interest in the world of true crime fans, that this may, and I had no idea about publishing or any of the details of what was involved, what the market really entailed until I became--till I researched this specifically for the book proposal, I had no idea. All I thought was, instinctively, maybe even intuitively, that this was an interesting story.
Q All right. And you told him that he was going to get 30 percent of the profit on the book?
A Yes.
Q And that would be on the first printing, and then there would be more printings after that in all likelihood?
A Well, his idea of how things work I was not familiar with.
Q But you told him that. You told him--the 30 percent came from you?
A Yes, but not about the printings. Thirty percent of the entire profit of the book split between his cell-mate...
Q Who?
A His cell-mate.
Q Who? Who was his cell-mate?
A Don Abbott.
Q This unreputable, disreputable fellow that you told him about?
A I never said he was disreputable. He has a criminal record, and you want to depict people with criminal records as disreputable, then that's your decision.
Q You didn't tell him that he wasn't trustworthy; you didn't tell Sydney Teerhuis that he wasn't trustworthy?
A I may have told Sydney Teerhuis he was untrustworthy.
Q Okay.
A But that's a little different than disreputable.
Q Okay. You know that Mr. Abbott was in constant communication with Mr. Teerhuis? They were locked up together and they were...
A Yes.
Q In constant communication?
A Yes.
Q And you were in constant communication with Mr. Abbott?
A Correct.
Q And what Mr. Abbott was doing was telling you what kind of questions to ask Mr. Teerhuis?
A No.
Q And telling you what he had found out?
A No. Mr. Abbott did very little except introduce me to Sydney Teerhuis and impart to Sydney Teerhuis that he could trust me as a journalist.
Q But as the year went on, Mr. Abbott was continuing to talk about this incident and letting you know what he had found out lately?
A He had found out very little and he imparted very little to me about anything involving the crime whatsoever. Sydney did not impart any relevant information to Don Abbott. Don Abbott told me what he observed in that jail, in that cell block.

Q Did you ever see the letters that were tendered that were written to you from Mr. Teerhuis? Did you...

A Have I...

Q Do you know what letters were tendered and which letters were omitted?

A Basically.

Q Let's talk, then, about some of the ones that are not there, or some of the things that are contained therein. At the beginning of your dealings with Mr. Teerhuis, he was talking to you about the voices. Can you tell the jury what he was telling you about the voices?

A He told me that when he was young, an aboriginal man appeared, a voice, which guided him to find objects in the woods, and of course he found those objects in the woods. Later he said that his mother came to him in some apparitions. I really didn't take too many of these things seriously because he didn't pursue any one of those courses of a potential defense.

Q But he told you the voices were there at the time of the offence. Tell the jury what he told you about the voices at the time of the offence?

A He didn't tell me about any voices at the time of the offence.

Q Did you request that Sydney write you a letter and speak more about the voices in relation to Greene's murder?

A I may have written that, that statement.

Q Right.

A In response to his talk of voices, I asked if the voices had any relation to this, to Greene's murder because he spoke of the voices in other instances when he was in other cities residing.

Q Didn't you note the fact that he was talking about the voices or as you put it, guiding voices? What does a "guiding voice" mean?

A A guiding voice may be a voice that would instruct someone to do something, very much like the aboriginal voice that instructed him to look for certain objects in the woods.

Q So he told you that he had the voices, he told you that?

A Two different voices, yes.

Q What's that?

A Two different sources of voices.

Q Okay. And he told you that the voices come to him more when he's drinking or doing drugs?

A Yes.

Q He told you at the time of the death of Mr. Greene he was drinking and doing drugs?

A Yes.

Q He told you that he tries to ignore the voices but when he drinks, the voices are intensified?

A Yes, I think that's correct.

Q And you were concerned that he would end up with an insanity defense here?

A No. I know the definition of insanity. I didn't believe he was insane.

Q I didn't ask you that. I asked you that he was going to come up with an insanity defense?

A I don't know where I wrote that I believed that he would come up with an insanity defense. I may be incorrect.

Q Well, you may be incorrect. Don't want to fool you. Did you write: "*I believe all the talk of sexing the headless corpse and bathing with*

244

certain body parts and the guiding voices is a misguided attempt to create an insanity defense. Sydney clearly loves attention and craves celebrity. He's very interested in the book I'm writing." Did you make that note?

A Yes, I did.

Q Did you believe it when you wrote it?

THE COURT: Mr. Brodsky, sorry, what's that from?

MR. BRODSKY: It's from a phone interview and a note the witness made for himself.

THE COURT: Okay.

MR. BRODSKY: Which my learned friend has a copy of. And for my learned friend's benefit, it's the January 22nd, '05 document entitled "Phone Interview".

Q Do you remember writing that?

A Yes, I do.

Q Did you believe it when you wrote it?

A I believe that if he continued with the voice excuse, that he may be trying to trot out an insanity defense.

Q Well?

A That's what my notes...

Q You were concerned also that he was going to have an automatism defense; would that be fair?

A I thought since you had defended people with automatism that you may use automatism as a defense.

Q Right. And what did you do about it?

A I just researched what automatism actually is.

Q Didn't you plot with Sydney to put me on a radio show?

A No.

Q Didn't you want a radio interview with me?

A Well, you're saying I plotted. I asked you for an interview.

Q Right.

A We didn't talk about the Sydney Teerhuis case whatsoever.

Q Didn't you try to on many occasions during that interview?

A No.

Q And wasn't the plan to undermine his defense?

A No.

Q By having that radio show interview?

A I offered the Crown attorney the interview between myself and you.

Q Yes.

A To show that there wasn't any impropriety in that interview.

Q And nobody ever put forward an insanity defense; it was just in your head. Would that be fair? Or an automatism defense?

A I said there would be some possibilities. At the time I was naïve as to what actually could happen in a murder case. This has been an education of sorts. I don't know what defense you're likely to raise and how you're going to conduct yourself.

Q Didn't you write that, *"I don't have anymore information about the offence than Brodsky does, except maybe the necrophilia, which he's denied?"*

A You know, my assumptions may have been wrong, and at the time, again, I might have suffered from naivety. Those notes were not gospel and were not for public consumption. They were my private notes. If I thought there was something wrong with what I had done, I would just not have given them to the authorities.

Q Can you tell us about the necrophilia?

245

A Can I tell you about the necrophilia?

Q Yes. What is Sydney talking about when he talks about necrophilia?

A He talks about sexing the headless corpse of Robin Greene.

Q And digging up a grave, having sex with a body in a grave?

A That's another, that was a different subject for a different time, and that was a different conversation.

Q Okay. Did he talk about it?

A Yes, he did.

Q And did he say there was an East Indian from Bangladesh involved?

A Yes.

Q Is that the same thing as the necrophilia or is that different?

A That's different.

Q Okay.

A That's cannibalism.

Q Deal with the necrophilia first of all. The necrophilia is when he was in Vancouver. Was it Vancouver? You're the one who suggested it must have happened in Vancouver, didn't you?

A I didn't suggest.

THE COURT: Wait a minute, Mr. Brodsky. One moment. You have to help me out here, so I can follow the cross-examination. I don't mean to interrupt, Mr. Brodsky, but you're referring to portions of a reference to what either Mr. Teerhuis-Moar said or what Mr. Zupansky said. I have no idea at what point in the conversations between Mr. Zupansky and Mr. Teerhuis-Moar these are coming, from whom they're coming. In fairness to the ladies and gentlemen of the jury, I think they need to know that just so they can make the necessary assessments they have. I'm not following portions of this.

MR. BRODSKY: I'm going to deal specifically with a specific letter in a little while. I just want to get the general topic.

Q Did you ask him about whether he'd ever engaged in necrophilia, that is, the digging up and having sex with bodies in a grave?

A He raised the subject and I asked him about the subject that was raised. I asked him if he'd ever fantasized or engaged in necrophilia before, so...

Q And did you suggest a place?

A Well, he was living in Vancouver. I probably asked him while he was living in Vancouver. He didn't reside in Winnipeg except for the last few weeks before the murder.

Q And did you tell him, that shouldn't be in the book, I don't believe you, that is, digging up a corpse and having sex with it?

A It, to me, I wasn't positive but I thought it didn't ring true, that portion of it. But I thought it was a little over the top, maybe even the cannibalism. To me it's just so unbelievable that there are some things that he has imparted to me that are hard to believe, even for someone that's willing to believe many things.

Q Okay. Let's now deal with the cannibalism. Tell us about the cannibalism.

A He said that he fantasized about being cannibalized, killed and eaten by some prospective person that he wanted this fantasy to come true with.

Q And what did he want?

A He wanted to be killed and eaten by this person.

Q That wasn't a fantasy person, that was a real person, was it?

A Well, I don't know if it was fantasy.

Q He told you it was a real person, didn't he?

A That's fine.

Q Didn't he?

A That's fine.

Q And he told you what country that person came from?

A Yes.

Q What country?

A India.

Q Bangladesh?

A I don't recall.

Q Okay.

A India.

Q And he said that that person, who he described as, gave an age, made him sound real. Would that be fair?

A I suppose so.

Q And he wanted to cannibalize, he wanted to eat Sydney, to use terms in the letter, would that be fair?

A Right. That's correct.

Q And when questioned, eat meant really eat, eat his flesh?

A Right.

Q And Sydney was going to go along with that?

A Right.

Q And be eaten? Right?

A That's what he said.

Q What he said. And you didn't, after a while you said to him, come on now, that can't be true. Or is that one of the things that he told you later on was just chain-yanking or pulling your leg or just not true?

A Well, in the last letter he said there was no grave digging. He didn't say that he didn't actually plan not to be cannibalized.

Q He said there was no East Indian in that last letter of April 4th, 2005. He said there was no East Indian.

A Okay. Well, I'll be more specific. He didn't say that he didn't ever have a fantasy of being cannibalized, because he said there was another attempt at it as well. He talked about, well, that it didn't work out here so maybe I'll ask somebody else if I can do it with them.

Q You don't think that there was a problem here of Mr. Teerhuis taking real facts and building fantasies on them?

A I don't know. My job is just to take the details down and if I doubted something, that was not, as part of my job as a journalist, it's just my own gut feeling, I would imagine, that he may have lied about some things, may have exaggerated. That's a possibility since almost everyone I've ever encountered, that can be said of them as well.

Q That they lie?

A That they may be dishonest or exaggerate.

Q Well, he was pretty specific. For instance, with the necrophilia, he told you it was a metal coffin?

A Right. That was reported in the news, as well.

Q And he told you about George being there?

A Yes.

Q Who's George?

A Supposedly it's someone that they were drinking with that afternoon.

Q And?

247

A And apparently at some point he left but came back because he forgot his six-pack of beer.

Q And you said that's not believable either?

A I said it isn't... I wanted clarification. I wanted to understand this more. If he wanted to tell me something like that, which seemed improbable then--and he never followed it up.

Q My suggestion to you is that you told him not to mention George anymore because there was no verification that there ever was a George, that George was there, if he came back for his six-pack that somebody would have seen him, if nobody saw him it would just destroy...

A That's not what I said.

Q The book that you wanted to sell.

A That's not what I said at all. I said it seems--in fact, in the letter I said that it seems quite odd that no one is talking about this George person. If George was there--he had originally told me that there was George's fingerprints on a plastic drinking cup.

Q But he never said that. That's the reason you told him not to talk about George because there wouldn't be any fingerprints of George.

A No. I never said not to talk about George. I said, in fact, that it seemed odd that no one would mention this George: Why don't you mention this George to your lawyer. I mean, unless it's just not true, then you should mention this.

Q *"Why would you make this up except to cast some doubt on someone else, that someone else may have done the killing."* That's what you said.

A That's right.

Q *"If I were you, I would push to locate this George, at least mention George to your lawyer."*

A That's right.

Q Right.

A Well, that doesn't sound like...

Q Didn't believe him.

A The contention you, what you just said. I'm not dictating to Sydney Teerhuis.

Q You spoke of George returning around 4:30 because he forgot his six-pack. That sounds suspect. How can anyone forget a six-pack? That does not make sense. That's what you said to him?

A That's correct.

Q Did he ever have sex with George?

A He's had sex with everyone else. I asked him the question.

Q You asked him, in fact, on that page you asked him about 80 questions; would that be fair?

A Probably.

Q And it was his answers that allowed you to build up this fictional account of what transpired in that room?

A I didn't think that any of it fundamentally was fictional.

Q Did you tell him there's a problem about why he would go to the police to turn himself in if he was trying to get away with something?

A I asked him why, again, these are just questions, that I was curious and a person that's trying to write a complete story. *"Why did you turn yourself in?"*

Q That created a problem. The reason Sydney turned himself in to the police rather than attempting to evade arrest is unknown, is what you wrote, right?

248

A Well, it is. It's unknown.

Q And then you wrote: "*He very well may be embellishing the entire story to make for a better book.*" Would that be fair? That's what you wrote, isn't it?

A Those are my early notes.

Q Yes.

A There is much that predates the information where he sends detailed information about the murder, post-killing and the organ removal. I'm not a calculating person so if I thought...

Q He...

A If I knew the procedure, I would have taken that note and kept that from authorities. Being an honest person, I gave all of the information that I had and I didn't look over it, over the possibility that it might trip me up later. I just gave all the information...

Q But be that as it may, when you wrote, he may well be embellishing the entire story to make for a better book, what did you mean by that?

A "Embellish" means exaggerate. Doesn't mean fiction. Means exaggeration.

Q The reason for turning himself in to the police is a real mystery but it certainly does make for a far more intriguing story?

A Yes. In terms of true crime there are very few incidences where anyone has turned themselves in to police. Other killers or accused killers have contacted authorities, contacted the media. And as far as I knew, it sounded like this was quite unusual for a person to contact police then claim that they didn't remember anything about the killing.

Q Did you ask him for a complete description of the interviews he had with his own lawyer?

A Yes, I did.

Q And other professionals?

A Yes, I did.

Q Why did you do that?

A I was curious as to that information as well. He seemed to dislike you and mistrust you, as he wrote, and mistrust and dislike his own psychiatrist.

Q That was at the beginning?

A Yes.

Q And then he got to like me?

A I don't know. I haven't asked him.

Q At least he said so, right?

A Oh, yeah, he liked you a little more, yeah.

Q He liked me a little bit more.

A Little bit more.

THE COURT: No bragging, Mr. Brodsky.

Q I'm not bragging. All I want to suggest is, there was no reason for him to hide anything from his lawyer. He never gave you a reason to hide anything from his lawyer, did he?

A As far as I knew, it took me a fair amount of time. I thought that he was only imparting this information to me.

Q And then you found out what?

A And then at some point he said, yeah, I'm going to be seeing a psychologist or psychiatrist and I'm going to tell them about this and that, and I asked him in a subsequent telephone interview, and he said, yeah, I gave this information to Mr. Brodsky, same information you have, in the summer of 2004.

Q "*The only information that I have that Brodsky does not have*

is the accounts of necrophilia Sydney alleges to have engaged in
while living out west for some nine years."

A That's according to Sydney.

Q That's according to your note.

A According to Sydney. I wrote down what he said.

Q Now, you know that he had seen the autopsy photographs on a number of occasions and the photographs of the scene as the police discovered it on a number of occasions. You know that. He told you that?

A He told me that. I found it hard to believe that, because I had no experience as to that would be the procedure, but again, I just wrote it down, whatever he told me.

Q So he said that from my office I came out on lots of occasions with the photographs and the police report and the autopsy report?

A That's what he told me, yes.

Q And that my assistants came out with the police report and the autopsy report, pictures, and the photographs and the police descriptions, and he went over them again and again, and then another assistant came out and did the same thing. And he made notes and he made diagrams. And then that's what he told you, isn't it?

A That's right.

Q And from all of these many visits to go over the disclosure that every accused is entitled to, he then had a basis to tell you a story?

A Well, I don't know that. If you assert that, maybe.

Q If he was which?

A If you assert that. But I don't know that. I don't even...

Q Well, he told...

A I don't even understand why you'd show him autopsy photos, to tell you the truth.

Q Well, whether I had a reason or I didn't, the fact is he told you that he saw them?

A That's right.

Q All right. And he told you that he saw the cut-up body in the tub, the pictures of them?

A I don't recall that specific reference. But he said he saw the body chopped up on an examining table.

Q All right. And he told you that he read the autopsy report?

A I believe so.

Q So when you asked him what organs were missing, you didn't ask him, are you repeating what you read from the autopsy report or from what you know? You never asked him that did you?

A I had no reason to ask him that. He was dictating what he told me. He said...

Q Well you...

A He said...

Q Go ahead.

A He said to Don Abbott, at one point, that he was surprised, when he did see the photo on the autopsy table, of the shrinkage.

Q All right.

A He never intimated or indicated or insinuated that the only reason he had this information is because you gave it to him.

Q But he was comparing the autopsy, the photographs at autopsy to the earlier photographs of the body in the tub; that's what he was comparing, wasn't he?

A I don't know that.

250

Q Well, isn't that was Mr. Abbott told you? You're..

A No.

Q Telling us what Mr. Abbott told you?

A No.

Q Not what Sydney told you; is that right?

A Can you repeat the question?

Q Sure. The shrinkage is what Mr. Abbott told you that Sydney told to him. You're repeating what somebody else got from Mr. Teerhuis?

A Okay. Yes.

Q Isn't that fair?

A That's right.

Q I don't want you to say anything if it's not accurate.

A Okay.

Q And Trophy Kill, where did that name come from?

A Sydney.

Q And he wanted you to call the book Trophy Kill?

A Yes.

Q Because he put the trophy on the dresser in the bedroom?

A I don't know. I still don't know to this day why he wanted me to call it Trophy Kill. I kept asking him, why do you want to call it Trophy Kill? It's important for me to ask you why you're calling it Trophy Kill.

Q And every time he talked about, or most of the times he talked about the book being called Trophy Kill he talked about the torso being on the dresser, right?

A I wouldn't say that. He didn't talk about and specifically mention the word Trophy Kill over and over again. He had originally had an earlier title for the book.

Q Drunken Defence?

A No, that was mine.

Q That was yours. He didn't like that?

A No, he didn't like that.

Q Not enough pizzazz, couldn't sell enough books?

A Maybe he just didn't feel it was appropriate.

Q Because it couldn't sell enough books?

A Well maybe he just thought it would be a better title for the book.

Q Right.

A More appropriate.

Q He was really interested big time in celebrities and being famous?

A Well, many people are, but yes.

Q So he asked you to go get Susan Sarandon's autograph on a picture so that he could have it included?

A Yes.

Q You never told him that Susan Sarandon wouldn't want to be associated with a person who pretended to have sex with a headless corpse, did you?

A I don't know what--did I? No. No.

Q No. But he told you to go get the autograph and...

A Well, he told me to do quite a few things that...

Q ...And go talk to Richard Gere?

A Yes.

Q Because he was here on the movie *Shall We Dance*.

A Well, he was deluded in thinking that you just contact celebrities and get their autographs.

Q Okay. He was pretty good at getting that himself wasn't he, autographs of famous people?

A I don't know.

Q Well, you know that he wrote to the Queen?

A Oh, I don't know that.

Q You don't? He didn't tell you that he wrote to the Queen and got a reply from Buckingham Palace?

A I never read that.

Q Okay. He told you he was brutally beaten by the police?

A He said he was brutally beaten by police. He said the police put a gun to his head.

Q Right. And he gave you the name of the police officer?

A No. Not that I recall.

Q Detective Mathez.

A Okay. I just didn't recall that he had actually said the officer's name.

Q So did you report that when he advised you of that? Did you report that criminal act when he reported to you that it happened?

A No.

Q Why?

A Well, because I think the police have the ability to police themselves if something like that were to happen. There are witnesses.

Q Right.

A A police officer wouldn't be in a room all alone with him, so I think the police would be able to determine. And if he was interested, just like he was in the future, he could have reported. There are means and ways of him reporting that type of crime to the proper authorities, and then they can address that.

Q If I were to suggest to you the reason that you didn't report it is because that would be one more witness to say that he's fantasizing and making things up and yanking your chain, what would you say to that?

A I say you're incorrect.

Q He told you that he cupped a correctional officer's ass, as he puts it, in his letter, didn't he?

A He may have.

Q Did you report that?

A Of course not.

Q Why?

A Again, he has the ability to report these crimes as he's reported other things that he felt needed to be reported.

Q My suggestion to you is that you didn't report it because that would be just another person who would say it never happened, he's a liar, he's fantasizing, you can't believe what he says, he's yanking your chain.

A That's not why I did what I did. I'm sorry. You're incorrect.

Q He was really interested in publicity, publicizing his case, wasn't he?

A Well, you're interested in publicity and so am I.

Q But I don't sell T-shirts...

A Well, neither do I.

Q ...Outside the courtroom. No, but he wanted you to sell T-shirts.

A Well, sure.

Q And what was supposed to be on the T-shirts during the trial?

A "Eat me."

Q Eat me? You didn't think he was again yanking your chain and just fooling with you?

A I'll repeat it again, that I assumed that there may be some minor, again, fundamentally I thought he was telling the truth, that there were certain things that he may have exaggerated. That's what I believed was a possibility. I had no information where he did exaggerate or where he did lie, but all I had was my instincts and my impressions but...

Q You don't think he was yanking your chain and telling you fantasies and telling Don Abbott fantasies for the purpose of getting cash, even small amounts of cash?

A No. I don't.

Q Didn't he ask for cash and small amounts of cash, and didn't you promise to give it to him?

A I sent him $20. I promised to send him a little bit more cash. It was certainly not part of our book proposal.

Q No.

A I realized that he needed money for envelopes. He said he needed money for stamps and envelopes, $20 would cover a fair amount of envelopes and stamps, not much more.

Q So when he writes on April 13th, again--Exhibit 16--in 2004: Tell Don, who he refers to a number of times in the letter to, quote, "Send me cash fast." How much were we talking about?

A But if he's writing a letter to Don...

Q No tell Don.

A Not to me, okay.

Q To send me cash fast.

A Well...

Q As the P.S.

A I don't know if Don's agreement was with Sydney in terms of just sending him money as a friend. So I'm not sure what the agreement was, and I probably told Don what Sydney had said and left it at that.

Q And on June 14th, 2004, when he writes, "*It has been proven to me Mr. Abbott is not a man of his word, I have no respect for him.*" Do you know what he was referring to?

A Probably sending him some money as he had promised he would send him, since he'd be working and he would send some money because Sydney didn't have any money.

Q So your promise to him, when he writes, during the incarceration-- and I'm at Exhibit 61, My Lord, page 847:

> *During the incarceration of Mr. Abbott, your friend, he had mentioned the financial aspect of this matter depending on book sales and if there is to be a second or even a third printing. For each printing I believe it is safe to agree on 30 percent hypothetically for the first printing, 30 percent for the second printing, 30 percent, et cetera.*

Q That's what he wrote to you, isn't it?

A Yes.

Q And he already had, at that time, the release and he wasn't sending it back?

A Well, the release was sent in 2005.

Q Okay. He certainly was interested in getting paid?

A Yes.

Q And when he writes on October 6, 2004: *"To Dan, I had just received your letter only recently."* Do you know what letter he's referring to?

A No.

Q If we have it?

A Well, if you continue then I might be able to...

Q *"I have received your letter only recently since you only addressed it to Headingley Correctional Centre and not Sydney Teerhuis, that the guards read it and photocopied everything."*

A Yes, I'm familiar with it.

Q So you're telling me that he knows that everything is being photocopied?

A No.

Q Well, he says so.

A I sent...

Q The guards read it and photocopied everything.

A Yeah, well, all I know is that I sent that letter specifically so that the authorities might intercept that letter and read what he was sending to me.

Q All right. And nothing happened, though?

A That's right.

Q So you think that Sydney knows that, he's the one telling you about the photocopying, and you're asking him questions now about where are the organs, what did you eat first, what did you do with the decapitation, what order it took place, would you have sex with the body or Mr. Greene or a portion of the body, and all of that's being photocopied, according to the accused, Mr. Teerhuis, by the Headingley Correctional Centre?

A Right.

Q And he's writing to you anyways in that fashion. Is that right?

A Well what preceded that was that he said that when we visit, it is likely that the interview can be tape-recorded.

Q Right. And when you write, it's going to be photocopied.

A And when we write, it's not censored; they don't read incoming or outgoing mail. That's what he told me.

Q But it says here, the guards read and photocopy everything.

A No. They read. They read, not read...

Q And photocopied.

A Everything was photocopied because I didn't put his name on the letter. He told me they don't read ingoing and outgoing mail, and that's why I sent that letter that way.

Q In that same letter, he's very interested in all this money that you're promising him.

A Okay.

Q Would that be fair?

A Yes.

Q I quote: *"I still need a list of offshore banks in the Bahamas that are not affiliated with the United States or Canada. I will have to set it up so the check will go directly into the offshore account."* That's what he writes?

A Right.

Q Did you tell him that when we publish the book and I put all this material in that you say, you're not going to be able to go to any offshore account; you're going to be in jail?

254

A You know what, I don't know the rules of what you can do with your money in an offshore bank account. I mean, I may have my ideas but I just thought that Sydney was ill informed about how things work. I don't know how banking works in the Bahamas.

Q Even if he had money in an offshore account in the Bahamas or anywhere else in the world, how in the world was he going to ever spend any of it if he was writing in the fashion that you were encouraging him to do, explaining all of these things, fictional or otherwise, how in the world was he going to spend any of that money?

A When he got out of prison.

Q When would that be?

A He was planning to be out of prison fairly soon, I would imagine.

Q But he never said that. He never ever said that to you?

A No, he didn't. No, he didn't say that. But he talked about being out for the 2010 Olympics being his dream.

Q But he never said that he was talking about being in prison for a very long time and taking advantage of the system?

A No.

Q Because he was going to be in prison for a...

A No. If.

Q Very long time.

A If he was to spend a long time in jail, rather than manslaughter, he would take the taxpayer for every nickel and much, much more.

Q By doing what?

A I don't know. I don't know how he was going to milk the system. I have no idea.

Q He wanted to go on CJOB?

A Correct.

Q And he wanted you to go on CJOB?

A Correct.

Q And he wanted to talk about his case?

A Correct. He wanted me to talk about his case.

Q And talk about the detail in his case?

A Right.

Q So even if it wasn't going to be photocopied, the letters, or the words on the telephone were going to be listened to or not, he wanted you to go expose it on CJOB?

A He had said to me that he wanted this information to come out after the trial was finished.

Q He doesn't say that.

A He did say that to me.

Q *"If you do this appearance on CJOB with Charles Adler, I will give you an interview right after the preliminary hearing, not trial."* Preliminary hearing. That's what he writes.

A In that letter, yes.

Q On October 6, 2004.

A In that letter, yes.

Q In this letter.

A Yes.

Q And he tells you to be dramatic, use human trophy or room 309 or murder at 6:20 p.m. on the radio with Charles Adler?

A Right.

Q Did you not think that he was just fooling with you?

A Absolutely not.

255

Q And does he not say to you, after the preliminary, I will send you a chapter in graphic detail of how Greene ended up in the tub. He said that?

A That was earlier. And later, in subsequent letters he sends me the details. At one time he said, *"You're going to have to wait till the trial to find out any details."* By December, he gave me every single detail.

Q Because you were pushing him and he had more disclosure and he knew what he could say and that there was no witness too and what he could fictionalize and make things up?

A Well, I don't know that to be true.

Q That could be true?

A It could. I don't know that to be true.

Q And he told you that closer to the trial he would tell you about the East Indian man and how that relates to this crime of passion, right?

A Well, he never did tell me how the East Indian related to this, what he called a crime of passion. The East Indian story is totally separate.

Q Would it be fair to say that he hadn't worked out the detail yet of this fictional account when he wrote you this letter on October 6, 2004?

A What fictional account?

Q The fictional account of how the body came to be dismembered and having sex with a dead body and all of that?

A I don't know it is a fictional account. He never said it was a fictional account. I never believed it to be a fictional account.

Q Would it be fair to say that he wrote to you and told you that he grabbed Mr. Greene by the ankles and dragged him into the bathroom?

A Yes, I believe so.

Q Did he tell you that there was no sign that the body had been dragged into the bathroom?

A I don't recall that.

Q Did he tell you that he was drinking rye and Coke at the time?

A The time of what?

Q At the time of the dragging of the body?

A I don't know if I can recall that specific reference. He said he smoked crack after.

Q After or before and after?

A You know, he may have--before or after. It's either before or after dismemberment, according to him.

Q Where did he get the crack from?

A I don't know.

Q There was no doubt that he'd been using considerable amount of crack, according to what he told you?

A I have no idea how he could afford to buy any crack.

Q But that's what he said he did?

A Yeah. But I have no idea how he could afford to buy any.

Q He said it was readily accessible in the Royal Albert Hotel?

A I don't know. I don't know anything about crack.

Q And aside from crack, he said that in that room, around the time of this gruesome incident, he was using Oxycontin?

A Yeah, that's what I believe he said he had some Oxycontin.

Q What is that?

A It's a prescribed painkiller.

Q And it, taken in too large amounts, produces hallucinations?

A Oh, I don't know that.

THE COURT: Mr. Brodsky, one second, this witness can't answer that.

Q Do you know what its adverse affects are?

A No.

Q Or side effects are?

A No.

Q Would it be fair to say that he wrote to you in this letter of March 26, 2004 that the first time he put a condom on was after the body was decapitated and cut up?

A I don't know if that's the first time. All I remember is he said he used a condom.

Q Did he tell you he'd used a condom before that?

A He didn't say he had anal sex before. He said he only had oral sex before.

Q Without a condom?

A Without a condom.

Q And the first time he mentions using a condom is after the dismemberment?

A Well, he claims to have engaged in oral sex. Oh, pardon me, claims to have engaged in anal sex before the murder.

Q Right. And so did George, or some stranger by the river?

A That's what he claims. No, he didn't have sex with the victim. Oh, yes, oral sex by the river, yes.

Q Right. Didn't you tell him that the police would look for evidence of DNA findings if you had sex without a condom?

A No.

Q You didn't tell him that in order for your story to be true you have to say you were wearing a condom otherwise the police would see that you didn't ejaculate as you claim?

A I didn't say anything like that. I don't know what the police procedure is. I don't know much about DNA really.

Q He wrote to you asking what you wanted, what you wanted to hear for the book?

A Could you, could you read it?

Q *"Would you like me to make some drawings of the trophy on the dresser and the pelvic area in the sink?"* Would that be fair?

A Yes.

Q *"Do you want me to describe what his penis looked like inside or what it was like?"*

A Well, I wanted to encourage him about anything that he is already imparting to me anyway, that's what...

Q *"Do you want what's written in a particular form, the writing in a particular format? Get back to me right away."*

A And I didn't get back to him right away about whatever, I didn't understand what he was talking about anyway.

Q *"I want you to write back a.s.a.p. with your thoughts."*

A Well, there are lots of things he commanded me to do that I didn't do.

Q All right. But wasn't he writing you to see if this would go over, how does that sound?

A No.

Q If that doesn't sound good well and maybe this? Wasn't he trying to work out a story for the book, a fictionalized account of... I won't use the word "fictionalized," a more marketable account?

A I never saw any evidence whatsoever of that account.

Q He wanted to make a movie, too, not just a book. Would that be fair?
A Sure.
Q And he wanted Susan Sarandon to be in the book and a variety of Hollywood people?
A Right.
Q And he was telling you where it should be, in New York City. He wanted to know how the first chapter was coming. He wanted to talk about the dialogue and the jewelry and how to sell this book of his, of yours?
A Well, fine. But the jewelry in the room might have been an attempt, as well, to have some notoriety from the crime. I don't know.
Q And he, again, was fooling with you by saying, "*I expect Sarandon's photos by mid-week.*" Did you write him back?
A Well, he asked for certain things, he would demand certain things, and then not mention them again. Since I couldn't see how on earth I could possibly do it and nor was I inclined to do it, I'm not taking orders from Sydney Teerhuis, and then the issue was dropped. Then we moved on, we continued our correspondence.
Q And he wanted to know from you, or he wanted to tell you, according to your letter, about the conversations with the police that he had?
A I asked him for every bit of information about the truth concerning this entire case.
Q And his background?
A And his background.
Q Including the fact that he had no charges or record?
A Right.
Q He told you he had no charges or record?
A Correct.
Q And he told you that he told the police that?
A Right.
Q You don't know anything about any charges or record?
A Not that I know of.
THE COURT: Mr. Brodsky, it's 3:05. I think it might be time for a brief break.
MR. BRODSKY: Sure.

(JURY OUT AT 3:05 P.M.)

THE COURT: Mr. Zupansky, you're going to still be under oath so I'm going to ask you again not to talk to anybody about the evidence you're giving or anything about this case. Okay?
THE WITNESS: Yes.
THE COURT: Thank you.
THE CLERK: Order, all rise. Court is in recess.

(BRIEF RECESS)

THE CLERK: Court is re-opened. You may be seated.
THE COURT: Mr. Brodsky, just so I don't have to interrupt you, how long do you expect to be this afternoon?
MR. BRODSKY: Rest of the day.
THE COURT: Okay. All right.
MR. BRODSKY: I have never, as Your Lordship probably knows by now, have ever stayed within the, my expected time.
THE COURT: Okay.

THE CLERK: My Lord, all 12 jurors are present.

BY MR. BRODSKY:

Q You didn't do all of the things that Mr. Teerhuis asked you to do; would that be fair?

A Yes.

Q For instance, when he wanted to jazz up the book or the movie and get you to go down and see Ben Affleck and Jennifer Lopez who were part of the movie, you didn't just do that, did you?

A I don't remember any reference about Ben Affleck and Jennifer Lopez, any instructions regarding those two people.

Q It's at page, it's the letter of January 3rd, 2004. It's page 785. For my learned friend's benefit, it's Exhibit 64. *"How is the first chapter coming? I was actually thinking we could start it off in New York City, Sarandon and Gere being interviewed on 'Shall We Dance'. Gere looked at the back at a reporter, raised his eyebrows and said, 'There was a murder?' He goes on to say, 'The murder puts a slight damper on things,'"* and so on and so forth. Sarandon starts laughing. And he says later on, *"You may have to do some research on this point because Jennifer Lopez wasn't in Winnipeg at the time the jewelry was stolen, she was in Vancouver with Ben Affleck. It was his birthday."* And he talks about checking the July 2nd to July 5th Free Press, and then he talks about, I could go on and on. Talks about those people and what you should do to investigate and get interviews...

A Right.

Q From them and get them in as part of the movie, to make money.

A Okay.

Q In this incident. You didn't do all of that?

A Well, I researched when Jennifer Lopez actually came into the city. I knew, I didn't have to research, I just read celebrity stuff, like a lot of people, and I knew that Ben Affleck was in Vancouver. It was pretty well fodder for all the newspapers, not just celebrity tabloids.

Q You didn't think that he was pulling your leg, making things up and making you do things, seeing how far you could jump?

A Everything that he asked me that I thought was unreasonable, I just decided not to do it.

Q So when he said in that same letter that he never meant to hurt or kill Greene--for my learned friend's benefit, it's page 8, it's page 773 numbered, same exhibit number--what did you take that to mean?

A You'd have to--you can't take that out of context.

Q *"I never meant to hurt or kill Greene."*

A Well, you have to continue otherwise it's out of context.

Q Okay. *"I never meant to hurt of kill Greene. There was something about him I liked. He gave good head."*

A I don't have that letter in front of me, or at least if you give that to me I can...

Q Sure. With my learned friend's permission and court's permission, I've got it highlighted, what I've just read out.

THE WITNESS: Thank you.

Q Take a look at page 8, the very top. You see that? *"I never meant to hurt or kill Greene?"*

A Yes. However, in another letter he talks about that he didn't mean to hurt Robin Greene, he said he enjoyed the crime at the time.

Q Well, he says: *"I fell in love with his body."* You can see that three lines down.

A Right.

Q *"I never meant to hurt or kill Greene. I fell in love with his body."*

A No, but I'm talking about, there's another reference in the letter where he talks about he was not in his... he enjoyed the murder at the time. He feels sorry... I can't use the exact words; I'd have to reference it.

Q Right.

A But he said that he...

Q *"Was saddened for his family."*

A Again, that's out of context because in the other...

Q But that's what he says right in that thing, later, at the bottom?

A This one, yes. Yes. In this one.

Q Now, he's talking again about his being intoxicated and not being in his right mind. His actual words are: *"Remember at that time I wasn't in my right mind. Today I'm saddened for Greene's family. I didn't enjoy what I did."*

A And in brackets...

Q *"At the time, July 1st, 2003, I did."*

A Well...

Q That's what he says, right?

A That's what I'm referring to, yeah.

Q All right. It would be fair to say that what he's talking about is his being in such an inebriated state that he wasn't in his right mind at the time these things were happening. That's what he's talking about?

A He didn't say that, though.

Q But that's what he's talking about. That's the impression that you got from reading these words?

A That's not the impression I got from those words. There is an incredible amount of information where he has a callous disregard for Robin Greene, so in one, in one sentence where he says he does care, that has to be put in perspective too.

Q So he does a diagram for you and he has Mr. Greene's body being hung up in the bathroom?

A Right.

Q And then he tells you later on: *"I lied about that, there's no place to hang anybody, and I didn't hang him."*

A Right.

Q Which one was true?

A Well, all I can assume that maybe he didn't hang the body from the ceiling.

Q But he told you that he did.

A Originally, he had told me that he did. But he has the opportunity to recant many things and he only recants very little specifically.

Q And he's clear again that the trophy, that is, the torso was on the dresser. You see on page 773, that page 8, the one we're just looking at.

A Yes.

Q About 10 lines up from the bottom. That the trophy was on the dresser. He says that clear as can be, right there in that letter.

260

A Okay.

Q And then he retracts that later on, too, saying when I told you that, that's not true. Does he?

A I believe so.

Q Which one is true?

A I'm not sure which one's true.

Q When he says, in Exhibit 65, some of your questions, he's writing to you, this is January 3rd, 2005, *"I can't answer simply because certain things haven't even crossed my mind."* Do you remember him saying that?

A Yes.

Q Would it be fair to say that what he's telling you is, I haven't figured out, if I'm going to make a story, the boundaries within which I have to make up the story yet.

A I don't know where you're getting these conclusions, but I don't agree with them.

Q In that letter. Let me start a different way. He never, at any time, said that he was interrupted in his activities; would that be fair?

A Activities? Could you be more specific?

Q Sure, cutting up a body.

A No, he didn't say he was interrupted by anyone.

Q He never said anybody came or the phone rang or any interruption at all. He never said anything about an interruption at any time?

A What I know of your definition of 'interruption', I do not recall him saying that he was interrupted by a phone call or a person knocking on the door, or anything of that sort.

Q Or anything. What he said was, these activities happened and he went to sleep, or he passed out, or he blacked out, whatever the term is that you would like, and when he came to he found the body chopped up in the bathtub?

A He never gave me any details about blacking out and waking up and finding the body in the bathtub.

Q Okay. He said to you that in any event, that he was not interrupted in any way, even whatever version he gave to you?

A I don't recall him saying he was interrupted by a phone call or a knock on the door, as you use as an example, no.

Q Or in any other fashion?

A Well, you'd have to be specific what you mean by 'any other fashion'?

Q Well, I mean a loud noise on a TV, somebody knocking on the door or any interruption?

A I don't believe so. I don't recall any specific interruption, no.

Q So when he writes to say, *"I hadn't gotten a chance to smash Greene's skull and dissect his brain or dissect his hands and feet."* Do you know what that means he didn't have a chance? *"I hadn't gotten a chance?"*

A I don't know what he's referring to. I obviously think it refers to some form of disposal. He doesn't specify why he said that.

Q You don't think he's not making up a story as he goes along?

A I don't know what he made up or what he didn't make up.

Q Well, he wasn't disposing of the body; it was in the bathtub. Would that be fair?

A Well, he disposed of the organs.

Q And then he left the rest in the bathtub and told the police to go find him there.

THE COURT: Mr. Brodsky, the witness says he doesn't know what was made up or not made up, and now you're providing details in which you want some type of evaluation. I think the witness has already declared himself incapable of doing that, so...

MR. BRODSKY: Well, let...

THE COURT: Maybe we can dispense with a lot of questions that he just can't answer.

MR. BRODSKY: With deference, My Lord, let me ask this one:

Q He was asking for your input on what happened?

A He was? No, he wasn't.

Q Well, did he write to you saying, at page 4 of that letter: *"What did I do with Robin Greene's internal organs, were they (a) flushed down the toilet? (b) Did I sell them to George for $50? c) Did I eat them in a cannibalistic ritual? (d) Were they tossed into a BFI dumpster near HSC? (e) Were some tossed in a vacant lot and a dumpster near HSC?"*

A He was giving me multiple choices. I had asked him where the organs were. He said, *"You seem to be fascinated about the whereabouts of these organs, let me give you a multiple choice."* And then he asked, he posed the question: *"What do you think?"* I didn't write back and say, this is what I think till he told me that he disposed of them in a garbage can and in a vacant lot.

Q You don't think he was asking you what would sell better in the book?

A I have no indication, I don't know what he's intimating or insinuating. I just go by what he asked me and what I asked him.

Q Now, he told you that he has pictures of Mr. Greene sitting on his lap and Mr. Greene sitting on George's lap.

A Correct.

Q Do you know where the pictures are?

A All I know is what information was in the media, and just recently I read this last week, that there were certain photos of Robin Greene naked and Robin Greene in underwear posing for photos.

Q Right. I'm asking you specifically, about a photo of Greene sitting on George's lap. You never read that in the paper?

A No.

Q He told you though he took that picture. Was it in the same roll as the other pictures of Mr. Greene? Didn't he tell you that?

A That's correct.

Q But you don't know what became of those pictures?

A I don't know if there were any photos of this George. I have no indication that there are any photos of George. I know nothing about George except from what Sydney told me.

Q Now, in that same letter he wrote to you talking about necrophilia, right?

A Okay.

Q And he told you that he'd dug up a grave and opened the coffin?

A Okay.

Q Right?

A Haven't we gone through this already?

Q Yeah, we have.

A Okay.

Q Did he tell you what condition the body was in of this grave that he dug up?

A I can't recall exactly what he said about the body in the coffin. Since it had nothing to do with this murder, I was not as interested.

Q Wouldn't it be fair to say that he was just making stuff up to see if he could get a reaction from you or what kind of reaction he could get from you?

A He may have wanted to see my reaction. But again, my job was to seem impartial and that I was not shocked by anything he said to me. So, I continued with that.

Q So when he writes to you on January 12th, 2005 and says, talking about the police, they said there was very little or no blood?

A Yeah, he said that, yes.

Q He didn't say, I know there was no blood because I drained the body, or, I know there was no blood because I saw that. He says in the letter, they said there was little or no blood. The first page. It's, in black it's written 781, and it's dated January 12th, 2005.

THE WITNESS: Right.

Q And it's a little past halfway: *"They said there was little or no blood. There was no blood to be found in Greene's carcass."*

A Well, all I can assume is that he told me he washed the body. I don't think for a second I realized that he could have cleaned up all the blood, or at least that was my thought at the time, that I thought it might be inconceivable that he cleaned up all the blood in the entire room.

Q But he's not talking about what he did. He's talking about what they said, what they found, right?

A He thought...

Q Would that be right?

A It seemed like it was an important point to him. He made it more than once, that there was little or no blood, and he said 'in the body'. If he said he washed the body in the bathtub, then it would seem to me that the blood had washed down the bathtub.

Q Do you know why he was writing to you in that same letter, on the next page, about going on a program called Crime and Punishment, CJOB, to talk about what the papers had said and speculated, and all the rest of that? When he's talking about having sexual fantasies about Jeffrey Dahmer?

A Okay. Can you repeat the question, please?

Q Yes. Do you know what he was talking about, going on Crime and Punishment, to talk about what the papers are speculating?

A Well, I think it's just keeping--I thought it just kept in line with he wants to be on Charles Adler, then he would want to be on the other, you know, Mike McIntyre's famous radio program.

Q Right.

A CJOB being the biggest radio station in Winnipeg.

Q When he talks about--I'm at Exhibit 67, My Lord, at the very top of the page. When he talks about your speaking to him over the telephone, how many times did you speak to him over the telephone?

A Well, I'm not sure specifically how many, but I estimate about 50 times.

Q Five-o?

A Yes.

Q Did you keep notes of them, of 50 times?

A I kept notes, yes.

Q What happened to them?

A I gave all of the notes that I had to police--there were some phone calls possibly that I can't recall when I did not take notes, possibly because the conversation had nothing to do with the crime itself.

Q But mostly it had to do with the crime because that's the reason you put to us for speaking to him?

A I spoke to him to establish and continue the relationship that we had, the rapport.

Q When he writes to you in that same letter, on that same page, saying: *"Write up what you have so far on the first chapter and send it to me, I need to get a sense of your style of writing, I'll read it and make any necessary adjustments and send it back to you."* Remember receiving that?

A Yes.

Q Did you let him proofread or read for accuracy the first chapter?

A No.

Q Why?

A I didn't have the first chapter written. I didn't even start writing the book to well after I had contacted the authorities. I just considered the first, that period of time as to what's considered research.

Q Did Gere and Sarandon call the book The Shall We Dance Murder?

A I don't know.

Q That's what he said in that same letter; isn't that right?

A But I don't know if that's true.

Q Trophy Kill, The Shall We Dance Murder, is what Gere and Sarandon called it?

A Sydney gave me some information about Susan Sarandon talking about the Winnipeg Police fingerprinting her trailer. I did find that reference on MSNBC on the Internet.

Q Right.

A So the other information about Richard Gere and Susan Sarandon having the discussion, despite not having been able to find it, didn't mean that it didn't occur, so I had no evidence that it occurred or didn't occur.

Q And he was big again into profit from this, I recall, a fictional event when he writes to you in that same letter, the next page, talking about the royalties if you ask Hollywood's permission. Would that be fair?

A Yes.

Q Did you promise him royalties?

A No. I didn't really know. I think he doesn't quite understand the publishing world, especially now that I've looked into it. I mean in my estimation anyway, I don't think that royalties would be an issue.

Q And would it be fair to say it took till February 7th of '05 for him to finally tell you where the organs were?

A If that's what you're reading, then that's true, then.

Q Do you know why it took so long? Did you ask him or did he tell you why it took so long to divulge that?

A I think because I was so adamant and so interested in that detail, that he held back that information while giving me all kinds of other details. I think he realized that that was a very important issue.

Q Would it be fair to say that he waited that long because he wanted to make sure that no one could check to see if it was accurate?

A I don't know that to be true.

Q And then in Exhibit Number 68, again he talks about the dresser where he displayed Greene as a human trophy?

A Right.

Q That's repeated many times, on the dresser he displayed Greene as a human trophy, and that's the trophy kill and that's over and over again?

A Right.

Q Emphasized?

A Okay.

Q That's the diagram at the back I'm looking at.

A Well, this one is of the crime scene drawing that he made.

Q Right. And on the right-hand side it says: *"Dresser displaying Greene as a human trophy."*

A Okay.

Q Right under where it says: *"Chair I sat to smoke crack after killing Greene."*

A Right. That's correct. And your question is, sorry?

Q That he emphasized over and over again the fact that Greene was a human trophy on the dresser?

A Well, I didn't fixate on where exactly the body was. I was more shocked that he considered a human being a human trophy, and the drawings were equally disturbing and shocking.

Q Did you ever ask him if he was making things up as he went along?

A No.

Q So when he says in that letter, the front page of that letter: *"There are certain things I did to Greene's body that I'll never tell anyone. Something happened right before Greene died that I'll never tell either--as sort of a respect for the dead."* Did you ever ask him what he meant by that or whether he had made something up yet?

A Again, you know, I wouldn't ask him if he made up stuff yet. All I know is what he talks about. I just lost my train of thought for one second. Could you just repeat that question, please?

Q Yes. We're talking about his saying that he'll never tell anyone about certain things he did to Greene's body right before Greene died because he has a sort of respect for the dead.

A Well, number one, it seemed almost laughable that he has a respect for the dead. And that he was holding back certain information. I couldn't even fathom what else he could be telling me.

Q And it's in this letter that he writes that he's seen photographs of Greene's mutilated corpse on the examining table and, as well, some really awesome pictures of Greene's body parts. Would that be fair?

A Yes.

Q And then on April the 4th, 2005, he writes you the letter saying he gave you a lot of false information. It's Exhibit 69.

A Okay.

Q *"If you look back to all the false information I gave you about the necrophilia, about Greene's death, if you put two and two together, I took excerpts from Dahmer, Gacy, Nilsen, Wuornos and put them together and gave you a story."* Open bracket, *"fiction"*, close bracket. You see that?

A Yes.

Q That was a surprise to you that he would say that it was all fiction?

A That was a surprise, yes.

Q It included not just the necrophilia but also Greene's death? He says that specifically, right?

A It's all fiction? His death wasn't fiction.

Q *"If you look back to all the false information I gave you about the necrophilia, Greene's death."* No, he agrees that he died, but he says that he got the story of what happened from excerpts from Dahmer, Gacy, Nilsen and Wuornos and put them together and gave you a fictional account?

A Well, yeah, but that's nonsense.

Q That's what he says?

A Well, that's what he says but that's nonsense.

Q He goes on to say: "*In your letters you say many things don't make sense. Well, of course not. You have four different stories put together. Did you honestly think I'd tell you so voluntarily about July 1st, 2003? I don't want you to make a fool of yourself or spend money on a book of lies.*" He wrote that?

A Yes.

Q Did you talk to him again after that?

A No. I wrote him after he sent me that letter. I never spoke to him after that.

Q There was no East Indian, on the next page, no grave digging and no necrophilia?

A Right.

Q You don't know if that's accurate or not accurate?

A Well, I took it as he had, again, the opportunity to recant many things specifically, and yet he only recanted very few things specifically.

Q Do you know why he said: "*I've also made Mr. Brodsky aware of who you are and gave him your home address and phone number?*"

A Was I aware of that?

Q Yeah.

A Yes.

Q And, when he says, as for the drawings, I had gotten the basic drafts from text books in the jail library, including a biological text of the human body, did you verify that there is such a text or make any attempt to do that?

A There's a drawing of him on top of Robin Greene with a knife, saying in the caption, "*Please don't kill me*". And Sydney Teerhuis has a hard-on. So I don't understand how, you know, that doesn't lend any credence to his claim.

Q Well, what's the human body got to do with a hard-on?

A Nothing. I can't see how he got that drawing from any book and in any conceivable way.

Q He's talking about the body, isn't he?

A He talks...

Q Not talking about the drawing of him straddling Mr. Greene, he's talking about what a body looks like, the skin and the eyes and the tendons, the way he has it all laid out in the drawings.

A Well, that's fine, but I don't--that wasn't part of my research and my responsibility, and I felt that I would just wait for the trial and the pathologist to get on the stand to discuss that.

Q When he writes to you: "*Do you recall the fictional story about the bathtub murders in it?*" on that same page.

A Yes.

Q "*Sorry I wasted your time.*" Did you recall the fictional story about the bathtub murders?

A Yes.

Q And where was it told?

A I asked him for that fictional story because according to Don Abbott, that there was a book, a fictional book, which he specified as fictional, about a murder, multiple murders, a man who is sexing his own child.

Q Right.

A And bodies end up in a bathtub. And he called it Murder and Mayhem. It was clearly a fictional work. I asked him for that fictional work, if I could derive anything from that whatsoever and relate it to Robin Greene's murder. I was just curious.

Q When he told you--this is Exhibit 70, My Lord. When he told you that he had taken alcohol, crack cocaine and Oxycontin, was that the first time he told you about the Oxycontin?

A I'm not sure if that's the first time. He may have mentioned it another time, because he had mentioned that he had asked Robin Greene to his suite in exchange for drugs and alcohol.

Q And in exchange for sexual pleasures, as he puts it?

A Well, his sexual pleasures.

Q Well and he writes as well: *"Teerhuis and Greene spent the early afternoon by the Assiniboine River, drinking?"*

A Correct.

Q And did you ever ask him where he got the alcohol and how much he had to consume by the river?

A He pointed out that he'd been drinking for a considerable amount of time.

Q He used the word 'binge'; he'd been on a binge for a considerable amount of time, hadn't he?

A I can't recall if he said specifically the word 'binge'. He said he was an alcoholic years before. He said he drank alcohol. He said they picked up some beer. It seemed if I could recall, that there were always small amounts of beer that he was picking up. There was no time when he picked up four cases of beer or had copious amounts of alcohol available.

Q Or two-liter containers of beer? He never said he got those?

A He said he bought big beers.

Q Big beers and strong beers, at a different place?

A Well, they can only go up to about six and a half percent, as far as I know, or seven point five, pardon me.

Q And he told you that he went to the Garrick and got some more beer?

A Yes.

Q Him and Greene, Mr. Greene?

A Yes.

Q And he told you that he partied with the hotel staff at the Royal Albert, smoking pot?

A He said that, yes.

Q Do you know who could verify that, who of the Royal Albert staff...

A No.

Q Were smoking pot with him?

A No.

Q Or if that's just a fictional account again?

A I don't know what's fictional or what's true in regards to that.

Q You told us that he had treatment already in the past for his alcohol and drug addiction?

A Correct.

Q That was at Poundmaker's Treatment Centre in St. Albert, Alberta? And he told you as well that he'd had a relapse after he got out of Poundmaker's at the Totem Resorts in Lake of the Woods?

A Yes.

Q And he told you all about his being a fancy chef, culinary artist?

A Yes.

Q And he worked for five star hotels all across this country?

A That's what he told me.

Q And there was nothing that he told you about that which seemed to be untrue?

A Again, it didn't seem untrue, but when he depicted himself as a rising star in the culinary world, it sounded maybe like he may be exaggerating.

Q And he told you that not only that he was a rising star, that he served very fancy people, royalty?

A Well, he said he was at a party with Jim Pattison of Pattison Signs and Donald Trump and Ivana Trump were there.

Q And he was the chef, he was the organizer?

A He was one of the chefs, yes.

Q Yes. And he was very concerned about your appearance to tell his story on CJOB?

A He was interested in me appearing on CJOB, telling his story.

Q When did you first find out about that this East Indian male—I'm at Exhibit 72. When did he first tell you about this East Indian male from Bangladesh?

A Probably in this letter here.

Q There's lots of detail in the letter, isn't there?

A Yes, there is.

Q Lots of detail in a letter that seems to be, in the end, fictitious?

A Possibly. I don't know. So much information is incredible that this very well could be true.

Q On the next page, he writes to you about what the autopsy report showed.

A Okay.

Q Would that be fair, at the top?

A Yes.

Q The autopsy report concluded that the accused must have had some knowledge of human anatomy.

A Correct.

Q And that gave you the idea that he read the autopsy report, right?

A Well, he told me he read the autopsy report, that you, your office provided it to him, so...

Q And the result was, he was able to draw the diagrams that appear on that page?

A Well, given the shrinkage that he claims, I don't know if this depicts the shrinkage or...

Q The shrinkage is not something he told you. That's something somebody else told you?

A Okay. That's right.

Q He said to somebody else.

A Okay. Well, this looks like drawings of the autopsy.

Q As does the next page?

A Okay.

Q Right?

A Okay.

Q He writes in that letter: "*From what I have seen, it looked as if the victim, Mr. Greene, had been dismembered in a chaotic fashion, but let them, the panel of 13, the jury will decide what happened that day. You see that?*"

A Yes.

Q He's not telling you that I know what happened, he's telling you that they'll have to decide?

A Yeah, but all he says...

Q And if I say "I", I mean Sydney Teerhuis.

A Well, he said it looked like to him at that point that the body was dismembered in a chaotic fashion, yes.

Q But he wants a jury to decide what happened that day?

A Yes.

Q Not trying to get away with anything here?

A Oh, I can't make that conclusion. Can't agree with you there. I don't know that.

Q In the next exhibit, Exhibit 73, this is an exhibit where he talks about going to the bus terminal, getting some scotch, going to the Royal Albert, smoking crack, drinking some sherry, his job at the Medicine Rock, smoking more crack, having some vodka, continuing his drinking binge. That's the word he uses, 'drinking binge'. That's all right, isn't it?

A Yes. But based on my experience, I realize that one drug often counteracts another drug.

Q But when he's talking about—it was 8:30. I'm on page 6: *"It was about 8:30 a.m. I was heading back to the Albert to continue my drinking binge."* He's not talking about drugs there.

A Right.

Q Had not been talking about drugs: *"And then we started walking, headed for the Woodbine. They opened at nine and we drank for a bit."* And then he talks about his friend joined us and a tall native guy tried to sell me a $15 bus ticket and a gold necklace, which seems to be his recollection of the events of that day.

A Okay.

Q Would that be fair?

A Yes.

Q When we got outside, he said his name was Robin, and then we went to room 309.

A Correct.

Q And then they went drinking again.

A Correct.

Q And at page 7, after they were drinking inside, they finished their drinks and headed outside. Right? And then he bought some strong beers at the Windsor and headed towards the library?

A Correct.

Q And then they walked down to the river and sat by the Royal Crown?

A Correct.

Q So he's drinking and drinking and continuing his binge and drinking and drinking, is what he's talking to you about?

A Correct.

Q Now, in the next exhibit, Exhibit 74, which I take it follows the letter we've just read, you now challenge him on *what do you mean you didn't have time or opportunity to smash his skull*, which means you did not finish what you had started; is that the real reason? You didn't believe that either?

A Oh, you can't put, you can't conclude what I thought at the time. I just was asking questions. I needed clarification: What do you mean by not having enough time to smash his skull? That's simply what it is. There's nothing else, nothing else intimated or insinuated in that. That's just a simple question.

269

Q And why would you say to him, other than alcohol--on the next page, halfway down--other than alcohol, were you under the influence of any other drug, if he's already listed the drugs for you?

A Well, sometimes I ask questions again. Sometimes I was repetitious. And if I might add, part of the reason is that I believe that, like I was starting to say, that in my experience, based on what I've read and what I've observed, is that a drug, which is a stimulant, and another drug, which is a depressant, one will counteract the other, at least in terms of intoxication or visible intoxication. So the effects of that might include what people would experience while they're drunk but might be counteracted by the other drug itself.

Q But you don't know that to be the case?

A No. Just based on my experience.

Q Your experience using these drugs?

A No, based on my experience reading about these drugs and observing other people on those specific drugs.

Q Do you have a degree in?

A No. No, I don't.

Q You don't. Why did you want to know what his statement was to the police? This is Exhibit 75.

A Just part of all the details that I was interested in. I was interested in the entire story, so part of the story is what happened when he met with police.

Q And that's the letter that, December 16, 2004, where you want to make sure that you have all of the notes of all of the meetings with the lawyer and the shrink?

A Right.

Q In full. Did you ever get them?

A He gave me some letters detailing meetings with Dr. Shane. He did have...

Q And me?

A Yes.

Q He gave you letters detailing his meetings with me?

A With your office, with meeting you.

Q And did he write out the conversations?

A Not specifically with you, no.

Q No. This is 2004, December 16, 2004. You want him to give you that release back. So he's already had it in 2004; would that be right? I'm on page 2, second page, and I'm quarter way down.

A What line is it, sorry?

Q Quarter way down. Right under the: *"All the subsequent meetings with Brodsky should be recorded in full and sent to me. They are very important notes so write them down at the actual time of the meeting or phone call,"* exclamation mark. *"I need to get that. I need you to get that release back to me before we make arrangements to visit you and record the visit."*

A Well my friend, the documentary producer told me we would need a release in order to be able to put anything on air, we'll say.

Q All right.

A And so it's a standard film release, as I understood it.

Q And that's to release, the book release and the film release?

A No. No. It's the film release. We were scheduled to interview Sydney Teerhuis at Headingley jail, and since he was going to be on camera, we needed, as far as I knew, according to the advice I had, was that we needed a release for that.

Q And you were going to send him some money, you tell him: *"Send me back the release and I'll send you some money."* You look at last two sentences on that page.

A Well, I didn't put it that way. I didn't say, send me the release and I'll send you some money. Send me the release, I need it, to get this project done that you're interested in. And by the way, as I had promised, I'll send you a little bit of money despite being broke like a church mouse.

Q In his big description of where he walked and the beer he got here and the beer he got there and the drugs that he drank or had, he never said, at any point at that time or at any other time, that he plied Mr. Greene with alcohol to make him drunk, did he? Ever did he say that?

A Ply, he didn't use the word 'ply'.

Q He never gave Mr. Greene sufficient alcohol to make him drunk, more drunk than he, Sydney, was. Would that be a fair statement?

A Well, of course he didn't, he didn't make that reference. But that doesn't mean that...

Q Well, anything could have happened, but he...

A Yeah.

Q Never said that?

A No, he didn't say, no, *"I plied him with alcohol so he was much drunker than I was."* No, he didn't say that.

Q Or, *"I attempted to get him drunk so he wouldn't be able to resist me."* He never said that either?

A No. No. He didn't.

Q He said a lot of very awful things, mutilation and mutilating the corpse and a lot of awful things, but he never said that he tried to incapacitate Mr. Greene by having him drink more than he, Sydney, was drinking?

A But I wouldn't ask that question since in previous letters he talks about his method of operandi and talks about meeting people and drugging them and then raping them and sodomizing them.

Q But he didn't say that's what happened with Mr. Greene?

A That's right.

Q That was a different scenario that you're talking about?

A That's right. But that's why...

Q In this case he didn't talk or even hint at doing that with Mr. Greene, did he?

A No, he didn't.

Q Well, why were you telling him to be wary of Don Abbott: That you have a good reputation but I can't say that for Don, however. Why were you telling him to be wary of him?

A Well, Don Abbott, when he was released from jail, he needed a place to stay so I'd offered him a room at my home, and I had a real hard time collecting the paltry amount of rent that I charged him each month. He would disappear. So that's what I was referring to.

Q And what did you mean by suicide by cannibalism?

A Well, Sydney referred to...

Q Sydney what?

A What did I mean by suicide, by cannibalism?

Q Yes.

A Well, what I was referring to is Sydney's talk of wanting to be cannibalized--or, pardon me, murdered and then cannibalized by someone. So...

Q Did this precede that?

A Pardon me?

Q Did this come before his talk of cannibalism? Were you the one who put the cannibalism?

A No. No.

Q In his mind?

A No.

Q There are those who wish to fantasize about suicide by cannibalism and you spoke of guys who would like to literally eat pussy, do you think there might be those who would like to die this way, that is, being sexed and then killed and used for sex again? Isn't that directly putting in his head what you expect to hear back from him?

A He already wrote me a letter talking about a killer, his friend the bank robber who had told him about a famous serial killer who ate the breasts of his victims.

Q Why did you tell him to drop the eight piece references?

A What I saw from that was how he was counting the eight pieces didn't correspond with, if you counted the eight pieces and then the eyeball, which is another separate piece.

Q Yes.

A Technically, that I thought--I don't know why I wrote "drop the reference" but at least I thought that's what I was referring to, that the eight pieces makes sense but if you add, with the new information he gave me, that he had dissected one of the eyeballs and the other one he took out of the socket, then that's nine pieces.

Q So you weren't saying, *if you keep on talking about eight pieces, that reference to eight pieces of silver, eight pieces of gold, eight pieces is too fantastical for anyone to really believe.* You weren't saying that?

A You're going to have to rephrase the question. I don't quite understand what you're trying to get me to answer.

Q Where did you get the idea that the weight of Mr. Greene was 240 pounds and his height was six foot four and that he was a big guy?

A That came from Sydney Teerhuis.

Q A number of times?

A At least once, maybe twice. I'm not sure.

Q Did he tell you that he had spent the night before, that is, most of the night, drinking and smoking crack and drinking vodka?

A I believe so.

Q And he was very big into notoriety and being on CNN and Celebrity Justice in L.A.?

A He was interested in those programs.

Q And he told you that he himself, as a child, had been sexually molested on many occasions?

A He had told me that.

Q And he told you the names of the people who sexually molested him on many occasions?

A He stated what he claimed, yes.

Q And he told you that he had been physically abused as a child?

A Yes.

Q And he told you that he had been a male prostitute?

A Yes.

Q He told you a horrid story of his upbringing?

A Yes, and I investigated that claim.

Q And?

272

A His guidance counselor in high school, the person that Sydney claimed to be the closest to and still had a relationship after, that was maintained after the murder, after he was charged...

Q Yeah.

A This person, I asked him, he said, no, he never mentioned any physical abuse; he never mentioned any sexual abuse.

Q That doesn't mean it didn't happen, obviously?

A That's correct.

Q And if it is a fantasy, that would be just continuing on with his fantastical story, wouldn't it?

A I, I...

THE COURT: The witness has already said, sorry, that he can't say what is fantastical and what's not, Mr. Brodsky.

Q Did you ever tell the police that Sydney told you that one of them held a gun to his head?

A I can't recall if I told police in my video statement. I don't believe I did.

MR. BRODSKY: With respect, My Lord, that is the cross-examination.

THE COURT: Thank you, Mr. Brodsky. Any re-examination, Ms. Leinburd?

MS. LEINBURD: No, thank you, My Lord.

THE COURT: I just have one question for you, Mr. Zupansky, if I might.

EXAMINATION BY THE COURT:

Q At what point after the correspondence ended or during the correspondence did you consult the individuals that you say you sought advice from with respect to whether or not the police ought to be spoken to?

A It was around late in the year of 2004 when there was so much information had been imparted to me.

Q Was that near the beginning of your correspondence with Mr. Teerhuis-Moar or near the end?

A It was closer to the end.

THE COURT: All right. Any questions arising from that?

MS. LEINBURD: No, thank you.

MR. BRODSKY: I have two, My Lord. One is not arising from that and I'm asking permission to ask it.

Q You told us two journalists. Who did you get the advice from? Who are the two journalists?

A One journalist is named John Webb, and the other is a former journalist named George Jacub.

Q And, two, on the website that you have, Zupansky.com, do you get paid for that?

A Oh, no.

Q If people go onto your website and buy what's advertised on the left-hand side, do they...

A The web designer derives the income from that because I didn't pay anything for the website. It's a free--it's Peg City Works, I think it's called. It's a free website. You have to upload information, video, but I don't know anything about web designing so...

Q I'm not talking about that.

A I make no money.

Q The 7900 hits either that have been on it. I'm talking about if someone orders something that's advertised, when they pull up your blog, or whatever it's called, do you get paid every time someone goes to an advertiser?

A I don't make any money from that website.

Q Does your web designer get it?

A He gets the money from whatever person advertises on that website.

Q And your advice to us is that you don't know how much that is?

A When we spoke, it was about $30 at one point, maybe after...

Q Earlier.

A Pardon me?

Q Earlier.

A I just spoke to him recently. He didn't talk about all the money he was making from it.

MR. BRODSKY: All right. Thank you.

THE COURT: All right. Thank you very much, Mr. Zupansky.

THE WITNESS: Thank you.

(WITNESS EXCUSED)

THE COURT: Ladies and gentlemen, that's everything for today. We'll see you back here at ten o'clock. Thank you very much.

(JURY OUT AT 4:27 P.M.)

THE COURT: Just one second. Mr. Zupansky, just before you leave, I just wanted to direct you that, to remind you that—you do have a website, I understand, and you have some interest obviously in this case. There was some conversation earlier today about a lunch you may have had with a gentleman that I've spoken to and we'll hear about that in a moment. But just to remind you, you know this, I hope, and I'm not accusing you of anything, but you are not to in any way utilize any information you have about the jury. If you have any possession of pictures of the jury, obviously that can't go on your web page. The web page is not to be a format for anything with respect to this jury either their identity, names, photos, anything like that. Do you understand?

MR. ZUPANSKY: Yes, and it hasn't been.

THE COURT: All right. Good. Thanks very much.

MR. ZUPANSKY: Thank you.

THE COURT: You can leave. Thanks.

Figure 28: December 8th, 2008, Winnipeg Law Courts. Dan Zupansky leaves court after a full day of testimony. Courtesy of Sun Media.

21

More Controversy

DECEMBER 9/08

ON THE FRONT-PAGE OF THE WINNIPEG SUN, REPORTING ON THE PREVIOUS day's testimony was the following headline: **Accused Killer Lied For Book Deal? Teerhuis-Moar made up grisly details about murder, lawyer argues.**

The article began with the statement that Brodsky was arguing that Sidney had fabricated grisly details of the murder in order to secure a lucrative book deal.

The reporter quoted Brodsky, "*You don't think he was yanking your chain and telling you fantasies to get cash? You don't think there is a problem here of Mr. Teerhuis taking real facts and building fantasies around it?*" The story quoted me as replying that Sidney, "*may have exaggerated... (but) I didn't think any of it was fundamentally fictional.*"

The story continued stating I had said that Sidney only 'backpedaled' regarding his earlier revelations when I informed him that a law had been passed that prevented criminals from profiting from their crimes.

In the article much information was taken verbatim from the previous day's accounts such as the disposal site of the missing organs and the plot to be killed and then cannibalized. The newspaper reported that Sidney later 'had retracted the claims'.

They mentioned that I had offered 30% of the profits from the book for his cooperation and incorrectly stated that the correspondence ended when I contacted authorities, quoting me saying, "*He (Sidney) said he had not read about the law and he thought it was a ploy to rip him off.*"

Completely out of context but more importantly confusing for readers, they included me saying, "*I had always planned on contacting authorities, but given the flood of information that was coming, I wanted to get information on the motive first. I thought that was important.*"

The Sun also stated that Brodsky had painted me as a dishonest opportunist using the case to further my professional ambitions.

The Sun claimed that I was a former University radio show host who had a website 'devoted' to Sidney and that on the website I had expressed concern that prosecutors "*would have to settle for a manslaughter conviction.*"

They included Brodsky's allegation that I had tried to convince him to be a guest on my radio program in an attempt to discredit the case. "*Wasn't the plan to undermine the defence with that radio show?"* Brodsky said. They wrote that I had denied the allegation.

In the Free Press was a story, **Accused in killing saw book deal**. The article was not as bad as the Sun's but it stated that, *"Zupansky admits he repeatedly pleaded with Teerhuis for gory, graphic details of the killing."* Again misinformation. Mike McIntyre did get one thing right, stating, *"The letters are the heart of the Crown's case."*

To say I was disappointed with the newspaper articles would be an understatement. I was incensed. It was as if the reporters were not even there or had not bothered to listen carefully to my testimony whatsoever.

I had been on the witness stand for almost four-and-a-half hours and this was what these so-called journalists had gotten from all of that. What? They couldn't comprehend the proceedings? Were they so confounded by Greg Brodsky's 'brilliant' cross-examination that they couldn't grasp that I had been a completely convincing and effective witness, entirely dismissing Brodsky's relentless attempts to have me admit that Sidney's letters and drawings were all fiction? The sheer misrepresentation of the proceedings by both the Free Press and the Sun was irresponsible and I was glad that a jury would be deciding this case, and—thanks to the newspapers—not the misinformed public.

✳   ✳   ✳   ✳   ✳

DECEMBER 9/08 — IN COURT

THE CLERK: Court is open. Please be seated.
MR. BRODSKY: As a courtesy I would indicate to Your Lordship that I've advised my learned friend that it is still my present intention to call the accused. I've told my client that I'm going to be meeting with him...
THE COURT: Yeah.
MR. BRODSKY: ...After court today, and I told him he's going to be testifying tomorrow and that nothing, nothing has...
THE COURT: I appreciate that.
MR. BRODSKY: ...Nothing, absolutely nothing has changed.
MR. BRODSKY: Did Your Lordship have an opportunity of watching whatever that tape was?
THE COURT: I was briefed on its contents and my indication to the owner of the apparatus will be that I think it's something that ought to be destroyed. I don't know that I can order destruction, but if I can't order destruction I will probably be referring it to the Winnipeg Police Service. There is on the digital film, film of the jurors, and at one point one of the juror's turns around. The gentleman indicates that he wasn't intending to do that. I'm at this point not making any evaluation on that. But for my purposes and for the purpose of just ensuring that there is nothing by way of a recording, still or moving, of any of the jurors, I think that ought to be ideally destroyed.
MR. BRODSKY: I hesitate to get involved in something that may not be my providence, but I'd be nervous if you destroyed it. I think it might be better off given to the police or the Crown to maintain. I mean, you're--
THE COURT: My destruction would be done with the consent of the, of the owner of the camera. It's not going to be a court order, but I appreciate your point.

277

THE WITNESS WAS PETER MCLAREN, A CIVILIAN MEMBER OF THE RCMP WORKING in the capacity of forensic DNA specialist.

Through questioning from Sheila Leinburd the expert witness verified that Robin Greene's DNA in the form of blood was found on Sidney's body and some of his clothing. Also that both Sidney's and Greene's DNA were discovered on the two knives that were used in the killing. Leinburd's direct examination was quite extensive and thorough.

Greg Brodsky's cross-examination was very brief, asking only six questions in total. Sheila Leinburd announced with that, she had completed presenting the evidence for the Crown.

Judge Joyal thanked her and told the members of the jury that court was finished for the day.

(JURY OUT AT 11:01 A.M.)

THE COURT: Sir, yeah, at the back of the court, I forget your name, again, would you come forward, please? What's your last name, again, I'm sorry?

MR. SMITTY: Smitty.

THE COURT: Smitty. Mr. Smitty, yesterday members of the sheriff's department had an opportunity, with your assistance, and I appreciate your willingness to address my concerns about the possible identification of one or others of the jurors because of what you say was perhaps an inadvertent attempt to film them. Apparently there was on the film that was viewed images of the jury, at least their back, and at one point during the film one individual, I guess, turned around. At this stage, what I'm going to do is I'm going to refer the cassette that is currently in possession of the sheriff's department to the Crown attorneys' office, who in turn will just distribute it or rather refer it to the police department. That's not to say there'll be charges, but there has to be some orderly fashion to pass the film on to someone. It may be that the film is simply destroyed; I don't know, but that's going to be for the police and, perhaps, the Crown to decide. All right. But at this stage I just wanted to advise you, based upon your willingness to turn over the cassette yesterday, which I appreciate, at this stage you can't have it back. I don't think you expected it back. But any further inquiries should be made really of the police who will be getting that in due course once they get it from the Crown. Okay?

MR. SMITTY: Sure. Thanks.

THE COURT: Thanks very much.

(PROCEEDINGS ADJOURNED TO DECEMBER 10, 2008)

22

The Killer Takes the Stand

THE WITNESS: M-O-A-R.
SIDNEY TEERHUIS-MOAR, sworn,
THE CLERK: Thank you. Please have a seat.

DIRECT EXAMINATION BY MR. BRODSKY:
Q Mr. Teerhuis, the jury doesn't know much about you except what they saw in the letters so I'm going to ask you to give us a little of your history. First of all, how old are you?
A Thirty-nine.
Q And when were you born?
A August 23rd, 1969.
Q Sixty-nine? Okay. Where were you born?
A In St. James Assiniboia.
Q And can you tell us a little bit about your early life?
A I was taken away from my birth mother because she was only 15 years old and I was placed in foster care with the Teerhuis family, who resided in North Kildonan, here in Winnipeg.
Q And that was in 1979?
A 1969.
Q And you were adopted by them?
A Yes, I was.
Q And how many children did they have?
A They had four of their own children. Mrs. Teerhuis had suffered a miscarriage, so she would have had five.
Q But she had five and there was how many in the household when you grew up there?
A There was myself, a French girl named Isabel, who was also adopted by them, and their daughter, Ann Shirley and their son, Bill.
Q And can you tell us about growing up in that household a little?
A One of my earliest recollections was my birth mother being very overprotective of me. I was molested by their second oldest son.
Q Now, the Teerhuis' second oldest son?
A Yes.
Q And what happened as a result of that?
A Mrs. Teerhuis had caught him in one of the acts and she just told him to stop what he was doing and she told me never to speak of it again.
Q And how many times had you been molested? I take it that's sexually molested?

Figure 29: Sidney Teerhuis, shortly after his arrest in July 2003. Courtesy of Sun Media.

A Yes.

Q And how many times had that happened?

A From 1973 up until about 1975.

Q And after she told him not to do that again, did he?

A A few times after that, yes.

Q Few times? Is that the only time you've been sexually molested?

A No. There was an incident with Mrs. Teerhuis when I was about nine years old.

Q And, and what happened there?

A She had me touch her vagina.

Q Did anything happen as a result of that?

A No.

Q Besides memories? No?

A No.

Q All right. Can you tell us about any other unhappy incidents of that nature?

A A grade six music teacher, who was convicted for that, he...

Q When was that and what happened?

A It was in 1981.

Q Yes?

A At Donwood Elementary School. It happened prior to a Christmas concert and with a promise that I would be in the Christmas play, he would touch me and have me touch him.

Q And over what period of time did that go on?

A From October until school commenced in, in June.

Q Of what year?

A 1981.

Q 1981? And how did it get to the police' attention?

A I never said anything until I was 17 years old. I was going through an adoption breakdown at that time.

Q All right. And what did the police do?

A I was told by Child and Family Services, the woman who was investigating it, and they had gone to the school to interview him and he admitted it right away.

Q All right. And you told us he was convicted?

A Yes, he was.

Q And do you know what the sentence was?

A He got one year for that.

Q So you had a pretty unhappy childhood? How would you describe it?

A I wouldn't say an unhappy childhood. My total childhood wasn't a complete tragedy, but I have some very happy childhood memories from growing up with Isabel.

Q And as a result, or moving it along, you became employed?

A Yes.

Q Can you tell us about your employment history? Oh, before we get to that, I take it you have somewhat of a minor criminal record?

MS. LEINBURD: Can you give it to me, Mr. Brodsky? I've never seen it.

A Yes.

MR. BRODSKY: You haven't?

MS. LEINBURD: No.

MR. BRODSKY: I haven't filed that, actually.

Q Well, you have a record that consists in 1991 of being intoxicated and picked up for being drunk in a public place?

A I believe that was in 1990.

Q All right. And in 1991, on February 22nd, you were convicted of flashing a paperboy?

MS. LEINBURD: I believe it's an indecent act. I don't see...

MR. BRODSKY: Yes.

MS. LEINBURD: ...flashing a paperboy anywhere on the record.

MR. BRODSKY: Given the, with respect, My Lord, that's what happened and that, anyway...

THE COURT: Well, Mr. Brodsky, if I...

Q I was about to add, and convicted as a result of committing an indecent act; would that be fair?

A Yes.

Q And you received a probationary term?

A For two years, yes.

Q For two years? In fact, you were convicted twice on the same day of doing an indecent act; would that be fair?

A I'm not too sure on those particulars. All I know was that I had gone out to get the paper in my underwear, so.

Q In your underwear?

A Yes.

Q All right. Then I understand that in 1988, you were picked up drunk under the Intoxicated Persons Detention Act?

A I believe so, yes.

Q And that's the entirety of your record up until the incident that brings you to court?

A That is correct.

Q Tell us about your employment history.

A My very first job was a dishwasher and food prep.

Q And you moved along and became a chef?

A Not right away. My second employment was at the Relax Plaza and then I did the grand opening for the Royal Crown Revolving

Restaurant, where I became a dining room manager.

Q That's on Broadway?

A The Royal Crown Revolving Restaurant.

Q Royal Crown? Okay. And how long are you there?

A Three years.

Q And then, what happened to you then?

A My mother died of breast cancer.

Q Which resulted in what happening to your life?

A I decided, because I had differences with certain members of the Teerhuis family, that we had nothing in common anymore and, because I had spent so much time in Vancouver since 1972 over the years, that I would make a new life for myself in Vancouver.

Q And did you?

A Yes, I did.

Q And what did you do there?

A I completed my grade 12, I wrote my Dogwood, their equivalent of a GED out there.

Q Yes?

A I went to the Native Education Centre, I took a computer course, I took what is called a first host diploma, which is for the hospitality industry, specifically, for aboriginal people. And then I got my culinary arts degree.

Q All right. For aboriginal people, the course was established? You are treaty?

A Yes, I am.

Q Out of what band?

A Little Grand Rapids First Nation.

Q Now, in the course of your culinary training in British Columbia, did you have an occasion to see or attend at meat processing plants?

A Yes, I did.

Q And under what circumstances did you do that?

A They were on field trips. They wanted everyone to know all the different facets of the culinary industry because not everyone was going to become a chef.

Q So what did you do at the meat processing plant, meatpacking plant?

A We would watch, whether it would be hogs or cattle come in, depending on what plant we went to, and they would put them on an assembly line and we, basically, we watch them start at the beginning as an animal and then they would end up ready to go to a supermarket.

Q So all of the processes between their being on hoof and alive to their being packaged as steak and hamburger and everything in between, you were part of and learned about?

A Yes.

Q And participated in?

A Yes.

Q Along with the rest of your class?

A That is correct.

Q And how long did you stay in Vancouver?

A About nine or 10 years.

Q And then you came to?

A I lived in Washington state for one year in Bellingham.

Q And what did you do there?

A I wanted to be close to my son and I, I stayed there for one year. I had, I was on income assistance at that time as well.

Q And then you came back to Canada?

A Yes.

Q And what did you do and where did you do it?

A I worked at a restaurant called the Hart House Restaurant in Burnaby, British Columbia.

Q Yes?

A I was one of their executive chefs. I had worked for a place called A Kettle of Fish in downtown Vancouver, which is actually a very well known restaurant to local celebrities and Hollywood celebrities. And I worked for McCann's Catering, a high-end catering in Burnaby, British Columbia.

Q And then you went to?

A I went to a fine dining restaurant in Rocky Mountain House, Alberta. That was in 2000.

Q And you worked in the culinary field then in Alberta for some time?

A Yes.

Q Until you were taken into a treatment centre?

A That is correct.

Q Can you tell the jury about the treatment centre?

A I was working at a luxury hotel called the Thornton Court Hotel in Edmonton and I was having some health problems at the time, but I was also drinking and using a drug called OxyContin, which is a pain killer for severe back pain.

Q And what happens when you overuse it, over prescribe it?

A You hallucinate.

Q All right.

A Or if you mix it with alcohol, you, you have blackouts or loss of memory.

Q So you went to the treatment centre?

A Yes, it was called Poundmaker's.

Q Poundmaker's? And you were there for how long?

A It's a 28-day program, but I was allowed to have a two-week extension, so I was there for 42 days.

Q That's because of the extent of your addiction?

A Yes.

Q And the addiction was to the OxyContin and to alcohol?

A That is correct.

Q And then you went to another treatment facility?

A Yes.

Q And what's it called?

A It was called Recovery Acres.

Q And how long were you there?

A About six months.

Q And why did you stay so long?

A Their program was about an eight, nine-week program and they wanted to make sure that people would, would try the best they could to stay off their addictions.

Q Yes?

A So you either could stay at the facility or they had halfway houses in the area that you could stay at as well.

Q And you took the program?

A Yes.

Q And you stayed an extra long time to make sure your addiction was gone?

A That is correct.

Q And was it gone when you got out?

A No.

Q What happened?

A The day I got released from that program, I went out drinking right away, which is not uncommon for people who attend treatment centres. They call it a relapse and they just say if you have a relapse, then either you go to a meeting or try to get back into another treatment centre.

Q But you didn't?

A No.

Q You'd already had two extensions at the recovery treatment facility and you didn't go back?

A No, I did not.

Q This was in what year?

A 2003.

Q Where'd you go?

A When I'd left Edmonton, I had a contract to work for Totem Resorts for the summer in Lake of the Woods, Ontario.

Q All right. Is that, north of Kenora?

A Yes. I was hired to be one of the executive chefs for Wiley Point. Unfortunately, because I had just come out of a treatment centre, I had relapsed almost instantly there, causing me to lose my job there when I only had enough money to come back to Winnipeg.

Q And after Totem, where did you go?

A I went to Winnipeg.

Q And this was around when?

A I believe it was the beginning of May 2003.

Q Okay. And where did you go, what happened?

A I well, because I grew up in Winnipeg, I know my way around here, so I, I went to the Sally Ann.

Q Right.

A They have a policy when, when, when you stay there, if you have no money, that you have to go to the welfare office the next day, get an intent to rent form and find a place to live before they will issue you a check.

Q All right.

A Which is what I did.

Q So you stayed overnight at the Salvation Army?

A That is correct.

Q And then you went to the welfare office, and tell us about that day?

A They usually give people a hard time when they apply for welfare, but because I had documentation showing that I had just come out of a treatment centre, they were willing to help me out with what they considered a loan, meaning that I would have to pay it back.

Q Right.

A They gave me an intent to rent form and I had spent the rest of the day looking for a rooming house. I went to the Woodbine and another hotel on Main Street. Both places were full. And then I went to the Royal Albert on Albert Street.

Q And what happened there?

A There was an older lady working at the bar since they didn't have a reception desk there and I had asked her if there were any rooms available. It was a small room that had its own washroom for; I believe it was $295 a month.

Q And that room number was?

A Room 309.

Q And how many days before July 1st was this?

A About 60 days, I believe.

Q All right. And what happened in those 60 days? Did you get a job? Did you stay on welfare? What...

A The first few days, I had gone to my old neighborhood, just to see how it changed, and I went to go see the house I grew up in, which was rather disturbing. It brought back a lot of unpleasant memories for me. And then I found this ad in the newspaper for the Medicine Rock Café. I met with the owner Mr. Vann. I had brought my resume with me. I gave him a list of well-known people that I had prepared food for in the past and basically, we talked about his restaurant, his menu and possible changes that we could make to it.

Q And the prominent people you had prepared meals for included the people set out in these letters that were filed?

A That is correct.

Q That's Ivana Trump and Donald Trump and....

A No, it was Ivana Trump.

Q Right.

A She was filming a television show called Beggars and Choosers.

Q Yes?

A Where she was playing herself in that TV show. And over the years, there were people who attended the Hart House Restaurant, such as Richard Gere, Cher, a local celebrity named Judy Tyabji and at one time, Margaret Trudeau had dinner at Kettle of Fish.

Q All right. And after hearing about your activities and employment history and reading your resume, were you hired?

A Yes.

Q And when did you start?

A I believe it was about four days after that interview.

Q All right. And how many days prior to July 1st was that?

A Perhaps 14 days.

Q Tell us about chefs and knives and things like that, the tools of your trade?

A Yes.

Q Are they kept at your work or they kept someplace else?

A Any good chef would keep his knives with him. These knives are very, very expensive.

Q Yes?

A They're commercial knives. They're knives that you would not have in a regular household. Some of them are made out of titanium or stainless steel. A lot of people would keep them in, in a large metal toolbox. I didn't have one yet, so I kept it in a folder, a leather folder.

Q Right.

A But I would never leave them at work because I paid so much money for them, people would steal them and I've had stuff stolen in the past.

Q So when you were at the bus shelter, or when you went to get the strong beer, where were the knives?

A I had them in my backpack.

Q On your person?

A Yes.

Q All right. Now, tell us about where you went for the strong beer?

A To the Windsor Hotel.

Q All right. And how much strong beer did you buy?

A That time it was two bottles.

Q What size bottle?

A They're like giant Pepsi bottles.

Q Right. Two liter bottles?

A Two liters, yes.

Q All right. You were alone?

A Yes, I was.

Q All right. Tell us what happened after that?

A I went back to the Royal Albert. I had consumed some of the beer. I had a bath because it was hot. There was a gentleman who lived down the hall from me his name was Louis.

Q Yes?

A Everybody in the building knew that he sold crack cocaine and I had purchased some from him.

Q Was this the first time you had purchased crack cocaine?

A No.

Q For how long had you been using crack cocaine?

A Since about 1993.

Q So aside from the alcohol and the OxyContins, you are now into crack cocaine also?

A Yes.

Q All right. You bought some crack cocaine from Louis and what, what happened to it?

A I went back to my room and I smoked it.

Q And what time was that around?

A I would have to say it was past ten o'clock because it was getting dark outside.

Q All right. And what happened after that?

A I don't really remember much after that.

Q What about the beer?

A I had consumed maybe one and a half bottles.

Q You consumed one and a half bottles and half a bottle was left?

A No, there was still a full bottle left.

Q Okay. How many bottles did you buy?

A Two at that time.

Q Two? So you drank how much?

A I would say half a bottle.

Q Half a bottle? All right.

A So that would be one liter, perhaps.

Q Right. And when you talk about strong beer, what are we talking about?

A Normal beer is usually, I think, four, five percent and this was either seven or eight percent.

Q All right. And what happened after you consumed the beer? You say you can't remember?

A I can't remember exactly what I did, but I know I went downstairs and outside. I went there for a few drinks.

Q Okay. And how long were you there?

A It'd be safe to say about an hour, maybe.

Q All right. And then what happened?

A Then I returned to the Albert.

Q And?

A I believe I passed out.

Q All right. And let's talk about passing out. Had you passed out ever before?

A Yes.

Q Can you tell us about what happens when you pass out?

A Well, I'll either wake up on the floor--there are times when I lived at home, I'd woken up in the back yard or in my parent's RV. One time I woke up in the back seat of my father's car.

Q With no memory of how you got there?

A No.

Q No memory of how you got to any of these places?

A No.

Q So your experience is that your last memory is of being one place and because of your consumption of alcohol and drugs, ending up someplace else without knowing how you got there?

A Yes.

Q Or how long it took you to get there or what you did while you're in that state?

A That is correct.

Q And for how long prior to 2003 had you been having these periods, passing out periods or how, blackout periods, whatever you call them?

A Since about the age of 16.

Q What's that?

A Since about the age of 16.

Q Sixteen?

A Yes.

Q How frequently did you have these periods?

A In the beginning, not that many. As, what they would call in the treatment centre, your alcoholic career, it intensifies, you consume more alcohol because your body becomes used to it, so over the years it became more frequent.

Q So on the day before July the 1st, you went to the St. Charles after having consumed the litre of beer, you drank there and you went home and passed out?

A Yes.

Q And what happened in the morning, when was it that you woke up?

A That would be July 1st.

Q But what time, around?

A According to my alarm clock, which is a windup clock, it's not electrical...

Q Yes?

A And I purchased that in case there was a power outage, so I wouldn't be late for work, probably around 7:00 or 8:00.

Q All right. Tell us about this day now, July the 1st?

THE COURT: Seven or 8:00 in the morning?

THE WITNESS: That is correct, yes. I was hungry, so I got dressed, I left the Albert and I walked down Ellice. The place that was closest was the Winnipeg Bus Terminal.

Q And the restaurant there is called?

A The Salisbury House.

Q And did you have breakfast?

A Yes, I did.

Q A regular breakfast? What happened there?

A A young gentleman sat across from me and didn't have any money, so I gave him my coffee and then he left.

Q All right. This was a person known to you or unknown to you?

A Unknown to me.

Q And instead of giving him money, you gave him your coffee?
A Yes.
Q How old was he?
A In his 30s, maybe.
Q All right. And then where did you go?
A Then I started walking down Portage Avenue.
Q You're alone?
A Yes, I was.
Q That young fellow wasn't with you?
A No, he was not.
Q Okay. And where did you go?
A On, near the TD tower there's a bar; I don't know if it was called the Beachcomber, but it had beaches or something. There was an older...
Q What is the TD tower?
A Portage and Main. There is a little bar or tavern there, but it wasn't open yet and there was an older aboriginal male...
Q Yes?
A He was waiting there, too, for it to open and he suggested that we go to the Woodbine because it was going to open soon. And I believe the Woodbine opened at 9:00 that morning.
Q Nine in the morning?
A We had to sit outside for a few minutes.
Q You and the aboriginal older gentleman?
A That is correct.
Q All right. And did you go into the Woodbine?
A Yes, we did.
Q Around 9:00? And what did you do when you got inside? You went to the bar I take it?
A We sat down. There was a bartender serving drinks. So we pooled our money together and, and bought what, what they call a pony, which is a pitcher of draft.
Q Do you know how many ounces there are in a pony?
A Not per se, no.
Q That's a big jug, though?
A Yes.
Q Not for one person, that's for a number of people?
A I'm not familiar with the liquor laws in Manitoba, but I've, I've seen people in other provinces purchase them for themselves.
Q That's a lot of liquor?
A Yes.
Q Lot of beer. So you order up a pony. You were with...
A Yes.
Q The elderly gentleman still?
A That is correct.
Q All right. And what happened?
A One of his friends came to join us.
Q Did you meet anybody else?
A There was sort of a tall, skinny aboriginal male going from table to table.
Q Yes? What was he doing?
A He had a $15 receipt from a bus ticket that he was trying to sell and he had a gold necklace he was trying to sell for $15 as well.
Q Did he tell you where he got the gold necklace?

A No, he did not.

Q Was he trying to sell it at all the tables or many of the tables?

A He went from table to table.

Q All right. And he came to your table?

A Yes.

Q Had you ever seen him before?

A No.

Q And did he stay at your table?

A Not at first.

Q All right.

A I was not interested in the necklace. He sat at the table. And then he dozed off for a bit, but that's not uncommon for people to do that in places like that. Some people are homeless and they just would come in there and fall asleep at a table.

Q You're not saying that he passed out from drink?

A No.

Q You're talking about his just going to sleep?

A Yes.

Q Which you say is not uncommon for homeless people?

A No.

Q And how long did he sleep for?

A I'm not totally sure, but the waitress had woken him up.

Q Yes?

A I bought him a beer.

Q How much had you consumed in that place up to that point?

A By then, I'd say maybe we ordered another pitcher.

Q Right.

A I was already starting to feel the effects from the alcohol. I wouldn't say drunk, but when, when you consume alcohol, eventually, you become more talkative, more sociable. I'm usually an introverted person. I'm usually pretty quiet.

Q So now you're on your second pony or pitcher of beer?

A Yes.

Q And it's you drinking it and one other person?

A Yes, and...

Q And now you invited a third over?

A That is correct.

Q The fellow who wanted to sell the necklace?

A Yes.

Q He had the necklace in his pocket or did he succeed in selling it?

A No, he did not.

Q All right. And did he consume some of the beer also?

A Yes, he did.

Q And how long did you stay there?

A Well, if we arrived there at 9:00, I believe it was close to 12:00 when we finally left.

Q And how many pitchers of beer did you drink?

A About two.

Q All right. Did you order anything else?

A Yes.

Q What?

A Every now and then we would order little shots of scotch.

Q Right.

A Some people call them boilermakers when you take a shot of scotch, then you wash it down with a swig of beer.

Q And how many boilermakers do you think you had between 9:00 and 12:00?

A Maybe three.

Q All right. And how were you feeling when you, when twelve o'clock came?

A I would say a little tipsy.

Q All right. And where did you go then?

A We went--the older gentleman that I was sitting with didn't want to come with us, so the other gentleman and I went back to the Royal Albert.

Q All right. What happened at the Royal Albert?

A We went up to suite 309.

Q Yes?

A And we had a few beers from the beers that I purchased the day before.

A Again, he took out the necklace. I wasn't interested in it, so he put it on the desk. I distinctly remember him saying it was a beautiful day and that he wanted to go outside again.

Q Right.

A So we went to the Garrick.

Q And what did you do there?

A He didn't have that much money on him, so we stayed there for one drink, quickly, which was a draft.

Q Yes?

A And then we had purchased some ice beer.

Q That's two liters?

A Yes.

Q And how many of them did you purchase?

A At that time, only two.

Q Right.

A And then we sat by the Millennium Library. I don't know the name of the park, but there's a park behind the Royal Crown Revolving Restaurant.

Q Right.

A And we sat...

Q That's by the river?

A Yes.

A And then we sat there for a while and finished our beer.

Q So that's called Bonnycastle Park?

A Yes.

Q All right. And the park is down to the river?

A That's at the river and then there's kind of like a hill and then they have benches there where you can sit. And that's where we sat for quite some time.

Q Were you joined by anyone?

A We were joined by two people at first. There was an older Caucasian male.

Q Yes?

A And the gentleman that I was with and him went into the bushes and engaged in anal sex.

Q How do you know that?

A I went with them.

Q Yes?

A I didn't engage in anything at that time.

Q All right. Had you been drinking in, when you were down by the riverbank there?

A Yes.

Q And what were you drinking?

A Beer.

290

Q The beer that you had purchased earlier?
A From the Garrick, yes.
Q How many beers did you have with you?
A Just the two two-liter bottles.
Q All right. And you were drinking and the other fellow was drinking?
A Yes.
Q You later found out that the other fellow's name was, fellow who tried to sell you the necklace?
A His name was Robin.
Q Robin Greene?
A I didn't know his last name.
Q All right. So he engaged in anal sex with the Caucasian fellow that came by?
A Yes.
Q Did he know him from before?
A No.
Q Is just a casual pickup, casual meeting?
A No matter what city you're in, when you have places like that where gay men, what they call cruising, engage in that sort of thing, you don't particularly ask what their name is or their background or anything like that.
Q You're better off not knowing?
A Yes.
Q And that's what happened here?
A Yes.
Q So after this activity was over, what happened?
A There is a picnic table in a grassy area near 85 Garry or the Royal Crown area.
Q Yes?
A And then we sat there. This gentleman named Robin was interested in a street hustler that was in the area, but I wouldn't agree with it because this person seemed too young. And then we started walking back towards the Albert.
Q Around how old was he?
A Fifteen or 16, maybe.
Q All right. You walk back toward the Albert?
A Yes.
Q That's where room 309 is?
A That is correct.
Q And did you go right there?
A At first we did, yes.
Q And what happened when you were there?
A We went upstairs.
Q Yes?
A There was a bottle of whiskey.
Q All right.
A We had consumed some of that, but we didn't have any mix or anything and because it was hot, we decided that we wanted to drink beer instead. So once again, we had left the Royal Albert and went to the Windsor Hotel and purchased three bottles of strong beer again.
Q All right. Did you drink anything at the Windsor or just take the beer away?
A We just took the beer.
Q And where did you go?

A Back to the Royal Albert.

Q All right. And what happened then?

A We stopped off in the tavern first.

Q Yes?

A The bartender, Diane...

Q That's the lady that testified here?

A That is correct.

Q Yes?

A Was working that day. She was by herself.

Q Yes?

A So I had introduced the gentleman I came to know as Robin as my cousin. I normally do things like that. It's sort of a joke between aboriginal people that we're all cousins.

Q Right.

A I'd asked her to watch him because I was going to go downstairs to get some ice.

Q Why did he need watching?

A I figured he would wander off or get himself into trouble or something.

Q All right. Up to that point, had either one of you been drinking more than the other one?

A I'd say we were sort of on the same level.

Q All right. And then you went down to get some ice?

A Yes.

Q And you came back up?

A Yes.

Q And what happened?

A Then we went upstairs.

Q The two of you?

A Yes.

Q And where, you went to 309?

A That is correct.

Q All right. Now it's just the two of you in 309?

A Yes.

Q What did you do? What happened?

A We had a few drinks. I went to see if Louis was home and he was. I had purchased...

Q Louis is the crack dealer?

A Yes, he is.

Q All right. And what happened with Louis?

A He only had three rocks and I purchased them.

Q Yes?

A And then I took them back...

Q Three rocks meaning three rocks of?

A Crack cocaine.

Q All right.

A I don't think he smoked any.

Q You consumed the three rocks of cocaine?

A Yes. That wasn't all at once, though. I mean, you have to break pieces off and...

Q Yes?

A And smoke them in small amounts.

Q So while you're in the room over a period of time, you smoked the three rocks of crack cocaine?

A Yes.

Q Did you take anything else?

A Sometime during the afternoon, I had taken some OxyContin as well.

Q How much?

A I can't say per se.

Q All right. And how long were you there?

A At that time?

Q Yes.

A I'd say maybe it was past three o'clock.

Q And did anything happen between you and Robin in that period?

A We had engaged in oral sex.

Q And how long did that take?

A Not that long.

Q All right. And what happened, or what time was that, approximately?

A I'm not sure. I don't know. Sometime during the afternoon, anyways.

Q All right. And then what happened?

A I had these disposable cameras that I needed to get developed.

Q Yes?

A And in a jokingly manner, we decided to play around with the cameras, where I had photographed Mr. Greene in a pair of my blue underwear.

Q Right.

A And I had photographed him in the nude.

Q Yes?

A We, I believe we, we engaged in sex again.

Q Right.

A And then he was photographed sort of sitting in the bathtub, smiling.

Q Did you use a condom?

A No.

Q Was this oral or anal sex?

A Oral.

Q All right. And then what happened?

A He went to go lay down on the bed for a while and...

Q He was in the bathtub, he was wearing no clothes, you took a picture of him?

A Yes.

Q With a disposable camera?

A Yes.

Q Was anybody else there?

A No.

Q All right. And then you--what happened after that?

A I went downstairs.

Q Okay. What happened, where did you go, what did you do?

A Mr. Greene wanted to take a nap.

Q Yes?

A And I didn't have a problem with that because I didn't have much personal belongings up there anyway. So I went downstairs and I ordered a beer.

Q Yes?

A From the bartender, who was Diane Last. I sat at the bar for a few minutes just watching her work. There was, I think his name is Damien, a young gentleman who worked in the hotel.

Q You'd seen him before?

A Yes.

Q And you'd seen him working as a bartender on the evening shift?

293

A That is correct.

Q On earlier occasions?

A Yes.

Q Other occasions? And what did you do with Damien?

A I approached him and asked him if I could sit down with him for a while.

Q Yes?

A And he must have said yes because I ended up speaking with him.

Q He must have said yes; do you remember that?

A No.

Q Why?

A By then with taking the OxyContin, things are starting to get a little, I wouldn't say fuzzy, but I'm starting to feel a bit dizzier.

Q Yes?

A We had gone outside. We had some marijuana.

Q Yes?

A I had consumed some of that.

Q And you were out there with Damien and anyone else?

A His girlfriend and there was another gentleman.

Q All right. So when you were outside, where were you outside? So you were in the parking lot?

A That is correct.

Q And what happened to you?

A We stayed outside for maybe an hour, 45 minutes, maybe.

Q And smoked pot?

A Yes.

Q And what else, anything else?

A No.

Q And what's your next recollection or memory?

A We had gone back inside.

Q Yes?

A Damien ordered some more beer for us.

Q Yes?

A I didn't purchase any. And I can't, I don't know what time it was because I didn't see a clock or anything, but I started to feel that maybe I had enough, then I decided to go back upstairs.

Q And did you?

A Yes.

Q And where did you go?

A Back up to room 309.

Q And what happened when you got in there?

A I don't remember if I had my key with me or not, so I might have, not sure.

Q Tell us about--you say you don't remember. Tell us about your memory of events around this time of day?

A This was usually around the time, if I had consumed masses amount of alcohol or when you cross-use different types of alcohol, where I start to, I wouldn't say have memory loss or--I become forgetful.

Q Right. But you have some memory of going into 309?

A Yes.

Q And what memory do you have of what happened in 309?

A I can vaguely recall getting undressed.

Q Yes?

A And lying on the bed.

Q Was anybody else on the bed?

294

A Mr. Greene was still on the bed.

Q And what was he doing?

A Sleeping.

Q Sleeping?

A Yes.

Q So you...

A I remember him snoring. He snored really loud.

Q All right. And you're dressed now, when you got into the bed, in your underwear?

A Yes.

Q Anything else?

A I don't think so, no.

Q All right. And then what happened?

A Then I woke up the next morning.

Q How many hours later?

A Maybe seven or eight hours later.

Q Do you know for sure?

A No.

Q So a number of hours, maybe seven or eight hours later, you woke up?

A Yes.

Q And what did you see or hear, or what happened on awakening?

A The windows were all dark because the, the drapes had been closed. I distinctly remember an unusual odor in the room. It smelled like tin or copper.

Q And what did you do as a result of that, or what did you do while that was happening?

A Well, I had to use the washroom, so I entered the bathroom and when I peered over to the bathtub, there was Mr. Greene in the tub and he was deceased.

Q He was more than just deceased?

A Yes.

Q He was in what condition?

A He had been dismembered.

Q All right. Do you know how he got to be in that condition?

A No, I do not.

Q Do you have any recollection whatsoever of how he got to be in that condition?

A No.

Q Do you have any recollection whatsoever of how he became deceased before he was dismembered?

A No, I do not.

Q Do you have any recollection at all of how he got to be in the bathtub?

A No.

Q Do you have any recollection at all of what happened in those seven or eight or so hours that you, from the time you laid down on the bed to the time you woke up in the morning?

A No.

Q What did you do?

A I threw up.

Q Where?

A Into the toilet.

Q Yes? Because?

A Because of what I have seen. Just the intense odor of the bathroom.

Q This is odor of?

295

A From, in the bathroom. It was, it smelled like, it had a very sickening smell.

Q Yes?

A I can't really describe it.

Q And you threw up?

A Yes.

Q And what did you do? What happened next?

A I went back into the bedroom and I had seen the blood on the bed.

Q Yes?

A On the pillow.

Q Yes?

A There was a blanket on the floor.

Q Yes?

A That had a blood stain on it. And, I guess, maybe for the next half an hour I kept going back and forth trying to figure out what had happened.

Q What had happened?

A I don't know.

Q All right. And what happened in the half-hour, what else did you see the bathroom?

A There was what looked like a towel on the floor that had blood on it.

Q Yes?

A There was a large knife on the floor by the bathtub.

Q Whose?

A I believe it was mine.

Q Right. How did it get there?

A I don't know.

Q All right. What else did you see?

A There was some blood on the sink.

Q And after the half-hour, what did you do besides going back and forth to the bathroom, to the bedroom and back to the bathroom, what do you do then?

A I figured that this would have to be something for the police to investigate.

Q Right.

A So I just grabbed whatever clothing I had that was on the floor, put them on, put on my baseball cap and decided to go report this incident.

Q And did you?

A What I had found. Yes, I did.

Q Where did you go?

A I had walked to the Winnipeg Remand Centre.

Q Yes? Did you intend to go to the Remand Centre?

A I was under the impression that the Remand Centre was actually a police station.

Q And what did you tell them?

A When I walked in there, I went to the front reception desk and I had asked if there was someone I could talk to.

Q And what did they say?

A They wanted to know about what I wanted to talk about and I just asked that I wanted to speak to somebody in private.

Q And what happened?

A They summoned a gentleman from an office that was adjacent to the front lobby for what they call a duty officer.

Q And that was Mr. Steenson?

A That is correct.

Q And what happened with him?

A We went into the office. It is a very small office, so when I entered the office, his desk was here. He had gestured for me to sit.

Q His desk was in front of him?

A Yes.

Q Right.

A And then he walked around the desk and then sat in front of me.

Q All right. And what did you tell him?

A I didn't say anything at first. I was, I was pretty scared at that time.

Q And you finally said?

A I said I wanted to report that there was a dead body in my bathtub and that it had been chopped up.

Q Right. And what did he say or do?

A He told me not to say anything. He said something about Charter rights or something. And then he said that I should speak to the Winnipeg Police on this matter and then he picked up the phone, he dialed the number and there was a woman on the other end of the receiver.

Q Yes?

A I don't remember what her name was and then I recounted the same thing that I had said, that there was a dead body in my hotel suite.

Q And how did he meet his death?

A I had told her that this person had been chopped up and I had told her that there was a knife on the floor.

Q Yes?

A And I guess, at that time, she had radioed or contacted who was ever on patrol to come to the Remand Centre.

Q And who did you say did this thing to Mr. Greene?

A I said that I believed that I was the one who killed Robin Greene.

Q And what words did you use?

A I think I killed someone.

Q All right. And why did you think that or why did you say that?

A Because I was the only one who was there.

Q You were taken into custody?

A Yes.

Q And you have been in custody since then?

A That is correct.

Q And while you were in custody, you met a number of people, including Mr. Don Abbott?

A Yes.

Q And Mr. Dan Zupansky?

A That is correct.

Q Can you tell us about your relationship with them?

MR. BRODSKY: Maybe, My Lord, this is an appropriate time for a recess.

THE COURT: Okay. Let's take the morning break, please.

(JURY OUT)

THE CLERK: Order, all rise. Court's in recess.

(BRIEF RECESS)

THE CLERK: Court is reopened. Please be seated.

THE COURT: Jury, please?

(JURY IN)

THE CLERK: My Lord, all 12 jurors are present.

THE COURT: Thank you. Mr. Brodsky?

Q You were taken to the Remand Centre from the police station and you were taken to Headingley Correctional Institute and Brandon Correctional Institute?

A Yes.

Q In the course of your confinement, you met, as we spoke just before the break, of a Mr. Don Abbott and a Mr. Dan Zupansky?

A That is correct.

Q Can you tell us about meeting them and the circumstances under which you met them and your dealings with them, please?

A My first encounter with Mr. Don Abbott was in unit A at the Brandon Correctional Centre. He, his first impression was he was a very evasive individual towards the staff and some of the inmates; something, in jail terms, you call a heavy; somebody who bullies and picks on people that are weaker than he is.

Q Yes?

A I was playing cards with fellow inmates when he made a collect call to Winnipeg that I would assume would be Mr. Danny Zupansky.

Q He's the witness who testified?

A Yes.

Q Yes?

A And Mr. Abbott's exact words were: *You're not going to believe who I'm on the same range with.*

Q Referring to you?

A That is correct.

Q And as a result of that, you talked to him, met with him, what happened?

A We were, at that time, hired as trustees.

Q Yes?

A So whenever breakfast, lunch or supper came out; we would dish out food for the other inmates. At first, he seemed like a pretty normal inmate, I guess. Then he started talking about Mr. Zupansky, that he was friends with him, that Mr. Zupansky wanted to talk to me.

Q Yes?

A At first, I didn't really do anything about it, but I'm assuming through telephone conversations, Mr. Zupansky kept pestering Mr. Abbott to get me to say something.

Q And did you?

A Not at first. He left me Mr. Zupansky's number, which I couldn't call from Brandon anyways. I didn't have access, or I didn't have the funds for making long-distance phone calls. I had first contacted Mr. Zupansky from the Winnipeg Remand Centre when I was transferred back to Winnipeg.

Q When was that, around?

A February or March of 2004.

Q And as a result of your... who contacted who?

A I contacted Mr. Zupansky because I was curious as to what he wanted.

Q Right.

A And he said he was interested in writing a book.

Q About?

A About my being arrested. About what had happened to Mr. Greene.

Q And you said?

A I don't recall my exact words, but I had agreed to meet with him.

Q And meet with him means what to a locked up person?

A They have visiting booths on the main floor of the Winnipeg Remand Centre.

Q All right. And did you meet with him?

A Yes.

Q How many times?

A In person? Just that one time.

Q Okay. And what happened?

A He was really interested in what he called the motive for the killing, what the police had to say, what we said in the papers. He had a radio show called Off the Cuff that was broadcasted from the University of Manitoba.

Q Right.

A And he had asked me if I wanted to be on his radio show that night and I said no.

Q And what happened after that?

A I didn't really have any contact with him after that until I was transferred to the Headingley Correctional Centre to the ISU, which is a maximum-security unit.

Q And when was that?

A I would say maybe the end of April of 2004.

Q Right.

A I was on a unit called Charlie.

Q Right.

A Mr. Abbott was in the unit called Delta. Now, Headingley Correctional Centre has a policy. You do not get to pick and choose who your cell-mates are. You're assigned a cell-mate. Whether you two beat each other up or not, that's, not much of their concern. I was on Charlie unit maybe no less than an hour when suddenly, Mr. Abbott was made my cell-mate. At first, I didn't really think anything of it, but then I sort of became suspicious as to why they chose him to be my cell-mate when he was already at Headingley Correctional Centre for some time.

Q And he would talk to you about?

A He didn't really say anything at first. He had spoken to Mr. Zupansky numerous times and Mr. Zupansky, apparently, was giving him instruction on getting my personal background, my childhood, my upbringing, information about my adoptive mother. She came from a very wealthy European family, so her family is quite known, well known over in Europe. So we had, he had these little Hilroy notebooks and he started taking notes about my childhood, growing up at 373 Foxdale, what my life was like, the physical and sexual abuse that I suffered, where I went to school, about my life in Vancouver, time that I had spent with my son in Bellingham in Washington state, all the places that I've worked at throughout western Canada, which included British Columbia and the Yukon Territory and my life in Edmonton as well, me going to the treatment centres, me working in hotels, me going to Totem Resorts.

Q And this is over what period of time?

A I'd say over a three or four week period.

Q And did you meet with Mr. Zupansky or write to him or correspond with him or communicate with him during that period?

A Not during that time, no.

Q All right. And then what happened?

A Mr. Abbott was due for release. He had packed everything up and he packaged it in such a way that the correctional staff couldn't open it. He had a piece of cardboard he had folded numerous times and then he had used, really, about one inch clear, thick tape and he just wrapped it all around, constantly. It contained the notebooks, he had stolen toenail clippings from me, he had stolen a pair of my underwear that he said he was going to sell on eBay and he had some of my pubic hair as well that he said he was going to sell on eBay.

Q How do you know he had them and how do you know he was going to sell them?

A He told me.

Q All right. On the day that he left?

A Yes. He also wanted me to sign a waiver.

Q Waiver of what?

A That if anything happened to me, that I would be cremated and him and Mr. Zupansky would sell my remains over the Internet.

Q Right.

A I totally disagreed with that, so I signed nothing. He left me Mr. Zupansky's number.

Q Yes?

A His exact words were that Dan was a sympathizer for people who are incarcerated and that he wanted to help, was his exact words.

Q And what did you do as a result?

A I contacted Mr. Zupansky.

Q Yes?

A And got more information as to exactly what he wanted.

Q What did he want?

A He wanted to write a book.

Q About?

A About the account that took place on July 1st, 2003. He was fascinated with Susan Sarandon's necklace. There was a necklace and a silver bracelet, I believe, that had been stolen.

Q How do you know that?

A From police reports, from when I was questioned by Winnipeg City Police, they had showed me a photograph of the necklace. They asked me if I had recognized it. At first, I said no.

Q I'm showing you Exhibit 80 in the cause; recognize that?

A It looks a little different from how I remember it, but yes, this is it.

Q That's the necklace?

A Yes.

Q And the bracelet? He wanted to know about the bracelet?

A He was interested in who stole the necklace.

Q He was interested in which?

A Who had stolen the necklace.

Q Who stole it? Who did steal it?

A Mr. Greene.

Q How do you know that?

A Because he tried to sell it at the Woodbine.

Q So that's the same one that he was trying to peddle to the different tables at a time when you were there?

A That is correct.

Q That you've told us about already?

A Yes.

Q All right. So he wanted to talk about the incident?

A Yes.

Q And the decapitation and all of that?

A Yes.

Q Did you tell him what you've told us?

A No.

Q No? Why not?

A Not at first, because I started going into great detail, more about my upbringing.

Q Right.

A Those are the first few letters; about my work in the Yukon...

Q Yes?

A About me coming to Winnipeg.

Q Yes?

A Then I started getting death threats from inmates and I was placed in segregation, where I had spent the rest of the year locked up in solitary confinement.

Q That's 23 and a half hours a day?

A That is correct.

Q And as a result of that loss of contact with the world...

A At that time, Mr. Zupansky was the only person that I had outside contact with other than correctional staff.

Q And?

A And...

Q Your lawyers?

A Yes.

Q And tell us about the visits with your lawyers?

A I wanted to see the photographs from the crime scene, from suite 309.

Q Yes, why?

A The photographs from the forensics, I wanted to see the police reports.

Q If, by the forensics, you mean the autopsy photos?

A That is correct.

Q All right. And you saw them?

A Yes, I did.

Q And you saw them on many occasions?

A Yes.

Q And who brought them out?

A The first person to bring them out was Bonnie MacDonald.

Q And she was a lawyer in my firm?

A That is correct.

Q And she brought them out on a number of occasions?

A Yes.

Q That is the photos, the autopsy report and the police report?

A Yes.

Q To the, what they call the disclosure?

A Yes.

Q And you reviewed and went over that on a number...

A Yes.

Q Of occasions?

A I took notes.

Q Yes? And who else showed you those things?

A I don't remember the names, but you had about three or four articulating students.

Q Right.

A A woman named Kathleen Fotheringham.

Q Yes?

A And another gentleman, but I don't remember his name.

Q Here, Mr. Newman?

A Perhaps.

Q Okay. And they brought them out in the disclosure?

A Yes.

Q And you made notes?

A Yes.

Q And they brought them out again?

A Yes.

Q And you made notes?

A Yes.

Q And you reviewed them, so you are familiar with the findings in the room and the investigation?

A Yes.

Q Why did it stop?

A You had started becoming suspicious as to why I wanted to see them all the time.

Q Okay.

A And you had put an end to it.

Q I put an end to it?

A Yes.

Q Now, getting back to Mr. Zupansky, he wanted to know what happened?

A Yes.

Q And what did you tell him happened?

A He kept implying that things didn't make sense for whatever was said in the newspapers.

Q Right.

A He wanted to know if there was a motive.

Q Right.

A He wanted to know--I can't remember that one word. I think it's called premeditated.

Q Right. Whether it was premeditated?

A Yes.

Q Right.

A I didn't have an answer for him at first.

Q Why?

A I was taking all the information that I had gotten from the reports, from the photographs, the layout of suite 309. I wanted it to sound accurate. He started writing me letters and asking for specific things, such as the layout of the bathroom, of the bedroom area, where the window was, where the bed was. He wanted to know certain things about Mr. Greene. I had to look through reports to find out where he came from. I knew nothing about Mr. Greene at all. I had to look at reports to find out how tall he was, how much he weighed.

Q Is that how you came up with six foot four, 250 pounds?

A That is correct.

Q So in, some of these reports described him that way?

A Yes.

Q All right. So you were answering his questions, not as best you could, but you were answering his questions because you wanted to?

A He was the only person that I had contact with on the outside.

Q Right. And he promised you a reward?

A Yes.

Q What was the reward?

A In exchange for him writing this book, that he would give me royalties from this book.

Q That's the 30 percent to you, depending on the number of

302

printings, a minimum of 30 percent?

A Yes.

Q And he promised Mr. Abbott what?

A In exchange for Mr. Abbott for his note taking, he guaranteed Don Abbott a two-week paid vacation in the Barbados.

Q All right. And we heard or read in Exhibit 62 about an offshore account. What was all that about?

A Prior to that, there was an inmate named Barry Antel. He was an American bank robber who robbed a bank on McPhillips in order to be incarcerated so he could receive treatment for cancer.

Q Yes?

A And he told me about his lifestyle, about him having offshore bank accounts in the Bahamas, other places around the world, where he would deposit money that he had stolen from banks across United States.

Q So you communicated that to Mr. Zupansky?

A Yes.

Q If you were agreeing and told the police that you killed someone, that it wasn't self-defence, you just killed someone and decapitated him in the fashion that he was found in, how did you ever expect to use an offshore account?

A I don't really know anything about offshore accounts, so I don't know how that works.

Q All right. How did you expect to spend the royalties he was promising you?

A I was very naïve back then. I, like Don Abbott said he was, assuming he was trying to help.

Q So you were trying to help?

A Yes.

Q And you were talking about names for the book?

A Mr. Zupansky wanted to call the book "drunken stupor" or something like that.

Q Yes?

A Or "drunken defence" or something like that.

Q And you didn't?

A I started getting caught up in his ploys, with promises of large amounts of money.

Q Yes?

A He said he was going to send me money periodically to Headingley. He said he was going to send me magazines.

Q Yes?

A He said he was going to send me books.

Q Yes?

A Which he never did.

Q This is all at a time that you were incarcerated in a lockup 23 and a half hours a day?

A That is correct.

Q You knew that the staff, Headingley staff was looking at your mail?

A Not at that point.

Q Okay. At some point?

A At some point, yes.

Q Did you stop writing when you knew that?

A No.

Q Why not?

A The information Mr. Zupansky wanted and how I obtained that information, there are also books in the Headingley library.

Q Yes?

A Where I could make it sound realistic.

Q Books on what?

A Where I, I could get details on other true crime stories, other fictitious stories, either science or biology textbooks, that was a high school level type of book that showed diagrams of the human body. It had transparency pages in it so that if you were to open the book, you would see a person...

Q Yes?

A And then you would turn the page, then you would see, I guess what you would call the muscles on the person. And then if you turn the page again, you would see the internal organs, the brain, and then you could turn the page and then you would see the skeletal structure.

Q And you copied that?

A Yes.

Q And you read about these crime stories?

A Yes.

Q And as a result, you told him about the story or a story of what happened in that room?

A That is correct.

Q Was it a true story?

A No.

Q Where did you get it from?

A There was one book, called Murder in Milwaukee.

Q Yes?

A And it had testimony and, I guess in his own words from Jeffrey Dahmer when he made his statements to police on his crimes, on his dissection of his victims.

Q His which?

A Dissection...

Q Right.

A Of his victims. There was another book on John Wayne Gacy.

Q Yes?

A Dennis Nilsen.

Q Wait. Gacy was another serial killer?

A Yes, he was.

Q And he was prosecuted and widely publicized?

A I only know about him from American Justice, which is a television show.

Q All right. And Dennis Nilsen was who?

A Another serial killer.

Q Yes?

A He lived in...

Q And you know him from?

A He lived in the United Kingdom.

Q Right. How do you know about him?

A There was about a four-page write-up in one of those books that I had from the Headingley library.

Q And who else?

A And a female serial killer named Aileen Wuornos, from the United States.

Q And what did you do with this collage of stories of serial killers?

A My time was idle at that time. I was locked up 23 and a half hours a day, so I would read and I would take notes as to what their specific crimes were.

Q Yes?

A What their specific, I guess you could say, forte was.

Q Yes?

A Or their, their signature.

Q Yes?

A And then I put them all together in rough drafts, which was very time consuming. If something didn't sound real enough, I would edit it over and over, since Mr. Zupansky had said not to embellish, or keep it real. So I figured if it sounded as real as possible or as horrific as possible, it would sell more books.

Q So why did you tell him about voices?

A Just to make it sound more interesting. I believe one of those serial killers heard voices as well.

Q Did you hear voices?

A No.

Q And if it was more interesting, interesting to who to tell that you heard voices?

A To Mr. Zupansky.

Q And the book?

A To make it sell more books.

Q What about George?

A There was nobody named George.

Q Well, why would you tell him, as we see in one of the letters, that George is captured on film by one of the disposable cameras?

A Again, to make it sound more interesting. To make it sound like there was a party going on or to make it sound like maybe there's a party that went bad or went sour.

Q So you were setting up in the book, I take it the film, you were talking about a film there, too?

A At one point, Mr. Zupansky talked about a possible film.

Q You, you were talking about a plot in which there could be options as to who the real killer was?

A Yes.

Q But that was just for the book?

A Yes.

Q That's not, in fact...

A No.

Q What happened in the, room 309?

A No.

Q When he wanted to know the time of the killing, when you said 6:20, how'd you come up with that number?

A In many of those letters, there are, I guess, gaps or inconsistencies.

Q Yes?

A And Mr. Zupansky would write back and say, well, this doesn't make sense or that doesn't make sense and in order to make it sound more realistic, if I chose a timeframe as to the demise of Mr. Greene, it would sound more realistic.

Q So where did you get 6:20 from?

A I just picked it randomly.

Q You wanted to design a title page or a cover and a title for the book, called Trophy Kill?

A Yes.

Q Why?

A Mr. Zupansky's title for the book didn't seem appealing enough. If

305

you looked at Jeffrey Dahmer, his book was called Murder in Milwaukee and I'm assuming to a lot of people, the word 'murder' would, would be eye-catching if they're walking by a bookstand. So if it said "Trophy Kill", people would pay attention to the word 'kill' and purchase the book.

Q And you connected 'trophy' to what?

A In one of the letters, I had drawn a diagram...

Q Yes?

A Of Mr. Greene's torso displayed on a pine dresser that...

Q That's the dresser in one of the photographs?

A Yes.

Q Or many of the photographs?

A Many of the photographs, indeed.

Q And so the torso was on the dresser?

A In the diagram.

Q In the diagrams? But not in real life?

A No.

Q In real life, how relevant was the dresser to anything?

A It wasn't. It was, from the police photographs to the investigation, it was undisturbed.

Q So you don't know anything about a torso being on a dresser?

A No.

Q Was it on a dresser?

A No.

Q Why did you say it was on a dresser?

A To make it sound more appealing.

Q And you didn't give him all the detail, I see, in the letters or we see in the letters right away; why was that? That is, the detail he was asking for?

A As the correspondence went on, his inquiries or questionings became more elaborate. He wanted to know specific details. He wanted to know if there was any form of necrophilia.

Q Yes?

A So I thought if he's asking these questions, if he's being truly sincere and if I tell him what he wants to hear, is he going to figure out that I'm lying to him or not? But he just kept asking more interesting questions as our correspondence went on.

Q So you told him about necrophilia?

A I told him what he wanted to hear, yes.

Q Well, what did you tell him?

A I told him, I introduced it to him first as living in Vancouver that I had dug up a grave and pulled the body out of its casket and viewed the body while I masturbated.

Q Yes?

A Which was untrue.

Q Did he ask you about how you could do that to a body? Don't, because they decompose in graves.

A No.

Q Did he ask you anything about that?

A No.

Q So you told a story about masturbating over a body you had taken out of a casket that wasn't true and he never challenged you on that?

A No.

Q And you told him that story because?

A That's what he wanted to hear.

306

Q To sell the book?

A Yes.

Q You told him about other stories of necrophilia?

A Yes.

Q What?

A I told him that I worked at a funeral home, which, if you look at all of my tax receipts and my T4 slips dating back to 1986, I have always worked in the hospitality industry.

Q But why would you tell him you worked in a funeral home?

A Again, for the book, to make it sound more appealing.

Q So did you tell him anything about necrophilia in that funeral home?

A I believe only once.

Q That is one act of necrophilia?

A One act, which...

Q Or one time you told him, which?

A One act of necrophilia.

Q Okay. Did that ever happen?

A No.

Q Why were you trying to sensationalize the content of the book by telling untrue stories?

A I had nobody to talk to. I was locked up 23 and a half hours a day. I guess in a sick way, you could say it was a form of entertainment for me.

Q Were you getting visits from the lawyer?

A Periodically.

Q Did you tell--you asked for a trial, which is in the letters, you asked for trial in an aboriginal court?

A Yes.

Q What would be different about an aboriginal court to a court like the one we have here?

A I, in the beginning of my incarceration, I knew nothing about the law or how the court system works or the legal system. I was reading an article in Reader's Digest and they had a particular section called Section 718, Section 718(1), Section 718(2) of the Criminal Code that dealt with specific needs of aboriginal people. I didn't know that for something so serious of this nature that they wouldn't deal with something like that. This is more of Circuit Court or some sort of community involvement with the aboriginal community, where the entire community will decide what sort of punishment is appropriate.

Q As a sentencing circle?

A Yes.

Q But you weren't...

A And I read a book from Crown attorney Rupert Ross.

Q Right.

A Called *Dancing with a Ghost*.

Q Right.

A And his second book, called *Returning to the Teachings*.

Q He's a Crown attorney from Kenora, Ontario?

A The Kenora district, yes.

Q You weren't trying to or expecting to be released as a result of going to an aboriginal court?

A No.

Q And insofar as your necrophilia is concerned, you were talking about that with regard to Mr. Greene in your letters?

A Yes.

Q Exhibit 63?

A I spoke of that, yes.

Q You talked about putting on a condom and having sex with a headless body?

A In the letters.

Q You recall that?

A In the letters, yes.

Q In Exhibit 63; right. That's right after lighting a cigarette. Did either of those things happen?

A No.

Q That is, you didn't sit with a chopped up body?

A No.

Q And smoke a cigarette, either crack cocaine or regular?

A No.

Q You didn't put on a condom after the body was chopped up?

A No.

Q You didn't have sex with a headless body?

A No.

Q Why did you say you did?

A To sell a book.

Q You talked about hanging the body?

A In one of the letters, yes, and I drew a diagram of that as well.

Q Why?

A Again, to, to feed Mr. Zupansky's appetite for this, sale of this book.

Q Did you hang a body?

A No.

Q Headless or otherwise?

A No.

Q Could you if you wanted to in that bathroom?

A It would be next to impossible. Their ceilings are, like, 13 or 14 feet high.

Q Yes?

A I'm only five eight, so it would be impossible.

Q You told him in one of the letters, Exhibit 64, that you weren't in your right mind?

A That is correct.

Q You're talking about an insanity or you're talking about a, a drunkenness, a lack of intent?

A Was talking about a blackout.

Q The blackout caused by over-indulgence in alcohol, OxyContin and crack cocaine?

A That is correct.

Q Did he challenge you on that?

A I believe at one time he said, *"Oh, come on,"* during a telephone conversation; that it didn't make any sense.

Q What didn't?

A The blackout.

Q Yes?

A About this George person that I spoke of in the letters.

Q Yes?

A Forgetting his six-pack, he says that doesn't make any sense.

Q The six-pack that you said George bought?

A Yes. I think it was the six-pack of Budweiser.

Q All right. And George came back about 3:30 in the afternoon in, in your story?

A In the story, yes.

Q But did he?

A No, because there was no George.

Q All right. Well, didn't you think that he would look at the film to see that there was no film of George sitting in Mr. Greene's lap?

A Do you mean Mr. Zupansky or...

Q Yes.

A I don't know how he would get a hold of the film.

Q But you knew what was in the film?

A The film had been confiscated by police, so there would be no way Mr. Zupansky could view what was on that film.

Q But you knew because you had the disclosure?

A Yes.

Q There was no George?

A No.

Q In any of the films?

A No.

Q So why would you say to Mr. Zupansky there was?

A If there was a third party involved, it would sound more realistic or interesting.

Q Right. In Exhibit 65, you say: *I can't answer your questions because I haven't figured out the answers. I haven't figured it out yet.* What did you mean by that?

A I started running out of ideas for his letters. I don't know what exhibit it was, but it is in one of the typed letters from Mr. Zupansky.

Q Yes?

A Near the top of the letter, he makes a reference to Mr. Greene where he says he doesn't care about Robin Greene, he's not interested in Robin Greene. He's only interested in what happened that day.

Q You said, in that Exhibit 65: *I didn't get a chance to smash Greene's skull.* You recall that?

A I recall writing that, yes.

Q Was that true?

A No.

Q Why did you say it?

A Jeffrey Dahmer had done something similar to that to one of his victims.

Q He would smash the skull?

A Yes.

Q Nobody interrupted you while you were sleeping in that room, 309; that be fair?

A That would be fair to say, yes.

Q So what did you mean by, "*I didn't have the chance*"? Why would you say something like that in the letter to Mr. Zupansky?

A To make it sound more interesting for his book.

Q It was truly a figment of your imagination?

A Yes, it was.

Q Now, would it be fair to say that your intention at the outset, when you first found the body, was to go to the police and tell them that you found the body and that you killed him while in a blackout?

A Yes.

Q And was it your intention to say that to the court?

A Yes, it is.

Q And the only thing that happened in between was Mr. Zupansky?
A Yes.
Q He asked you details like: Where are the organs?
A He was fascinated with the organs, he was fascinated with the necrophilia. He was even suggesting that there were forms of cannibalism.
Q Yes?
A And he kept harping on that.
Q So as a result of that, you did what?
A I told him what he wanted to hear.
Q Which was?
A About the necrophilia, about the disposal of the organs.
Q All right. Let's do both of them one at a time. First of all, the necrophilia means the East Indian fellow from Bangladesh?
A Yes.
Q Is he a real person?
A No.
Q Why did you make him up?
A Just to make it sound more realistic.
Q What did you say about him?
A To make it sound--I told him about the East Indian guy, **I** wanted the East Indian to kill me.
Q Because?
A Because I wanted that East Indian person to consume my body.
Q Because?
A It came from an idea from Jeffrey Dahmer and Dennis Nilsen is how I came up with that idea.
Q You want to be part of somebody, the East Indian?
A In some sort of macabre way in, through those letters, yes.
Q And you made that up because?
A I wanted to tell Mr. Zupansky what he wanted to hear.
Q And the organs, where were they dumped?
A I don't know.
Q And where did you say they were dumped?
A I said they were dumped in a dumpster near the Health Sciences Centre.
Q Why?
A To give it more, this is going to sound horrible, but to make it sound like it was a really vicious act to sell more books.
Q Where were the organs found?
A I don't think they were found.
Q And you know that because?
A From police reports, from the media, from a Dr. Shane, from you.
Q He asked you to sign a release?
A Yes, many times.
Q You never signed the release?
A No.
Q Why?
A I started to question his sincerity for he promised to send me money in small amounts, which he never did. He never sent the books or the magazines. Around this time we already had a falling out due to Don Abbott. He told me not to trust Don Abbott. He said he was having problems collecting rent from Mr. Abbott as well. There was one time we were going to do a radio interview on his show, Off the Cuff, but Mr. Abbott didn't come to his residence at the time the show

was supposed to start because he was out drinking, so that never commenced at all.

Q And what about the part of the release that said you had to have independent legal advice? You already had a lawyer. Why would you have in the release the requirement of having independent legal advice?

A He had sent me, according to him, three letters with these release forms in it.

Q Yes?

A Out of those three letters, I had only received one letter that had two release forms in it. One was for a phone company located on Dufferin Avenue.

Q Yes?

A And the other one, I believe, was a standard release form for a publishing company or something.

Q And what were you supposed to release when you were releasing your moral obligations? What was all that about? What sense does that make to you?

A From what I understood, how I read it, it was so that he could take his rough drafts to a publisher so that they could read the proofs and see if they needed corrections to be made or if he had to word things differently.

I had asked him one time about the first chapter and he said that he's going to start the book off saying, *"oh, it's a beautiful day in Winnipeg. It's a sunny day."* And that's when I started realizing that this guy is not a writer and he's not a reporter as he claims to be. And eventually, our correspondence stopped.

Q Before we get to that, be fair to say that you were looking for some publicity? You wanted to be on CJOB; would that be fair?

A Yes.

Q Did you go on CJOB?

A No.

Q You wanted CNN involved?

A I believe I wrote that, one of the letters, yes.

Q And you wanted Celebrity Justice involved?

A I think so.

Q And why was that?

A To gain notoriety.

Q And you wrote to Buckingham Palace?

A Yes.

Q To the Queen?

A Yes, I did.

Q And she replied?

A I wrote a very lengthy letter to Her Majesty, Elizabeth II, regarding systemic discrimination in the Manitoba courts when involving aboriginal people and all people with ethnic origins, whether they have access to proper legal advice, whether they know what their legal rights are and it also involved the jury selection process in Manitoba, which I had a copy of the Manitoba Jury Act. And by reading it, it is very outdated and doesn't meet the needs of a modern Canadian society.

Q And so you wanted some more publicity by writing to Buckingham Palace?

A No.

Q What did you want with the Queen?

A I have always been told that I have, it's my constitutional right to a fair trial.

Q Yes?

A And my beliefs at that time were if the jury panel only consisted of white people, that there would be some sort of biasness or jaundiced or swayed attitude towards an aboriginal accused, so I wanted the jury panel to represent the Canadian multicultural community, meaning Asians, Arabs, blacks, Caucasian and aboriginal.

Q But in this case, you had an aboriginal deceased and an aboriginal accused?

A Yes.

Q So where would the bias be?

A From having an all white jury, is what I believed.

Q Okay. Now, on April the 4th, 2005, you wrote Mr. Zupansky a letter. Right?

A I believe so, yes.

Q And you told him, this is before the trial, you told him that what you had said to him in your correspondence was not true?

A That is correct.

Q Why?

A By then, I started realizing, you know, this—I don't want to sound evasive or smart alecky or anything, but this person is a nobody who had a recording studio in his basement that was on the verge of bankruptcy and then along comes his friend, Don Abbott, and is conveniently made my cell-mate at Headingley. These people see that I am naïve; they see that I am, never been in jail before. I don't know how the system works or how people prey on each other in prison. And I started getting tired of it. I mean, I started to realize that by writing these letters it could be very damaging to how a jury or how the public or how the media sees me.

Q But you wrote them?

A Yes, I did.

Q Nobody made you write them?

A No.

Q Why did you write them?

A To sell Mr. Zupansky's book, I was bored, I was locked up 23 and a half hours a day, nobody paid attention to me, I'm an attention seeker and Mr. Zupansky was the only person corresponding with me other than my legal advisor.

Q And you told him what I told you in the letters is not true?

A That is correct.

Q The necrophilia is not true?

A It's not true.

Q George is not true?

A George is made up.

Q The hanging from the rafters in the bathroom is not true?

A That is correct.

Q The trophy is not true?

A That is correct.

Q You told him that you didn't want to fool around anymore?

A No.

Q You didn't...

A I told him I didn't want him to make a fool out of himself, which

312

is basically what he was going to do if he went ahead with this.

Q And that's because you were going to go to court and do what?

A I was going to testify in court.

Q Right. And you told him that various times, wait until the preliminary hearing, wait until the trial, you'll find out the truth?

A Yes.

Q And is what you've said today the truth?

A To the best of my abilities, that is correct.

Q You said: *You have to wait for the trial or at least the preliminary inquiry because that's when the truth will come out*?

A Yes.

Q And all the letters then were sensationalized, a fictional account, based on a true event?

A Yes.

MR. BRODSKY: Thank you.

THE COURT: Ms. Leinburd, I trust you'll have some questions. It's 1:10. Can we take the lunch hour break?

Thank you very much, ladies and gentlemen. We'll see you back here at--is 2:15 reasonable, counsel? Two fifteen, how does that sound? Okay. We'll see you back here then. Thank you very much.

(JURY OUT)

THE CLERK: Order, all rise. Court's adjourned.

(LUNCHEON RECESS)

THE CLERK: Court is reopened. Please be seated.

THE COURT: Okay. Thank you.

(JURY IN)

THE CLERK: My Lord, all 12 jurors are present.

THE COURT: Good afternoon. Ms. Leinburd?

CROSS-EXAMINATION BY MS. LEINBURD:

Q Good afternoon. Mr. Teerhuis, you admit you killed Robin Greene?

A Yes.

Q And you admit to writing all of the letters to Mr. Zupansky that have been marked in this court as Exhibits 60 to 73; is that correct?

A That is correct.

Q And Mr. Brodsky spent some time this morning on your background and I just want to add to that, sir. You are a self-described person who enjoys kinky sex; is that correct?

A Yes.

Q You are also a man who has a fetish for men's underwear, used; is that correct?

A Yes.

Q At one time, you had a collection of over 3,000 pairs; is that correct?

A That is embellished, actually.

Q Sorry?

A That is embellished, actually. I had 30 pairs.

Q Oh. So you lied?

A Yes.

Q Okay. You're also into sadomasochism, as I understand it?

A At one point, in Vancouver, yes.

313

Q You like sex slaves? This is self-described. I'm reading from Exhibit 70, which is your handwriting.

A Yes.

Q If you might look at it, bottom of page 1. You like sex slaves?

A Yes.

Q Okay. And water sports?

A Yes.

Q That's when people urinate on one another, isn't it?

A That is correct.

Q Now, you would have this court believe that you, in fact, were Mr. Zupansky's puppet in the sense that he told you what he wanted to hear and you puppeted it back or told him back what you thought he wanted to hear?

A That is correct.

Q Okay. And that this went on for a year or so; is that correct?

A I would say almost a year, yes.

Q Okay. And you would like this jury to believe that everything in those particular letters that you sent to Mr. Zupansky is fabrication; is that correct?

A That is correct.

Q And you would like this court to believe that you were naïve and you were the person who was being toyed with by Mr. Zupansky; is that correct?

A Yes.

Q Okay. You wanted notoriety, didn't you, Mr. Teerhuis?

A Yes, I did at one point.

Q At all points. When did you not want notoriety?

A When I started realizing that this could be very damaging.

Q Oh, the part that, you mean you confessed to mutilating the body, dissecting the body, dismembering the body, decapitating the body, you mean that damaging evidence?

A What was written in the letters, yes.

Q Yes. And that's what was written in the letters, was it not?

A Yes, it was.

Q Now, you say that you were sucked in by Mr. Zupansky; is that correct?

A And Mr. Abbott.

Q Both of them?

A Yes.

Q And that you are the victim in this ploy; is that correct?

A I wouldn't say I was exactly a victim because I, I'm the one who wrote the letters.

Q We'll get to that in a few minutes, Mr. Teerhuis. Is that correct?

A Yes.

Q Why did you write to Mr. Pomplum then? He didn't solicit you.

A No.

Q He didn't put Mr. Abbott in the cell with you, did he?

A No.

Q He wasn't someone who was interested in you at all, was he?

A No, he wasn't.

Q You wrote to Mr. Pomplum, telling him that you had killed the deceased; is that not correct?

A In the letter, yes.

Q Why did you do that?

A There was an inmate who brought with him a copy of Graphic Comics.

314

Q Yes, we know about that.

A Okay. And in those Graphic Comics, which Mr. Pomplum describes as classics, there was a comic strip in there called The Terrible Old Man.

Q Um-hum?

A And there was another comic in there that was quite graphic, depicting a mad scientist dismembering a body.

Q Oh, so another book from which you took the facts; is that right?

A Yes.

Q So not only did you take the facts from Dahmer and Nilsen and Gacy's book, but also from Mr. Pomplum's book?

A That is correct.

Q So what were you trying to do, fool Mr. Pomplum on his own books by putting forward a story that he already published?

A There was an inmate named Trevor Syznowski.

Q Yes?

A Who did a comic called 'A Crappy Comic.'

Q Does that have anything to do with what I just asked you? I asked you, sir, why it was that you would think that Mr. Pomplum would be interested in something that he'd already published?

A I'm, I don't know.

Q Well, then why would you write to him?

A I'm not sure. Something to do, I guess.

Q You told us that was something to do because you were bored and you were in solitary confinement for the killing; is that right?

A I was in solitary confinement because I was getting death threats from certain inmates.

Q But you were in solitary confinement nonetheless and you were bored, you said?

A Yes.

Q And that's why you wrote, you say, to Mr. Zupansky?

A Yes.

Q Well, a year before you wrote to Mr. Zupansky, Exhibit 59, Madam Clerk, September the 4th of '04, a few months after the killing, you wrote to Mr. Pomplum; is that correct?

A Yes.

Q You couldn't have been that bored then. You worked there that long; isn't that right?

A No.

Q You weren't bored?

A I wasn't there that long. I'm sorry.

Q That's right. So the boredom hadn't yet set in?

A No.

Q Going to refer you to the letter that you wrote to Mr. Pomplum, sir, Exhibit 59: Greene was decapitated. I then performed sex acts on his headless corpse after he was chopped into pieces and internal organs scooped out. Your handwriting, your words?

A Yes.

Q *"Greene was then emasculated (cutting off the penis and testes in one large piece)."* Your words?

A Yes.

Q Now, you said that that's the sort of stuff that Mr. Zupansky wanted to hear; isn't that right?

A That is correct.

315

Q Mr. Pomplum certainly did not want to hear that, did he?

A No.

Q Then why would you write to him and tell him the details of what you had done?

A What I had told Mr. Zupansky.

Q I'm sorry, I didn't ask you anything about Mr. Zupansky. I asked you about Mr. Pomplum, sir.

A Yes. What I mean here, it sounds like I wanted to give a false background.

Q To who?

A To Mr. Pomplum.

Q Why?

A Well, I'm the one writing to him in this letter. I mean...

Q Yes, and you're hoping...

A Yes.

Q That he's going to publish one of your comics, right?

A Yes.

Q So why would you give him any false information if the reason that you wrote to him was so he'd know who you were and publish your work?

A Because Mr. Zupansky was going to publish a book.

Q So?

A So if it sounded the same, then he would think that there was some sort of validity to it.

Q Well, how would Mr. Pomplum ever know that you wrote to Mr. Zupansky unless you told him? He lived in Madison, in a little town...

A That is correct.

Q In the United States.

A Yes.

Q So how would he ever know?

A I was assuming eventually, he would find out.

Q How?

A Either by book sales or through the media or some sort of...

Q So you were hoping that this book would be published, I gather?

A With the help of Mr. Zupansky, yes.

Q Yes. Now, let's get back to Mr. Pomplum and the questions I was asking you. Now, you indicate to him as well that you, in fact, had a claim to fame in this particular case. Those are your words: *My claim to fame was that Robin Greene was killed and he was decapitated*; is that correct?

A No, it says: *My unfortunate claim to fame.*

Q It's still a claim to fame; correct?

A Correct.

Q Okay. Now, you go on to indicate that, bottom portion: *I have news that will shock the world on what happened that day, July the 1st, in room 309 of the Royal Albert Arms.* What did you mean? Your words?

A Um-hum.

Q What did you mean?

A The phrase, *"I have news that will shock the world,"* I got that phrase from Princess Diana before she died.

Q Had she spoken to you?

A No, but she had said that in a media conference.

Q And why would you use those words?

A I've used many phrases from other people as well.

Q Well, what was the news that you were going to tell the world that was going to shock it?

316

A That these letters were phony.

Q Well, why on earth would you write to this man telling him the facts and then suggesting that you're going to take those facts away?

A They're not facts.

Q What are they?

A They're fictitious.

Q Well, why would you have to take fiction away, sir? It's made up.

A That's correct.

Q Anybody can make anything up, can't they?

A Yes.

Q So there's nothing to take away, is there? Is there?

A I suppose not.

Q Let's move on. "*I'm the only one who really knows what happened to Robin. I know his last words. I was the last person to have consensual sex with him, the last person to swallow his semen after oral sex.*" That's what you said to Mr. Pomplum; correct?

A Is that still on the first page?

Q Yes, it is. Bottom of the first page.

A Okay.

Q Your handwriting.

A That is what is written, yes.

Q That's what you wrote, not what is written, what you wrote; correct?

A Correct.

Q You were the only one that knew his last words; isn't that correct?

A Incorrect.

Q Who else would have known his last words if you admit that you killed him?

A I don't know what his last words were.

Q But there was no one else in the room, you said?

A No.

Q So then you would have heard his last words?

A No.

Q Why not?

A I'm assuming at the time of Mr. Greene's death, which was some-time on July 1st.

Q Yes, you've told us that.

A I was suffering from a blackout.

Q Sorry?

A I was suffering from a blackout or some sort of psychosis from mixing alcohol and drugs.

Q A psychosis?

A Yes.

Q We'll deal with your psychoses in a minute, but I want to get back to the fact that you tell him that you knew what the last words were. You would be the last person with him?

A That would be correct.

Q So whatever words he spoke last were spoken to you, correct?

A Correct.

Q And as a matter of fact, in your letters to Mr. Zupansky, you tell him what the deceased's last words were, don't you?

A In the letters?

Q Yes.

A But in reality, I don't know what Robin Greene's last words were.

Q You say that he begged for his life?

A In the letters.

Q Yes, the letters that you wrote?

A That is correct.

Q And you say the same thing in this letter to Mr. Pomplum. You know his last words?

A In this letter, yes that is correct.

Q Yes. You go on to give detail about what happened in this particular letter to Mr. Pomplum. You say that it was really hot and that you told the bartender that Greene was your cousin; is that correct?

A Are we on page 2?

Q Yes, we're on the second page of this letter.

A Okay. Yes.

Q Okay. And the reason that you told the jury that you called him your cousin was because that was a joke, as you say, between aboriginal people, isn't it?

A That is correct.

Q And here you say that the reason that you said he was your cousin is *"so that they wouldn't think I was gay"*?

A Yes.

Q Well, which one is it? Were you telling the truth to Mr. Brodsky or are you telling the truth in this letter?

A To Mr. Brodsky.

Q Then you lied to Mr. Pomplum?

A Yes.

Q Why would you say something *"so they wouldn't think I was gay"*? You are gay, are you not?

A Bisexual.

Q Bisexual, sorry. Why would you care if anyone thought you were gay?

A That's always been an issue through my whole life, so.

Q Mr. Pomplum wouldn't know that?

A Well, I didn't really know anything about Mr. Pomplum at first.

Q Except that you wanted him to publish your comic strip and you confessed to killing and dismembering a man to him, but you were denying you were gay to him?

A Yes.

Q Now, he said he thought your comments were too crude to be published. He would never think of touching anything like what you sent him. You heard that?

A Yes, I did.

Q Okay. And you described the issue of your forgetting everything this morning to the jury. That is there was great detail before you actually killed him; correct?

A Yes.

Q And there was great detail after you actually killed him; correct?

A The morning after, yes.

Q And the part that you don't remember is the killing?

A That is correct.

Q In any of the letters that you wrote to anybody, Pomplum or Zupansky, did you ever mention a blackout?

A Yes.

Q When?

A In the Zupansky letters.

Q Where?

A I don't recall. There have been so many letters written to Mr. Zupansky. Not all of them are called as evidence.

318

Q But all the ones here, go through them if you'd like, is the word "blackout" ever mentioned? It's all right, sir. During the recess, you can certainly have the opportunity to look through it. You cried this morning in the courtroom, Mr. Teerhuis?

A Yes, I did.

Q And yet, when you went to the Remand Centre after having seen as horrific a site as a man disemboweled and decapitated and chopped up into eight pieces, you were calm and collected?

A I wouldn't say calm and collected. I was in shock.

Q The witnesses called you calm, every one of them?

A That's their perception. People handle situations differently.

Q Well, let me try to understand this, then. You wake up, you say, with a chopped up body in your bathtub; correct?

A Correct.

Q You spend half an hour with a chopped up body in your bathtub; correct?

A Correct.

Q Why? What did you intend to accomplish in that half an hour except maybe cleaning up, moving things around? What would you do with a dead body that was chopped up for half an hour?

A Nothing. I tried to figure out what happened the night before.

Q Well, if you say you couldn't remember, how could you possibly spend any time figuring it out? You had a blackout, you say?

A Yes.

Q So what was there to figure out?

A What happened.

Q Well, what did you figure?

A Why did Robin Greene end up the way he did.

Q Well, let's start there. Robin Greene was a homeless man, you say. He was clearly an alcoholic; is that correct?

A Yes.

Q And, in fact, you came into contact with him for the purpose of sex; isn't that correct?

A Not at first.

Q Well, what did you do with him if not have sex?

A Well, I met him in the bar first.

Q Yes, so you had liquor?

A Yes.

Q He had liquor?

A Yes.

Q And then your intent was to take him back to your suite for sex, plain and simple?

A Plain and simple.

Q Correct. So you solicited sex from this man. You had him drink liquor and then he ended up dead in your room, so what was there to figure out?

A How he came to be dismembered, how he came to be deceased.

Q Well, how were you going to do that by yourself in a locked room with a dead body if you had no memory?

A It's not every day you wake up in the morning and you find somebody dead in your hotel suite.

Q That's precisely my point. Spending half an hour with a chopped up body is not something a reasonable person would do. Why didn't you call the police?

A That's where I went.

Q Why didn't you call the police? There are phones in the hotel.
A They're pay phones.
Q Yes, you had enough money for liquor, you say? You say you like Diane Last. She would have let you use the phone?
A The bar wasn't open at that time.
Q You could have knocked on anybody's door, gone to the office, gone across the street, could you not?
A Half these people don't have telephones in their hotel suites.
Q You think it's reasonable not to phone the police from the scene of a crime when you're the only person in the room and find a chopped up body?
A I had just woken up.
Q We understand that.
A Yes.
Q Why didn't you phone the police?
A I thought the Winnipeg Remand Centre was a police station, so I walked there. That never crossed my mind, picking up a telephone.
Q Okay. Now, let's get to your contact with the people. You say that you approached Mr. Steenson and you told him there was a chopped up body in your bathtub. That's the Remand Centre on duty man?
A Yes.
Q Why were you not upset or crying or hysterical for that matter?
A I was in shock.
Q You managed to walk and find your way from the Royal Albert Hotel to the Remand Centre in order to turn yourself in?
A Yes.
Q So you could put that much together?
A I used to live in Winnipeg for 19 years.
Q But the point I'm making, sir, is you were together enough to decide that you wanted to turn yourself in. You didn't wander the streets for hours on end not knowing you were going. You went straight to what you thought was a police station to turn yourself in?
A Yes.
Q Well, then what shock? You knew where you were going, you knew what you were going to do and you did it; correct?
A Yes, there was a dead body in my bathtub and I felt that it was for the police to investigate.
Q Exactly. Rational thinking. *I'm going to turn myself in because I killed someone. He's in my bathtub. I'm going to go and report it.* Where's the shock? Very clear thinking.
A Have you seen the pictures?
Q I have seen the pictures.
A Yes.
Q Why weren't you visibly shaken, crying, upset?
A I was in shock and like I said, people handle things differently.
Q Okay. Let's deal with the 911 operator. She says you were collected, calm and responsive. Correct?
A Correct.
Q You told her exactly what you wanted to tell her, that you had killed someone and that the knife could be found underneath the sink in the bathroom, which is where it was?
A That is correct.
Q What shock? You remembered where the knife was?
A No.
Q You didn't? You told her.

A No, I was in shock because of what I had discovered that morning.

Q Okay. Well...

A And her interpretation of me being calm is her interpretation.

Q As was Mr. Steenson's. Let's move on.

A Yes.

Q To the police officers. Each one of them, particularly the woman, described you as calm, collected, responsive; yes?

A Yes.

Q Why didn't you break down and cry at that point? You're certainly capable of crying because you showed us this morning.

A Well, I am human, aren't I?

Q Then why weren't you crying?

A I don't know.

Q You took them back to the hotel room in which you found this dismembered, decapitated body; correct?

A Correct.

Q And yet, even when you went back to the hotel room, you did not cry or display any emotion whatsoever?

A No.

Q Why?

A I felt it was inappropriate.

Q What's inappropriate about crying when you see a dead body?

A Not about seeing a dead body. It's just in general, the way I was brought up. I was brought up that men are not supposed to cry.

Q So what happened this morning? Jury was here and you broke into tears?

A Yes.

Q For the first time?

A In court, yes.

Q Yes. For the first time in respect of anybody that came into contact with you about this killing. First time is in front of this jury this morning as you sobbed; isn't that correct?

A That is correct.

Q You weren't even concerned when you were arrested for murder; didn't show any emotion then either, did you?

A I was confused.

Q What were you?

A I didn't know what was going to happen. I have never been arrested like that before. I've never been in a situation like that before.

Q But you were turning yourself in for murder. How was that surprising to you?

A I had woken up to discover Mr. Greene in the condition that he was.

Q Yes?

A Me being the only person that lived there, I had assumed that I was the one who was responsible for that.

Q Yes, you've admitted that.

A Yes.

Q So? The point I was making, sir, is that why would you find it surprising if you, in fact, admitted that you murdered the man, which you were turning yourself in for murder, why would you find that surprising? What did you expect would happen, they'd let you go?

A No.

Q Well, then what was surprising about that series of events?

A I've never experienced anything like that before.

Q Um-hum. In terms of your drunkenness, you're an alcoholic?

A Yes.

Q It takes a lot to get you drunk?

A Yes.

Q There was not a lot of liquor found in the room, was there?

A No.

Q Okay. And as a matter of fact, there were two of you in that room; isn't that correct?

A Yes.

Q You and Mr. Greene, who also was unfortunately an alcoholic; is that correct?

A Correct.

Q So there wasn't much liquor, we know how drunk he was because he was almost three times over the legal limit, two six seven, three times over the legal limit. He was falling down drunk; isn't that correct?

A I don't know.

Q Why don't you know? You were with him.

A I was drinking just as much as he was.

Q Well, that's interesting, Mr. Teerhuis, because Dianne Last; you remember her?

A Yes.

Q She was the bartender at the Royal Albert?

A That's correct.

Q An experienced bartender; correct?

A I wouldn't say experienced, but...

Q She'd been there for 20 years.

A Well...

Q Correct?

A Still doesn't make you experienced.

Q Well, maybe in your view. I won't argue with you. But in any event, she'd been there for many, many years and she told this court that she knew a drunk when she saw a drunk. Did you hear that evidence?

A Her interpretation of a drunk, yes.

Q Well, she's a bartender. She serves liquor. If someone is too drunk, she's the one that cuts them off, isn't she?

A Yes.

Q Well, then she would have to know, wouldn't she?

A People can hold different amounts of alcohol and still appear sober.

Q We'll come to that momentarily. She said she spoke to you?

A Yes.

Q She said she served you a beer?

A That's correct.

Q She said she had no trouble understanding you?

A No.

Q She said you walked normally?

A Correct.

Q She said you displayed no signs of impairment whatsoever?

A That's what she said, correct.

Q And she saw you at about 5:30 that evening.

A According to her, yes.

Q Yes, according to her. So at 5:30 the night of the killing, according to the barkeeper at the Royal Albert Hotel, you were sober, correct?

A Her interpretation, correct.

Q Absolutely her interpretation. She talked to you?

A Yes.

Q On the other hand, she saw the deceased swaying by this point in time. As a matter of fact, you asked her to watch Mr. Greene while you went downstairs and got some ice?

A Yes.

Q You had no trouble going downstairs, getting the ice or asking her to watch your friend?

A She never saw me go down the stairs.

Q But you did go downstairs?

A Yes.

Q You were capable of doing it?

A I'm capable of doing many things.

Q Yes, I'm sure you are. You said you went downstairs and you got the ice...

A Um-hum.

Q You brought it back up?

A Yep.

Q Why did she need to watch Robin Greene?

A Well, he doesn't live there.

Q Why does she need to watch Robin Greene? He was in a public area, a bar. Why would you ask her that?

A I don't know.

Q Because you didn't want him to leave, did you?

A Possibly.

Q Now, you say that in the past that you have drank and passed out?

A Yes.

Q Particularly, when you mix alcohol and drugs?

A Yes.

Q And you said as you told your story to Mr. Brodsky that, in fact, every time you'd done that in the past, you would wake up in a strange place, a car, an RV, somewhere like that?

A Yes.

Q And that's been your experience when you've blacked out before?

A With living with my parents, yes.

Q Yes. And this time, you say that you went to sleep on the bed?

A Yes.

Q Next to Robin Greene?

A That's correct.

Q And then seven hours later, you woke up in that same bed?

A Yes.

Q You didn't fall out of the bed, you didn't end up in a different room, didn't end up in the hallway, you ended up exactly where you went to bed?

A On the mattress, yes.

Q On the bed?

A Yes.

Q And did you not notice the bed was blood-soaked when you woke up?

A Not at first, no.

Q I'm going to deal with your memory, if I might, in terms of the events that occurred just prior and during the whole day, as a matter of fact, that you spent with Robin Greene. Your memory is exceptional, sir. Every detail is in fact, remembered by you. You told Mr. Brodsky details about a picnic table, about it being a beautiful day, about the sun shining, about the fact that you'd gone to the water's edge; is that correct?

A Yes.

Q Why is that memory not impacted by your drinking?

A That was earlier on in the day.

Q Yes, I understand that, but you passed out for seven hours and yet you have a perfect recollection of absolutely everything that happened before the killing, to the minutest detail. How can that be, sir?

A I wouldn't say the minutest detail, but to the best of my abilities.

Q Well, let's deal with some of that detail. You know every place you stopped at with Robin Greene; isn't that correct? You listed them this morning.

A Yes.

Q Okay. You know what you ate for breakfast at the bus terminal?

A Yes.

Q You know what restaurant you went to?

A Yes.

Q You know how much you paid for the food?

A Yes.

Q You know that you initially bumped into Robin Greene at the bus depot?

A No.

Q What? You found out that you did, didn't you?

A There was a young aboriginal man that I bumped into there.

Q Yes, and you say in your letter, Exhibit 73, page 6: "*I ate breakfast, got some food. Native guy sat across from me, asked if I could buy him something to eat. I know that was my first encounter with Robin Greene.*"

A That's what I said to Zupansky, yes.

Q So you lied about that, too?

A To Mr. Zupansky, yes.

Q Why would you lie about something as ordinary as that? What difference would that have made?

A Thought it would make it sound more interesting to Mr. Zupansky.

Q And why would he care when you met him?

A Why did he care at all? He said in one of the letters he didn't care about Robin Greene at all.

Q Well, that's the point. He had no contact with Robin Greene. He wouldn't have cared.

A No, he had no interest in Robin Greene whatsoever.

Q He had no contact with Robin Greene?

A No.

Q You had no interest in Robin Greene; isn't that correct?

A I wouldn't say I had no interest with him.

Q Well, other than sexual?

A I drank with him, I spoke with him, I partied with him.

Q You describe him as a slab of beef. Isn't that what you described him as in your letters?

A To Mr. Zupansky.

Q That's your description of him, regardless of who you were writing to; you called him a slab of meat, didn't you?

A In the letters.

Q Yes, in the letters; correct?

A Correct.

Q You said he was like a turkey that you could cut the arms and legs off; isn't that correct?

A Yes.

Q He was disposable to you, wasn't he? Completely disposable, wasn't he?

A I suppose.

Q A piece of meat to be butchered, as you described him; correct?

A Correct.

Q Let's get back to your memory, if we could, for a moment. You indicate that, in fact, you dealt with Robin Greene at the Woodbine Hotel as he approached you about the particular necklace in question?

A Yes.

Q And you say that you didn't want to buy the necklace, but, in fact, it was opportune that you met Mr. Greene at that point in time because you say in one of your letters that it was at this point in time that he put his knee or his hand on your knee; isn't that correct?

A I believe so.

Q So the sexual connection was made at the Woodbine?

A Yes.

Q So you knew you were taking him home for sex?

A I would assume so, yes.

Q Sex was a huge part of your lifestyle, was it not?

A I guess from anybody who's gay or bisexual, yes.

Q Would that be different than heterosexual?

A I don't know. I'm not heterosexual.

Q Well, every letter that you wrote to Mr. Zupansky has the word "sex" in it?

A I'm sure every letter I wrote to Mr. Zupansky has the word "I" and "the" in it, too.

Q But those are a little different than the word "sex", would you not agree?

A I would agree, yes.

Q All right. Now, you say that you can't remember anything, except you were able to tell the jury this morning when you had anal sex with him, when you had oral sex with him, whether you had a condom on; isn't that correct?

A Yes.

Q Why are those memories so vivid before the killing? You were drinking, you say?

A Yes.

Q You had taken the drugs, you say?

A Yes.

Q You say you had smoked the crack?

A Yes.

Q So all of those things happened and yet your memory is detailed, why is that?

A Perhaps the, the OxyContin hadn't started taking effect yet.

Q Well, what about the crack cocaine?

A A crack high is only a five-minute to three-minute high. It's momentary.

Q Okay. So boom, you're finished with the crack high. What about the liquor you say you drank?

A That has long-term effects.

Q Well, then why didn't that impact the detail of your letters to Mr. Zupansky, Exhibit 73, page 6, and I'll read to you: *"July 1st was a beautiful day, it was sunny, there was a nice breeze coming from the window, I told Greene to take off his clothes. I watched him undress then offered him a beer he sat... naked for a bit."* Then you go into the detail

325

of your sexual encounters with him. Why is your memory so clear?

A In the letters?

Q Yes.

A I had to give Mr. Zupansky a scenario.

Q But interestingly enough, that's exactly what you told Mr. Brodsky happened, not what you wrote in the letters. Your testimony this morning...

A Um-hum.

Q In response to Mr. Brodsky's questions were, what happened that day in the suite and this is exactly what you told him, Mr. Teerhuis?

A Yes.

Q Word for word. There's no lies in this letter, Mr. Teerhuis, is there, unless you were lying to Mr. Brodsky?

A No.

Q Well, then they're true, aren't they?

A Some of them are, yes.

Q Yes. Most of them were true, in fact; isn't that correct?

A Some of them, yes.

Q We'll go through all of the truths momentarily. Going to ask you about the necklace that you've made so much of. You say that the necklace was, in fact, something that Robin Greene was selling?

A Yes.

Q And as a matter of fact, Greene put the necklace on you at one point in time; isn't that correct?

A Yes.

Q And he put it around your neck, you said it was rather tight, you said it was cute that he did that--isn't that what you said in your letter, Exhibit 73?

A I believe so, yes.

Q And then you say: *"I took it off after a while and I put it on the table or the dresser."* Do you remember that?

A Yes.

Q And, in fact, if you look at the photographs, that's exactly where you did put it. Going to direct you to the booklet of photographs, Mr. Teerhuis, photograph number 10. Where you said you put the necklace is exactly where you put the necklace and where the police seized it from. Exhibit 10, the necklace is right on that table; you'd agree with me, Mr. Teerhuis?

A Yes.

Q True again, isn't that right, Mr. Teerhuis?

A Where the necklace is located? Yes.

Q Sorry?

A Where the necklace is located? Yes.

Q What you wrote to Mr. Zupansky as well about what you did with the necklace; correct?

A Correct.

Q So the truth again, correct?

A Yes.

Q Interesting this necklace, you describe it in great detail in your letter, Exhibit 70, page 3, when you want Mr. Zupansky to go on the Adler show for you?

A Um-hum.

Q And you describe it as: *Gold chain necklace with an amber pendant depicting the three St. Christophers.* Is that correct?

A That is correct.

Q Those are your words?

A Yes.

Q You remember that clearly?

A From news reports and the police report, yes.

Q Did you ever...

A They said it was a 1932 antique necklace.

Q Never said what was on it, did they, Mr. Teerhuis?

A No, that's what Susan Sarandon said.

Q That's right. So the detail is provided by you. You remembered what was actually on the necklace, didn't you, to the point...

A Yes.

Q That you told that to Mr. Zupansky--correct?

A After I had gathered all that information, yes.

Q But that information wasn't anywhere to be had?

A Yes, it was.

Q Where was it?

A The Winnipeg Free Press.

Q The Free Press never reported what was in that particular amber pendant?

A No, Susan Sarandon reported that.

Q Not in the Winnipeg papers?

A Yes, it was.

Q Going to show you photograph 18. Look at it. You can't tell what's on the face of that particular necklace, can you, from that photograph?

A No.

Q So that means it would be something in your memory, correct?

A I was shown a photograph of this by the police.

Q Yes?

A Yes.

Q Still, there were no three Christophers on it?

A It's on the other side.

Q How would you remember that?

A That's what Susan Sarandon said.

Q Oh, so you remember what Susan Sarandon said, but you don't remember what you did that night?

A There was a full-page ad or write-up about what Richard Gere and Susan Sarandon experienced while filming *Shall We Dance*.

Q Yes, that's right. Everyone knew there was a necklace. Not everyone knew...

A Yeah.

Q What was on it.

A No, but Susan Sarandon did because it was her necklace.

Q I see. Now, let's deal with the issue of your memory or, or lack thereof again. You indicated that you don't remember what happened at the time of the killing?

A No.

Q But you do remember that the killing occurred at 6:20; is that correct?

A Incorrect.

Q Why is that incorrect?

A Mr. Zupansky wanted a timeframe, so I gave him a timeframe.

Q But you're the one that picked 6:20?

A I could have picked 7:20, I could have picked 9:30.

Q But you didn't.

A No.

Q You picked 6:20?

A I picked 6:20.

Q So within an hour, if one believes what you wrote, of Dianne Last seeing you sober, you say that Robin Greene was dead, correct?

A I suppose.

Q Don't suppose. You say within an hour of that woman seeing you stone cold sober the deceased was dead?

A Incorrect.

Q You said it in your letter, Exhibit 62.

A I never said I was sober.

Q No, she did. You're right.

A That's her interpretation, yes.

Q But the point I'm making is that within an hour of her seeing you in that condition, Mr. Greene was dead. You say that in...

A According to the letter.

Q Your letter, your writing, your words, Exhibit 62?

A Yes, according to the letter.

Q Yes. You also, in one of your letters, particularly the one to Mr. Pomplum, say that photographs were taken of the deceased within hours of his death; is that correct?

A Yes.

Q And that's true, isn't it?

A Yes.

Q You took photographs of Robin Greene within an hour of his dying and being killed, correct?

A Incorrect.

Q Sorry?

A Incorrect.

Q Sorry, what was incorrect about it then?

A You said an hour before his killing.

Q Yes, that's correct. That's what I did say. And you say its hours?

A I believe so, yes.

Q So you remember that?

A Well, I'm...

Q You corrected me?

A I'm assuming.

Q Well, don't assume. Here it is, Exhibit 59: *"There were photos of him posing nude and modeling underwear hours before his death."* Your words to Mr. Pomplum--correct?

A What page is that?

Q It's on the first page of the letter to Tom Pomplum, bottom line?

A Yes.

Q So you corrected me when I said "hour", I was wrong and you remembered 'hours' from a letter you wrote over four years ago...

A No, I just...

Q Without looking at the letter, correct?

A Incorrect because I saw this letter yesterday. It's part of my disclosure.

Q Oh, and you remembered that out of the 13 letters and maybe 50 pages? Quite a memory. In any event, I want to deal with those pictures for a moment. Take the booklet of photographs, Mr. Teerhuis, and go to photographs numbers 75 through to 78. Those are photographs you took of Robin Greene before he was killed?

A In the afternoon, yes.

Q Okay. Every one of those photographs, you'd agree with me, is in focus--correct?

A Yes.

Q None of them are out of focus?
A They wouldn't be. It's a disposable camera. It's an automatic focus.
Q If a camera is in your hand and it's shaking, it's going to be out of focus--wouldn't you agree? Clear photographs, correct?
A Correct.
Q Not the sign of an impaired man--you'd agree?
A Depends who the individual is.
Q You. That's who the individual, it is you. You took those photos?
A Yes, I did.
Q Within hours of that man being killed and they're in focus--correct?
A Within hours, I suppose, yes.
Q You say that there was alcohol in the room and...?
A Yes.
Q You had not consumed it all--isn't that correct?
A I had consumed alcohol, yes.
Q Was it all gone, all the alcohol in the room?
A The next day, yes, I suppose.
Q Don't suppose. Take your time. Think about it. Remember.
A All I remember of the police saying that there was some...
Q Never mind what the police said, sir. What do you remember about the alcohol in the room?
A There could have been some left, I guess.
Q Not only was there some left, but you drank after the killing, didn't you?
A No.
Q You didn't drink after the killing?
A No.
Q Then why did you write to Mr. Zupansky under the date of November the 26th of 2004, Exhibit 63, page 3, you said you sat down to rest and drink after you killed Robin Greene and you were admiring your work twice, taking time to have a drink. After killing Greene, the actual killing took less than three minutes, you say. I'll let you catch up, Exhibit 63, page 3, sir.
A I don't need to see it.
Q You remember it?
A No. It was a scenario given to Mr. Zupansky.
Q Yes.
A They were excerpts taken from Murder in Milwaukee and from Dennis Nilsen.
Q I'm going to continue on. You say: "*I felt Greene's body relax, his eyes become unfocused toward the ceiling. I got up off the bed, walked towards the window, lit a cigarette. My hands are caked with Greene's blood. They smelled of copper.*" That's what you told Mr. Brodsky this morning, that you...
A No, I told Mr. Brodsky...
Q Remember the smell?
A That morning the room smelled of copper.
Q Yes, the room smelled of copper. Your hands smelled of copper--correct?
A That's what I said in the letters.
Q That's what you told Mr. Brodsky this morning, not what you wrote in the letter. You wrote that as well.
A I told Mr. Brodsky this morning that the room smelled of copper.

Q Yes, you remember that smell. It smelled of copper. You wrote that in your letter to Mr. Zupansky as well?

A Yes.

Q So you say you went to the window, the room smelled of copper, your hands smelled of copper: "*I washed my hands in the sink. I poured myself a drink.*" Do you remember that?

A I remember writing that.

Q Rye and Coke--correct?

A What I wrote in the letters? Yes, correct.

Q And the bottle that was found at the scene with the deceased's blood on it was a bottle of rye whiskey; correct?

A Correct.

Q True again--correct?

A That it was a bottle of whiskey? Yes.

Q Yes. That the deceased's blood was on it? Proven.

A I had no idea there was the deceased's blood on it.

Q Well, you sat here in this courtroom; you heard that his blood was on the bottle?

A That's what I heard, yes.

Q Yes. And you say that you were looking at Greene's body on the bed. You had oral sex with him as he lay on the bed. And then you say: "*Prior to that, I pulled the knife out from his neck. I rolled Greene's body off the bed, grabbed him by the ankles and dragged him into the bathroom.*" Do you remember writing that?

A I don't remember writing that, but that is what is in the letters, yes.

Q Yes. And you say that you had an erection. The idea of having sex with his corpse somehow aroused you. You say you lay him on the tile floor, went back into the bedroom, got the knife from the bed, finished your rye and Coke; remember that?

A That was written in the letters, yes.

Q Why would you put that detail into the letter if it were not correct?

A To make it sound gruesome. It's a fictitious letter, Ms. Leinburd.

Q Oh, I see. So the...

A All these details about dismemberment, necrophilia...

Q Um-hum.

A Was to feed Mr. Zupansky's appetite for his so-called book.

Q Or yours--isn't that correct?

A Partly correct, yes.

Q Completely correct. You wanted that book as badly as he wanted it...

A Yes.

Q If not more, isn't that right?

A Yes.

Q You respected these serial killers. They were your heroes, Dahmer, Gacy, Nilsen--isn't that correct?

A No.

Q Why do you mention them six or eight or 10 times in the letters that you wrote?

A To make it sound more sensational.

Q The only thing that was...

A Mr. Zupansky wanted a book. He was interested in serial killers; he was interested in necrophilia, so I told him what he wanted to hear.

Q And he was writing a true crime story?

A He said he was writing a true crime story.

Q Yes, that's what he said. He asked you for the truth--is that correct?
A Yes.
Q And you knew that he had also researched Gacy, Nilsen, Dahmer--he knew about those writers, didn't he? Because you two talked about and wrote about it?
A Yes.
Q So he knew the plots to those particular murders as well as you did, didn't he?
A Perhaps.
Q Not perhaps. You discussed them. He knew the stories of those killers as well as you did?
A After I told him about them, I'm pretty sure he did.
Q After he told you and you spoke about it?
A No, I told him first about them.
Q Either way, if you told him that those were the cases of those murderers, he would have known that this was fabrication. If the facts were the same and you've stolen them from the serial killers who committed those crimes, these facts would be the same; correct?
A Did you ever read the stories from the...
Q Actually, no.
A No.
Q Now, answer my question?
A Incorrect.
Q The facts would be the same if you'd stolen them from these three serial killers, would they not?
A Yes.
Q He would have known that; correct?
A I would assume so, yes.
Q Then why on earth would he keep writing to you for over a year if he knew that these were not truthful accounts?
A I can't answer that. Only he can answer that.
Q He did. He said he thought that, in fact, he's getting the truth from you. You heard that in this courtroom; isn't that right, Mr. Teerhuis?
A That's what he said, yes.
Q Yes. He was prepared to write a book, you say, based on what you wrote to him; correct?
A Correct.
Q And he was, in fact, interested because you were telling him about a killing that you had done; correct?
A Correct.
Q No fiction there?
A Was telling what he wanted to hear.
Q You told him about a killing that you admit to having committed; correct?
A Yes.
Q No fiction. As a matter of fact, the way you describe dragging the body is very interesting. You say in your letter that you dragged him by the ankles and his body banged against the doorway of the bathroom; correct? I can read the line back to you if you'd like?
A Yes.
Q You do remember saying that?
A No, read the line to me, please.
Q Okay. It says: "*I rolled Greene's body off the bed, dragged him by the ankles and dragged him into the bathroom.*" Do you remember that? Those are your words. You can look at it, Exhibit 68, sorry, 63, page 3.
A That's what's written there, yes.

331

Q Yes. Your writing?

A My handwriting, yes.

Q Yes. And you will recall that the blood splatter expert, Sergeant Ellis, and if the jury looks to photographs 31, there's blood on the door jam leading from the bedroom into the bathroom. He pointed out that blood. Again, that's true then, isn't it?

A You said 31?

Q Yes. He pointed out the picture while you were sitting here. It's in the lower bottom portion on the door jam. You may not be able to see it, but it was pointed out. Is also blood in photograph 32?

A By the doorknob?

Q Yes. And further down. The expert gave that testimony. Rest assured there was blood found there consistent with what you said in your letter to Mr. Zupansky?

A That doesn't sound consistent with the claim to drag the body, but blood on the door handle seems pretty high.

Q I'm not talking about the blood on the door handle. I'm talking about the blood near the bottom portion of the door.

A Okay. I can't see anything there.

Q Yes, it was pointed out. Consistent with the body being bumped into that door?

A That blood could have gotten there anywhere, or by other means. I don't know.

Q But isn't it odd that dragging the body and the witness described the fact that the object that had the blood would have to be close to the floor when it hit that door jam in order for there to be blood on there? Coincidence?

A Possibly.

Q You go on to say that in terms of the dismemberment of the body, that you were, in fact, good at it. From what you tell the court, you were a chef, you knew how to do it. You describe it as gutting a turkey at one point in your letters?

A Yes.

Q You knew how to dismember bodies; let's put it that way?

A I wouldn't say bodies, but when we get turkeys or whatever from suppliers, you, there's some sort of portioning that needs to be done.

Q Yes, so you cut through the joints, through the tendons, isn't that correct?

A They're already processed like that.

Q But if you were, let's say, cutting a whole turkey, cutting a chicken, you would know how to cut through the tendons; isn't that correct? Part of your job, isn't it?

A For a turkey, yes.

Q Okay. If you were doing a leg of beef, same thing, you would be cutting through the joint at one point, would you not?

A No.

Q Why not?

A It would come partially processed already.

Q Oh, so the fact that you went to the abattoir and took these lessons really was of no value to you, was it?

A That wasn't my expertise or the expertise that I was going to take as a chef.

Q But it was somewhere that you went?

A Everybody, everybody who was in my class had to go through everything the same.

Q I see. Why raise that? Why would you speak to an abattoir? I mean, what difference does it make?

A It's part of culinary training because you spend the first year doing nothing but cutting vegetables.

Q Um-hum. And the next year is cutting animals, meats?

A Yeah.

Q Now, you say that some of the information that you got for these letters about the anatomy of Mr. Greene, you got from a book?

A From textbooks, yes.

Q Yes. And you say that in that book, that you could see how different portions of the body were dissected?

A Yes.

Q And you could see the tendons and the veins and the muscles?

A On the transparency pages, yes.

Q Yes. And you said you saw that in jail?

A Yes.

Q So that would have been after the dismemberment of the deceased, is that correct?

A Yes.

Q Going to show you photograph 107. That looks almost like a classic anatomy textbook with a dissection of an arm; is that right? Looks like what you saw in the books, isn't it?

A I wouldn't say that's what I saw in the books, no.

Q Well, it shows a dismembered or disarticulated hand with the veins and the tendons and the muscles; isn't that right?

A Yes.

Q Exactly the sort of thing you saw in the book; right?

A They were hand-drawn sketches.

Q Yes, but similar to this; you'd agree?

A Similar, I suppose, yes.

Q Except that this happened before you got to jail and looked at the books, isn't that correct?

A Yes.

Q So you have your order backwards. You didn't see the anatomy books before the decapitation or dismemberment...

A Well, that would be impossible, wouldn't it?

Q That's right. You saw them after. Now, I want to deal with the tools of the trade, as Mr. Brodsky called them, the knives. You said you took them home with you...

A Yes.

Q Because they were precious to you. They cost you a lot of money. You didn't want them stolen?

A Yes.

Q And yet, you left a complete stranger in the room with them, Mr. Greene?

A So?

Q Well, how did you know he wouldn't steal it? Why on earth would you leave the tools of your trade that were valuable to you with a complete stranger?

A We don't rationalize or, or think straight when we're drinking, do we?

Q I see. But what you do is you take particular care of your tools, Exhibit 64, page 5. It's in the section that you titled:

Dismembering.

A Oh, sorry.

Q You have different headings in that letter. One of them is: Dismembering. Just look to that paragraph.

A Top of page 5?

Q Page 5, Exhibit 64: *I like to take care of my culinary tools.*

A That's what's written there, yes.

Q Yes. You go on to say: "*Greene was no exception. I placed my sharpening stone beside his bodice, cleaned knives in the sink until they sparkled and began to sharpen them, anticipating the dismemberment. I was looking forward to cutting him up.*" Do you remember writing that?

A I don't remember writing that or when I wrote it, but that's what's written there, yes.

Q It's your handwriting?

A Yes, that's correct.

Q And you did, in fact, have a sharpening stone in that room, photograph 53?

A Yes, it was in the pine dresser.

Q Yes. You say as well that it added some sexiness to this dismemberment. Odd choice of words?

A Well, Mr. Zupansky's an odd man, isn't he?

Q Well, you're the writer?

A Yeah, well, he...

Q Did he ask?

A Kept asking for bizarre information, so that's exactly what I supplied him.

Q And you are certainly capable of giving bizarre information, from what you've said?

A I assume that's what he wanted.

Q Did he ask you about a sharpening stone?

A No.

Q Did he ask you about how you'd use the sharpening stone?

A No.

Q Did he ask you about which knives you'd used? No?

A No.

Q Why give him all that detail if he hadn't asked for it? Because you had it.

A No, he wanted it to sound realistic. In one of his letters, he said to keep it real or keep it sounding real, so.

Q And you did, didn't you?

A Yes, it sounds very grotesque, doesn't it?

Q Just sounds real, unfortunately. You also say in that particular letter that you remember sitting in your chair, looking at Greene's headless body on the floor; do you remember that?

A Is it on page 5 still or no?

Q Yes, it should be or further on. You say: "*I remember just sitting in my chair, looking at Greene's headless body on the tile floor.*"

A I don't see that on page 5. Are you sure that's the same page or...?

Q No, I didn't say it was on page 5. I said it was in the letter.

A Oh.

Q In any event, whether you can find it or not, you, in fact, wrote that you sat in that chair, watching the body; do you remember that portion of your letter?

A Vaguely.

Q Okay. And you also, as a matter of fact, drew, in Exhibit 68, if you want to turn to it, the room. Diagram of the room; you see it, sir?

A Yes.

Q And you write in that diagram: "...*chair, I would take a smoke break and masturbate and look at Greene's dismembered body.*" Correct?

A That's what's written there, correct.

Q Yes. And you remember that the blood splatter expert said that there was blood on the back of the chair; do you recall that evidence in this courtroom?

A Yes. Yes.

Q And you say you sat in a chair as you watched his dismembered body?

A It doesn't say which chair though.

Q Oh, I agree with you.

A It just says a chair, so.

Q Yes.

A Could be any kind of chair.

Q But the facts marry with your version. There's blood on a chair.

A There could have blood on more than one chair.

Q I don't deny that for a moment, but it's only something the killer would know?

A Or something Ms. Leinberg (sic) is trying to fabricate.

Q I'm fabricating?

A Well...

Q Those are your words.

A You're the one cross-examining me; right?

Q Yes, look at those words?

A Yes. I've read it, so?

Q Your words. Why would I fabricate anything about you, Mr. Teerhuis?

A Well, that's your job, isn't it?

Q My job is to make up evidence about you?

A No, your job is to cross-examine.

Q Yes.

A Yes.

Q What does that have to do with making things up, Mr. Teerhuis?

A Do you recall the thing with Chris Cornell?

Q I don't even know who Chris Cornell is, sir.

A Yes, you do.

Q No, I don't.

A Yes, you do.

Q Mr. Teerhuis, you seem to know a lot about me?

A Well, you prosecuted me when Chris Cornell said I was bringing drugs into the Remand Centre.

Q Now, my job is to fabricate part of it? Tell me which parts I would be fabricating?

A When I was accused of uttering threats.

Q I'm talking about here today. You accused me of fabricating. That's a very serious allegation.

A That's my assumption, I guess, I suppose.

Q What's your assumption based on, Mr. Teerhuis? This is a court of law.

A Yes.

Q I'm an officer of that court. You just accused me of fabricating evidence. Better be very clear in your explanation.

A I'm just getting the impression you're trying to twist everything around in the Zupansky letters.

Q I'm not twisting anything. Those are your letters, sir. What part did I fabricate?

A I don't know.

Q Why would you say it?

A Why would I say anything then?

Q Hitting too close to home? Now, Mr. Teerhuis, let's get back to where we were, the dismembering of the body. You say, and this is also in your dismembering portion of the letter, that when you were actually dismembering the body of Mr. Greene, that the fireworks at the Forks were going off; isn't that correct?

A In the letter, correct.

Q Yes. It's true that on July the 1st at midnight, fireworks went off in the city as they do every July the 1st at the Forks; do you remember that?

A No.

Q So you just made up the fact that on July the 1st in Winnipeg at the Forks, the fireworks go off?

A Well, they could go off at ten o'clock or 11:00 or midnight.

Q Yes.

A Midnight would seem kind of odd, wouldn't it, though? Fireworks usually would go off at around 9:00 or 10:00, wouldn't they?

Q Then why would you write that that's when the fireworks went off?

A I don't know.

Q Well, you wrote the letter?

A I wrote many letters.

Q Why would you write that?

A I don't know.

Q Now, you say that you filled the bathtub with water and bathed with Mr. Greene; do you recall that, Exhibit 64, page 7? Diagram C, you also drew it?

A Yes, that's what's written there.

Q And what did you caption that particular cartoon that you drew of you in the bathtub with Mr. Greene?

A In diagram C?

Q Yes.

A It reads: "*Bathing with Robin's corpse, the water was red like tomato soup.*"

Q The water was red like tomato soup?

A Yes, that's what it says there.

Q Now, you recall that Dr. Littman said that, in his expert opinion as a forensic pathologist of some 25 years, that the body had been washed or bathed, correct?

A I believe so, yes.

Q And you say that you bathed with the body; correct?

A Well, that's what I say in these letters.

Q Yes. As a matter of fact, you even draw it?

A Yes, in diagram C.

Q Strange that you and he would come to the same conclusion, that is, the body is washed, you have it in the bathtub?

A It also says in one of the letters that I...

Q Answer my question, Mr. Teerhuis.

A I am answering the question.

Q Bathtub, water, Littman?

A Yes, that's what Dr. Littman said, yes.

Q Yes. As a matter of fact, in one of your letters, you say that you washed the corpse and dried both Mr. Greene's body and yours after you bathed; do you remember that?

A In one of the letters, yes.

Q Yes. Particular detail again only the killer would know; wouldn't you agree?

A No.

Q How would anyone other than the two people in the room know what happened to that corpse that night?

A These letters are fictitious.

Q And yet they match the truth?

A I went through a lot of detail from Jeffrey Dahmer. I had to make rough copies.

Q Yes, we've heard that, but the Dahmer stories were already...

A Dahmer, Nilsen, Wuornos...

Q All the stories Zupansky and you both knew? Nothing new? This was a unique murder. It was yours. You admitted to killing this man. Had nothing to do with the other murders, did it?

A I suppose not, no.

Q No, it did not. Now, let's look at the pictures of the body. Photographs 40, 41, 42; you'd agree with me, sir, that the body is neatly positioned in the bathtub; isn't that correct?

A I wouldn't exactly say neatly, but it's in the bathtub.

Q Well, the head is on top of the neck; isn't that correct?

A Looks like it's beside the neck, sort of.

Q Yes, but where it should be, in the neck area; correct?

A Correct.

Q And the bottom half is positioned against the waist, correct?

A Yes.

Q Where it should be, correct?

A Yes.

Q And the two feet are side-by-side, correct?

A Correct.

Q And the two arms are side-by-side, correct?

A Yes.

Q And the penis is between the legs in one piece; correct?

A Yes.

Q Neatly positioned. Correct?

A Well, I'd say it was in some sort of position, but I wouldn't agree as to neatly.

Q Now, look at the picture that I'm going to direct your attention to, picture 78, Mr. Greene lying in the bathtub?

A Yes.

Q Similar positioning of the body, lying on its back in the bathtub, the head portion up; correct?

A I wouldn't say correct, no.

Q How are they different, except that, unfortunately, Mr. Greene is dead in one of the pictures?

A They're very different, from what I'm seeing, so.

Q Yes, one's chopped up and one's alive, but other than that, they're both lying back down in a bathtub, facing up; correct?

A Yes.

Q Now, even the clothing, as Constable McLean described it, is neatly folded. His jacket in Exhibit 41 is on top of his jeans, neatly folded, as Constable McLean described it?

A Looks like it's bunched up.

Q Well, all that I can tell you is that you and I heard the same evidence. The police officer said both items were folded in that particular position. And now, look at photograph number 99; 27 stab wounds on one side of the chest, 28 stab wounds on the other side of the chest. Dr. Littman described them as symmetrical, precise and defined; do you recall that?

A From what Dr. Littman said, yes.

Q And you looking at this picture, would you not come to the same conclusion?

A I wouldn't say they're symmetrical, though.

Q Well, 27 on one, 28 on the other, they look evenly spaced.

A Well, they could have...

Q Why are they not symmetrical? Do you know what the word means?

A No, not really.

Q Same on both sides?

A Well, if there are 27 on one side and 28 or 29 on the other side, then I guess it's not...

Q Well, there's one less.

A The same.

Q They're symmetrical, they reflect each other; you'd agree with that, wouldn't you?

A I suppose.

Q And the nipple has been cut off and you'll recall that Dr. Littman said that there was one stab wound that went right through the center of the nipple; do you remember that?

A Yes.

Q Precise, defined; you'd agree with that?

A I recall him saying that it went right through the nipple, yes.

Q Yes. The center of the nipple. And yet, when Mr. Brodsky asked you about this particular crime scene, you described it in one of your letters as chaotic?

A Yes.

Q How so?

A Look at the photograph. It's...

Q Nothing chaotic about...

A It's disturbing. It's...

Q Oh, it's disturbing.

A Yes.

Q All right, but look at the room. There's no blood in it, very little, except on the bed. In the bathroom, the two towels are neatly put on each side of the sink, hot water and cold water. Even the bottles aren't disturbed; they're all upright in the bathroom, neat and tidy. I'll just direct you to that particular photograph. If you look at photograph 33, the bottles are upright; none of them are knocked over?

A They're sitting in the corner, yes.

Q Yes, not on the floor, not rolling around?

A No.

Q Exhibit 38, photograph 38, the nail brush on one side, two pieces of towel, one on either side of the sink, neat and tidy again; you'd agree with me?

338

A Yes.

Q No chaos in that bathroom other than the body itself. Let's look at the bedroom. Go to photograph 13. Again, the chairs are upright, there's a glass on the table that's upright and it hasn't been knocked over. The rye bottle is neatly put behind the chair; it's on the left-hand portion of the photograph?

A You say the left-hand?

Q Yes. Again, no chaos in that room. Even the plastic mug is upright. Where is the chaos that you want this jury to believe?

A Well, there's some...

Q What?

A Not quite sure what it is by the dresser, but there's something on the floor.

Q Chaos, you described it as chaotic?

A To me, it looked chaotic. It's...

Q That to you is...

A When I woke up, it looked chaotic, so.

Q So did someone clean it up? It was only you and the deceased.

A There's some blood on the wall in photograph 16.

Q Yes, and you'll recall that the blood splatter expert and Constable McLean said that there was an attempt or a number of cleaning swipes through the blood on the wall; can you remember that?

A I recall him saying that, yes.

Q Yes. Now, you say that when you woke up, you were in a bed and you ultimately discovered that the bed was bloody. Huge pool of blood on the bed. And I'll direct you to photograph number 20; do you see it?

A Yes.

Q That huge pool of blood?

A Yes.

Q How is it that you showed up at the police station with virtually no blood on you?

A It's in the corner of the bed.

Q Well, how do you know that?

A The photograph's right there.

Q But how do you know you weren't on that side of the bed? You were passed out, blacked out. How on earth can you remember your positioning through the night if you were blacked out?

A Well, when I woke up, I was one side of the bed.

Q You had no blood on you when you went to the police station?

A Not according to them.

Q You had a drop on your head that was covered by a baseball cap and a drop on your toe. You'd just come from the scene of a dismembered body. Did you wash?

A Well, washed my face in the morning. That was...

Q You washed your face where?

A In the sink.

Q Next to the chopped up body in the bathtub?

A Well, yes.

Q How on earth could you have done that? Stood there at that sink within two feet of the body that we see displayed in those pictures and washed your face?

A I don't know.

Q And then you got dressed?

339

A Yes.

Q And then you calmly walked to the police station?

A I walked to the police station, yes.

Q Yes. Now, you didn't shower, did you?

A No.

Q Reason that you didn't shower is because there was no shower in that suite?

A That is correct.

Q And yet you tell this court that you drank a great deal of liquor the night before; correct?

A Yes.

Q To the point where you were drunk to the point where you passed out?

A Yes.

Q And yet you recall that nobody smelled any alcohol about your person or your clothing, correct?

A In their statements and testimonies, yes.

Q So the police officers that sat in a closed car with you, and it was only 9:30 the next morning, so 12 hours had passed, 13, 14 hours had passed, you didn't wash, you say?

A No.

Q And yet you did not display one sign of having been drunk?

A According to them.

Q Yes, according to Steenson; correct? I asked him.

A I don't recall.

Q Smell any liquor.

A Don't know what his name was, but...

Q Yes. You were in the room, you were as, closer than you and I are?

A Yes.

Q No smell of alcohol, no smell of alcohol on your breath, correct?

A According to him, yes.

Q According to the two police officers who were in the car with you, who walked with you to the bloody hotel room, no smell of alcohol on your breath, no smell of alcohol about your clothes. How is that possible?

A Well, in the police cruiser, there's a partition between who's ever in the back of the car and the police officers themselves.

Q And when they're walking you and arresting you and handcuffing you and standing within inches of your body, there's no guard there. How do you explain it then?

A We were outside.

Q You were in the police station; you were in a hallway that is tiny, as depicted in the photograph. They're barely standing within six inches of you. No smell of liquor whatsoever?

A According to them, yes.

Q Yes, according to two sworn police officers who are trained in picking up symptoms of drunks. You had none of those symptoms?

A According to them, yes.

Q Yes, according to them. They fabricated their evidence?

MR. BRODSKY: With respect, My Lord.

THE COURT: Mr. Brodsky?

MR. BRODSKY: That's inappropriate.

THE COURT: Ms. Leinburd, that's not an appropriate question.

Q Well, you say according to them?

A That was their testimony.

Q Yes. And you hadn't washed?

340

A No.

Q And you say that you started writing letters to Mr. Zupansky after you contacted him?

A Yes.

Q Why did you ever contact Mr. Zupansky? You didn't like Mr. Abbott or what he was doing, did you?

A Not at the beginning.

Q Not ever. You still dislike him intensely, don't you?

A Yes.

Q Well, why on earth would you then phone a friend of Mr. Abbott's to tell them your story?

A I was bored, I guess.

Q Don't guess.

A I was locked up 23 and a half hours a day.

Q You didn't trust Mr. Abbott. You say he snuck your information out of the jail?

A Yes.

Q You knew that?

A Yes.

Q And yet you knew that Abbott and Zupansky were connected?

A Yes.

Q And yet you chose to write to Mr. Zupansky, isn't that correct?

A That is correct.

Q Why would you do that?

A I don't know.

Q Well, think about it if you need some time, but certainly, you know why you wrote to him. Why did you write to Mr. Zupansky?

A He had an idea for a book, so I decided to follow up on it with him, I guess.

Q You wanted to be famous, your 15 minutes of fame; is that right?

A I suppose.

Q Just like the other serial killers, Dahmer and Gacy and Nilsen; isn't that right?

A I suppose, yes.

Q And you maintain that all of the detail about the decapitation and the disembowelment and the mutilation is fabrication?

A Yes.

Q You confess to doing those horrible, monstrous things to Robin Greene's body in minute detail in the letters before this court?

A Yes.

Q Why did you do that?

A I don't know. I don't have an explanation for that.

Q Well, this morning it was boredom. Do you not have that explanation now? Why would you confess to such cruel, monstrous actions if you didn't do them?

A I don't know. I don't know why I would write something like that. I, because I read them again and I actually myself can't believe I would write something like that.

Q And yet you did?

A Yes, I did.

Q You are telling this jury that you confess to all of those actions just to have a book written?

A Yes.

Q You would sell your soul to a nobody?

A In the beginning, yes.

Q In the end, you wrote to him for a year, over a year, detailing

341

everything that happened to Mr. Greene's body. You sold your soul to a nobody for nothing. He gave you $20?

A Actually, I received nothing from him.

Q Well, then...

A I got $20 from Don Abbott.

Q Why would you ever to confess to something you didn't do?

A I don't have a logical explanation for that.

Q The only logical explanation is that it's true, that you remembered it--isn't that true?

A No.

Q Weren't you concerned that you were putting yourself in the position of confessing to something that you didn't do?

A Not at that time. I was pretty naïve back then.

Q At any time, at any time, Mr. Teerhuis, at any time?

A I don't know.

Q Sorry?

A I don't know. I'm...

Q Can't answer that question?

A No.

Q Now, it's interesting that your letters are very detailed, very precise and then as soon as you get the letter from Mr. Zupansky in which he says to you that you can no longer profit from your own criminal acts that you and he have a disagreement?

A We've had many disagreements.

Q But after that letter, you stopped writing to him, didn't you?

A Eventually, yes.

Q Not eventually. That was the last letter you wrote to him--isn't that right?

A I'm not sure which letter you're referring to.

Q Oh. Let me help you out. It's the one where you say to him, he actually says to you, it's Exhibit 76 and in this particular letter, it's actually Zupansky writing to you, but he references your letter and this is what he says to you: *"When we last spoke..."*

MR. BRODSKY: With respect, My Lord, if my learned friend could give the date of this letter because the letter that she's talking about is an April 4th letter, 2005.

MS. LEINBURD: Well, I'm talking about a letter that was sent by Mr. Zupansky in answer to your letter, Exhibit 76. April the 4th is a letter that you wrote to Zupansky.

THE COURT: Do you want to see the letter Mr. Teerhuis-Moar?

THE WITNESS: My Exhibit 76 says September 13th '05.

MS. LEINBURD: It says: Sent 13th. Not September.

THE WITNESS: Oh, okay. I'm sorry.

THE COURT: Do you have it in front of you, Mr. Teerhuis-Moar?

THE WITNESS: Yes, I do.

THE COURT: All right.

Q And I'm going to direct your attention the mid-portion of the 1st paragraph: *"When we last spoke and you hung up on me, I was telling you only what I read, that's it. You completely overreacted."* Do you see that in the mid-portion?

A Yes.

Q And the reason that he was writing to you is because you had, in fact, hung up on him when he told you that you couldn't make any money from your killing--isn't that right?

A No. He has something written here, but it's scribbled off.
Q Why don't you then look at Exhibit 64, which is your letter to him?
MS. LEINBURD: Wondering if we might have a brief recess?
THE COURT: Sure. Ladies and gentlemen, we'll have a brief break.

(JURY OUT)

THE COURT: Mr. Teerhuis-Moar, you're in the middle of your cross-examination...
THE WITNESS: Yes.
THE COURT: So you ought not to talk to anybody. Okay?
THE CLERK: Order, all rise. Court's in recess.

(BRIEF RECESS)

THE CLERK: Court is reopened. Please be seated.

(JURY IN)

THE CLERK: My Lord, all 12 jurors are present.
THE COURT: Thank you, Madam Clerk. Ms. Leinburd?
Q Mr. Teerhuis, we were just at the point where I was referring you to Exhibit 69, which is your letter to Mr. Zupansky. It's written April the 4th of 2005?
A That is correct.
Q And it says: "*I didn't find any article in the Winnipeg Sun pertaining to that law that you claim that offenders or whatever can't cash in on their crimes or anything related.*" Do you see that?
A Yes.
Q What were you referring to?
A To his previous letter, I believe.
Q And what information did he give you in that letter?
A That was 76?
Q Yes, 76.
A Something he said that had to do with people cashing in on their crimes or something.
Q So basically, what Zupansky told you after you've written all of these letters confessing to this decapitation and mutilation is that you can't now make any money from any book you write about your own killing—isn't that right?
A So to speak, yes.
Q Not so to speak. That was your understanding. You can't make a red cent from the killing now, can you? That's what he said to you?
A That's what he said in the letter, yes.
Q So now, all of these letters that you'd written to him confessing to this murder and the monstrosity of the murder, you couldn't profit from anymore, could you?
A No.
Q And so therefore, you wrote to him saying it's lies now—isn't that right?
A It always was lies to begin with.
Q Well, why pick this time to cut off the communication?
A Was going to cut off the communication anyway at some point.
Q But you didn't until the money was out of the picture, did you?
A I suppose so.
Q Don't suppose.
A I suppose so.
Q You were told no money from your book. Zupansky could still make

money, you couldn't, though, and you understood that, didn't you?

A From his letter, yes.

Q So now, you had to find a way to get out of all of that incriminating confession letters that you had written, didn't you because now, he had the book, he had your letters, he was going to make the money and you were out in the cold--is that right?

A I was always out in the cold to begin with anyway.

Q Well, no, you thought you and he were writing a book, didn't you?

A As soon as Mr. Abbott only sent me $20, Mr. Zupansky never sent me a cent, like he promised with magazines and books and stuff...

Q Yes?

A So I didn't believe him anymore anyway.

Q You never believed him at all, from what you're saying?

A No.

Q Then why did you write all of those letters, invest hours and hours of time, if you didn't think he was writing a book?

A I had nothing else better to do.

Q Except confess to the gruesome dismemberment of a body of a man that you met?

A To make up a fictitious story of a man that I had met, yes.

Q Then why were you so angry with Mr. Zupansky? Your anger...

A Who says I was angry? I don't see anywhere here where it says that I'm angry.

Q You're in disdain of that man. You almost growl when you say his name, Mr. Teerhuis--isn't that correct?

A I wouldn't say growl.

Q Well, you hate him.

A Well...

Q Don't you?

A I hate lots of people.

Q Yes.

A Doesn't mean anything.

Q But you hate Mr. Zupansky--isn't that right?

A I hate Mr. Abbott, too.

Q Didn't ask you about him. I asked you about Mr. Zupansky--do you hate him?

A Yes.

Q And the reason you hate him is he managed to get all of this incriminating evidence from you and you got nothing out of the deal--isn't that right?

A That's your interpretation, I suppose.

Q Your back-pedaling starts in this letter of April the 4th of 2005 and you say it's all false information--isn't that right?

A Yes.

Q Why didn't you take back the fact that you chopped up the body? I don't see it anywhere here. There are only three captions. There was no East Indian?

A No.

Q There was no grave digging?

A No.

Q There was no necrophilia?

A No.

Q You never once said, I did not cut off Mr. Greene's head, did you?

A No, it says I took excerpts from Dahmer, Gacy, Nilsen, Wuornos...

Q Didn't ask you that.

A And put them together.

Q Look at me, Mr...

MR. BRODSKY: Wait, wait.

THE COURT: Just wait.

MR. BRODSKY: He's giving an answer. Why can't he give his answer?

MS. LEINBURD: Because his answer's not related to the question.

THE WITNESS: I'm answering your question, aren't I?

MR. BRODSKY: Well, how do you know until you...

THE COURT: All right.

MR. BRODSKY: Hear he makes it?

THE COURT: One second, please. Okay, Mr. Teerhuis-Moar, provide the answer that you were going to provide it.

THE WITNESS: I am providing her with an answer.

THE COURT: That's fine. Just provide it and then we'll let Ms. Leinburd continue with her next question. Go ahead.

THE WITNESS: Yes.

Q Did you...

A Repeat the question, please.

Q Did you ever once deny cutting the head of Mr. Greene off? Did you ever say that?

A Not in this letter, no.

Q In any letter?

A I'd have to read through all of them.

Q Go ahead.

A Okay.

Q Did you ever once deny cutting off the head of Mr. Greene? This is the only letter, maybe I can just help you along, but this is the only letter in which you say anything is false. Am I wrong, Mr. Teerhuis? What exhibit was that?

A Sixty-four.

Q Definitely not in 64, was it?

A No.

Q And while you're looking, did you ever once in any of those letters deny that you mutilated Mr. Greene's body, disemboweled his body, eviscerated his body?

A Not in 69, no.

Q No? Keep going.

A But it's my understanding we don't have all the letters here either. You've edited some of them and didn't submit all of them, right?

Q That's, your counsel and I edited the letters, your lawyer and I. I didn't do it by myself. But if there was a letter, I'm sure Mr. Brodsky would have produced it and he didn't submit it, did he?

MR. BRODSKY: Wait a minute; I'm not on trial here.

THE COURT: Okay.

MS. LEINBURD: He's suggesting that there was a letter that was not, in fact, tendered that puts forward a denial. Mr. Brodsky, in fact, examined his own client this morning and all I'm suggesting to his client is if a letter did exist, that it would have been put forward through his testimony this morning, if it existed.

THE COURT: Did you want to object to something, Mr. Brodsky? You do?

MR. BRODSKY: Yes, yes, I do.

THE COURT: Okay.

MR. BRODSKY: Yes, I do.

THE COURT: All right. Well, ladies and gentlemen, could I maybe ask you to excuse yourself for just a few moments? We'll discuss this very briefly; we'll bring you back, all right? Thank you.

MR. BRODSKY: I'm not on trial here. It's unfair to ask the witness why a lawyer or anyone else, why a lawyer does or doesn't do anything. If there is such a letter, I don't know—the point is, I'm not going to be here to testify as to what the letters said. If I was—I'm a little uncomfortable, My Lord, because my client is in the, the witness is in the witness box and I'm going...

MS. LEINBURD: Well, perhaps we could have him excused?

THE COURT: No, we can't have the witness excused.

MS. LEINBURD: Well, then...

THE COURT: The witness can never be excused.

MR. BRODSKY: I'm going to suggest that in the Exhibit 69, he makes a blanket denial of all of the events that he's previously relied on. To suggest that I would take some other letter with some other denial in it or some other phone conversation...

THE COURT: But, Mr. Brodsky...

MR. BRODSKY: Is it an issue of trial tactics.

THE COURT: Here's how I saw the exchange, Mr. Brodsky. And I think, with the greatest of respect, and you can correct me if I'm wrong, but I think we're exaggerating the whole thing. The exchange took place as a result of your client having invoked what he said were other unedited letters that weren't tendered into evidence. Those other unedited letters, according to your client, might have provided an answer that at this point he can't provide because he can't find what he's looking for. Ms. Leinburd, in response to something your client said which suggested that there were these other letters that were more complete, perhaps, said, well, we edited them. I don't think there's any suggestion that you were specifically, Mr. Brodsky, doing anything, either improper or that you had done anything in silence this morning. It was just that if there was a letter that might have assisted on this point...

MR. BRODSKY: That I had, but there are letters that, there are 50 conversations and there are letters that we don't have. We don't even have notes of them and there are letters that we don't have, I don't have. That was the evidence from the cross-examination of the...

THE COURT: So what is the, so what is your objection?

MR. BRODSKY: The suggestion is that I would be able to tender something that I don't have when I don't have it. It's an argument about trial tactics. I should, I don't want to give any, start giving evidence before the jury that, of what I have and what I don't have and why I did or didn't do any particular thing or whether or not I thought, on a separate point, on whether or not I thought that the denial, the, halfway down the page in Exhibit 69 is a denial of the accuracy of the, all of the events, the fictitious events.

THE COURT: All right.

MR. BRODSKY: I mean, the fictitious story.

THE COURT: Where does this leave you, Ms. Leinburd, I mean...

MS. LEINBURD: I didn't make any suggestions about Mr. Brodsky, nor did I intend to and if he got that impression, I apologize, but certainly, it has nothing to do with Mr. Brodsky. His client suggested that there was, in fact, another letter. I was asking his client whether or not that letter existed and surely, if it did, he would have tendered it during the course of his exam.

THE COURT: I mean do we need to...

MS. LEINBURD: We don't need to go there.

THE COURT: Pursue this much further? I don't see this as a...

MS. LEINBURD: I don't see the issue either, but...

THE COURT: Huge point. In fact, I see trouble arising if we carry on with it because we're into areas that, as I think you're rightly saying, Mr. Brodsky, are somewhat delicate--the edited letters and all the rest. So I would prefer, Ms. Leinburd, unless you want to pursue it in a slightly more nuanced way, although I think even that's dangerous, we simply move on.

MS. LEINBURD: No, it's fine. We're just at the point where we're asking about his denials.

THE COURT: All right. Before we excuse the juries, I also want to address counsel once, if the cross-examination is concluded today, so can we bring the jury back, please?

(JURY IN)

THE CLERK: My Lord, all 12 jurors are present.

THE COURT: Thank you. Ms. Leinburd?

MS. LEINBURD: Thank you.

Q Mr. Teerhuis, we were just at the point where I was asking you if any of the letters that you have before you contain a denial by you as to the decapitation, dismemberment, disembowelment, evisceration or mutilation of Robin Greene?

A The letters that I have before me, no.

Q So you don't, in fact, write to Mr. Zupansky in this letter that part of the fiction, you say, is not true--isn't that right?

A In this particular letter, it doesn't mention anything like that, no.

Q And this is the letter when you say to him, everything I said to you was lies, isn't it?

A Yes.

Q So why didn't you put in those very, very important comments about the fact that you didn't do any of those things? This would have been the place, would it not?

A Perhaps I forgot to answer it.

Q You forgot to say you didn't decapitate the man?

A It was a letter I've written more than five, four years ago, so.

Q Yes, but the point of your letter is that these are all lies.

A Everything, yes.

Q But you didn't say anything about the actual dealing with that body in this letter?

A Not in that letter, no.

Q No. Did you write any such letter?

A Not that I have before me.

Q No. Now, after this, you no longer corresponded with Mr. Zupansky-- isn't that right?

A I believe so, yes.

Q Yes. You said, it's over, these are all lies, I take it all back, end of game--right?

A Yes.

Q And he told you he was going to write the book anyway, didn't he?

A In not so many words, yes, on his radio show.

Q Yes.

A He said this book will be written.

Q So this was the last time that you dealt with the man. You did

347

not deny any of the particulars of the killing in this letter and it was your only method of telling him that the whole thing was fabricated, wasn't it?

A In that letter, yes.

Q Yes. Now, in terms of your other letters, you say at one point in time that the joke is on the legal system. What did you mean by that?

A I had started pursuing other things around the same time involving the legal system and how the legal system, especially in the province of Manitoba, is biased against aboriginals, so I was somewhat vehement towards the legal system.

Q Okay. But why did you say the joke is on the legal system—what joke?

A Those were just words written on paper.

Q Your words?

A Yes.

Q What did they mean?

A I don't know what I was thinking at the time.

Q Well, it's in Exhibit 68 and it says: "*Upon my release from jail...*" So it's in the context and you said you were rather naïve about the law to Mr. Brodsky?

A What page is that on?

Q It's page 2, Exhibit 68. You say that the reason that the joke was on the legal system had something to do with the fact that aboriginal people are not treated fairly by our system—is that correct?

A Yes.

Q Let me read you the rest of that sentence: "*The joke is on the legal system, if they decide to put me away for a long time, I'm going to milk the taxpayer for every cent they are worth and sooo much more. I'll demand that they build me a special cell with my own shower, my own bathtub and send me to Club Fed in beautiful British Columbia.*" That doesn't have anything to do with aboriginals, does it?

A Not in those sentences, no.

MS. LEINBURD: Thank you.

THE COURT: Mr. Brodsky, re-examination?

RE-EXAMINATION BY MR. BRODSKY:

Q Do disposable cameras have a focus? Can you focus a disposable camera?

A They have automatic focus.

Q Automatics, which means they're point and shoot?

A Yes.

Q When you wrote in Exhibit 69 that you took excerpts, in the middle of the page: "*...From Dahmer, Gacey, Nilsen, Wuornos, and put them together and gave you a story (fiction).*"

A Yes.

Q Were you referring to the detail?

MS. LEINBURD: With all due respect, these areas were canvassed by my colleague in his direct examination.

THE COURT: Where's the novelty or the need for clarification there, Mr. Brodsky?

MR. BRODSKY: The denial. The issue that my learned friend was raising about if Mr. Zupansky knew already about the collage, the mixing up of the four stories, then why would he tell the story that Mr....

THE COURT: All right.

MR. BRODSKY: Zupansky knew. That was the thrust of my learned friend spending considerable time in her...

THE COURT: All right. Put the question to your client.

348

MR. BRODSKY: All right.

Q When you talk about in that letter: *"I took excerpts from Dahmer, Gracy, Nilsen, Wuornos and put them together and gave you a story (fiction)."* In your letters, your letters with an S on the end, you say, *"Many things don't make sense. Well, of course not. You have four different stories put together. Did you honestly think I'd tell you so voluntarily about July 1st, 2003?"* When you were saying that, what was the fiction that you were talking about?"

A All the gruesome details.

Q Pardon me?

A All the gruesome details I had written to him.

Q Like what?

A Me bathing with the corpse, the necrophilia, the hanging of the body in one of the letters.

Q The dismemberment?

A The gruesome dismemberment of Mr. Greene, the graphic and great detail of the different organs.

Q All of that was fiction?

A Yes.

Q And that's what you've said in this letter?

A That's what it says there, yes.

Q And that's what you meant?

A Yes.

Q In this letter?

A Yes.

Q Three months earlier, you write in Exhibit 66: *"You feel my situation is shockingly similar to the likes of Dennis Nilsen. I find it interesting."* Is that as a result of some comment--or let me just be open with that. Why did you write that? Why is that there? What prompted that in your letter, that comment?

A I believe that came from a telephone conversation.

Q So in the next three months, when you wrote the letter of April 4th, in that period of time, were there more conversations, telephone conversations about the similarities between the Nilsen story and the, your fictional account?

A From April 4th or...

Q No, from...

A Sorry.

Q January 12th to April 4th?

A I believe there was some correspondence.

MR. BRODSKY: I have no further questions. Oh.

Q When you referred in the, that April 4th letter to the fictional story about the bathtub murders, that's the last two lines of that letter...

A Yes.

MS. LEINBURD: Objection. That's not something that was raised at all on cross and it was available to my colleague to raise on direct.

THE COURT: Mr. Brodsky, why is this coming up in direct?

MR. BRODSKY: Again, insofar as the, what he was denying, as raised by my learned friend, I want to ask him the words are there, what was the, the fictional story about the bathtub murders that, with the emphasis on the word "fictional" as opposed to what my...

THE COURT: We, we've covered that already. It's not new.

MR. BRODSKY: I have no further questions, My Lord.

(WITNESS EXCUSED)

THE COURT: Thank you. Ladies and gentlemen, I think we're finished for the day. I'm going to confirm that in a moment with counsel. If nothing else, what I do want to confirm for you are our plans for tomorrow, so I'll ask you to excuse yourself briefly and if we need to call you back, I'll call you back fairly quickly, but at the very least, we'll hopefully be able to advise you as to what's going on tomorrow and for the rest of the week, all right? Thanks very much.

(JURY OUT)

THE COURT: Do you want to bring Mr. Teerhuis back, officers? Two things, counsel, arising from the cross-examination. Mr. Brodsky, at one point during the cross-examination, it rose inadvertently as a result of your client's response in an exchange with Ms. Leinburd that he, at one point, was being prosecuted for a drug offence with respect to bringing drugs into the Remand Centre. I don't recall that being one of the enumerated convictions that you brought out. Did you want me to instruct the jury on that, on that point? It wasn't a conviction.

MR. BRODSKY: It's not a conviction, no.

THE COURT: No, precisely. It came up.

MR. BRODSKY: Yes, I do want you to instruct them on that.

THE COURT: Well, well, there's two times I can do that. I can do it now or later. Sometimes it's better to do both. I'm asking for your...

MR. BRODSKY: Both.

THE COURT: Okay. I'll bring them back in a moment. The other issue that arose, and it may not be an issue and I know it was inadvertent if it occurred, Ms. Leinburd, and maybe I'm being just a tad too exquisite in terms of my hearing here, but I thought at one point you referred to: "...and other serial killers." It was done in a context with reference to...

MS. LEINBURD: The other named...

THE COURT: I know that. It came up in a way that seemed just a tad bit awkward. Mr. Brodsky, again, you didn't pick that up?

MR. BRODSKY: Let me put it in this way and I hesitate because this will be one of the few times I don't answer directly. This is not a direct answer, but if Your Lordship picked it up, I'm concerned that the jury may have picked it up, whether I did or not. That may not be a direct answer, but Your Lordship gets my meaning.

MS. LEINBURD: Well...

THE COURT: All right. I'll--Ms. Leinburd, go ahead.

MS. LEINBURD: If Mr. Brodsky didn't pick it up, and given his training and expertise, I doubt that the jury picked it up, but in any event, it was in the context of the other serial killers.

THE COURT: I know that. I know that. So you would prefer that I instruct them on it?

MR. BRODSKY: I would say that to put in their head that he might be a serial killer would be inappropriate. I would not ask you to instruct...

MS. LEINBURD: Well, first of all, let me say that that was never put into his head nor was it ever asked and frankly, I don't think that Your Lordship should say anything about it. And what are you going to say? That he's not a serial killer, that he is a--what can you say? I mean, the question wasn't asked, it wasn't answered and it wasn't raised. And how is Your Lordship going to put it? By the way, he doesn't happen to be a serial killer. I mean...

THE COURT: No, I think I would be...

MS. LEINBURD: That just flags the issue.

THE COURT: Think I would be a tad subtler than that.

MS. LEINBURD: Well, I hope, but I don't know how you're going to approach it other than that.

350

THE COURT: I think...

MS. LEINBURD: He wasn't asked.

THE COURT: Well, the question's a good one, Ms. Leinburd. What I would say if I was to say anything was simply that there was a reference made where the phraseology was: "Other serial killers." All counsel and I want you to know that Mr. Teerhuis-Moar is charged with one offence here. No other convictions are in existence. Even that's complicated. You know what, Mr. Brodsky?

MS. LEINBURD: Well, yes, that's the problem.

THE COURT: I think we're going to get into something here that I'm not...

MR. BRODSKY: I don't think it's--I think we should just leave it...

THE COURT: All right.

MS. LEINBURD: That's what I think we should do.

THE COURT: Okay.

MR. BRODSKY: I know about serial killers because I know that they, if we would have gone through the history of the investigation by the police, they wanted to see if he was involved in other offences. The jury doesn't know that.

MS. LEINBURD: The jury doesn't know that.

THE COURT: I know. All right.

MR. BRODSKY: So I'm asking whatever was said shouldn't be underscored.

THE COURT: Okay.

MS. LEINBURD: My view, too.

(PROCEEDINGS ADJOURNED TO DECEMBER 11, 2008)

23
The Defense and Prosecution Re-State Their Cases

MR. BRODSKY: My Lord. I apologize, but I want to get a little closer to you so that I don't have to yell and you can hear me and we can have a dialogue of sorts about this case and about your function and about what your duties are.

First of all, before I start I do have to thank you, and I do, sincerely, for the attention, the careful attention you've paid to the evidence. Don't think that this is an ordinary case that all juries go through what you did. This is not an ordinary case and all juries don't go through what you did. The facts in this case are gruesome. The pictures in this case are horrid. You need a very strong stomach to get over the descriptions and the pictures and the autopsy. You need a very strong character to be able to look at them, listen to them, and still pay attention to the evidence and through all.

From what I've seen, and I only speak for myself, you seem to be trying very hard, you're very intent, you seem to be paying significant attention and I appreciate it. I appreciate the fact that I can't talk to you, that is, I can't get you to answer me back, but you seem to be paying attention to the evidence and I hope you will pay attention to the law.

Now that's important because we all have different roles in this courtroom. My job is to argue all of those facts that I think are beneficial to my client and, and will persuade you or tend to persuade you to see things in a way that allows the benefit of a reasonable doubt to be applied to him. That's my job.

You can't decide this case on emotion. You can't decide this is a horrible case, my client is involved in a horrible crime, he's dangerous, he might be dangerous. Those are not the rules. That's not what the case is about.

We accept the fact that this is a horrid case and the horrid thing happened, and we accept the fact that he's not trying to run away from it. We accept the fact that he went to the police station right away, he didn't go get advice from his whoever, friend, neighbor, spectator, lawyer. He didn't get advice from anybody. He thought it was, as you clearly will find or have already have noticed, it's a horrible thing that happened and he went to the police to tell them. He didn't try to blame anybody else. He didn't say he was acting in self-defence. He didn't say he had it coming. He didn't say "I was in Pittsburgh" or "down the hall." He didn't say any of those things. He didn't concoct an alibi, or try to. He went directly to the police station.

Now guilty doesn't mean--find that he's the killer beyond a

reasonable doubt. We've already admitted that. The trial wasn't about that. It never was about that. "Beyond a reasonable doubt" means you have to find that he was more than probably in a sane and sober state of mind at the time of the killing of Robin Greene. That's what you have to find. You have to find that he wasn't drunk. You have to find that he knew what he was doing. You have to find that he intended what he was doing before you can find him guilty of the charge of murder that he stands accused of. If you can only find that he probably intended his actions, he probably knew the consequences of his actions, and, as you already heard His Lordship at the beginning of the trial when you first took your oath, then you find him not guilty because the case isn't about whether he's probably guilty. The case is about whether he's guilty beyond a reasonable doubt.

And you can't decide because it's gruesome he must have known what he was doing. I mean to argue that after the first stab wound he would have known that the body would be killed, or after the seventeenth the body would be killed, is an exercise of futility. I mean after the sixtieth it's an exercise in futility anyways. We're talking about a dismembered body. The fact of the matter is, it's a dismembered body. No use getting caught up in an argument about, well if it was one blow maybe it was an accident. I'm not talking about that. We're talking about whether he was so impaired by alcohol that he wasn't able to judge the consequences, couldn't understand what he was doing and what this was about. Or, as His Lordship will tell you more properly, like I said before the rules come from him, whether he did intend, not whether he had the capacity to judge, but whether he did intend the natural consequences of his actions. Or whether in fact he woke up with a scene before him such as was described in this courtroom and said, oh my gosh, what happened? What must have happened? What do I do now? Anybody else here? Holy mackerel. It was awful. It's awful.

And I'll be a little longer than I would otherwise if I had her address before me because I'm dealing in the dark a little bit, and I'll be dealing with things that I think she'll be saying, but I may not know. I don't know what she's going to say about Mr. Abbott, who was the intermediary, not being here to testify about what was going on with those letters and how it was all set up and why he got into that room right away.

You can't presume, you can't guess that he was plied with liquor. That's a speculation and His Lordship and I apologize to His Lordship who is going to tell you the law because it really is his realm, not mine, but I expect that he's going to tell you that speculation is only valid if it's an inference from proved fact. If it's an inference from proved fact. And there is not proved fact here that the deceased was being plied with liquor, that is, drank more than Sydney Teerhuis. I say that again, or it's going to ring and ring and ring: There is no proof of that. There is no proved fact.

Now why is that important? It's important because you know how drunk Robin Greene was. Really intoxicated, according to the pathologist. Why really intoxicated? Because his blood alcohol, in fact his urine alcohol was 296, almost to the point of unconsciousness in most people. And it was higher before, he said. And if it was higher before and they were drinking together, what does that say about the intoxicated state of Sydney Teerhuis?

Well he told the police right away, before he got any advice from anybody and before he was spinning off the fantastical stories, that he blacked out and came to and when he woke up, is what he said, the awful scene confronted him. No one else being there, he told you or he told them, he found at the time of the blackout he assumed what he must have done and reported to the police that he was the killer based on his assumption: Nobody else there when he went to bed, nobody else there when he woke up. What happened?

After he was locked up, he decided to spend his time playing with the media, which includes Mr. Zupansky, merely on the facts of the case as disclosed by the autopsy report, the police report, the photos of the crime scene, and what he had seen in the room. And what he had seen in the room; that is what he had seen in the room after he woke up in that half hour before he went to the police station.

Now he didn't have, as he told you and as the letters show, he didn't have all of the autopsy reports with him all of the time. There were repeated visits by a variety of people from my office, including, unfortunately, me, to prepare for this case, to go over what the police reports said and what the police investigation showed, what the autopsy pictures showed, what the pictures of the scene, crime scene, and when I say crime scene I mean in room 309, showed. And he looked at them repeatedly. Why? Why did... why?

Well my suggestion to you is that he was trying to play this game with Mr. Pomplum, 14 months after the incident in September of 2004; killing being on July the 1st or 2nd, 2003, and with Mr. Zupansky he had to get the factual part correct so it wouldn't be just a total fiction. The case itself would be sensational enough. So, the cameras would be there and the papers would be there. But in order to play out this book deal he had to sensationalize, which is what he did, what must have happened. But he couldn't be contradicted by anything in the police report. You see, as Mr. Zupansky said, as long as Sydney was there the Crown couldn't prove its case of murder; he'd have to be convicted of manslaughter. So Mr. Zupansky, not trusting the police to do their job or being able to do their job, and without giving them a chance to do their job, decided that he would do the job of the police.

Would you want anything that happened to you or your family investigated by Mr. Zupansky? You heard about his friend who was incarcerated with Sydney. Would you want him investigating because he knew the justice system, because he was involved in it, not the way the police are but from a different angle? Would you want him to investigate whether or not there was an insanity defence because he knew what that was.

So those, with those credentials he's going to become the investigator. And he's going to say, as the Crown I suspect will say, rely on his investigation. You don't have all of his letters. You don't have the 50 phone calls that he made. You don't have what was being told to Sydney in the cells with his cell mate, Don Abbott, who was promised a trip, well if you believe Sydney he says Bahamas, in the letters it says Jamaica; but, whatever, he was promised a two-week all expense paid trip.

Decide the case. Decide it as if it were a jigsaw puzzle and you only have some pieces, what the jigsaw puzzle really shows--because if you do that, you're doing a wrong thing. If you're missing pieces and you're guessing at what the picture really shows, that tells you that you have a reasonable doubt.

Sydney always maintained that the truth would come out at the trial and this truth would come out, and did come out, in the same fashion he told the police. He didn't try to blame somebody else. He didn't try to create an alibi. He didn't argue self-defence. He admitted responsibility to the police. He admitted responsibility to the court and to you.

He is a chronic alcoholic. He is a drug abuser. He has been treated in in-house treatment programs. He's not a regular drug abuser, not

354

an ordinary alcoholic because the programs, which he told you were 28 days and he had to go through two extensions, weren't long enough for him. And the recovery program, which was whenever it was, weren't long enough for him, which tells you that when we're using the word chronic, spelt in capital letters and it's underlined and he lasted, when he got out of the recovery program, one day. So that's his background. Not talking about someone who suddenly has no explanation for a crime and says, I forgot, like your kids do. What happened at school today? I forgot. We're not dealing with that. He didn't have that kind of an excuse. He does have a background that shows you it's not, I forgot. It's real. He relapsed. He has had a horrid upbringing.

Was there a George? I mean Sydney, in the letters, writes that George is captured in the Fuji cameras, which you'll, they're not here, but you can have them in the jury room, the disposable cameras. What about George? Remember about George? Yeah? Do you remember George sitting on his lap? Yeah? Where is the picture of George sitting on his lap? Where is the explanation as to why you don't have it? And you can't ask the Crown any questions, but you can ask with your eyes, let's hear it, let's hear the explanation.

He doesn't have a memory of the things that he must have done, but he does have a memory of the things he made up: the East Indian from Bangladesh who wanted to cook him in a pot, or whatever it was. Made up. The necrophilia: I dug up some bodies in a grave and I had sex with them or masturbated over them, whatever he said. He knows that's not lack of memory. He knows that's plainly made up and that's what he said in that letter of April 4th, 2005.

I use the term 'yanking his chain', that's what he was doing, fooling around. He was bored. He ought not to have done it because you can't tell when some Crown attorney is going to take it seriously.

He blacked out. He drank too much. He did too much coke. He did the oxycontin. And he didn't tell you; by the way, this is a cocaine high, I was hallucinating. He could have. He said: No, crack cocaine only causes a temporary high. So he's not maximizing everything. He's not trying to turn everything to his benefit. He's minimizing. I'm not sure. We don't have any medical evidence here. Nobody asked the pathologist, the doctor, or the toxicologist: What is the effect of oxycontin? What is the effect of cocaine? What happens if you mix them? What happens if you mix them with alcohol? We don't have that. But you have the job of finding guilt beyond a reasonable doubt.

He could have made up any story if he was the only witness; but he didn't.

How much dope did he smoke? Did he smoke any? Maybe he went out with the two people, the night clerk and his girlfriend Sherry. What did they say about how much dope he smoked and the effect on him?

Remember the onus in this case is on the Crown to prove its case beyond a reasonable doubt. There is no onus on the accused to prove anything, to prove anything.

Remember you can't draw inferences unless from proved fact. One of the things you're going to have in that room is the Profits of Criminal Notoriety Act, five pages, Exhibit 81. Sydney says: I never saw it. I never read it. I looked for it in the paper. I don't see what you're talking about. I don't know what you're talking about. Does he say to anybody else, I have it? Does he have a copy of it? The fact that it's filed and in your jury room doesn't mean he read it.

355

Dr. Littman testified next that Sydney -- that a chronic alcoholic can exhibit no signs of impairment. They're able to hide the signs of impairment. They can drive and drive long distances and they can walk. The problem is their reflexes; their ability to react to unexpected things is affected. Somebody, a child runs onto the street, that's unexpected. A deer comes out, it's unexpected. A car changes lanes it's unexpected. But as long as you're doing what you're used to doing, you don't exhibit signs of the impairment. If you're uninterrupted and you're doing what you're accustomed to doing, you can.

When you're dealing with what Sydney knew, remember and keep in mind all the disclosure he had, all of the photographs he had, and remember things like 6:20, time of the killing, is not the time of the killing. Dr. Littman didn't testify that the killing was at 6:20. He never did that. Sydney just made up a number. He just made up a number. Was he even asked, Dr. Littman, was that number accurate, correct? No.

Dr. Littman said that the evisceration was done by a steady hand, but that a chronic alcoholic would be able to do that. A chronic alcoholic you heard about who was treated, went to rehab, treated, relapsed, could do that.

It's true that Mr. Zupansky is key to the case, like he says, because without him there is no case.

Sydney told Mr. Zupansky that he hung the body from the ceiling. In 2005 he told him that, in 2005. It's now 2008. Had anybody checked? Did you hear any evidence? Did you hear any evidence? Now why wouldn't you hear any evidence if it wasn't true? Told him in 2005. You can't guess, well we don't know, it must have happened. If it couldn't have happened, or it could happen, why didn't you hear any evidence? Remember, the Crown must prove its case beyond a reasonable doubt.

Sydney testified that pardon me, in the letters, when he was building this fantastical story to sell books and make a movie, he said the body, the torso was put up trophy style on the dresser. That he was going to call the book, Trophy Kill. Did you hear any evidence that anybody went back there to see if the torso had been put on the dresser? It hadn't, unless Sydney cleaned off the top of the dresser because it's full of objects and pictures and you'll have the pictures in the jury room to look at it--put the torso on, took the torso off, put it in the bathtub, cleaned up the top of the dresser, put the dust back, put the picture back, put the necklace back, put the articles back the way they were before. It's ridiculous. But did anybody check to see if there were any wipe marks at least, wipe marks from 2005 to 2008?

According to the Crown Sydney had a clear head, clear mind. Least I suspect that's what she's going to say. But listen to her explanation for why he would hide evidence of the crime. Put it another way, he took the organs out and he took them away from the room and he hid them. Took him about seven months to figure out that I guess by going through the police reports enough times to find that they weren't found, to make up the Health Sciences Centre BFI bin in a vacant lot. Why would you hide the organs? Why would you hide them? So that people wouldn't find them and you would be able to get away with the crime? But you still had the body. Why would you hide the body in the bathtub? Do you really think that people wouldn't see it in the bathtub? Or is this evidence that he clearly had disorganized thinking, impaired judgment from which there's only one explanation, and that is a high degree of intoxication. Why clean up some of the blood and leave the rest? You heard the blood splatter expert say he made a zed on the wall. It's impaired thinking. No judgment. He took pictures and he left the cameras. If he was trying to hide things, why? Impaired judgment, inability to judge consequences, and drunk.

There's lots of review of the autopsy results, the crime photos, the autopsy photos and, by the way, you're going to see two pictures in there of the autopsy with the skin removed that weren't referred to by anybody. Why were they in there? Why did you have to be exposed to that? Don't let your passions get inflamed. Don't find they are so grotesque and awful that you can't listen to what the judge says when he tells you to decide the case based on the facts, not based on your emotion.

He had the foundation for his fantastical book. Sydney worked, you will recall, on the photos and the police reports. And the photos, same as the bloodstain analyst, had the same basis for deciding what happened, the photos. The bloodstain analyst came and told you that's what he worked on. He wasn't there at the time.

When you think of the cut up body you think of something organized or do you think of something with a grossly impaired judgment? And if it is a grossly impaired judgment and we're dealing with the alcoholic that we know he was, with the background he has, you have to have, in my respectful submission to you, a reasonable doubt.

Mr. Steenson from the Remand Centre said that at 9:20 he walked in and said that he went out drinking the day before, that he blacked out and when he came to he had a body chopped up in his bathtub. That's how he knew, that's how Sydney said he knew he killed him. He said the same thing on the phone to the dispatch as he told me, that is, Sydney said on the phone the same thing as he told me and I marked it down. So if you're comparing the notes of Robyn (Sabanski), the dispatch operator, remember that the conversation from Sydney Teerhuis was overheard by Mr. Steenson from the Remand Centre and that's what it was. She says, I even had, I marked it down on my dispatch log. You've got the CV's of everybody. You've got the reports of nearly everybody. Do you have that log, or is that gone with the tape with no explanation?

Dr. Littman said that whoever did this had some degree of movement and dexterity, of manual dexterity. He was a chef. He listed off all of the or not all of them, but a lot of the restaurants and experience that he had. This was his day job. This was his day job. And because he put it in the letters and because Mr. Zupansky knew that too, it's easily verified because the names and the dates of the places that he worked show that. Show that. If you hide the organs but leave the body, chopped up, keep in mind the 296 urine alcohol reading and Dr. Littman says it would take two or three hours to cut the body up like that. He's talking about in a normal situation, but he certainly doesn't know the experience of Sydney Teerhuis-Moar and his background. There were no signs of necrophilia that the doctor found.

Dianne Last told you that it was Damien and Sherry that went out with him. He says to smoke pot. She says to have a cigarette. You have to decide what they had to say. The fellow had a small sway, fellow that she couldn't identify in the photographs, a small sway. She wasn't even asked in this courtroom to see if she could identify a picture of Robin Greene.

He didn't tell you that he heard voices. He didn't pretend to have an insanity defence. Mr. Zupansky says the voices should be told to his lawyer and a psychiatrist. I mean, it didn't happen. He just came to court to tell the truth. There was no voice. There was no insanity. There was no automatism. It never came out on the radio program that there was. What there was is what was from the very start.

Dianne Last can't say whether Sydney was drunk or sober. She didn't know what was going to happen five years ago.

If the Crown says only the killer would know in his right mind that the body was void of blood, remember that Sydney saw that and was there with the body for half an hour before he went to the police.

If the Crown says that only the killer would know in a clear mind that the killing was at 6:20, remember that's just a made up story, a made up time. Nobody knows when the killing was.

If the Crown says there were two knives, if she says that only the killer would know that, a killer with a clear mind, remember he had the pictures. He knew how many knives he had. They were his.

If the Crown says the organs were livery, or whatever they say about the organs, remember Sydney's background, remember his training in British Columbia.

If the Crown says there was a frenzy at the killing, remember her cross-examination of Sydney when he wrote that maybe the jury will find this was a chaotic scene that he awoke to.

Remember, I can't be there with you when you're deliberating. Remember another term, at least I ask you to remember another term, that is a 'functioning alcoholic', that is someone who can be drunk and still do his job, still come to work and do his job. Can be drinking the night before and still go to work and do his job is still a functioning alcoholic. Remember in these horrible letters that they make events even more horrible by a vivid imagination and intertwining fiction for entertainment, as opposed to truth telling which is what happened here.

No sane and sober person wants to put a human torso on a dresser or even pretend that he did. No sane and sober person cuts up a body into eight pieces and hides it in a tub. First of all, he wouldn't cut it up in eight pieces, a sane and sober person. And two, wouldn't hide it in a tub. It's not really hiding it. No sane and sober person. It's not like making sure he's dead so he's going to stab him again. The body was cut up in eight pieces and reassembled. He's not taking aim; it was just disassembled and reassembled. This is a drunk acting crazy while you're drunk. A sane and sober person doesn't cut off someone's head. A drunk.

What about the suicide by cannibalism raised by Mr. Zupansky? They want to hear about suicide by cannibalism? Well I'll tell you, there was an East Indian in Indonesia, or Bangladesh, rather. I'll tell you whatever you want to hear and this is how I spend my time, twenty-three and a half hours a day locked up. There was no George. There was no necrophilia. There was no human trophy.

There are many, many letters. We only have some. They have many, many unrecorded, 50 unrecorded phone calls, which wouldn't have happened if the police were involved.

You have the release and by the way, I apologize for taking so long. It's not when you look at your watches that I know that I'm talking too long, it's when you shake them that I'm taking too long, and I'll be watching for that. Unfortunately you can't leave when you want, you can only leave when I'm finished. And no you can't have a lawyer for a bail application you have to just sit. I know I shouldn't be light hearted but this is a very stressful thing that you're doing.

This is a very serious charge and sometimes, even Shakespeare has some comic relief in the middle. And comic relief could be ridiculous, absolutely ridiculous, in my respectful submission.

He knows he has a lawyer, so he wants him to sign a paper acknowledging that he's already received independent legal advice, independent legal advice for announcing that he's a killer. So who would sign a thing like that? And why would he go to another lawyer aside from the lawyer he already has? I mean, why would he sign it? Why would anybody put that in a release? And how do you give away moral rights? Take a look at the release they wanted him to sign. How do you give away moral rights? What does that mean anyways? What does it mean? I have the moral rights and you can't talk to anybody, only me, and I have to give you written permission. I want you to sign that. Old habits right there.

We know and Mr. Zupansky knows that he's dealing with a self-avowed publicity seeker. Do I know that? Do you know that? When was the last time you wrote to the Queen? When was the last time Buckingham Palace replied to you? I mean he knows how to get people's attention. He likes that. Get me the autograph of Susan Sarandon. Richard Gere should be saying this at the beginning of the movie. He likes that.

When Sydney writes that letter of April 4th, 2005 and says that what he's told in the letters previously is a work of fiction, what he means is he's made up what he can't remember, and the rest of it, the necrophilia and East Indian, all of that, are plain lies. Some are purely imagination or sensationalism and some is filling in blank spaces with more imagination and sensationalism. He says repeatedly: Wait for the trial. Wait for the truth to come out. Well he never told anybody he never did it. He warned Mr. Zupansky that it would be wrong to publish the fiction as if it were true. Mr. Teerhuis says: I said I had 3,000 pair of underwear. I never did. And he says that he's playing around with Mr. Zupansky and Mr. Pomplum because of the graphic comments, which there is no denial. He says he's playing with Mr. Pomplum and he says in that letter, if you look at it, 14 months later, that his lawyer showed him the photos from his camera months later, that the photos exist showing a third party, being George, having sex with Mr. Greene. No, they didn't. You would have seen it. But it's good to have George. The sequel will be: Did George do it? If you're writing a fictional book: Did George do it?

Dennis Nilsen bathed his corpses, made love to them he says in that letter. Well he got the letter. He got the idea. And you know that even Mr. Zupansky is upset: *"You feel my situation shockingly similar to the rights of Dennis Nilsen? I find that interesting. You think Nilsen had any influence?"*

This is three months before that April 4th, 2005 letter. That's when things went downhill, when this letter was written, when you figured me out. I'm just recanting, or repeating, rather, what I picked up from another case, another person.

You can't say that he washed himself up in order to... I mean I'm just guessing again of what Crown might say, you can't say he washed himself up in order to hide evidence of the crime because, what did he do? He washed himself up and he went to the police station and said, I committed the crime, I killed somebody. He says I stole the ideas from Dahmer, Nilsen, and Gacy. He said that in 2005, rather, and 2004. And it's now 2008 and there's no denial of that. You weren't given anything to show that Nilsen never said that, Gacy never said that, Dahmer never said that.

So what are you going to make with the blood on the swipes on the chair? I mean how many chairs were there in that room? And, too, he was there for half an hour.

You know, Mr. Zupansky said his object from the start was to convict Sydney Teerhuis. The police couldn't do it. The evidence was lacking. So let him pay money, or offer to pay money, and suggest this and that to Sydney. But you didn't hear an insanity defence and you didn't hear voices and you didn't hear self-defence or somebody else did it or George did it or you didn't hear any of that. You heard that bathing with bodies and body parts is from Murder in Manhattan, but you don't have that.

You know I have a lot of stuff here. You can figure out the rest. I trust that you will. Remember the onus is on the Crown to prove that Sydney Teerhuis-Moar guilty of the crime of murder beyond a reasonable doubt. Sydney Teerhuis-Moar doesn't have to prove anything. He doesn't even have to raise a reasonable doubt. You have to find the Crown has proved its case beyond a reasonable doubt before you can do your duty. Thank you.

THE COURT: Mr. Brodsky. Ladies and gentlemen, why don't we take a brief break and then we'll hear from Ms. Leinburd. Okay. Thank you.

(JURY OUT AT 3:08 P.M.)

THE CLERK: Order. All rise. This court is in recess.

(BRIEF RECESS)

THE CLERK: Court is re-opened. Please be seated.

(JURY IN AT 3:26 P.M.)

THE CLERK: My Lord, there are 12 jurors present.
THE COURT: Thank you. Ms. Leinburd.
MS. LEINBURD: Good afternoon. I promise you I won't be as long as Mr. Brodsky, and I concur in his thanks to you. This was a very difficult case for you to hear. The facts were extraordinarily violent, gruesome, atrocious, and I do thank you for your patience and your attention.

And I agree with very much of what Mr. Brodsky said in his opening at the beginning, that is that you are the triers of fact, that's your job. Nothing I say and nothing Mr. Brodsky says, regardless of how elegant and persuasive he was a few minutes ago, is evidence. That's his opinion. That's his surmising. But you can only make your decision based on the evidence. And on Monday morning Justice Joyal, the judge, will tell you what the law is and how you can use that law. So you don't take that from Mr. Brodsky and you don't take that from me. And on Monday you will be instructed on what you can and cannot do.

Mr. Brodsky is also correct in the fact that he did, in fact, anticipate a lot of what I have to say, and the reason he pointed it out to you is because, in fact, he has to overcome all of those issues, and in doing so he says to you there is no evidence of this and there is no evidence of that. My job is to prove the case against Mr. Teerhuis beyond a reasonable doubt and I do that with evidence that is relevant to this particular charge. Because there's an absence of evidence means nothing. You've heard that from every single expert that came before you. Nobody can disprove something that did not happen. So we aren't about to venture into that particular area.

As I indicated to you, my function is to prove beyond a reasonable doubt that Sydney Teerhuis-Moar killed Robin Greene. He murdered him. Mr. Brodsky was very eloquent when he said no sane, no sober man would do to any human being what Sydney Teerhuis did to Robin Greene. The word he left out is 'evil'. That's the difference. We all know there is evil in this world. We all know there are killings in this world. We all know that we can't explain them because there's never a good reason to kill anybody.

Now, if you listen to Mr. Brodsky, as I did intently, he would have you think that this was a normal Saturday night out drinking and someone falling asleep and then waking up to find something out of the ordinary. That's not what happened here at all. And, let me tell you why that didn't happen.

First of all this accused admitted to killing Robin Greene. In that admission, and in the admission of the fact that there was no one else in that particular room with him, you can draw the inference. Remember Mr. Brodsky said you can draw an inference based on fact is absolutely correct, and the inference that you can draw from the accused admitting that he killed Robin Greene is that there is no other logical inference but that he also decapitated him, dismembered him, mutilated him, washed him, put him back in the bathtub, washed himself and left the room. He stacked the body neatly in the bathtub, eerily looking very much like the photograph that you saw of Mr. Greene alive. He had the wherewithal to change his clothing, to wash his face and to go down and turn himself in. There was a dead body, a chopped-up dead body in his bathtub. You can't walk around that kind of physical evidence. He turned himself in and he admitted that he did, in fact, do the killing.

In the end when you retire to the jury room you will take with you the letters that the accused wrote. I've referred to them. Mr. Brodsky has referred to them time and time again. But when you get into that jury room, you read those letters. You pass them amongst yourselves. You touch them. You feel them. You look at them.

This is a very simple case. You've heard that Mr. Teerhuis is an admitted sadomasochist. He admitted that he likes sex slaves. He admitted that he was an individual to whom sexual activity was vitally important. He admitted all those things. So let's begin with that premise. We're not dealing with the ordinary man. Disabuse your minds of that completely. He likes serial killers and follows their books. Not an ordinary man. Not many people follow serial killing. Not many people respect serial killers and yet you heard Mr. Teerhuis say that he does. Evil.

This particular accused befriended Robin Greene who was, unfortunately, an alcoholic, a homeless man, basically picked him up. He shared liquor with him. He brought him to his room in suite 309, Royal Albert Hotel, performed numerous sex acts on him, stabbed him 68 times, and those stab wounds are on the chest and the neck. If you stab a person in the areas of the vital organs you can anticipate that they will, in fact, either suffer bodily harm or die. Those are the consequences of the actions of this particular accused.

Now the accused disposed of the organs, I agree, and that has to be dealt with. He removed them, not because he was hiding them. I mean there was nothing to hide. How do you hide a corpse that you chop up? This isn't a function of hiding anything. You can't hide a chopped-up dead body unless you have a means of moving it and things of that nature.

The evidence is very fresh in your mind. And remember Mr. Teerhuis on the witness stand. You watched him. You listened to him. You saw his demeanor. He thought of Robin Greene as no more than a piece of disposable meat. He agreed with that suggestion when I put it to him. Evil.

You will also recall the actual evidence in this case. The accused admitted to you that he not only wanted celebrity and notoriety, that he still wants celebrity and notoriety and this is his vehicle to get it. He butchered a man. Evil.

You're right; no sane, sober man would do that. But how could a man be so drunk that he does not remember stabbing another human being 68 times, chopping up his body, mutilating his body, taking out all of his organs, draining his blood, putting him back in the bathtub, cleaning up the room, because he had to have done that. You've heard the evidence, there had to have been a lot of blood there at one point. Well he didn't have a washing machine so the bedding wasn't washed. He tried to wash off the wall, fairly useless. But that's not a function of hiding. He toyed with that body. He says he had sex with that body. And then he washes his face and he goes to the Remand Centre.

The killing was merciless. You heard him say that the last words that Robin Greene said to him were, don't kill me; only words that a killer would hear from the man that he was killing.

In looking at the photographs and the letters one questions how any human being could do something like this to another human being. Mr. Brodsky says his accused was sane, but he says he was drunk. How drunk does a man have to be to be able to do this to another human being? It's incomprehensible. It's incomprehensible that you could do these things and forget that you did them. This isn't a man who passes out at a party drunk and wakes up to find out that he spilled liquor on himself or insulted someone. This is a man who wakes up and realizes that he's chopped another human being into eight pieces and carefully and clinically and surgically. Not the actions of a drunk man.

The evidence against him, the physical evidence, you saw 90 exhibits, is overwhelming. That is, there is no doubt whatsoever that this particular man killed Robin Greene. He's admitted that. I want you to examine the evidence for a moment. As clearly the body is decapitated, dismembered, nowhere, not once does the accused actually deny doing any of these things. Nowhere in his letter to Mr. Zupansky, as Mr. Brodsky anticipated I would say, does he deny that he did any of these things. And ask yourself, why would a man confess to something that he did not do? He wouldn't. It's not reasonable.

In terms of the body itself you will recall that Dr. Littman said that these were the actions of a focused, delineated and methodical person. No drunk, regardless of how well he carries his liquor, could possibly surgically remove parts of that body, cut up pieces of that body, and be so drunk that he didn't realize he did it. You're right he had to have knowledge of anatomy, and this accused does. He's a chef. That's why he's so good at cutting up carcasses.

Dr. Littman said that it would take several hours to cut up this body, two to three hours. That's how long it probably took this accused to chop up Robin Greene. Could you possibly be so drunk that you couldn't remember that?

And let's deal with the issue of memory and the issue of intoxication. Mr. Brodsky says that his client was a seasoned alcoholic. He was. That means that he can handle his liquor better. That's true. That means that he can drink a lot more and perhaps not have the same symptoms that anyone else would have. What we do know about these two men is that while they were drinking together it doesn't mean that they drank equal amounts. There's no evidence about that at all. We do know that the deceased was very, very drunk when he died, to the point where he probably couldn't defend himself. The only evidence that we have about Mr. Teerhuis's state of drunkenness is his own testimony.

In terms of his finding of the body, you heard him say that he spent half an hour in the suite with this decapitated corpse. If it were you and you woke up from an otherwise ordinary evening, as this man would believe or have you believe, you saw this body in the bathtub, you realized that he was not only dead but completely mutilated, would you calmly go to the sink and wash your face two feet away from this corpse? You would only do that if you'd spent the night chopping him up because any reasonable human being who woke up to find that scene, if Mr. Brodsky's correct, run to the nearest phone, run out of that room. Instead he stays in that room. To do what? Figure out what he did? Well if you can't remember, you can't remember. Evil. Who would spend half an hour in a room with that body? For what reason? Who wouldn't run from that sight? Each one of you would.

He can't get around the physical evidence. He's admitted that he killed him and now we have to address his state of drunkenness, or lack thereof. As I said to you, he can't remember those things that are most incriminating, that is, he says he surmised he killed him and yet the inference can be drawn upon his admission that he chopped up the body and did all of those atrocities to that particular body. As I say it's not a lack of memory that he suffers from, it's convenient memory that he suffers from.

The problem with the accused's story about being so drunk that he can't remember what he did is that the evidence is all to the contrary. Not one of the civilian witnesses, that is the police included, say that this man showed any signs of intoxication whatsoever.

You will recall that Dianne Last, who was the last woman who, in fact, saw this accused about an hour before the timing that he put on the killing, 6:20. He put that time on the killing. At 5:30 she sees him in the bar. She serves him liquor. If he were that drunk she probably would not have. She speaks to him. She understands what he wants. She watches him walk. She watches him go get ice. She watches him come back. No slurred speech. No faulty walking. Nothing to speak to impairment. And she would know, she's been a bartender at that hotel for 20 years. She would know a drunk when she saw one.

You will recall the evidence of Mr. Steenson, the guard at the Remand Centre. This accused walks in off the street. He's calm. He says I want to speak to someone. I killed someone. And, again, hours after this killing, there's no smell of liquor on him, no signs of impairment. He's lucid. He's calm. He answers everybody's questions. No signs of impairment.

Much has been made of Mr. Zupansky, and I want to deal with that issue for a moment. Mr. Zupansky, understand, is not on trial. You may not like what he did. You may not agree with what he did, but the reality is he didn't do anything wrong. He, in fact, read about this killing and he contacted the killer. He wanted to write a book. The investigation that my learned friend spoke of, he didn't do any investigation. The murder had already occurred. He couldn't have changed anything about the facts. He couldn't have implicated this accused. He couldn't have exculpated this accused. Everything had already happened. All he was a fact gatherer. No investigation like Mr. Brodsky would have you believe. He couldn't do anything. It was over. He didn't come into contact with this accused till several months after this had happened.

And remember that it was Mr. Teerhuis, despite his hatred for Mr. Zupansky, who contacted Mr. Zupansky. He didn't need to. He didn't have to.

He chose to. And the reason that he chose to is because the only thing of any value is that this man had to sell was the truth. The murder was sensational. It had the garbs of Hollywood. There was a mutilated, dismembered body. Those were the facts. No fiction. Those were the facts. That was sensational enough. No need to embellish. He just told him what he did in the interim with the body when he and the deceased were alone.

I ask you to remember the accused's words, as well, that this killing was his claim to fame. That's what he wrote to Mr. Pomplum. And it was this accused who in fact solicited Mr. Pomplum. Take away everything that Mr. Zupansky said for a moment and we still have this man giving the same information to Tom Pomplum, an American publisher. That publisher didn't solicit him. He wrote to him asking to be published, telling him about the crime. He wanted celebrity and fame and he was going to get it one way or another. He tried to sell the truth to Mr. Pomplum, who was obviously disgusted by it, and so he tried another route. He sold his story to Mr. Zupansky.

The letters were written over a very long period of time, and when you get into the jury room you will have the opportunity to read them and read the detail that is in them. I couldn't read you every line of those letters, nor could Mr. Brodsky. But when you get into that room read those letters for yourselves. No man would confess to the things that were done to Robin Greene unless they were true. No amount of money could persuade any reasonable human being to confess to those atrocities. No degree of fame would persuade any one of you to do what he did.

And when he found out that there was no more value to his story, the law had been passed and Mr. Brodsky says: No, he didn't read the Act. You're right; he probably didn't read the Act. But Mr. Zupansky told him in a letter, and he acknowledged the fact that he knew that there was a law that said he couldn't make any money. So what's he left with? A bunch of letters that he confesses horrendous actions in and no way to get around them.

It's easy to lie. Mr. Teerhuis came into this courtroom and could say virtually anything he chose to say. And what could he say except I made it up? How could he get around it? I made it up. I don't remember. I blacked out. I have no recall.

I'm going to leave you with the accused's words, which are far more telling than anything that I could say. You will recall that Sydney Teerhuis wanted, or characterized this particular matter as a joke on the legal system. Do not let him perpetrate this joke on you. You're the jury in this case. You're the finders of fact. Convict him of murder. When you look at those letters where he's laughing about the fact that he killed Robin Greene, think about the jokes that he wants to perpetrate on you. When he jokes about body parts and slicing them open, think about the joke he will perpetrate if he's not convicted of murder.

You, as jurors, have to return a true verdict based on the evidence and there is certainly enough evidence before you to convict this man of murder, and I ask that you do.

THE COURT: Thank you, Ms. Leinburd. Ladies and gentlemen, as I said to you yesterday, I'm going to be bringing you back, not tomorrow, but on Monday morning at ten o'clock and I'll have my opportunity to instruct you, as a trial judge does in this case, on the law, and it's on that basis that you'll begin your deliberations sometime on Monday. All right. So we'll see you back on Monday morning for ten o'clock. Have a good weekend.

24

The Judge Address the Jury

DECEMBER 15/08

(PROCEEDINGS CONTINUED FROM DECEMBER 12/08)

I will explain what Crown counsel must prove beyond a reasonable doubt, to establish the guilt of Mr. Teerhuis-Moar. I'll also tell you about the other issues that arise on the evidence you have heard in this case.

Then I will discuss the issues that you need to decide and then review for you the evidence that relates to those issues. By doing this I hope I can help you recall the evidence and understand how it relates to the issues that you will be asked to decide.

You must always keep in mind, however, that to decide this case you rely on what you remember the evidence was, not what counsel or I say it was.

After that I will briefly summarize the positions that counsel have put forward in their closing addresses.

As judges of the fact your first duty is to decide what are the facts in this case.

The deciding of the facts is your job, it is not mine, it is not counsels. Our law does permit me to express and comment upon issues of fact. If I do that, however, you do not have to agree with me. You, not I, decide what happened in this case.

The evidence does not have to answer every question raised in this case. You may think it would be an unusual case in which a jury could say--we know everything there is to know about this case. You only have to decide those matters that are essential for you to say whether the charge has been proven beyond a reasonable doubt.

If I make a mistake about the law, justice can still be done in this case. The court clerk/monitor records everything I say. The Court of Appeal can correct my mistakes. But justice will not be done if you wrongly apply the law. Your decisions are secret. You do not give reasons. No one keeps a record of your discussions for the Court of Appeal to review. As a result, it is very important that you accept the law from me and follow it without question.

To return an effective verdict in this case requires that all of you agree on your decision. A verdict, whether of guilty or not guilty, is the unanimous opinion of the whole jury.

Mr. Teerhuis-Moar also testified about his letter to Mr. Tom Pomplum and his contact and correspondence with Danny Zupansky. Mr. Teerhuis-

Moar maintained that the descriptions and depictions provided to Mr. Pomplum and Mr. Zupansky were fabricated. Mr. Teerhuis-Moar testified that in reality he couldn't recall what happened after he blacked out. In your assessment of Mr. Teerhuis-Moar's evidence, as with all witnesses, you will consider, of course, the arguments of both the Crown and the defence respecting Mr. Teerhuis-Moar's credibility and reliability. As with any witness you may believe some, none or all of Mr. Teerhuis-Moar's testimony. It is for you to decide. Whatever your assessment, you must not forget that the burden of proof always remains with the Crown to prove beyond a reasonable doubt the essential elements of this charge, second degree murder. As I will remind you later, because of certain admissions the one essential element the Crown must still prove in this case is that Mr. Teerhuis-Moar had the necessary state of mind at the time of the killing to commit second-degree murder. Accordingly, if you believe Mr. Teerhuis-Moar's evidence that he did not have the state of mind for second-degree murder, then you must find him not guilty of second-degree murder. You will then find him guilty of manslaughter. If you believe Mr. Teerhuis-Moar's evidence, if it leaves you with a reasonable doubt that he had the state of mind necessary for second-degree murder, you must find him not guilty of second-degree murder and guilty of manslaughter.

As part of the exhibits in this case you will recall Exhibits 59 through to and including Exhibit 73. Those exhibits, ladies and gentlemen of the jury, encompass the letters that were sent by Mr. Teerhuis-Moar to Mr. Zupansky and the one letter sent to Mr. Pomplum. Exhibits 74 to 77 are letters sent by Mr. Zupansky to Mr. Teerhuis-Moar.

Now, as exhibits all of those letters are available for your examination and consideration. I must, however, give specific instructions concerning how those letters written by Mr. Teerhuis-Moar can be considered and how, if at all, they are to be used. I will do so in a few moments.

As I said at the beginning of this trial, the exhibits go with you to the jury room. You may but do not have to examine all of them. In the case of the letters, an examination of them is not only advisable but in my view necessary in your determination as to their truth and reliability.

Now, let me move to what I mentioned a moment ago, admissions.

I'll deal with one more section and we'll take a break: the testimony of Danny Zupansky.

Mr. Zupansky testified for the Crown. There is a special instruction that has to do with his evidence. It is an instruction that you must keep foremost in your mind when you are considering how much or little you believe of or rely upon his evidence in making your decision in this case.

You will recall that he gave evidence in respect of his contact with Mr. Teerhuis-Moar, both their telephone contact and their correspondence.

Now, in the circumstances of his correspondence with Mr. Teerhuis-Moar, Mr. Zupansky acknowledges that he wanted to use the book project to establish himself as a non-fiction book writer and in that regard he saw Mr. Teerhuis-Moar's case in 2004 as an opportunity to begin working in earnest.

Mr. Zupansky testified that, that if the book project made money, he would receive his share after the 30 percent went to Mr. Teerhuis-Moar, as promised.

Common sense tells you that in light of these circumstances, there is good reason to look at Mr. Zupansky's evidence with the greatest care and caution. You are entitled, however, to rely on Mr. Zupansky's evidence even if it is not confirmed by another witness or other evidence, but it might be unsafe for you to do so. Accordingly, you should look for some confirmation of Mr. Zupansky's evidence from somebody or something other than Mr. Zupansky before you rely upon his evidence in deciding whether Crown counsel has proven the case against Mr. Teerhuis-Moar beyond a reasonable doubt. To be confirmatory, the testimony of another witness or witnesses or other evidence should help restore your faith in relevant parts of Mr. Zupansky's testimony or evidence.

Mr. Zupansky and the circumstances in which he testified might well make you wish that somebody or something else confirmed what Mr. Zupansky said. You may believe Mr. Zupansky's testimony, however, if you find it trustworthy, even if no one else or nothing else confirms it. When you do consider it, however, keep in mind who gave the evidence and the circumstances under which Mr. Zupansky testified.

You will find that there is some evidence in this case that confirms or supports parts of Mr. Zupansky's testimony. It is for you, however, to say how much of that evidence is confirmatory and what parts of his testimony are confirmed or supported. It is also for you to determine how any such confirmatory evidence affects whether or how much you will believe of or rely upon his testimony in deciding this case.

The evidence to which I'm about to refer illustrates the kind of evidence that you may find confirms or supports Mr. Zupansky's testimony. It may help you, it may not. It is for you to decide.

Given that what Mr. Zupansky testified to relates to his correspondence with Mr. Teerhuis-Moar, you will find that some independent support for some important parts of what Mr. Zupansky testifies to can be found in the hard and real physical evidence that are the letters in Exhibits 60 to 77. In other words, the very fact of the existence of those letters may support some of what Mr. Zupansky tells you. There, in black and white, in Exhibits 60 to 77, are the words he, Mr. Zupansky, wrote and the words the accused, Mr. Teerhuis-Moar, wrote. It will be, as I will explain shortly, for you to decide whether some, none or all of what Mr. Teerhuis-Moar wrote in those letters was true or, rather, as the defence suggests, fabricated and/or embellished. Indeed, Mr. Zupansky candidly acknowledges that despite his requests of Mr. Teerhuis-Moar to keep it factual and to keep it real, Mr. Zupansky cannot say what in Mr. Teerhuis-Moar's letters is fact and what is fiction. However, insofar as those letters do exist, their very existence represents potentially confirmatory evidence for some of what Mr. Zupansky says in his testimony.

While the existence of the letters may confirm or restore your faith in material parts of Mr. Zupansky's testimony, remember, until you determine that some, none or all parts of the letters are true, those parts so determined, can't be used for the distinct purpose of deciding Mr. Teerhuis-Moar's guilt.

My mention of the letters is meant to be illustrative and not exhaustive of potentially confirmatory evidence for some of what Mr. Zupansky has said. It will be for you to decide whether there is such independent evidence and whether it confirms or supports Mr. Zupansky's testimony. I repeat, such evidence may help you it may not. It is for you to say.

Anything you find Mr. Teerhuis-Moar said, however, is only part of the evidence in this case. You should consider it along with and in the same way as all of the other evidence.

367

Now, let me deal with the letters written by Mr. Sydney Teerhuis-Moar. I'll deal with them as promised and provide you the instructions. We are, of course, talking about the letters marked as Exhibits 59 through to and including 73. Some of those letters may encompass as well, the letters written to Mr. Teerhuis-Moar from Mr. Zupansky. I'll talk about context and the circumstances of the correspondence in a moment.

But you will recall that those letters consist of what the Crown alleges are true depictions, details and diagrams respecting what were the horrific events of July 1st, 2003.

The Crown contends that these letters are declarations or admissions by Mr. Teerhuis-Moar. The Crown says that not only did Mr. Teerhuis-Moar write those letters and draw the diagrams, but also that the letters and diagrams are true descriptions and depictions of what actually happened as recalled and provided by the very person who committed the acts described.

Mr. Teerhuis-Moar admits to writing the letters but says that the so-called recollections, descriptions, details and diagrams were fabricated, embellished, made up. Mr. Teerhuis-Moar says that in reality he was blacked out at the time of the killing. He says that the contents and the details of the letters were fabricated or embellished for the purpose of encouraging and assisting a book deal, with the accompanying notoriety and financial gain that Mr. Teerhuis-Moar hoped would come to him. And Mr. Teerhuis-Moar testified that in providing the details he did, he was trying to make the story more interesting and at the same time he was giving Mr. Zupansky what he wanted to hear. Mr. Teerhuis-Moar contends that to provide those details and create those diagrams he used his observations on the morning of July 2nd, 2003 and the information and photographs, which he received as normal disclosure from the Crown for the preparation of his defence. According to Mr. Teerhuis-Moar, that information was the basis or reference for the details he made up about the killing.

In determining whether or not you can rely upon Mr. Teerhuis-Moar's letters to Mr. Zupansky and Mr. Pomplum as a true depiction of what Mr. Teerhuis-Moar actually did and remembered from July 1st, 2003, you must look at all of the evidence. It is for you to decide whether some, none or all of the supposed recollections, descriptions, details and diagrams in the letters are true, as remembered by Mr. Teerhuis-Moar.

To determine whether you rely upon some, none or all of the contents of the letters as truthful, you must consider the circumstances and context in which the letters were written.

Mr. Teerhuis-Moar's letter to Mr. Pomplum, for example, was unsolicited. You will remember that it was Mr. Pomplum's impression that Mr. Teerhuis-Moar wanted Mr. Pomplum to publish those or other of Mr. Teerhuis-Moar's cartoons. You may wish to consider that notwithstanding that Mr. Teerhuis-Moar's letter of September 7, 2004 was unsolicited and was his one and only contact with Mr. Pomplum, the contents of that letter contained many of the same grisly details that were included in parts of Mr. Teerhuis-Moar's letter or letters to Mr. Zupansky. In the context and circumstances of his first and only letter to Mr. Pomplum, the publisher of a series of book adaptations of classic literature, did Mr. Teerhuis-Moar have a logical motive to embellish, fabricate and tell Mr. Pomplum what he thought he wanted to hear? Was his purpose as he said it, was respecting his correspondence with Mr. Zupansky, the pursuit of a book deal? In his cross-examination Mr. Teerhuis-Moar himself seemed unsure why he wrote to Mr. Pomplum.

The letters written to Mr. Zupansky were part of a correspondence wherein both Mr. Zupansky and Mr. Teerhuis-Moar seemed interested in a book and documentary film project.

When examining the circumstances of the correspondence, what Mr. Zupansky writes in such correspondence may help you figure out what Mr. Teerhuis-Moar meant. It may also be used as part of the context for the written assertions of Mr. Teerhuis-Moar that you must assess for their reliability and truthfulness. But remember, Mr. Teerhuis-Moar can be held responsible only for what he actually wrote, assuming that it is true, and not for what anyone else says.

What another person writes may provide a context for understanding and assessing what Mr. Teerhuis-Moar has written but only Mr. Teerhuis-Moar's words, as understood in that context, if found to be true, are evidence of what Mr. Teerhuis-Moar has done or intended to do.

In determining whether or not some, none or all of the contents of the letters can be relied upon as true accounts of what Mr. Teerhuis-Moar did or intended to do, you should examine all of the evidence. In examining all of the evidence you should specifically look for evidence that might either support or rebut the Crown's suggestion that the contents of the letters can be relied upon as truthful recollections, descriptions and depictions of what Mr. Teerhuis-Moar actually did and intended to do on July 1st, 2003.

In determining whether the letters can, in fact, be relied upon as a truthful recollection, description and depiction of what Mr. Teerhuis-Moar did and intended to do on July 1st, 2003, you will consider the evidence of Mr. Teerhuis-Moar.

As I have already mentioned, insofar as he admits to writing the letters, he tells you that they were made up and fabricated. Mr. Teerhuis-Moar says that the fabricated details he provided were fabricated to enhance his story in order to secure the book deal that would give him the fame and financial gain he was seeking. Mr. Teerhuis-Moar testified that in writing those letters and providing what he says were fabricated details, he used his observations of the room after he awoke on July 2nd, 2003 and the information, the photographs and the general disclosure he would have received from the Crown to prepare his defence. He says that all of this made the fabricated descriptions and depictions more realistic and seemingly accurate.

Now, you will note that at one point in his correspondence with Mr. Zupansky, Mr. Teerhuis-Moar says that everything that he had previously written was false. He suggested to Mr. Zupansky that if Mr. Zupansky insisted on publishing the details that Mr. Teerhuis-Moar had earlier provided, he, Mr. Zupansky, would look like a fool.

When you consider Mr. Teerhuis-Moar's sudden change of position, whereby he suggests that the earlier descriptions, details and diagrams were false, you might consider the timing of that change. According to Mr. Zupansky's testimony, Mr. Teerhuis-Moar's claims about the fabricated nature of his letters occurred very shortly after being advised of the new Canadian law called the Profits of Criminal Notoriety Act. Simply put, it was a law that would prevent individuals from profiting from their own bad doing. Mr. Zupansky testified that he advised Mr. Teerhuis-Moar of the new law in a telephone conversation he had with him. Upon receiving that information, Mr. Teerhuis-Moar immediately hung up and subsequently sent a letter to Mr. Zupansky. Mr. Zupansky testified that Mr. Teerhuis-Moar accused him of trying to cheat him. It was at that point that Mr. Teerhuis-Moar expressed his retraction, saying that all that he had provided was fabricated or untrue. Mr. Teerhuis-Moar made no further contact with Mr. Zupansky.

As part of your determination as to whether the letters can be relied upon as truthful recollections, descriptions and depictions of what Mr. Teerhuis-Moar did or intended to do on July 1st, 2003, you might also consider the evidence of Mr. Pomplum.

Mr. Pomplum told you that he's the publisher of a series of book adaptations of classic literature. Those adaptations, says Mr. Pomplum, are typically accompanied by, by cartoon images.

According to Mr. Pomplum's testimony, some of the details in the unsolicited letter by Mr. Teerhuis-Moar seemed to be consistent with the facts of the case as he came to know them. However, Mr. Pomplum acknowledges that such information that was contained in the one letter he received from Mr. Teerhuis-Moar was information that Mr. Pomplum believed was available when he, Mr. Pomplum, first consulted the Internet shortly after receiving Mr. Teerhuis-Moar's letter. For example, Mr. Pomplum testified that the details about the missing organs and jewelry was information available on the Internet.

In determining whether the letters can be relied upon as truthful depictions and descriptions of what Mr. Teerhuis-Moar did and intended to do on July 1st, 2003, you might also consider the evidence of Constable McLean.

In his capacity as an officer with the identification unit, Constable McLean attended and observed Mr. Teerhuis-Moar's room in a fairly thorough manner. When presented with some of the details in the letters, Constable McLean acknowledged that some of his observations were, indeed, consistent with some of the details and descriptions provided by Mr. Teerhuis-Moar.

For example, Constable McLean observed, as the police photographs demonstrate, that the body parts were chopped up and positioned neatly in the bathtub as described by Mr. Teerhuis-Moar's letter.

Constable McLean's evidence would also seem to confirm Mr. Teerhuis-Moar's assertion in the letters that Mr. Green's organs were disposed of. In that regard Constable McLean testified that from his knowledge and observation at the scene, despite the efforts of fellow officers, the organs were never found.

Constable McLean's evidence confirms that consistent with some of the clean-up described in the letters, there was, despite the chopped up body parts, little evidence of blood in the bathtub at Mr. Teerhuis-Moar's room.

Constable McLean also commented that the big and small knives depicted in the diagram correspond accurately to the big and small knives found at the scene.

Some of the points that I just mentioned coming from Constable McLean could support an inference that the person who wrote those letters, Mr. Teerhuis-Moar, did indeed have knowledge and a memory of what happened on July 1st, 2003. On that basis you might conclude, therefore, that the details provided can be relied upon as true and sincerely recalled. That is one conclusion.

However, based on the evidence of Mr. Teerhuis-Moar, you must also ask yourselves: Did the details provided in the letters come not from Mr. Teerhuis-Moar's own memory but instead from his own observations during the one-half hour in his room on July 2nd, 2003 and the information he was able to obtain and discern, the information he was able to obtain and discern from police photographs and police reports provided to Mr. Teerhuis-Moar by the Crown during the period he was preparing his defence?

It will be for you to decide whether such details could be obtained and embellished from his own observations on July 2nd, 2003 and the information that Mr. Teerhuis-Moar received to prepare his defence.

It should also be noted that while there are details in the letters that are consistent with the observations of Constable McLean, there are other details in the letters, which are inconsistent or cannot be clearly confirmed or supported by his observations. It is for you to decide whether any such inconsistent or non-supported details are suggestive of fabrication or embellishment.

For example, notwithstanding the depiction in one of the diagrams, Constable McLean did not believe from his observations that a body could be hung from either a ceiling pipe or, for that matter, from anything else in the bathroom area.

Similarly, according to Constable McLean's observations, unlike the descriptions in the letter, there were no obvious marks in the carpet consistent with a body being dragged from the bedroom to the bathroom.

In your considerations as to whether the letters can be relied upon as truthful depictions/descriptions of what Mr. Teerhuis-Moar did or intended to do on July 1st, 2003, you may also look at the evidence of Sergeant Ellis.

You recall that Sergeant Ellis did state that the bloodstains on the bed in Mr. Teerhuis-Moar's room were consistent with the actions depicted in the diagram in Exhibit 64. That diagram depicts an individual straddling a victim who is being stabbed as he lay on, on his back on a bed.

Sergeant Ellis also testified that there was in the doorjamb or door frame area blood staining that could be consistent with contact from a bloody body being dragged in the bathroom, in the bathroom as described in one of Mr. Teerhuis-Moar's letters.

When examining the bloodstains in the bathroom area Sergeant Ellis noted that the bloodstains were consistent with decapitation occurring somewhere in the bathroom, as was described in one of the letters.

Sergeant Ellis testified that he observed evidence of diluted stains, which would have been consistent with a clean up or an attempt to remove blood as was described in one of Mr. Teerhuis-Moar's letters.

Sergeant Ellis further noted that in photograph 19 there was a pool stain consistent with the actions depicted in the diagram found in Exhibit 64.

It should be noted, however, that in cross-examination Sergeant Ellis acknowledged that the photographs on which he was basing his analysis could have been used by Mr. Teerhuis-Moar to create the details and the depictions in the letters and diagrams.

Furthermore, despite the details included in the letters, Sergeant Ellis found no evidence of blood staining to support an assertion that Mr. Greene's torso was placed on the dresser in the manner described in the letters. You may find such testimony from Sergeant Ellis as supportive evidence of the sort of embellishment testified to by Mr. Teerhuis-Moar.

Despite the assertion in Mr. Teerhuis-Moar's letters, Sergeant Ellis also acknowledges that the blood staining that he had observed cannot provide confirmation that the dismembering of the body took place in the bathroom.

It is worth noting that Sergeant Ellis acknowledged that his analysis of the blood staining in this particular case could neither prove nor disprove the truthfulness of the descriptions and depictions in the letters.

Also, in determining whether Mr. Teerhuis-Moar's letters can be relied upon as truthful depictions of what he did and intended to do on July 1st, 2003, you might consider the evidence of Dr. Littman, the forensic pathologist who, as you heard, performed the autopsy.

Dr. Littman's evidence suggested that his observations of the manner in which parts of Mr. Green's body were excised or dissected was consistent with some of the descriptions in Mr. Teerhuis-Moar's letters. Moreover, the list of organs that Dr. Littman noted as missing more or less corresponded to those listed by Mr. Teerhuis-Moar in one of his letters.

When confronted with portions of Mr. Teerhuis-Moar's letters wherein some of the detailed descriptions included the smell, feel and texture of Mr. Green's body and organs, Dr. Littman acknowledged that those detailed descriptions were accurate and plausible.

Corresponding to what Mr. Teerhuis-Moar wrote in the letter at Exhibit 64, Dr. Littman testified that the body appeared to have been washed. In your considerations of whether Mr. Teerhuis-Moar's descriptions and depictions were fabricated, you might ask: Was this a detail that Mr. Teerhuis-Moar could have obtained from the photographs, the reports or his observations after he awoke on July 2nd, 2003?

Dr. Littman did accept in cross-examination that it might be that some of the descriptions contained in the letters respecting body parts and/or organs are common to all mammals. Accordingly, some of the details contained in the letters may have come from a chef's past observations and experience with, for example, the cutting and preparation of animals to be cooked in a restaurant.

Similarly, Dr. Littman acknowledged that some of the descriptions of the injuries could come from a person's review or observations of the autopsy photographs.

So, ladies and gentlemen, concerning the written letters of Mr. Teerhuis-Moar, let me summarize. To determine whether some, none or all of what Mr. Teerhuis-Moar wrote in his letters to either Mr. Zupansky or Mr. Pomplum are truthful recollections, descriptions and depictions of what he did on July 1st, 2003, you will consider all of the evidence presented at this trial, including the testimony and letters of Mr. Teerhuis-Moar and Mr. Zupansky and the testimony of Mr. Pomplum. Consider, as well, the circumstances of the correspondence, the context of each letter and their contents. You should also consider any evidence, which might potentially support or rebut the Crown claim that the letters' contents were truthful and reliable recollections by the man who killed Mr. Greene.

Let me say something very quickly about motive. Motive is a reason why somebody does something. It is not one of the essential, one of the essential elements that Crown must prove in a case such as this.

Now, in the context of my instruction to you about the state of mind required for murder, I will tell you that if you determine that some or all of the portions of those letters can be relied upon as true descriptions and depictions of what Mr. Teerhuis-Moar did or intended to do on July 1st, 2003, you then may consider those letters to determine whether Mr. Teerhuis-Moar had the necessary intent or state of mind for murder. In that regard you might wish to consider the precision and detail represented by the recollections in those letters. From such precision and detailed recollection you may, but are not required to, draw an inference about what Mr. Teerhuis-Moar actually remembered and his state of mind at the relevant time.

Let me return to the matter of Mr. Teerhuis-Moar blacking out.

You obviously must consider all of Mr. Teerhuis-Moar's testimony, including his testimony about blacking out. Remember, however, that on the evidence at this trial, there is nothing that enables you to assume that a person who has blacked out cannot, nonetheless, possess the state of mind required for murder.

I remind you that it is up to you to determine whether Mr. Teerhuis-Moar blacked out as he described. Remember, as well, if you find that Mr. Teerhuis-Moar did black out as he testified, that the fact that he may have blacked out, is just one of the factors that can be considered as evidence that might throw light on the level of Mr. Teerhuis-Moar's impairment and its effects on his state of mind at the time of the killing.

The fact that Mr. Teerhuis-Moar may have blacked out, if you so find, does not by itself mean that he did not have the necessary intent or state of mind to commit murder.

Let me also address Mr. Teerhuis-Moar's absence of memory between the time he lay down on the bed with Mr. Green on July 1st, 2003 and his waking up the next morning, on July 2nd, 2003.

On the evidence before you, you cannot assume that the absence of memory equates with the absence of intent. The fact that Mr. Teerhuis-Moar may not remember what he did after he blacked out and before he awoke, does not, by itself, mean that he did not have the state of mind to commit murder at the relevant time. Again, remember it is for you to determine whether Mr. Teerhuis-Moar has, in fact, no memory of what happened. If you determine that, indeed, he cannot remember, the absence of such memory is, again, but one factor that can be considered in assessing Mr. Teerhuis-Moar's level of impairment by drug and alcohol and its effects on his state of mind at the relevant time.

Let's first of all deal with the Crown.

The Crown submits that Mr. Teerhuis-Moar befriended the deceased, Mr. Greene, solicited sex from him, plied him with liquor and then killed him.

The Crown submits that the letters written by Mr. Teerhuis-Moar that are evidence in this trial are true recollections, descriptions and depictions of what Mr. Teerhuis-Moar did to Mr. Greene. From those letters the Crown submits that you can obtain assistance in inferring the necessary state of mind required for second-degree murder.

The Crown contends that Mr. Teerhuis-Moar was not intoxicated when he killed Mr. Greene.

The Crown argues that it has proven its case beyond a reasonable doubt and, therefore, requests that you return a verdict of guilty on the charge of second-degree murder.

Let me deal with the defence.

The defence submits that Mr. Teerhuis-Moar, a chronic alcoholic, met Mr. Greene and spent the day with him drinking in one establishment after another, until he became totally intoxicated.

The defence reminds you that Mr. Green passed out in the bed with an alcohol reading of .296. Shortly thereafter Mr. Teerhuis-Moar himself blacked out.

When Mr. Teerhuis-Moar awoke, he found the dismembered body of Mr. Greene in the bathtub.

The defence submits that as no one else was there at the time of the killing or at the time he blacked out, Mr. Teerhuis-Moar assumed what he must have done and reported to the police that he was the killer.

The defence contends that during his pre-trial detention he played with the media, including Mr. Zupansky, building on the facts of his case based upon his own observations of what he found during the 30 minutes in his room on July 2nd, 2003 and based also on what was disclosed by the autopsy reports, the police reports and the photographs of the crime scene and body.

The defence reminds you that he did not try to blame someone else or claim self-defence. The defence also reminds you that he admitted his responsibility to the police as he has admitted his responsibility through his admissions that were earlier communicated to you, the members of the jury.

The defence argues that the Crown has not established Mr. Teerhuis-Moar's guilt beyond a reasonable doubt. The defence requests that you return a verdict of not guilty on the charge of second-degree murder and instead a verdict of guilty on the offence of manslaughter.

The defence does not believe the Crown has established beyond a reasonable doubt the state of mind necessary for second-degree murder.

I have already indicated to you that I think it's important, extremely important, that you examine the letters for the purpose of the determinations that you have to make about them.

Ladies and gentlemen, you have taken an oath or made a solemn affirmation to well and truly try this case and to render a true verdict according to the evidence. If you honor that oath or affirmation, as I am sure you will, you will have done everything that is expected of you as jurors in this trial. We ask for nothing more and as I said earlier on, we expect nothing else.

25

The Jury's Decision

DECEMBER 16/08

(PROCEEDINGS CONTINUED FROM DECEMBER 15/08)

THE CLERK: Court is open. You may be seated. My Lord, the jury has reached a verdict.

THE COURT: Thank you. Would you bring the jury in, please?

(JURY IN AT 10:48 A.M.)

THE CLERK: My Lord, all 12 jurors are present. Can you please stand? Members of the jury, have you agreed on your verdict and if so, who shall speak for you?

THE FOREPERSON: I will. And we have.

THE CLERK: And you have? Thank you.

THE CLERK: How say you. Do you find the accused Sydney Teerhuis-Moar guilty or not guilty of Count 1?

THE FOREPERSON: Guilty as charged.

THE COURT: Ladies and gentlemen, I have just one further task for you, you'll be perhaps happy or unhappy to hear, but it is a task that you must at least try to perform if it, if it is something that you choose to.

You have found the accused guilty of second-degree murder and the law requires that I now sentence him to life in prison. The law also states that he must serve a minimum of 10 years in prison. That's before he can apply for parole. But, that I, as the judge, can increase that minimum period of parole ineligibility of 10 years to a maximum of 25 years.

Before I make that decision, I am required to provide you, with an opportunity to consult in private and make a recommendation to me. Please listen carefully to this instruction.

You have found the accused guilty of second-degree murder and the law requires that I now pronounce a sentence of imprisonment for life against the accused, Mr. Teerhuis. Do you wish to make any recommendation with respect to the number of years that the accused must serve before the accused is eligible for release on parole? You are not required to make any recommendation but if you do your recommendation will be considered by me when I am determining whether I should substitute for the 10-year period, which the law would otherwise require you to serve when you're convicted of second-degree murder prior to release. So, it's between 10 years and 25. You're not required to make a recommendation if you choose not to make one.

I'm therefore asking you to return to the jury room once more and consider whether you would like to make any recommendation on the period of time during which Mr. Teerhuis cannot apply for parole, keeping in mind that the minimum period is 10 years and the maximum period is 25 years.

If you do not wish to make any recommendation, then it is your right to indicate that. You do not have to be unanimous in your recommendation. Once you have returned and your foreperson has given me your answer, you'll be free to leave, all right?

So, I'll ask you retire for however long you wish and you can indicate to me what it is you wish to do by again passing the usher a note and I'll be called back along with counsel, okay? Thank you very much.

(JURY OUT AT 10:51 A.M.)

THE COURT: Okay.
THE CLERK: Order. All rise. This court is in recess.

(BRIEF RECESS)

THE CLERK: This court is re-opened. Please be seated.
THE COURT: Okay, thank you.

(JURY IN AT 11:15 A.M.)

THE CLERK: My Lord, all 12 jurors are present.
THE COURT: Thank you very much. Mr. Foreperson?
THE FOREPERSON: My Lord, we're split. We have a seven/five decision, seven recommending 25 years and five with no recommendation.
THE COURT: All right. Thank you very much. Thank you very much. Before you're excused, ladies and gentlemen, I want to just make a few brief comments to you, if I might. .

To begin with, I have to remind you that, I think, at the outset of this trial, that you can't disclose, obviously, to anyone information about the nature of the discussions and deliberations that you have had in the privacy of the jury room. You know that. I don't think I have to insult your intelligence by telling you that again. I've repeated that a few times.

You will recall, also, that I pointed out to you that this is a concept that's so important that it's actually been enshrined in the Criminal Code and it makes any disclosure of the deliberations, the discussions you had, a criminal offence. Nothing that went on in the jury room is to be disclosed now or at any future time. I ask you to remember that whatever opinions may have been expressed in the jury room and however much your views or the views of any member of the jury may have changed during the course of your deliberations, nothing that went on in the jury room is to be disclosed. The verdict announced by your foreperson should be the last comments about your deliberation as a jury.

Second of all I want to thank you very, very much again on behalf of counsel. You've played an essential role, obviously, in this trial. It's been a difficult trial for you I can appreciate. Your fellow citizens, I know, are appreciative even if they're not always conscious of what jury duty is and what it means. It has resulted, obviously, in your expending time and money indirectly, and all of that is appreciated by everybody involved.

It brings with it, jury duty does, a level of inconvenience, expense and disruption to your normal lives. No one knows that better than a trial judge looking at jurors who are plucked from their ordinary lives and suddenly thrown into a courtroom, having to make very important decisions. Nonetheless, it's an important function and it's an important duty for all citizens and it really is a fundamental part of how our system works. So,

376

again I thank you very much on behalf of myself and on behalf of counsel.

I sincerely hope, as well, that the experience for you has been interesting and worthwhile.

I would also, before we finish, commend all counsel for the professional manner in which they performed their respective duties. They obviously are critical to this system. They make my job easier and they make the decisions that we have possible.

One last reminder: If it's necessary, please leave your notes with the sheriff's officer for shredding and destruction if there are notes taken.

This now completes your duties as jurors in this case and you are now formally and officially discharged. Once again I thank you for your time, for your consideration on my behalf, on counsel's behalf, and on behalf of all members of our community. You are now free to go. Thank you very much.

(JURY OUT AT 11:19 A.M.)

THE COURT: Ms. Leinburd?

MS. LEINBURD: I'm wondering if we can sentence this accused on December the 18th.

THE COURT: That's...

MS. LEINBURD: Thursday morning.

THE COURT: Tomorrow. Tomorrow morning?

MS. LEINBURD: No, today's Tuesday. Isn't it Tuesday?

MR. BRODSKY: I thought we were talking about Friday?

MS. LEINBURD: If you want it on Friday, that's fine. I have no objection.

THE COURT: What, what are we today? Sorry.

THE CLERK: Tuesday.

MS. LEINBURD: Tuesday.

THE COURT: No, but what...

MS. LEINBURD: Oh, the 16th?

THE COURT: Tuesday must be...

MR. BRODSKY: This is a little presumptuous, My Lord. I take it Your Lordship is not going to be sentencing today?

THE COURT: I'm in your hands.

MS. LEINBURD: If you want the 19th, that's fine, Mr. Brodsky. I have...

THE COURT: I, I just...

MR. BRODSKY: I'm fine with the 19th.

THE COURT: I just have to make sure that technically I'm available but, so, the 19th is Friday or...

MR. BRODSKY: Yeah, the 19th is Friday.

THE CLERK: What time, My Lord?

THE COURT: Time?

MS. LEINBURD: Ten o'clock?

MR. BRODSKY: Sure. Any time.

THE COURT: Ten o'clock? Sure, okay.

THE CLERK: Yes, you're available.

THE COURT: Okay.

THE CLERK: Make sure it's in this courtroom. It will be in this courtroom, My Lord.

THE COURT: So, that's fine with you, Mr. Brodsky?

MR. BRODSKY: Yes.

THE COURT: Okay. Thank you very much. Good morning.

MS. LEINBURD: Thank you. Good morning.

MR. BRODSKY: My Lord.

THE CLERK: Order. All rise. This court is adjourned.

26

The Sentencing

DECEMBER 20/08

O N THE FRONT PAGE OF THE SUN TODAY WAS SIDNEY'S SMILING FACE AND the headline: **Sex-murderer gets maximum sentence** by Dean Pritchard. The news piece began with the announcement that Sidney Teerhuis had been proven guilty of second-degree murder and sentenced to life in prison with no possibility of parole for 25 years, the maximum sentence in Canadian law.

There followed a reiteration of the basic, gory facts taken from the previous stories that had appeared in the paper since December 1st.

Judge Joyal disagreed with Brodsky's assertion that Sidney should not be given the same sentence as if he were convicted of first-degree murder; saying, "*Teerhuis-Moar showed a shocking lack of remorse for his crime and needs to be separated from society for as long as possible.*"

Judge Joyal stated that the letters may have contained certain 'embellishments' but he believed Sidney's account of the murder and the mutilation of Greene's body.

"*If there is a set of facts underpinning an offence of second-degree murder where the brutality is more gruesome than the case I heard, I have no shame in saying that my imagination is not yet capable of conceiving it,*" Joyal said.

"*When these acts are considered with his letters, they suggest frightening connections between murder and sexual pleasure and violence and self-aggrandizement,*" he said. "*The very existence of those letters and the accused's desire for a book deal and film agreement reveal not only his attempts at self-promotion for financial gain and profit, but also a shocking lack of remorse.*"

Robin Greene's sister Janice, cried as she explained how Robin's murder had 'scarred' her for life. She said Robin had come to Winnipeg to visit her, but instead met up with Sidney Teerhuis.

"*I felt bad enough, until I heard the gory details of his demise,*" she said. "*I was never to be the same again. I fell apart... His death made me question life, my creator, my spiritual being.*"

Sidney when asked if he wished to say anything merely stated, "*No.*"

The Free Press ran with the headline: **25 years for Winnipeg dismemberment killer**.

The paper called the murder, "*one of the grisliest slayings in Manitoba history*" and stated that Sidney's sentence also had been historic; being the first time a killer had received 25 to life for second-degree murder in the province.

Members of the victim's family traveled from Shoal Lake, Ontario to attend the trial. Robin Greene Sr. said it's been hard re-living his son's murder with the news coverage of the trial.

Several of the jurors were present in court and embraced members of Robin Greene's family after the sentence had been handed down.

Sheila Leinburd said, "*It's rare we have the opportunity to see into the mind of a cold-blooded killer.*"

Brodsky stated, "*The most horrible part of this case is what happened after death,*" claiming there is no evidence his client poses an ongoing danger to the public.

Epilogue

I HAVE MADE EVERY ATTEMPT TO 'show' and not 'tell' with this book. However if you were to go back to bartender Dianne Last at trial—she testified that Sidney had been in the bar for a drink at 2:30 p.m. Robin Greene was upstairs sleeping. Greene awoke and the two left the hotel and returned at 5:30 where Dianne saw them both. For some reason Sidney had told police and myself that he had been in the bar around 5:30 for a drink while Robin slept. Despite Dianne's testimony the Crown Attorney, Brodsky and the Judge didn't notice that during subsequent days of testimony they had all lost track of the actual sequence of events and reverted to Sidney's account instead.

Figure 30: March 2009, Victoria, B.C.—Dan Zupansky, a few months after the trial of Sidney Teerhuis.

Sheila Leinburd questioned Sidney as to why he wrote Tom Pomplum letters describing Robin Greene's murder in September 2003 shortly after his July 2nd arrest. She was trying to make the point that despite Sidney's claim that he had provided me the gory details because 'that is what I wanted,' he had no answer for why he would have contacted Pomplum and provided some of the same details, even before I came into the picture. Sidney couldn't answer the question. The order of events was wrong. I did not contact the Crown with my information till March of 2005, however I began corresponding with Sidney in March 2004. Pomplum received a single letter in September of 2004, not September 2003.

Sidney claimed that he was in segregation for twenty-three and a half hours a day during almost our entire year of correspondence. That did not occur along with a multitude of other events that Sidney claimed. Greg Brodsky said in our interview, *"First of all a lawyer cannot put a defense forward that he knows to be false. Second he can't put someone on the stand to tell a lie, he can't put a perjured defense before the court."* You decide for yourself. I say he's a liar.

*   *   *   *   *

Susan Sarandon's stolen jewelry was the motive for Sidney's murder-horror spectacle. Armed with the jewelry he decided to finally end his reign of horror when an incredible opportunity presented itself to him. He is an experienced serial killer—disposing completely of his previous victims—leaving absolutely no trace of any evidence linking him to any murder. When he discovered that he was in possession of Sarandon's jewelry, he hatched a plan to gain the fame he so desperately craved.

Very carefully and surgically dismembering his victim; staging and posing the reassembled ghastly creation, minus all of the internal organs, he calmly walked into a police station to claim that he had passed out and when he awoke found the man butchered.

The grisly horror spectacle alongside movie star Susan Sarandon's stolen jewelry, alone should have gained him the fame he so badly needed, but he went on to grant interviews and write letters to Winnipeg journalists that no one wanted or dared to know the entire story. I happened to get an opportunity to discover the truth and I took it.

*   *   *   *   *

It was January 20th, 2009. Sidney and his lawyer had 30 days in which to launch an appeal of the December 19th conviction. I had not seen anything about it in the Free Press or the Sun so I decided to call Manitoba Justice to enquire as to whether there had been an appeal filed. They informed me that Brodsky had appealed on behalf of his client. I notified Dean Pritchard at the Sun and he thanked me for the information. The next day a story about the appeal was in the Sun. The Free Press failed to mention it.

The story stated that court documents filed with the Manitoba Court of Appeal outlined 13 separate grounds for overturning the conviction.

In the appeal Brodsky claimed that Judge Joyal erred in deeming Sidney's letters and diagrams admissible at trial.

Brodsky also felt that Joyal had erred with his instructions to the jury regarding the issue of intoxication as it related to 'intent' and that the Judge should not have permitted the jury to view the crime scene photos.

*   *   *   *   *

I had a habit of routinely Googling Sidney's name to see what I might discover. This particular time I found a website called Can Art Coast to Coast and posted on it were three aboriginal-themed paintings by Sidney, alongside three newspaper articles which recounted the gruesome details of the murder he had committed.

One of the issues that arose during the trial was that I had offered Sidney a 30% share of the profits from the book. The law preventing criminals from profiting from their crimes was just being drafted in Manitoba when I first began corresponding with Sidney, and I was positive it would become law. I told Mike McIntyre from the Free Press that I knew the law would pass and that I would never have broken the law to pay Sidney for his story. Regardless, the fact that I had offered Sidney a share of the book's profits despite it being perfectly legal made me open to criticism.

382

On May 11th I contacted Manitoba Justice and The Canadian Press:

> *Sidney Teerhuis is attempting to profit from the notoriety of his crime. On a website called* Can Art Coast to Coast *under the heading* Sidney Teerhuis' Art Works *there are posted 3 paintings along with three articles recounting particulars of the murder Teerhuis was convicted of. The paintings can be purchased through the website. Posting of the newspaper articles, which in each article repeat details regarding the murder is a clear attempt to use the notoriety gained from the murder to sell his artwork. If his paintings were merely posted it would be different but he chose to post the accompanying articles along with his paintings.*
>
> *I would like first a response to my E-mail and secondly some sort of investigation into the information I have provided to you.*

A story appeared in Winnipeg papers and across Canada written by The Canadian Press on May 14th, **Criminal art for profit?**

It stated that Manitoba justice officials were investigating whether *Can Art Coast To Coast* was in violation of the *Profits of Criminal Notoriety Act*.

A man named Travis Findlay from the website said that he was Sidney's cell-mate a few weeks before the trial. He stated that he had four of his paintings and was selling them for "an exorbitant amount" which he claimed was forty-five to fifty thousand dollars each and called that figure "low end."

Findlay said Sidney had traded the paintings for a suit he had bought for him for trial. "They are some of the first ones he painted after the offence. His brain was in a position where it was like, when it poured out of him, it poured out."

The story included the report that as a result of convicted killer Colin Thatcher's plan to write a book, the Saskatchewan government was tabling similar legislation to that of Manitoba and other provinces.

The disappointing part was that all of the news agencies covering the story such as the Sun included with their stories color copies of Sidney's art. The C.B.C, our national news broadcaster who tax payers support, had chose not to attend the trial themselves, because as a reporter named Cavanaugh explained, the C.B.C. had decided that the graphic details recounted during the murder trial would upset their viewers—yet they had posted on-line the story about Sidney's potential violation and included three large color photos of his artwork. I shook my head in disbelief.

In the Winnipeg Sun the next day an article with the headline: **Killer's Art Probed – Cannibal comic investigated**. Included were three of the six cartoons sent to Tom Pomplum entitled *Munchie: Life in the Big City, A day in the life of a carefree, murderous cannibal,* which appeared on the Bookgasm.com website. Rod Lott, editor of Bookgasm decided to use red squares to cover parts of the cartoons that he felt were "overly gruesome." The story stated that Manitoba Justice was investigating the 'cannibal' cartoons that were sent to publisher Tom Pomplum. I had originally called the Sun about the *Coast To Coast* website, but they passed on the story and so it was interesting to see the Sun trying to now milk the same story they weren't originally interested in. I could only guess that someone may have called Justice officials just to generate the follow-up story, as the cartoons had been entered as evidence at the trial and as such were already known to Justice officials.

On July 20th the papers reported that Manitoba Justice was not going to charge either Sidney or the website promoting his art. There was mention that the other 'investigation' was not going to be pursued.

I simply asked Al Cameron from Manitoba Justice that if the law did not pertain in this case then when would it possibly pertain and why could the province not simply amend the legislation so that it would apply in a case like this?

$$* \quad * \quad * \quad * \quad *$$

A STORY APPEARED FRONT PAGE IN THE WINNIPEG SUN AUGUST 31ST, TITLED: **Killer crippled by rare infection**, written by Cary Castagna, Edmonton Sun.

It said that Sidney, a former Edmonton resident had contacted Castagna to say that he was recovering from a severe bout of flesh-eating disease diagnosed some seven months previous.

Sidney claimed that he had undergone three major surgeries in order to rid himself of the disease. "*I almost lost my left leg. To date, I am still recovering from surgery and deemed somewhat crippled for life. I'm dependent on a wheelchair, leg brace and walker.*"

Sidney is currently serving his life sentence in Saskatchewan Penitentiary near Prince Albert.

For a man that fantasized about being killed and eaten, I thought what had happened was quite ironic. For these microscopic flesh-eating creatures Sidney Teerhuis was "just a piece of meat."

$$* \quad * \quad * \quad * \quad *$$

ON SEPTEMBER 29TH, IN AN EDITION OF THE WINNIPEG FREE PRESS A STORY APPEARED with the headline, **Top lawyer must pay 39,000 for professional misconduct**.

The story reported that Brodsky, one of Canada's top criminal defence lawyers and the former chairman of the law Society's ethics and judicial committees has been found guilty of breaching professional standards for failing to act with integrity and receiving payment for legal services without accounting for such payments to his law firm, and breaching the law society's accounting rules for failing to deposit a retainer to a pooled trust account.

Basically Brodsky had asked a client initially for a $10,000.00 retainer, which was a check to be paid to Brodsky's law firm. Brodsky later called the client and asked for an additional $10,000.00—but instructed the client to make out the check to him personally. When the client received his invoice the second $10,000.00 amount was not included. The client contacted the Law Society and an investigation was undertaken.

Brodsky, through a plea-agreement, agreed to pay a total of $39,000.00—which included a $20,000.00 fine and $19,000.00 for costs relating to the court hearing, investigation and prosecution.

"*The panel considered the lengthy practice history of the member and his contribution to the profession and the community and accepted the joint recommendation,*" the decision read.

The Law Society has several available sanctions for lawyers found guilty of misconduct, ranging from a reprimand and a fine to a suspension or disbarment, however the fine imposed is one of the highest ever handed down. The sanction will remain on Brodsky's permanent record.

$$* \quad * \quad * \quad * \quad *$$

Sidney's appeal is to be heard on May 21st, 2010. Of course, I will be there. I believe that Greg Brodsky will read this book searching for any possible information that he can somehow use to argue that Sidney Teerhuis deserves another trial.

Regarding questions or requests, contact me at:
dan.zupansky@gmail.com

Look for TrophyKill on YouTube and visit TrophyKill.tv on the web for more!

Layout and design by **Prohyptikon Art & Media**

Cover design using the images:
  – TK Necklace, TK Knife, TK Clippings by Dan Caldwell, including relevant newspaper clippings courtesy of Sun Media.
  – Blood Splatter 1, 2, 3, & 4, by David Gurrea from davegh.com
  – Natural Black Leather by Sergiy Lukutin from dreamstime.com

Visit us on the web at:
www.prohyptikon.com

Please send your comments regarding this book to:
info@prohyptikon.com

CPSIA information can be obtained at www.ICGtesting.com
Printed in the USA
BVOW08s0859260814

364295BV00034B/1115/P